P9-CFJ-925

THE
HOPE OF
GLORY

THE HOPE OF GLORY

JOHN BRADSHAW

Pacific Press®
Publishing Association
Nampa, Idaho | www.pacificpress.com

Cover design by Gerald Lee Monks
Cover design resources from iStockphoto.com | Biletskiy_Evgeniy
Inside design by Aaron Troia

Copyright © 2021 by Pacific Press® Publishing Association
Printed in the United States of America
All rights reserved

The author assumes full responsibility for the accuracy of all facts and quotations as cited in this book.

Unless otherwise noted, all Scripture quotations are from the New King James Version® of the Bible. Copyright © 1982 by Thomas Nelson. Used by permission. All rights reserved.

Scripture quotations marked ESV are from The Holy Bible, English Standard Version® (ESV®), copyright © 2001 by Crossway, a publishing ministry of Good News Publishers. Used by permission. All rights reserved.

Scripture quotations marked KJV are from the King James Version of the Bible.

Scripture quotations marked NASB are from the New American Standard Bible®, copyright © 1960, 1971, 1977, 1995, 2020 by The Lockman Foundation. All rights reserved.

Scripture quotations marked NIV are from THE HOLY BIBLE, NEW INTERNATIONAL VERSION®. Copyright © 1973, 1978, 1984, 2011 by Biblica, Inc.® Used by permission. All rights reserved worldwide.

Additional copies of this book may be purchased by calling toll-free 1-800-765-6955 or by visiting AdventistBookCenter.com.

Library of Congress Cataloging-in-Publication Data

Names: Bradshaw, John L., 1967- author.
Title: The hope of glory : daily devotional / John Bradshaw.
Description: Nampa, Idaho : Pacific Press Publishing Association, [2021] | Summary: "A collection of 365 daily devotional readings"— Provided by publisher.
Identifiers: LCCN 2021013386 | ISBN 9780816367443 (hardcover) | ISBN 9780816367450 (ebook)
Subjects: LCSH: Devotional calendars.
Classification: LCC BV4811 .B665 2021 | DDC 242/.2—dc23
LC record available at https://lccn.loc.gov/2021013386

April 2021

Introduction

It could be said that Christianity is something like a Rubik's Cube. Virtually everyone has heard of it, most people have tried it, but few have figured out how to do it successfully.

When God called Abraham out of Ur of the Chaldees, His intent was to raise up a people that would be His witness to the world that God is love. But less than 1,500 years later, the ten northern tribes of Israel had ceased to exist, and only Judah and Benjamin remained. When Jesus came into the world, He extended an invitation to all: "Come to Me that you may have life" (John 5:40). But even before He hung on the cross, His closest friends "forsook Him and fled" (Matthew 26:56).

Six thousand years after the creation of the world, it might yet be said that the trend of former years continues. Jesus said as much when He described the church of the last days as "wretched, miserable, poor, blind, and naked" (Revelation 3:17). But far from being merely a rebuke, Jesus' summation of the spiritual health of His people is in fact an appeal to enter into the relationship with Him that He truly desires.

In his struggle to live a victorious Christian life, Paul recounted his experiences of falling far short of what he knew to be the will of God. But he went on to write about a Christianity that works, and about Christians who grow into a faith that connects them with the mind and heart of God.

Paul explained to his readers that vibrant Christianity rests upon "Christ in you, the hope of glory" (Colossians 1:27). In those words, Paul revealed the profoundly simple key to a successful faith. For the gospel to be truly experienced and lived, Jesus must dwell in the heart. As He does so, His presence—the reality of "Christ in you"—becomes the hope of glory to all who believe.

Jesus is coming back soon. He offers us His Word, that we might be ready to say on that day,

> "Behold, this is our God;
> We have waited for Him, and He will save us.
> This is the LORD;
> We have waited for Him;
> We will be glad and rejoice in His salvation" (Isaiah 25:9).

John Bradshaw
It Is Written

5

JANUARY

The Hope of Glory

To them God willed to make known what are the riches of the glory of this mystery among the Gentiles: which is Christ in you, the hope of glory.
—Colossians 1:27

We are embroiled in a great controversy, a battle in which the darkest forces in the universe have arrayed themselves in rebellion against the God of heaven. Fallen angels direct their malice toward those who, in the beginning, were created in the image of God. Satan targets his wrath toward human beings weakened by the debilitating effects of six thousand years of sin.

And yet God presents to the human family a pathway to full communion with the God of heaven. He exhorts us to "put on the new man who is renewed in knowledge according to the image of Him who created him" (Colossians 3:10), to "be holy in all your conduct" (1 Peter 1:15) and to "keep the commandments of God" (Revelation 14:12). Even better, the Bible tells us *how* we can be all that God wants us to be.

In Colossians 1, Paul discusses "the mystery which has been hidden from ages and from generations, but now has been revealed to His saints," and goes on to state that the heart of this mystery—the heart of the gospel—is "Christ in you, the hope of glory" (verses 26, 27).

Not a single person asked to be caught in this battle of epic proportions, a battle so intense it is necessary that angels surround and shield us from the unseen enemy (Psalm 34:7). Yet, in His goodness, God has made every provision for us to successfully navigate the troubled waters of this world. God is acquainted with the difficulties we face and with the weakened state in which we find ourselves. Recognizing that, after six thousand years of sin, we are no match for the enemy, He reveals the secret to being remade in the image of God: "Christ in you, the hope of glory." Sinners who have failed are promised restoration and re-creation through "Christ in you, the hope of glory."

God does not leave us to stumble alone through the darkness of this world. He is more than with us, more than near us. The great promise of the Bible is that Christ will dwell *in* you. And *that* is our "hope of glory."

Outnumbered!

*Then the LORD said to Gideon, "By the three hundred men who
lapped I will save you, and deliver the Midianites into your hand.
Let all the other people go, every man to his place."*

—Judges 7:7

The story of Gideon is one of the great stories in the Bible. God called Gideon to lead the armies of Israel against the Midianites, but with an army of thirty-two thousand, Gideon was seriously outnumbered. The Bible says Israel's enemies were "as numerous as locusts; and their camels were without number, as the sand by the seashore in multitude" (Judges 7:12). But despite the odds of victory being overwhelmingly against Gideon, God reduced the size of Gideon's fighting force to just three hundred men! Three hundred against a massive army, and yet Gideon was victorious.

So why did God reduce the size of Gideon's fighting force so drastically? Triumph with thirty-two thousand soldiers would have been impressive. Victory with the ten thousand soldiers who remained after the first wave of defections would also have been truly remarkable. In either case, Gideon's army would have been dramatically outnumbered. But with just three hundred warriors against an enemy army as large as Gideon was facing, there could be only one explanation for victory: God was with His people.

Often, God allows His people to get into a seemingly impossible situation before providing deliverance. And when He does, we may know without a doubt that it was God who saved us, rescued us, healed us, or strengthened us. David's numbering of Israel was the opposite of this. By numbering his people, David and Israel would have been tempted to claim credit for the victory. God wants us to know that our salvation, our prosperity, and our well-being are the result of His power, His might, and His goodness.

When your situation looks as impossible as that which faced Gideon, you can know that even if you're hopelessly outnumbered, you are in the majority if God is on your side. God can bring victory where no human could ever hope to do so.

Russian Roulette

*For the wages of sin is death, but the gift of God
is eternal life in Christ Jesus our Lord.*

—Romans 6:23

He had locked himself out of his fourteenth-floor apartment. Desperate to get inside, he went upstairs and asked his neighbor if she would let him onto her balcony. From there, he attempted to climb down to his own balcony. He was drunk after a night out with friends, which may explain why it didn't occur to him that what he was about to attempt wasn't a good idea. (I don't need to say "Don't try this at home," do I?) Unsurprisingly, he fell—thirteen stories, which is a very long way to fall—onto the roof of a neighboring building. Incredibly, he survived! He was badly injured—but not as badly injured as you might expect. He cheated death in a big way.

But don't most people do that very thing every day? "The wages of sin is death," and yet, people play with sin like it's a cute kitten when in fact, it's much more like a venomous snake. Sin is deadly. It introduced death into the world, led to the destruction of Sodom and Gomorrah, caused the Flood that inundated the planet in the days of Noah, and has caused untold woe and misery. Sin ultimately cost the life of Jesus.

But in today's world, sin is often considered nothing more than "fun," "edgy," maybe a little naughty, but certainly nothing to take too seriously. Consider the array of celebrities who have found themselves enmeshed in moral scandals only for society to collectively ask, "What's the big deal?" Incidents that once would have caused people to hang their heads in shame are now often the doorway to fame and fortune.

This familiarity with sin causes people to consider sin less dangerous than it really is. Being careless with sin is like playing Russian roulette or like climbing from one apartment to another 150 feet above the ground. It's better to play it safe and stay as far from sin as possible. Don't risk the painful, often deadly, fall that sin inevitably brings.

In the Heat of the Moment

"He shall call upon Me, and I will answer him; I will be with him in trouble; I will deliver him and honor him."

—Psalm 91:15

According to the Bible, sin begins with temptation. And temptation is a fact of life. Wishing for temptation to go away altogether is like wishing for the weather to disappear. One way or another, it's always going to be present.

What is key in your experience isn't so much whether or not you are tempted but what you do when temptation comes. If you are tempted to yell at your spouse or take something that isn't yours or say something that isn't true, there are moments in that temptation process when you can do something that will get you out of that situation successfully. To say that "there was nothing I could do" or that "it just happened before I realized what was going on" is to misrepresent the reality of temptation.

God promises that when we call on Him, He will answer. Not only that, but He also says, "I will be with him in trouble; I will deliver him, and honor him" (Psalm 91:15). When temptation comes, God will deliver you from its grasp if you call upon Him to do so. The problem is never that God is unwilling to help but that a person is unwilling in the heat of temptation to ask for or to accept the deliverance God provides.

When the temptation arises to say something cutting, God will intervene if you pray and ask Him for strength. A person who doesn't call on God is left to rely on his or her own human strength—or lack thereof. No one is a match for the power of temptation, but no temptation that could ever be imagined is a match for the power of God!

God promises to deliver His children out of temptation, and His promise is sure. When you have the presence of mind to respond to God's prompting, to call on Him in the heat of the moment, you can be sure God will provide His grace and power. If you learn to lean on Him when temptation comes and continue to do it, you will soon discover that turning to God becomes habitual. And when it does, victory over sin also becomes habitual.

The Call to Surrender

"King Agrippa, do you believe the prophets?
I know that you do believe."

—Acts 26:27

Y ou might have wondered why some people believe in God and others don't. Why some people maintain a faith experience and others choose not to. Two people may have the same spiritual advantages and opportunities—even the same upbringing—and the outcomes may be very different. While multiple factors may be at play, very often, the bottom line is that while people might have knowledge, they don't always choose to act on what they know.

Paul asked King Agrippa, "Do you believe the prophets?" Then he answered his own question. "I know that you do believe" (Acts 26:27). According to the apostle Paul, Agrippa believed! Agrippa knew that what he was hearing was true. He was aware that standing before him was a true witness for God and that the message Paul bore rang with truth. But King Agrippa wouldn't act. He wouldn't *surrender*. We can speculate as to what his issues were, but the salient point is that knowing the difference between right and wrong, between truth and error, and apparently understanding something of the gravity of the subject of eternity, Agrippa still chose not to yield.

While it's easy to criticize Agrippa's foolishness (for that's what it was), Agrippa's situation was not much different from ours today. We may be separated by culture and by millennia, but the question we all must resolve is the question of the heart. To whom will I surrender? Was it fame Agrippa coveted? Power? Admiration? Whatever it was, God was calling him to something higher, something more valuable, something *eternal*. Yet Agrippa, who believed, chose to chart his own course. As a result, Agrippa could not be saved.

If surrender was such an easy matter, we would all be 100 percent surrendered to God, and sin would have no place in our lives. But surrender is a test, a trial, a battle for supremacy in the life of every believer. When God calls, the best thing any person can do is yield. Surrender. Let God have His way, and you'll go in the right way.

Redemption

*"I persecuted this Way to the death, binding
and delivering into prisons both men and women."*

—Acts 22:4

It is common to hear stories of people who have committed truly awful crimes. News reports regularly share ghastly details of criminal acts, often causing people to respond with condemnation. There is frequently a temptation to think people who do these things are beyond redemption, that there's no help for them.

In Acts 22:4, Paul confesses that he was once a heartless persecutor of God's people. In another place, he calls himself the chief of sinners (1 Timothy 1:15) and "a blasphemer, a persecutor, and an insolent man" (verse 13). Paul was a scoundrel, responsible for the deaths of many of God's people. And yet, Paul went on to be a prolific Bible writer and one of the most significant figures in Christian history. No doubt, we will see him in heaven.

It is estimated that one former warlord in the west African country of Liberia was responsible for the death of twenty thousand Liberians during that country's civil war in the 1990s. He admitted to having committed unimaginable crimes. Investigations into his activities reveal that his claims are apparently true. Yet today, the man is a Christian pastor. He has personally apologized to dozens of people whose families he terrorized. He says, "I believe that God wishes to use me as a sign. No matter how far a person goes, he has the potential to change."

God is in the business of redemption and can turn around even the most hardened life. Even those considered to be hopeless cases are never beyond hope.

While you might not have done anything to rival the actions of a brutal warlord, every person has earned the wages of sin, which is death. How encouraging to know that God is in the business of restoration! He has shown us again and again that there is no project too hard for Him.

Calm Under Provocation

[Christ], when He was reviled, did not revile in return; when He suffered, He did not threaten, but committed Himself to Him who judges righteously.
—1 Peter 2:23

If you upset a snake, its response is to strike or to prepare to strike. A venomous snake coiled up just a few feet away from you can be a sobering sight. Angry dogs react to provocation by barking or biting, harried cats will scratch or hiss, obstreperous horses might kick, and people are much the same. It's sadly human for people to lash out—to react with hostility when they feel they've been poorly treated.

First Peter 2:23 is a challenge to sinful human nature. Speaking of Jesus, it says, "When He was reviled, did not revile in return; when He suffered, He did not threaten, but committed Himself to Him who judges righteously." Jesus, the Maker of humanity, the Savior of the world, was more than rejected. Wicked men plotted to end His life. His motives were misrepresented. The authorities "watched Him, and sent spies who pretended to be righteous, that they might seize on His words, in order to deliver Him to the power and the authority of the governor" (Luke 20:20). If anyone had reason to lash out, it was Jesus. But under intense provocation, He didn't react negatively. He remained calm, kind, and gracious.

It has always struck me as remarkable that after having been abandoned by His friends, betrayed by a disciple, and convicted by a kangaroo court; after having been beaten and spit upon and hearing crowds howl for His blood; after not having eaten for almost a day, and after staying up all night long, Jesus *still* didn't react in anger!

Can you be like that? The truth is, no. And yes! In your own strength, you cannot hope to get this right, but with Jesus living His life in you, you can react like Jesus did when He was provoked.

What a witness to the world it would be if God's people were gracious under fire and calm under pressure—if we learned to return blessing for cursing and love for malice. Jesus wishes for His character to be on display in the life of every believer. And if we allow that to happen, it will.

The Royal Birth

For unto us a Child is born,
Unto us a Son is given;
And the government will be upon His shoulder.
And His name will be called
Wonderful, Counselor, Mighty God,
Everlasting Father, Prince of Peace.

—Isaiah 9:6

They named him George. And it seemed as if the whole world was watching.

The media was covering the story moment by moment. Prince William and Princess Kate were having their first child, and it was global news. Royal watchers provided up-to-the-minute commentary, souvenir sellers anticipated brisk business, and a wave of goodwill washed over Great Britain.

It's astonishing that when a baby boy was born in Bethlehem two thousand years ago, the media was *not* covering the event. In fact, the birth was ignored by almost everyone. And yet this Baby was true royalty!

This was the royal birth that changed all of history. Born that day in Bethlehem was a child who would open the eyes of the blind, unstop the ears of the deaf, and cause the lame to walk and the ailing to be healed. Even better, this Royal Baby would offer peace in place of personal turmoil, mercy for condemnation, and forgiveness where there had been guilt and shame. He was a creative genius the likes of which the world had never seen, and He possessed wisdom that exceeded that of the most learned people of His day. Yet this royal birth was ignored. Though it had been prophesied long before, travelers arriving in Jerusalem in search of the Holy Infant discovered that the people were not excitedly anticipating a royal birth.

Although the media wasn't covering the events in Bethlehem, this Child changed the world, offering every person, in every age, the gift of everlasting life. Though the majority live without regard to that remarkable event, the humble Child born in Bethlehem still changes the world. If you let Him, He'll change your world today.

Waging War

Beloved, I beg you as sojourners and pilgrims,
abstain from fleshly lusts which war against the soul.

—1 Peter 2:11

The old saying is that familiarity breeds contempt. It is easy to lack appreciation for that which has become commonplace. When it comes to spiritual matters, there's a real danger that familiarity with sin can cause the gravity of sin to seem less serious than it actually is.

Believers in Jesus are at risk of failing to recognize how harmful some things are. Unbridled carnal desire is rampant in society, and it has become so common that we might fail to recognize how successful Satan has been in this area. Magazines sold at supermarket checkout counters routinely display extraordinarily suggestive headlines in full view of children. Store windows show pictures that would have been unacceptable a generation ago. News publications and websites geared toward the general public commonly discuss R- or even X-rated themes.

Before we dismiss such concerns as old-fashioned, we must remember Peter's caution that fleshly lusts "war against the soul." In other words, they are dangerous for us in light of eternity. Peter states that passions inappropriately indulged work against one's spiritual well-being. There are some roads that, when traveled, ultimately make it impossible for a believer to stay connected to Jesus. Sin is not harmless, and Satan knows how to weaken a person, often slowly and over long periods. For their own eternal good, the Bible urges followers of God to turn their backs on some things that society embraces.

Many lives that are irretrievably ruined would have turned out otherwise if temptations had been resisted. It would be wrong to suggest that resisting the sins of the flesh is always a simple matter. But it would be equally as wrong to suggest that such temptations cannot be resisted through God's power. For six thousand years, Satan has studied human nature with the purpose of presenting temptation in its most effective form. Peter's counsel reminds us that we are engaged in an intense spiritual war. God's grace is necessary to keep us from anything that would lead us out of the footsteps of Jesus.

Marvels of Creation

And God made the beast of the earth according to its kind,
cattle according to its kind, and everything that creeps on
the earth according to its kind. And God saw that it was good.
—Genesis 1:25

I marveled as I watched a large spider spinning its web. As it patiently and painstakingly labored, I wondered to myself how it is that spiders know how to create that masterpiece of engineering. How do birds know how to build nests and exactly when and where to migrate? Tiny hummingbirds migrate all the way from Mexico to Alaska. I recently read an article that explained how it is that flocks of birds—ducks, in particular—can land in groups on ponds or lakes without ever colliding with each other. Incredibly, ducks always land in harmony with the earth's magnetic field. It is believed ducks are constructed in such a way that they can see or sense the earth's magnetic field, which somehow enables them to land in groups without chaos ensuing.

You could call all of that—and more—instinct or accidents of nature. But there's a better explanation for the marvels of creation. Genesis tells us, "God made the beast of the earth." God *made* the animals, the birds, and the fish, and He put within them the knowledge they need to carry out the most remarkable things. Obviously, some animal behavior is learned: ducklings aren't born flying, baby lions learn to hunt, and grizzly bears learn to catch fish. But the incredible marvels of creation show us that we serve a good and a great God. It takes an enormous amount of faith to believe animals gained or gathered the remarkable knowledge and skill they possess as a result of evolutionary processes. Surely birds would have become hopelessly lost before evolution helped them figure out how to get from A to B.

God placed remarkable capabilities within animals that demonstrate not only that the creatures themselves are magnificent but also that the God of heaven is magnificent. Spinning spiders, migrating hummingbirds, and landing ducks reveal the greatness of the God of perfect plans and perfect love.

Keeping It Balanced

And having been perfected, He became the author
of eternal salvation to all who obey Him.

—Hebrews 5:9

It is important to keep things in balance when it comes to faith in God. Hebrews 5:9 describes Jesus as "the author of eternal salvation to all who obey Him." Is the Bible saying salvation is earned by obedience? The Bible is clear that the gift of salvation comes by grace, through faith. Nowhere does the Bible advocate salvation by works. But, along with many other passages in the Bible, Hebrews 5:9 says that salvation includes obedience.

A life centered on Jesus will be a life of continual spiritual growth. Not a single soul ever came to Jesus in faith and then never made a spiritual mistake from that time forward. When speaking to Nicodemus, Jesus made it clear that all who come to Him are "born again." They are remade as spiritual babies, not spiritual giants. After people accept Jesus as Lord and Savior, they experience a learning curve. Just as babies are born tiny and weak before growing to strength and maturity, Christians are born weak and in need of nurture and spiritual growth.

Many people become frustrated at their spiritual weakness. That is not entirely inappropriate—it is good to want to grow spiritually. But while we have no trouble understanding that our children, or our puppies, or the plants in our gardens need time to grow, that plain fact of life is frequently overlooked in regard to spiritual life. A person who comes to God in faith must experience growth. To not grow would be to stagnate. But to expect to come to faith in Christ and have no moments of weakness from that time forward is not only unrealistic but also demoralizing.

When Jesus enters a life, He brings into that life the gift of salvation. As days pass, old ways will start disappearing out of that life, like leaves falling from a tree in autumn. Let God do His work in your life today. Faith in Jesus will cause you to grow in grace, and your life will become more and more like His.

In His Presence

*But Jonah arose to flee to Tarshish from the presence of the LORD. He went
down to Joppa, and found a ship going to Tarshish; so he paid the fare, and
went down into it, to go with them to Tarshish from the presence of the LORD.*
—Jonah 1:3

A short phrase in the book of Jonah demonstrates how hopeful it is to be a child of
God. Jonah was commissioned by God to deliver an uncompromising judgment
message to the Assyrian people of Nineveh, located on the Tigris River near Mosul in
modern-day northern Iraq. There is little wonder Jonah was not eager to visit Nineveh.
The Assyrians were known for their cruelty and brutality. One writer described an
exhibition of Assyrian art at the British Museum as containing "some of the most
appalling images ever created."*

Jonah made an honest attempt to flee from God's presence. It seemed no trouble
was too great for Jonah if it meant avoiding Nineveh. He boarded a ship heading in
the opposite direction. Yet try as he might, Jonah could not successfully run from God.
God saw him on the dock in Joppa. He saw Jonah board the ship to Tarshish. He sent
a storm to trouble the ship, and "the LORD had prepared a great fish" (Jonah 1:17) to
retrieve the reluctant prophet. When Jonah encountered the sea creature, he thought
his life was over. But he discovered that rather than making him fish food, God had
apprehended him for a special purpose. Jonah realized that, try as he might, he simply
couldn't escape God.

God was with Jonah, even while he believed he was fleeing God's presence, which
tells us it simply isn't possible to escape God's presence. You can run from God, but
He'll run right after you and call you back to Him.

Even when you go your own way, God sees you, and He cares. As foolish as Jonah's
actions were, God didn't roll His eyes or lose His patience. God acted in love, and He
acts in love toward you to give you every opportunity to turn to Him. Instead of fleeing
from God, flee *to* God. His purpose is always to bless you in preparation for eternity.

---

* Jonathan Jones, " 'Some of the Most Appalling Images Ever Created'—I Am Ashurbanipal Review,"
Guardian, November 5, 2018, https://www.theguardian.com/artanddesign/2018/nov/06/i-am-ashurbanipal
-review-british-museum.

Converted

*"Repent therefore and be converted, that your sins may be blotted out,
so that times of refreshing may come from the presence of the Lord."*
—Acts 3:19

P eter spoke the words in Acts 3:19 under the inspiration of the Holy Spirit shortly after a lame man was healed at the temple gate in Jerusalem. The Holy Spirit inspired Peter to use the word *converted*, which means to turn, to turn around, or to turn back. A person without faith in God is walking in the wrong direction along the road of life. When Jesus comes into a person's life, He calls that person to make a U-turn, a 180-degree about-face that results in the entire trend of the life heading in a new direction.

Faith in Jesus results in a decided change in a person's life. Rather than simply modifying the old life of independence from God, faith in Jesus results in conversion. Transformation. The one who chooses faith in Christ is no longer the same. It isn't even possible for a person who has genuine faith in Christ to be the same person they were before conversion.

Three houses down from the home in which I grew up was a big old house. Even though someone was living there, it appeared for years to be abandoned. One day we noticed that the old house was beginning to change. The worn roof was repaired, weatherboards were replaced, and the entire house was painted. New windows were installed. Today it is a beautiful home, the type you might see featured in a glossy magazine. The house had changed owners. When a new owner occupied the home, the home was transformed.

The decision to allow Jesus into one's life brings the believer the dynamic, life-changing presence of Jesus through the Person of the Holy Spirit. Surrender to Christ allows Him to do the work He wants to do in the life of a believer. This is not a work of modification but a work of transformation, the work of conversion. Let Jesus do the work He wants to do and experience His miraculous ability to entirely remake you.

Mythical?

*"I am the living bread which came down from heaven. If anyone
eats of this bread, he will live forever; and the bread that I shall
give is My flesh, which I shall give for the life of the world."*
—John 6:51

In the north of Scotland, there is a twenty-mile-long lake famous the world over for being the home of a mythical creature known as the Loch Ness monster. For many years, claims have been made of sightings of a mysterious sea creature in the lake. Photographs and video footage have been taken of what is said to be the Loch Ness monster, and over the years, detailed scientific testing has been carried out at the lake in an attempt to verify the existence of "Nessie." But no one has been able to prove that the Loch Ness monster exists.

For thousands of years, claims have been made about the existence of a place that very few people can even *claim* to have seen. The first book of the Bible refers to this place, as does the last book of the Bible. In all, the Bible refers to it hundreds of times. In John 6:51, Jesus said He "came down from heaven." You haven't been there, and you know only one Individual who has. Nevertheless, we can believe heaven is a real place. Jesus said He came from heaven and that He was going back to heaven. And He said He was going to return to the earth to gather His people and take them to heaven to be with Him. We are told that in heaven, there will be streets of gold, a river of life, a tree of life, and mansions in which God's people will live.

It is hard to imagine that the Loch Ness monster truly exists. But heaven is for real. It is the assurance of our short earthly lives stretching on into the infinite. It reminds us that one day the darkness of a sin-stained world will be no more. It is our guarantee that one day neither pain nor tears will again be experienced.

God wants you to be in heaven, and He has done everything necessary to make that happen. Allow Jesus to have your heart, and heaven is yours.

They Did Nothing

And [they] said to the mountains and rocks, "Fall on us and hide us from the
face of Him who sits on the throne and from the wrath of the Lamb!"
—Revelation 6:16

It was a truly shocking story. Staff working at a computer store heard terrible sounds coming from the store next door. They heard a woman pleading for her life and what sounded like an act of terrible violence taking place. But they did nothing to intervene while a woman was being murdered by her female coworker just a few feet away. They didn't call 911 or even alert the security guard working at their store.

The thought that people would stand by while someone was being murdered defies belief. Yet every single day, many people—including many of God's people—stand by and do nothing to help those who are losing their eternal life. Not a day passes where Satan does not persuade people to be lost forever. But God has spoken clearly to His own, imploring them to do something to make a difference. Jesus said in Matthew 28:19, "Go therefore and make disciples of all the nations." God continues to call upon His people to do something to reach the dying.

What can God do through you to reach someone for Jesus? When a disaster strikes, people typically come out in force to help those who have been tragically affected. Disaster struck earth six thousand years ago, and today God is looking for people who are willing to help the victims of that tragedy. Missionaries must be found to travel to faraway places to tell people about a loving God they may never have heard of. And missionaries are needed in workplaces, on college campuses, in neighborhoods, and in households here at home.

On the great day when Jesus returns, the lost are going to call out to the mountains and the rocks and say, "Fall on us and hide us from the face of Him who sits on the throne and from the wrath of the Lamb!" (Revelation 6:16). One lost person is one too many. Tell God today that you are willing to be used by Him to reach someone for eternity, and He will use you to shine the light of the gospel into someone's life.

Unshakable

"For the Lord God will help Me;
Therefore I will not be disgraced;
Therefore I have set My face like a flint,
And I know that I will not be ashamed."

—Isaiah 50:7

Over five hundred years ago (April 18, 1521), a young monk stood before an august church council and was confronted with angry demands that he retract what he had written about the church and salvation. But Martin Luther would not retract. As he stood in a palace in the city of Worms, Germany, before one of the most imposing assemblies ever convened, he bravely declared, "Here I stand, I can do no other, God help me. Amen."*

If you visit the city of Worms today, you'll find a magnificent monument dedicated to Martin Luther and other heroes of the Protestant Reformation, including Philip Melanchthon, John Wycliffe, and John Huss. A nearby church has Luther's famous remarks inscribed on an exterior wall, and there is a humble marker set at the spot where Luther is said to have taken his bold stand for Jesus.

Isaiah 50:7 refers primarily to Jesus and His strong commitment to yield His life to the will of God. Derided, persecuted, and pursued, Jesus manifested solid, unshakable faith in His Father, faith that made Him choose to yield His life for the benefit of a sinful world.

Is great faith only an attribute of such people as Martin Luther and Jesus Christ? Every day, God gives each person the opportunity to demonstrate great faith: the mourner who chooses to trust in God in the midst of great sadness; the recipient of an unexpected, challenging diagnosis who holds fast to Jesus; the young man or woman who breaks off an engagement because of the sad discovery that their intended was not actually of God's choosing and moves forward claiming God's promises.

Every decision to trust in God, even in life's more mundane moments, is a decision of great faith. Martin Luther had learned great faith in the smaller details of life, and he demonstrated that faith on momentous occasions. His experience of faith in God can be yours.

---

* Merle D'Aubigne, *History of the Reformation of the 16th Century*, book 7, chapter 8, quoted in Ellen G. White, *The Great Controversy Between Christ and Satan* (Mountain View, CA: Pacific Press®, 1950), 160.

Living How Long?

And this is the promise that He has
promised us—eternal life.

—1 John 2:25

The Lancet, a prestigious medical journal based in the United Kingdom, reported that the majority of children now being born in wealthy nations will live to be 100 years old.* Yet as wonderful as it sounds, that announcement looks less exciting when considered in light of the Bible. In the beginning, God created a perfect world, where the inhabitants were intended to live *forever.* The apostle John affirms that "this is the promise that He has promised us—eternal life" (1 John 2:25).

It is true that living to be 100 years old is a wonderful achievement. In many British Commonwealth countries, it was customary that those who lived to 100 would receive a congratulatory telegram from the Queen. But God's plans are so much better. Compared to the patriarchs of the Bible, a person who lives to 100 is a spring chicken! Adam lived to be 930. Seth, the son of Adam, lived to 912. Seth's son Enos died at 905, and Methuselah died in the year of the Flood at the age of 969—making him the oldest man who ever died. The oldest man who ever lived is Enoch, who was translated without seeing death and is still living.

Sin has dragged the world down to the place where 100 years of life is considered a great achievement. The oldest person in the world at any given time is usually around 116 years old. But God wants us to make truly long-term plans.

I once met an elderly woman who told me she didn't want to live forever. "It seems like such a long time," she told me, "and I can't imagine what I would do." But God can! Those who hold the hand of Jesus can be certain of living a meaningful, fulfilling, exciting life that has no end. That is God's perfect plan for you. And you don't want to miss it!

---

* Joseph Brownstein, "Most Babies Born Today May Live Past 100," ABC News, October 1, 2009, https://abcnews.go.com/Health/WellnessNews/half-todays-babies-expected-live-past-100/story?id=8724273.

No Mistake!

For by grace you have been saved through faith,
and that not of yourselves; it is the gift of God.

—Ephesians 2:8

A man received the surprise of his life when his Paypal account was accidentally credited ninety-two quadrillion dollars. That's a thousand million million dollars—one thousand trillion dollars, eleven hundred times more than the combined gross national product of every country on the planet at the time. But within just a few minutes, Paypal had corrected its mistake, and the man's net worth was back to where it had been at the start of the day. The money had been removed from his account, and his balance was back to normal. The man in question said later that he was neither surprised nor disappointed that the money had been removed from his account. He said he never expected the "giver" to honor such an extreme "gift."

But think of what God does. Every person who accepts Jesus Christ as Lord and Savior receives from God the gift of everlasting life. Everlasting life is worth far more than ninety-two quadrillion dollars! Someone checking the balance of their spiritual bank account might be tempted to say, "This can't be right! Who gives such an extravagant gift?!" But God says, "No, that's not a mistake. It really is all yours. I've given you—an undeserving person—an extremely gracious gift, and I have no intention of taking it back." Salvation cost heaven the life of the Son of God. No earthly wealth could ever approach the value of the gift God gave the world in Jesus.

While unanswered prayer can lead some people to doubt God's goodness, the truth is that God's grace is extravagant. God is the giver of all good gifts. Jesus said He came to this world to give us life "more abundantly" (John 10:10).

Paul tells us we are saved by grace and through faith. We don't deserve God's grace, we cannot possibly earn it, and we will never be worthy of it. But by faith, we can claim the greatest, most incredible, and most valuable gift ever imagined. God gives the greatest gift of all.

"You're Terrible!"

And you, fathers, do not provoke your children to wrath,
but bring them up in the training and admonition of the Lord.
—Ephesians 6:4

The heartbreaking story said that the young boy used to enjoy soccer until his mother started watching his games and ridiculing him from the sideline. "She used to say, 'Why are you playing this? There's no point. You're terrible,' " he recalled. He never forgot the ridicule and rejection he had endured, inflicted upon him by his own mother. The very person who should have been demonstrating support was, instead, cutting him down.

Parents receive specific instruction from God when Paul says, "Fathers, do not provoke your children to wrath, but bring them up in the training and admonition of the Lord" (Ephesians 6:4). Although Paul addresses this to "fathers," it is clear this counsel applies equally to mothers—and certainly to mothers stalking the sideline of their children's soccer games. Parents say a lot of words to their children, and while no parent is going to get it right every time, it's essential to remember that words can either build up or tear down. And when dealing with the young and most vulnerable, it is crucial to realize there is power in words to do great good or great harm.

You don't get a chance to do it over again when it comes to raising children. Words that have been spoken can never be unsaid. Something uttered in anger might not have been intentionally malicious, something said in the heat of the moment might not have been deliberately cutting, but a word spoken cannot be taken back. Even apologies can't always reverse the damage done by careless words. It has been said that you can't unring a bell. You certainly cannot unsay a word.

Whether you are a parent or not, it is better to commit to speaking words God wants you to speak. The Spirit of God is able to tame even the wildest tongue. Pray today for the grace to speak kind words. When Jesus lives His life in you, His presence in your life will be noticed in your words. The God who changes your heart changes your attitudes and your vocabulary.

Easy Access

And the woman said to the serpent,
"We may eat the fruit of the trees of the garden."
—Genesis 3:2

A three-year-old boy in Australia found some eggs in his family's backyard, put them in a container, and placed them in his bedroom closet. Sometime later, his mother was surprised to hear strange sounds in her little boy's room, and when she investigated, she was alarmed to discover seven young eastern brown snakes. The eggs her son discovered and kept had produced a nest of the second-most venomous land snakes in the world—right in his bedroom!

A snake in the wild is one thing. Snakes belong in the wild. And while many people would rather they never encountered a snake anywhere at any time, to discover one in the great outdoors is to discover a snake on its own turf. Venomous snakes belong in the wild. They definitely do not belong in bedroom closets—especially the closets of three-year-old boys!

In the word of God, Satan is depicted as a serpent, and too many people are welcoming him into their home. In today's modern world, there are multiple avenues via which Satan is able to access our lives, the most obvious being television and the internet. And while nobody would think having seven eastern brown snakes in your home is harmless, all too often, the danger of Satan's presence is unperceived, even dismissed.

Consider sin's entrance into the world: "And the woman said to the serpent. . . ." Undoubtedly, the serpent through which Satan communicated was very beautiful, and Eve was fascinated by what she heard and saw. But if Eve hadn't parleyed with the snake, history would be altogether different. If Eve had dismissed Satan rather than granting him access to her mind, the Fall would not have occurred, and sin would not have entered the world.

While resisting temptation can often be a difficult thing, the truth is that Satan's job is often made easy by people who carelessly invite him into their life. Invite Jesus to defend you today and keep Satan out of the place he does not belong.

Consequences

"But if you do not do so, then take note, you have sinned against
the LORD; and be sure your sin will find you out."
—Numbers 32:23

When eight men took only eleven minutes to steal a shipment of diamonds from a plane at an airport in Brussels—the hub of the international gem trade—law enforcement officials were incredulous. The heist seemed to be meticulously planned and expertly carried out, and the crooks got away with $50 million worth of diamonds. But the thieves had a problem: how in the world were they going to get rid of $50 million worth of diamonds? And that's where they came unglued. Their attempts to unload the gems in Geneva were as ham-fisted as their theft was flawless. It was one thing to commit the crime, but getting away with it was another story.*

Numbers 32:23 speaks to this when it says, "Be sure your sin will find you out." It's one thing to tell a lie, but a lie told usually requires more lies to cover up the original lie. It's one thing to lose your temper or cheat on a test or go out and get drunk, but there are those troubling things called consequences, and they almost always have to be faced. Things done in secret have a way of eventually coming out into the open. This is not to say we should be motivated by fear of being caught. John wrote that we love God because He first loved us, not because we're scared of what will happen if we don't.

If more people stopped and thought, *Things could turn out very badly if I make this poor decision,* or *Someone will get hurt if I do this thing,* there would undoubtedly be less inclination to cave in to temptation and a greater likelihood of making a good decision. When temptation strikes, stop and listen. You will hear God's voice urging you to choose the path of right and encouraging you to surrender your will to Him. At that moment, choose to yield to the work of God in your life. Surrendering your heart to Jesus in the midst of temptation allows God to deliver you from it. Doing things God's way never has negative consequences.

---

* Associated Press, "Police Nab Suspects in $50 Million Diamond Heist After International Sweep," May 8, 2013, https://www.nydailynews.com/news/crime/police-nab-suspects-50-million-diamond-heist-cops-article -1.1338313.

Unfortunate Mishaps

Pray without ceasing.

—1 Thessalonians 5:17

B efore she went into the hospital, she put her wedding ring in a small wooden box and placed it in her closet for safekeeping. She tucked it under some padding, planning to retrieve it when she came home. While she was in the hospital, her kind husband decided he would clean up around the house and get rid of surplus items by selling them in a community yard sale.

As he searched the house, the helpful husband discovered the little box in his closet. He sold it for $10. His wife's wedding ring inside the box was worth $23,000. His problem was that he didn't know the valuable ring was in the little box. Just a little communication would have saved a lot of anguish.

Many of the spiritual problems people experience are due to a lack of communication. Paul encouraged his readers to "pray without ceasing" (1 Thessalonians 5:17). Prayer is communication with God. Anyone can pray, and it requires no special skill.

In all of life's details, we should sense a call to prayer. Our prayers can be prayers of thanks, praise, supplication, or confession, and they can be for ourselves or for others. There is never a shortage of things to pray about, yet many people regret that their prayer life is inadequate or powerless.

In the Bible, God communicated directly with people in remarkable ways. He communicated with Daniel through visions and dreams. He called to Saul on the road to Damascus and spoke to the young child Samuel in the darkness of night. The same God wishes to communicate with you in just as meaningful a way.

If your prayer life isn't what it should be, it isn't too late to turn things around. Incredibly, the person who purchased the wooden box saw a news story about the couple's unfortunate situation, and the ring was returned. If your lack of communication with God has complicated your life, it can still work out well. Make it your practice to speak often with God. As you do, your life will be richly blessed.

A Thief in the Night

*For you yourselves know perfectly that the day
of the Lord so comes as a thief in the night.*
—1 Thessalonians 5:2

One of the great themes in the Bible is the second coming of Jesus. Again and again, the Word of God urges us to be ready for that day. Paul wrote, "The day of the Lord so comes as a thief in the night" (1 Thessalonians 5:2). Thieves come unexpectedly, usually when people aren't anticipating them and most often when people aren't ready for them. If your home has ever been burglarized, then you know something of the shock and hurt of the experience. You know that thieves have a remarkable ability to carry out their criminal activity undetected.

In March 1990, two men posing as policemen gained entry to the Gardner Museum in Boston, handcuffed two security guards, and made off with artworks valued at $500 million, including masterpieces by Rembrandt and Vermeer. Although the FBI says it knows the identity of the art thieves, the stolen paintings have never been recovered, and no charges have been pressed. The thieves came in the night, and an outwitted museum suffered a great loss.

Paul says that for those who aren't ready, the return of Jesus will come as an overwhelming surprise. Even though the Bible clearly outlines the signs preceding Christ's coming, masses of people will not be prepared for history's greatest event. Just as people weren't ready for the Flood in Noah's day or for the first coming of Jesus, the vast majority are going to be surprised by Christ's return.

The purpose of this life is to prepare for the life to come. Rightly understood, all of the business and the busyness of life on earth are provided to us as a means of readying us to meet Jesus at His return. What are you spending your time on? What are you devoting your energies to? Jesus is going to return to this earth. Don't let His return take you by surprise. To live in preparation for the Second Coming is to live with Jesus in your heart. The second coming of Jesus is the one event you want to be ready for!

Ready for His Return

Therefore let us not sleep, as others do,
but let us watch and be sober.

—1 Thessalonians 5:6

Paul tells us that the day of the return of Jesus is going to come for many people like a thief in the night. The majority of people will not be ready, even though God has given them every opportunity. As he dwells on the theme of Jesus' return, he adds, "Therefore let us not sleep, as others do, but let us watch and be sober" (1 Thessalonians 5:6).

On the morning of December 7, 1941, two men operating a mobile radar unit were scanning the skies surrounding the Hawaiian island of Oahu. Intelligence suggested Hawaii was to be attacked. In fact, approximately an hour before the first bombs fell on Pearl Harbor, the two privates working at the radar unit saw the incoming Japanese aircraft and alerted the appropriate authorities. But the incoming aircraft were mistakenly identified as American planes, and the Japanese fighters and bombers flew unhindered over American soil. The result was the loss of more than 2,200 lives and America's entrance into World War II.* It isn't unfair to say that if America had been more vigilant, the Japanese attack on Pearl Harbor would have been, though still tragic, very different.

In recent years, humans have devised new ways to distract themselves. Texting while driving, or even walking, has created problems we never had to face before. A moment's carelessness results in lives being irrevocably changed. While you might expect "watching" to be fundamental to safe driving, you likely know from experience how common it is to see drivers distracted by their smartphones even though they know their behavior is potentially deadly.

There's nothing more important than being ready to meet Jesus when He returns. The distracted—the "sleepers," as opposed to the "watchers"—will not be saved. A simple, constant focus on Jesus will keep heaven in view and the Holy Spirit abiding in the heart. If ever there was a time to be living with eternity in mind, it is now. Soon, the last sermons will have been preached, the last tracts will have been distributed, and the last Bible study will have been given. Jesus is coming back soon.

---

* Gordon William Prange, Donald M. Goldstein, Katherine V. Dillon, *December 7, 1941: The Day the Japanese Attacked Pearl Harbor* (New York: McGraw-Hill, 1988), 98.

The Love of the Truth

*And with all unrighteous deception among those who perish, because
they did not receive the love of the truth, that they might be saved.*
—2 Thessalonians 2:10

The apostle Paul wrote about a certain group of people who "did not receive the love of the truth" (2 Thessalonians 2:10). It is important to note that Paul did not say that those who *know* the truth would be saved. He states that only those who "love the truth" will receive eternal life.

Churches are crowded with people who "know" the truth. It isn't hard to find people with an in-depth knowledge of prophecy or a deep understanding of doctrine. But painfully, often, people with a high biblical IQ have a weak grasp of what it means to be a true Christian. Someone once said that "the strongest argument in favor of the gospel is a loving and lovable Christian,"* yet it is clearly possible to major in knowledge while failing to experience transformation. You can possess all the truth you want, but only when Jesus touches your heart does the truth start to make a difference.

Salvation is about much more than theory. You can be right and still be wrong. The Pharisees in Jesus' day were right about an awful lot, but while practicing their religion, they were plotting to murder the Messiah.

When correctly experienced, truth results in transformation. For some, more truth merely allows them to be more "right." God's plan is that more "truth" will result in His children becoming more "*right with Him.*" The ultimate manifestation of truth isn't a doctrine or a prophecy or a scriptural interpretation. The ultimate manifestation of truth is a Person—Jesus. As we advance in the light shining from the Bible, our characters should continue to develop so that we become more like Him.

Loving the truth isn't simply a matter of loving pure doctrine or loving correct biblical principles. It is true that those things are important. *Very* important. But any form of truth that doesn't result in its possessor becoming more like the Truth isn't truth at all.

---

* Ellen G. White, *The Ministry of Healing* (Mountain View, CA: Pacific Press®, 1942), 470.

Man's Best Friend

*"Call to Me, and I will answer you, and show you great
and mighty things, which you do not know."*
—Jeremiah 33:3

Researchers say there will soon be devices that will make communication with pets possible. It is said that pet owners will be able to communicate with dogs and cats and possibly even farm animals. While humans and animals have been "communicating" for millennia, researchers say they are now taking this a step further than we have ever experienced.

If these claims prove to be true, people would be able to explain to their dog that they want it to stop barking or understand what the dog is barking about. But while animal behaviorists are working out how to talk to cats, it is more important what we learn how to effectively communicate with God.

God assures us, "Call to Me, and I will answer you" (Jeremiah 33:3). Prayer is a simple science. Even the most effective prayer is nothing more than a matter of opening up the heart to God just as you would to a friend. While prayer may result in God doing for us things He might not have done had we not prayed, the ultimate goal in prayer is not simply to get one's own way. If marrying a certain person was actually going to make you miserable, you wouldn't want God to answer that prayer in the affirmative. Or if getting a certain job would only result in life becoming less enjoyable, you would be thankful if God did not grant your petition.

Correctly understood, prayer is a matter of finding out what *God* wants in a given situation, which is why in Matthew 6:10, Jesus taught us to pray, "Thy will be done." This does not mean we aren't to have a will. Jesus' preference was that He not go to the cross (Matthew 26:42), but He submitted to His Father's will, and His Father's will was done.

Researchers suggest we might one day learn the language of cats and dogs. But it's the language of prayer that is essential. You can talk to God anytime. He really is man's best Friend.

Living It Up!

"The thief does not come except to steal, and to kill, and to destroy. I have come that they may have life, and that they may have it more abundantly."
—John 10:10

Ernie beamed as he spoke about the wonderful day he had riding a four-wheel ATV. The deer in the field fled as he took the machine up hills, down hills, and over downed tree limbs with the wind in his hair and a big smile on his face. This is all to be expected—except perhaps for one detail. Ernie was blind.

In spite of what most people would consider a major obstacle, Ernie rode a quad bike around a farm. His nephew whistled to warn him if he got too close to anything hazardous. Ernie had a great day!

Some people refuse to let what we might call disabilities get in the way of living life to the fullest. What is holding you back from enjoying God's blessings? Jesus came to give us life. And, even better, He came that we might "have it more abundantly." Jesus doesn't intend that we should live empty or unremarkable lives. His plans for us are vast.

God's blessings are realized by faith. When God says, "Get as many jars as you can so that the little oil you have may fill them all," our job is to take God at His word. Imagine the prophet's disappointment if the poor widow in the story had borrowed only two or three oil jars. And imagine the blessing she would have missed! A woman experienced miraculous healing because she believed Jesus could heal her. Touching the hem of His garment demonstrated that she expected God to do much in her life, not little. Four men who couldn't get their paralyzed friend into the presence of Jesus would not be turned back by the crowd. Instead, they took their friend onto the rooftop and lowered him down into Jesus' presence.

No one would have blamed Ernie if he had not ridden the four-wheeler. But his willingness to step out gave him a story to tell and memories he would always treasure. If we take God at His word and give Him the opportunity to fulfill His plan for us, He will shower us with blessings we will never forget.

The Process

I say then: Walk in the Spirit,
and you shall not fulfill the lust of the flesh.
—Galatians 5:16

With less than one hundred meters left to run in the women's eight-hundred-meter race during Olympic qualifying, Brenda Martinez was tripped by a fellow runner and stumbled. She failed to qualify in what was her favored event in the Olympic Games. But after the race, she didn't dwell on her disappointment. She said that she was focused on preparing for the fifteen hundred meters, and she had to put her disappointment out of her mind to give herself the best chance of qualifying to represent the United States in Rio de Janeiro.* Martinez was not focused on her goals; she was focused on the *process*.

Overly focusing on goals can have negative consequences. It can lead to irrational risk-taking and unethical behavior. In school, an unhealthy focus on maintaining a 4.0 grade point average could lead to cheating in order to get an A. Sportspeople fixated on winning may resort to using performance-enhancing drugs. And very often, achieving a certain goal might simply be out of a person's control. In such cases, an overemphasis on goals can easily lead to disappointment.

While goals undoubtedly have their place, focusing on the process may lead to better outcomes. This is especially true when it comes to spiritual goals. A believer whose goal is to be saved might easily look at the Christian life as a checklist. "I'm worshiping right, giving right, and acting right, so I'm all right." Except that focusing on behavior never saved anyone.

Paul focused on the process: "Walk in the Spirit." In other words, live your life connected to Jesus. Remain connected to the Savior. Paul emphasized the *process*.

If you focus on externals, on doing, Christianity will frustrate you. But if Jesus is truly the center of your experience, and you enjoy the process of being one with Him, faith in God will be nothing but joy. And eternal life will be yours.

---

* Seth Rubinroit, "Brenda Martinez's Emotional Week at Olympic Trials Ends in Triumph," *NBC Sports*, July 10, 2016, http://archivepyc.nbcolympics.com/news/brenda-martinezs-emotional-week-olympic-trials -ends-triumph.

Second Chance

When we were still without strength,
in due time Christ died for the ungodly.

—Romans 5:6

In 1849, Russian writer Fyodor Dostoevsky was arrested for alleged anti-government activities and sentenced to death. On December 22 of that year, Dostoevsky and others faced a firing squad. The condemned men were separated into groups of three. Dostoevsky stood to one side, awaiting his execution as he watched his peers being lined up and tied to posts. Guns were raised as the condemned men awaited the order to fire. Their hearts were heavy as they heard, "Ready . . . aim . . ." But the order to fire was never given. At that moment, a messenger arrived saying the czar had changed their sentence to hard labor in a Siberian work camp. The czar had already granted the men a reprieve, but he wanted it delivered as late as possible.*

In a novel he wrote years later, Dostoevsky described a character who, facing death at the scaffold, pondered what he would do if he was given one more chance to live. He said, "I would turn every minute into an age, nothing would be wasted, every minute would be accounted for."†

What would you do if you were given a second chance at life? How would it alter the way you live? The truth is that everyone has been given a second chance. Romans 6:23 says, "The wages of sin is death," and Paul wrote earlier in the book of Romans that "all have sinned and come short of the glory of God" (Romans 3:23, KJV). Everyone alive has earned the wages of sin. But God so loved the world that He stepped in to provide all people with a way of escape from the sin's penalty. Although we deserve death, "the gift of God is eternal life through Jesus Christ our Lord" (Romans 6:23).

Faith in Jesus provides every sinner with a second chance. Through Jesus' death on the cross, we all have the opportunity to start again. God offers a new beginning. The death penalty is gone, and life with all its possibilities stretches before us. It is too precious a gift to waste.

---

* History.com Editors, "Fyodor Dostoevsky Spared From Execution," *History*, November 13, 2009, https://www.history.com/this-day-in-history/dostoevsky-reprieved-at-last-minute.

† Fyodor Dostoevsky, *The Idiot*, trans. Alan Myers (New York: Oxford University Press, 1992), 64, https://books.google.com/books?id=5fyuj9x9UZIC&pg=PA64.

Father Forgive

Bearing with one another, and forgiving one another, if anyone has a
complaint against another; even as Christ forgave you, so you also must do.
—Colossians 3:13

I t is tempting to hang on to the anger or bitterness that can grow out of a sense of having been ill-treated. That is why Paul wrote, "Even as Christ forgave you, so you also must do" (Colossians 3:13).

It is true that people are frequently caused to endure extremely difficult circumstances through no fault of their own. An Olympic gold medalist said she would "never forgive" the woman who beat her at the Olympic Games but was later disqualified for drug use. It isn't uncommon to hear people say during or after a murder trial that they'll never forgive the guilty party for the crime that was committed. It isn't difficult to understand the hurt and pain that drives such emotions.

But bitterness toward another person is never justified. Holding on to hurt and pain is unhealthy physically, emotionally, and spiritually. It has often been said that choosing not to forgive is like taking a poison pill and waiting for the other person to die. Paul did not say that forgiveness is appropriate only when it seems justifiable. He said we "must" forgive, as Jesus has forgiven us.

Forgiveness is most powerful in the life of the one doing the forgiving. To choose not to forgive but to instead harbor bitterness is to allow the person who hurt you to have a measure of control over your life. Long after that person has forgotten what was done, he or she still inhabits your thoughts and causes pain in your life.

After the cathedral in Coventry, England, was bombed during World War II, cathedral provost Richard Howard wrote the words "Father Forgive" on the wall behind the altar in what was left standing of the church. A city had just been bombed by an enemy. Hundreds of people had been killed. And Richard Howard knew just what to pray.

The greatest Forgiver of all is Jesus. In Luke 23:34, as He was hanging on a cross enduring indescribable pain, He prayed, saying, "Father, forgive them." Today, He extends forgiveness to all, forgiveness no one deserves.*

---

* For more on forgiveness, see Dick Tibbits with Steve Halliday, *Forgive to Live: How Forgiveness Can Save Your Life* (Nashville, TN: Thomas Nelson, 2008).

I Forgive You

If we confess our sins, He is faithful and just to forgive us
our sins and to cleanse us from all unrighteousness.

—1 John 1:9

A man's careless driving resulted in the death of a motorcyclist. The wife of the deceased said to the very repentant driver, "I forgive you, and my family forgives you." As simple and as powerful as that. Clearly, forgiving the driver didn't make right the wrong that he had committed. But it did release the family of the deceased motorcyclist from unending hurt and bitterness, and it enabled them to move forward with their lives.

"I forgive you, and my family forgives you." That's the attitude God wants every person to have. Colossians 3:13 says, "Bearing with one another, and forgiving one another, if anyone has a complaint against another; even as Christ forgave you, so you also must do." Incredible examples of forgiveness shouldn't be the exception. As difficult as forgiveness may seem, God calls on His children to extend forgiveness to others.

A church that does not emphasize forgiveness has nothing to offer the world. Nonbelievers know that Christians claim a high standard. When we fail to meet that standard, we open up the church to criticism and even ridicule. But when we allow Jesus to live His life in us and to do what for us might be impossible, we give evidence to the world that there exists a power far greater than any human power. Forgiving another in the face of hurt and loss is evidence of the working of a divine Agency—a manifestation of the grace of an almighty God.

While human beings often choose to withhold forgiveness, we can only imagine our future if God took that same approach. Eternity has been opened up to us because God chose to forgive us of our sins. One of the most remarkable verses in the Bible assures us that "if we confess our sins, He is faithful and just to forgive us our sins" (1 John 1:9).

God is willing to forgive us for all of our many wrongs. He asks us to show the same love and mercy to others. And we may if our hearts have been fully opened to Him.

Willing?

"Whoever desires to come after Me, let him deny himself,
and take up his cross, and follow Me."

—Mark 8:34

A sign outside a church in rural northern Arkansas tapped into the very core of the gospel message. It said, "God won't change your will against your will."

Jesus came into this world to die for our sins, and He offers the gift of salvation to all who are willing. The difference between the saved and the lost isn't that the saved are better people or that the lost are undeserving of eternal life. God is willing that "all should come to repentance" (2 Peter 3:9). Jesus said, "Whoever desires to come after Me, let him deny himself, and take up his cross, and follow Me" (Mark 8:34). John 3:16 says that "whoever believes in Him" shall "have everlasting life." Salvation is offered to all.

But not all are willing to be saved. Salvation is received through a connection with God, and the only people who can have a thriving relationship with God are those who *want* to, those who are *willing*.

This simple thought opens to us the exciting possibilities Jesus offers. As humans, we have a selfish will, but God is able to blend our will with His own. That is what we refer to as conversion. As Ellen White once wrote, "Everything depends upon the right action of the will."* The person who is not willing to yield his or her will to be molded by the Holy Spirit cannot experience the new birth.

James tells us to "submit to God" (James 4:7), which is the key to the experience of the gospel. It is what the sign in front of the church in Arkansas was suggesting. If you are willing to let God have His way, He can then do in you what you could never do for yourself. If God has your cooperation, your permission, if God has your willingness, then He can do what needs to be done in your life. If you see areas where you need spiritual growth, don't feel as though there is no hope. If you are willing, then you are on your way to victory.

---

* Ellen G. White, *Steps to Christ* (Washington, DC: Review and Herald®, 1956), 47.

Treating Her Right

*Husbands, love your wives and do not
be bitter toward them.*

—Colossians 3:19

M arried people tend to spend a lot of time with each other. Marriage joins two people together for life. But for those whose marriages are not filled with happiness, that time spent together can feel like a life sentence.

Life can often challenge your Christian experience. Life can be busy, and busyness can cause stress. And that can affect the way you interact with others, even those you love. Many people vent their frustrations on those they should treat with the most tenderness. What God intended to be a blessing far too often seems like anything but.

While today's verse is directed toward men, there's no question that the counsel Paul offers is equally applicable to either spouse. However, Paul especially saw the need to say to men, "Treat your wife with love. Don't take out your frustrations on her, and don't let what she does—or what others do—allow you to become bitter, angry, or frustrated with her."

And Paul did not add an escape clause where he said, "Unless, of course, your wife is especially hard to deal with." Paul did not say, "Some of you are married to difficult women, and so I don't blame you for losing your cool!" Instead, Paul's intention—God's intention—was that every man would only be kind and loving, no matter the circumstances.

So where can a person get that kind of heart? Only the grace of God can do that work in a person's life. Couples who once despised each other have grown to deeply love each other after going to God in faith. God can give any spouse the grace to be tolerant and kind, and He can work in the heart of the most critical man to cause him to be truly supportive of his wife.

God wants to bless marriages and homes, and He calls husbands and wives to be all they can be through the power of the Holy Spirit.

Chosen!

"You whom I have taken from the ends of the earth,
And called from its farthest regions,
And said to you,
'You are My servant,
I have chosen you and have not cast you away.'"

—Isaiah 41:9

He was a "couldn't miss" college baseball prospect, but when he dived headfirst into second base during a college game, Cory Hahn broke his neck and was paralyzed. His playing days were over. But in an extraordinary gesture, Cory was drafted in the 34th round of the Major League Baseball draft by the Arizona Diamondbacks.*

Cory was selected for a professional team even though he would never play. Cory Hanh's story is a story of compassion and kindness. And one that has an obvious parallel.

Even though humanity has been injured by sin, out of His incredible kindness and grace, God chooses to draft broken sinners onto His team. God says through Isaiah, "You are My servant, I have chosen you and have not cast you away" (Isaiah 41:9). How much use were Adam and Eve to God after they fell into sin in the Garden of Eden? Sin had separated them from God, and to be on God's side, they would have to be rehabilitated—an incredibly painful process that would cost the life of the Son of God.

God did not redeem Adam and Eve simply to be magnanimous, to make a gesture, or to do our original grandparents a kind turn. God was motivated by love to save Adam and Eve. He redeemed Adam and Eve because God so loved the world that He couldn't possibly do anything else. It would cost Him the life of His own Son. Angels would be involved in a controversy unlike anything before or anything that will ever be. The most expensive rescue mission in the history of the cosmos saw God do something He didn't have to do for the most helpless creatures in the universe, and He did it because of the love He has in His heart for you.

God has chosen you to be on His team for eternity. Your abilities matter not. Your success or failure up to this point does not make you more or less likely to be selected. Out of love and by an act of amazing grace, God has chosen you to represent Him forever.

---

* Tyler Conway, "Arizona Diamondbacks Draft Paralyzed Arizona State Player Cory Hahn," *The Bleacher Report*, June 8, 2013, https://bleacherreport.com/articles/1666706-arizona-diamondbacks-draft-paralyzed-arizona-state-player-cory-hahn.

You Are Not Alone

Jesus wept.

—John 11:35

Even for followers of Jesus, not every day is filled with hugs and smiles and good news. Some days are difficult. Pain, grief, and loss are often the lot of even the most committed Christian believers. What the disciple of Jesus needs to know is not that days are going to be easy but that no matter what life brings, God is with you.

The shortest verse in the Bible is John 11:35, which says, simply, "Jesus wept." Jesus was affected by the grief of His friends as He stood at the tomb of Lazarus. Grief affected Jesus then, and it still does. Our compassionate Savior still feels for those who carry heavy burdens. Whatever you're going through, you are not alone.

Human beings weren't created to experience fear, death, or loss. These are intruders. When God created humanity in the Garden of Eden, He wired us for contentment, joy, and security. For six thousand years, people have been grappling with the gritty realities of life, and in all that time, the stark realities of hardship and loss have become no less difficult to process.

Witness a Middle Eastern mother mourning the loss of her son after a suicide bombing; a peasant woman struggling to make sense of the catastrophic flood that destroyed her home and swept away her livelihood; an elderly man walking numbly to his car following the funeral of his wife of sixty-five years. A lifetime of living in a world where death, grief, and loss are expected has not made it any easier to deal with such difficulties.

Where is hope to be found when emotions are raw and experiences are painful? There is a Savior who feels for you, who understands what it is to experience loss and hurt, and who will uphold you even in your darkest moments. There is a God in heaven who understands from experience what it is to lose the One most precious to Him. By experience, God understands the pain of loss. Heaven has demonstrated there is comfort to be found for those wrestling with life's difficult moments.

Carefree

Casting all your care upon Him,
for He cares for you.

—1 Peter 5:7

S omeone once stated that the vast majority of what causes people anxiety is that which either isn't true, isn't going to happen, or you can't do anything about. It seems reasonable to assume that if we didn't worry about what we cannot control, we would experience a lot less stress.

Stress is a fact of everyday life, but too much stress leads to distress. It isn't uncommon for stress to cause headaches, elevated blood pressure, and difficulty sleeping. And stress can exacerbate other symptoms and diseases.

It isn't possible to remove all stressors from your life, and some stress is perhaps even necessary. But there is something you can do when your burdens press you down. First Peter 5:7 suggests that we can turn to God and receive heaven's help in stress-filled moments.

If God really cares for you, you can face every day knowing that you have not been left to bear your own burdens. Understanding that God is ultimately in control of the universe means that even when we face dark periods in our lives, we can have the underlying assurance that, ultimately, things are going to work out well because God has a perfect plan for us. The Second Coming is referred to in Scripture as the "blessed hope" (Titus 2:13), a constant reminder that one day Jesus will return to earth and make all things new.

Today you can know that God not only cares about you but also wants to calm your anxiety and bring peace to your heart. "God is our refuge and strength, a very present help in trouble" (Psalm 46:1). Notice how the psalmist expressed the thought. God is a "very present" help. If you'll cast your cares on God—and then leave them with God—you'll have more peace than you have ever had. He is with you today. That knowledge doesn't take away all of our difficulties and stresses, but it does provide us with hope and help while we prepare for eternity.

Every Time

And God is able to make all grace abound toward you,
that you, always having all sufficiency in all things,
may have an abundance for every good work.
—2 Corinthians 9:8

Nobody wants to be a spiritual failure. But many people despair because they continually trip over the same ground: losing their temper, indulging immoral thoughts, using substances they know they shouldn't use, and so on. For many Christians, faith is a seemingly endless cycle of success and failure—a roller-coaster ride of ups and downs that invariably leads to spiritual defeat.

Yet there is a way out. Paul assures us God won't allow you to be tempted beyond what you are able to bear (1 Corinthians 10:13). In every temptation, there is a way of escape. No matter how hard a trial might seem, victory is available. However, victory does not necessarily come through trying harder or praying more.

Victory comes when the presence of Jesus, through the Person of the Holy Spirit, overtakes a life and makes that life His own. Jesus prayed that the will of the Father would be done in His life, and when we learn to pray the same prayer, we will see power at work in our lives that will leave us amazed and victorious! There isn't any victory Jesus cannot win, so as we grow toward God's eternal kingdom, we need not despair that pride, envy, or dishonesty has to be a permanent part of our character. The promise is made in Revelation 22:4 that God's name—in this case representing His character—will be reproduced in the mind of the child of God.

This is a work God promises to do. When temptation comes, God will provide you with a way of escape. If dependence on God in temptation becomes habitual, victory will become habitual, to the point that when obeying God, we shall be doing nothing but carrying out our own impulses. Remind God of His great promise: "Lord, You have promised to provide me with a way of escape." He will do so every time.

Kept

*Do not be conformed to this world, but be transformed by
the renewing of your mind, that you may prove what is
that good and acceptable and perfect will of God.*
—Romans 12:2

The average American is subjected to thousands of media impressions every day: billboards, television, radio, magazines, advertising, direct mail, and so on. Media pervades every area of society. Smartphones and Wi-Fi make it possible to take the media with you virtually wherever you go. Today there are video screens on the pumps at gas stations, videos playing in supermarkets, and televisions in the bathrooms at restaurants. It seems there is no place beyond the reach of the media.

Media is certainly not all bad. But most Americans spend more than five hours a day watching television and almost seven hours online. A constant barrage of media impressions assails our senses almost to the point of overload. While some of it is benign, much of what the media serves up is positively harmful.

So what is in your mind to counteract the secular and often spiritually dangerous influences that impress themselves on you? We are continually being bombarded by the media, but Romans 8:5 tells us that the Spirit of God can act as a barrier against the constant suggestions of the enemy and the endless distractions of society. Paul says, "For those who live according to the flesh set their minds on the things of the flesh, but those who live according to the Spirit, the things of the Spirit." A mind that is sustained by Scripture, the presence of Jesus, and the companionship of angels is a mind that won't be derailed by worldly attractions. In fact, a mind that has learned to appreciate what heaven appreciates will be far less interested in cheap entertainment and shameful gimmicks. One way to be less affected by media is to be less engaged with media. And much of it can easily be done without.

The great spiritual battle currently taking place in the universe is a battle for the mind. More than anything, Satan wants to affect and even control your thought processes. But if Jesus dwells in you today, He will keep your mind where it should be kept. As relentless as it is, this world does not have to overcome you.

Sudden?

"And I looked, and behold, you had sinned against the LORD *your God—had made for yourselves a molded calf! You had turned aside quickly from the way which the* LORD *had commanded you."*
—Deuteronomy 9:16

The earthquake happened suddenly. That tornado came out of nowhere. The cold snap occurred just like that. At least, that's how we often perceive it. But disastrous weather events are the culmination of many factors that develop over time. The hurricane that caused so much damage had been brewing for many days and was produced by the complexities of an intricate weather system.

Near the end of his life, Moses reminded the Israelites of a huge spiritual failure when he said, "You had turned aside quickly from the way which the LORD had commanded you" (Deuteronomy 9:16). It is interesting Moses said they had turned away "quickly." The people paused their wilderness wanderings to wait at the bottom of a mountain while Moses spent time in the presence of God. In no time at all, they had plunged deep into sin and rebellion. In one respect, it happened quickly. In a few short weeks, God's own people had gone from pledging their allegiance to God to worshiping a golden calf.

Viewed from another perspective, however, this apostasy was a long time in the making. Israel had spent many years living in the midst of heathenism, and those sinful influences had affected the people. It is difficult to lie on a beach without some sand sticking to you. The seeds of rebellion were in them. Their apostasy happened quickly in that they had recently committed to the service of God, but it happened slowly inasmuch as their sin was a harvest from seeds sown long before.

If termites are eating the heart out of your Christian experience, a fall that has been a long time in the making can happen suddenly. Our defense against a slowly produced sudden fall is surrender to Christ. If He has your heart, He will keep you in His way. Entrust yourself daily to God so that you don't experience a similar sudden fall.

Big Trouble, Small Troublemaker!

A fool's lips enter into contention,
and his mouth calls for blows.

—Proverbs 18:6

How many times has your mouth landed you in trouble? Not what you put into your mouth, but what comes out of your mouth. The words you use. It is easy to speak without thinking, to vent your frustrations, and to say exactly what you're thinking in a given moment, but doing so frequently ends in regret. A few small words can create major problems.

The Bible speaks a lot about the potential the tongue has to create strife. Your tongue can get you into a lot of trouble. James wrote,

> Indeed, we put bits in horses' mouths that they may obey us, and we turn their whole body. Look also at ships: although they are so large and are driven by fierce winds, they are turned by a very small rudder wherever the pilot desires. Even so, the tongue is a little member and boasts great things.
>
> See how great a forest a little fire kindles! And the tongue is a fire, a world of iniquity (James 3:3–6).

It takes only a moment of time to say something critical, cutting, angry, or condemning, and once words are spoken, they can't be unsaid.

God was gracious in giving each person the capacity to remember, but after you've said something you regret, you might wish the person you spoke to would forget your ill-chosen words. Many people can easily remember cruel or hurtful words that were spoken to them years, even decades, ago.

When you're tempted to say something harsh or unkind, it's often better not to say anything at all. Of course, that can be a real challenge. But remember that if Jesus has your heart, He'll also have your tongue. Cultivate the habit of asking God to guide your words, to touch your heart in such a way that what comes out of your mouth will be representative of Jesus. When God's Word gets into your mind, His words will come out of your mouth.

Delightful!

"Everyone who keeps from defiling the Sabbath,
And holds fast My covenant—
Even them I will bring to My holy mountain,
And make them joyful in My house of prayer."
—Isaiah 56:6, 7

It can easily seem as though the world is conspiring against us. Our parents and grandparents were told that automatic this and electric that would make life easier. But in reality, what labor-saving devices have done is give us more time so that we can accomplish more tasks! A washing machine means the family laundry no longer takes half a day to complete, but the time saved is often used to simply do more, which in some ways is good but, in other ways, is not so good.

Former US senator Joe Lieberman wrote a book called *The Gift of Rest*. The back cover says, "Our bodies and souls were *created* to rest—regularly—and when they do, we experience heightened productivity, improved health, and more meaningful relationships."* And in a 2011 interview, he said, "How wonderful it is to stop one day and disconnect all the electronics and just focus in on yourself, your relationship with your family, and God."† Senator Lieberman, who is Jewish, was referring to the Sabbath day, a day he recommends to people of all faiths. The response he received from the religious community was very positive because people recognize more and more that it is a good idea to step back from the busyness of life and connect with God.

God said in Isaiah 58:13, 14,

"If you turn away your foot from the Sabbath,
From doing your pleasure on My holy day,
And call the Sabbath a delight, . . .
Then you shall delight yourself in the LORD."

Society has changed radically in the last half-century or so. We're busier and more stressed. We have more stuff, and we've drifted from God's ideal. But God hasn't changed. He still offers us the same Sabbath He made for Adam and Eve. Take time to rest with God. Call the Sabbath a delight!

---

* Senator Joe Lieberman with David Klinghoffer, *The Gift of Rest: Rediscovering the Beauty of the Sabbath* (New York: Howard Books, 2011), back cover.

† Chana Mayefsky, "Joe Lieberman: Embracing the Sabbath," *Publisher's Weekly*, August 31, 2011, https://www.publishersweekly.com/pw/by-topic/industry-news/religion/article/48528-joe-lieberman -embracing-the-sabbath.html.

What to Do?

*"Is it not to share your bread with the hungry,
And that you bring to your house the poor who are cast out;
When you see the naked, that you cover him,
And not hide yourself from your own flesh?"*

—Isaiah 58:7

After a devastating tornado ripped through Oklahoma City, people came out of the woodwork to help those in need. One man who joined with a team of others to sift through debris and rescued many people said afterward, "It just felt good to help."

There's something about doing for others that brings blessing in its wake. God urges us to share our bread with the hungry, to care for the poor who are cast out, and to clothe the naked. Psychologists say it is good for a person's mental health to get involved in helping people. There's a reaction that occurs that brings blessing to the one who blesses others.

And perhaps this is where faith in God is most genuinely expressed. It doesn't take much to claim to have faith in God, but a demonstration of disinterested care for a fellow human being gives evidence that faith is real and not simply a theory. James emphasized this in James 2:15–17. "If a brother or sister is naked and destitute of daily food, and one of you says to them, 'Depart in peace, be warmed and filled,' but you do not give them the things which are needed for the body, what does it profit? Thus also faith by itself, if it does not have works, is dead."

God-given opportunities to turn our faith into action demonstrate to others that what we believe is not self-centered but other-centered. Faith in God produces in the believer concern for the well-being of others and a desire to actively be a blessing to the world.

Jesus brought this into sharp focus when He said in Matthew 25:40, "Inasmuch as you did it to one of the least of these My brethren, you did it to Me." Love for Christ leads to love for others. Love for others is a demonstration of love for God.

In blessing others, we are blessed. Look for the chance to make a difference in someone's life, and as you do, you'll be doing the work of Jesus.

Providence

As you do not know what is the way of the wind, or how
the bones grow in the womb of her who is with child, so you
do not know the works of God who makes everything.
—Ecclesiastes 11:5

Abraham Lincoln's son, Robert, was on a railway platform in Jersey City, New Jersey, when he slipped between the platform and a moving train. Someone behind him grabbed his coat collar and lifted him to safety, saving him from serious injury and possibly death. The man who saved young Robert Lincoln was Edwin Booth, the brother of John Wilkes Booth, who later murdered President Lincoln. The brother of Lincoln's assassin saved Lincoln's son.* A coincidence? Some might call it that. But when God is at work in our lives, there is no such thing as coincidence. Instead, the working of God is *providence*. Just as we "do not know what is the way of the wind, or how the bones grow in the womb" (Ecclesiastes 11:5), we can't see how God works in our lives.

Chance meetings are often much more than chance. A man attended a worship service with his family. Being the last people through the lunch line meant they had nowhere to sit to eat, so they opted to eat while standing. Church members urged them to join the group, but without a place to sit, it was impossible for them to do so. Several church members, realizing there were guests without a place to sit, cleared a space for the visitors. As they sat and ate, the man chatted with the person sitting opposite him. It turned out he was a surgeon who discovered the man had some health challenges. By the time lunch was over, the man visiting the church had an appointment to see the surgeon, who operated on the visitor only a week later. Before attending church, the visitor had not known he had a life-threatening illness. But God arranged the seating at lunch—and the timing of the seating—in such a way that a life was saved!

Even when you don't discern it, God is at work. He leaves nothing to chance and is constantly working to do for you what you cannot do for yourself.

---

* Brad Smithfield, "Edwin Booth, John Wilkes Booth's Brother, Saved the Life of Robert Lincoln, on a Train Platform," *The Vintage News*, January 23, 2017, https://www.thevintagenews.com/2017/01/23/edwin-booth -john-wilkes-booths-brother-saved-the-life-of-robert-lincoln-on-a-train-platform/.

The Right Response

What shall I render to the LORD for
all His benefits toward me?

—Psalm 116:12

The Bible asks some searching questions. One such question is this one found in Psalms: after all that God has done for us, how should we respond to Him? We can give offerings, we can share God's love by witnessing to others, we can do mission service, or we could dedicate our talents to God. We could do any or all of those things and yet still be in danger of missing the key point of David's question.

The first thing God wants from you is your heart. Better put, God wants your life. And once He has that, He has everything. Micah 6:8 says,

> He has shown you, O man, what is good;
> And what does the LORD require of you
> But to do justly,
> To love mercy,
> And to walk humbly with your God?

Recognizing what really matters, David wrote in Psalm 51:16, "For You do not desire sacrifice, or else I would give it; You do not delight in burnt offering." Religious activities without a clean heart and right spirit are meaningless. David continued, "The sacrifices of God are a broken spirit. A broken and a contrite heart—these, O God, You will not despise" (verse 17). A husband who wants to express love for his wife could build her a mansion or shower her with gifts, but if he can't treat her with respect and show her love, then his gifts would mean nothing.

What should we do in light of the Cross? In light of God's constant care and provision? Let Him have your heart today. And if you're unsure how to give your heart to God, simply ask Him to take it and make it His own. He will. And then, as your life increasingly becomes the possession of Jesus, He will direct your life more and more in the path that He wants you to go. Faith in God is an experience of growing in God's grace. If God does not have your heart, your experience can never be truly enjoyable. If God has your heart, everything else will follow.

Confidence in the Courtroom

For we must all appear before the judgment seat of Christ,
that each one may receive the things done in the body,
according to what he has done, whether good or bad.
—2 Corinthians 5:10

Over the years, numerous court trials have dominated the headlines. The State of Tennessee v. John Thomas Scopes (the Scopes Monkey Trial) in 1925, the trial of OJ Simpson seventy years later, and many other courtroom dramas have captured the attention of the masses and generated enormous media interest.

Every person alive will one day have his or her moment in court. The Bible says that "we must all appear before the judgment seat of Christ." This judgment has greater implications than any earthly court case. Decisions made in this judgment will be irreversible and will remain in effect for as long as time shall last.

The judgment in heaven is spoken of in the books of both Daniel and Revelation. Having painted a dramatic picture of the scene, Daniel announced that "the court was seated, and the books were opened" (Daniel 7:10). In Revelation, John writes of an angel flying in the midst of heaven with a message for the entire world to hear, announcing that "the hour of His judgment has come" (Revelation 14:7). At the core of God's end-time message, He alerts us to the solemn reality of the judgment.

Surely this is a sobering thought. God will examine our lives in a judgment that has eternal ramifications. Yet far from fearing a God who is looking for reasons to condemn faulty sinners, we should understand the judgment as functioning like an audit. In the judgment, God looks at the record of a person's life and judges according to the decisions we have made for or against Him. God simply recognizes and honors our decisions.

This means that you can face heaven's judgment without fear. Those who have repented of their sins and accepted Jesus as Lord and Savior will be recognized by God as having done so. Trusting in Jesus means any repentant sinner can approach the judgment with confidence. The One who has died for your sins gives you His own righteousness, and in the judgment represents you as your heavenly High Priest. The One who has borne your burdens declares repentant sinners to be forgiven and saved.

From Rags to Riches

If you confess with your mouth the Lord Jesus and believe in your heart that God has raised Him from the dead, you will be saved.

—Romans 10:9

Near the end of World War II in 1945, German forces occupying the city of Sastin, in what was then Czechoslovakia, began evacuating as the Russian army drew near. A German commandant filled several battered trunks to the brim with money that had been looted from the Czechoslovakian National Bank in Bratislava. His staff car wasn't large enough for the trunks, so he instructed certain Slovakian peasants to look after them, telling them he would one day be back to collect the trunks. "And when you hand them over to me," he said, "you will be richly rewarded."

When the Russians arrived in town a short time later, they inspected the Nazi headquarters and found the trunks filled with currency. Realizing the money would be of no use to the Russian forces occupied with pursuing the Nazis, a Russian lieutenant gave orders for the people of Sastin to receive a thousand korunas for every year of life they had lived. The money was quickly distributed.

In all, 300 million korunas were handed out, the equivalent of tens of millions of dollars today. People with large families ended up with between 150,000 and 200,000 korunas, a lot of money in that day and time.* Those downtrodden people went quite literally from rags to riches. When the day began, they could not have realized they were going to be the beneficiaries of a financial windfall.

God has something even better for you. You can go from rags to righteousness in as much time as it takes you to make a simple decision: "If you confess with your mouth the Lord Jesus and believe in your heart that God has raised Him from the dead, you will be saved" (Romans 10:9). Jesus offers us something of far greater value than money. Whether you have little or much in this world, eternal life is yours if you have Jesus. Make a decision for Jesus today, and you have the assurance that He will give you His righteousness and heaven will be yours.

---

* Theodore Irwin, "The Town That Got Rich Quick," *Des Moines Register*, September 8, 1946.

Tension

*"Strive to enter through the narrow gate, for many,
I say to you, will seek to enter and will not be able."*
—Luke 13:24

The beautiful sound made by a well-played piano is not in actuality produced by the pianist. While the pianist plays the instrument, the beautiful music is produced by *tension*. Each of the 230 strings on the typical piano is under about 160 pounds of tension. If the tension is not as it should be, not even Rachmaninoff or Mozart could make the piano produce beautiful music.

The gospel works on much the same principle. If the tension in the Bible isn't balanced correctly, a person's understanding of the gospel will be affected. Paul wrote that we are saved by grace through faith (Ephesians 2:8), while James wrote that "faith by itself, if it does not have works, is dead" (James 2:17). While Jesus urged us to "strive to enter through the narrow gate" (Luke 13:24), Romans 5:1 clearly states that we are "justified by faith." But rather than being in conflict, these concepts are complementary.

A person enters a saving union with Jesus by faith. The thief on the cross, the woman taken in adultery, and the publican who prayed in the temple had nothing to recommend them to Jesus. They reached out to God by faith and, as a result, received justification. They were forgiven and pardoned, made new by the grace of Christ.

Galatians 2:20 takes the believer's experience a step further. "I have been crucified with Christ; it is no longer I who live, but Christ lives in me; and the life which I now live in the flesh I live by faith in the Son of God, who loved me and gave Himself for me." The same writer stated in Philippians 2:13 that "it is God who works in you both to will and to do for His good pleasure."

Faith in Jesus lays hold on the gift of salvation. Then as Jesus works in a believer's life and continues to grow that person's Christian experience, the believer becomes more like Jesus. Old things pass away. An old life becomes a new life. God does the work to bring us to Christ and keep us in Christ. Our surrender to Him allows Him to work out His will in our lives.

Technology

Behold, I tell you a mystery: We shall not all sleep, but we
shall all be changed—in a moment, in the twinkling of an eye,
at the last trumpet. For the trumpet will sound, and the dead
will be raised incorruptible, and we shall be changed.
—1 Corinthians 15:51, 52

A Georgia woman who tragically lost her hands, a leg, and a foot to a flesh-eating disease received "bionic" hands. The remarkable prosthetic hands enable her to do most of life's regular tasks, including cooking, cleaning, and drinking.* This is reminiscent of *The Six Million Dollar Man*, a fictional television program from the 1970s about a severely injured man who was "rebuilt" with robotic body parts. As with so many technological advances, the Georgia woman's story has seen science fiction become a reality.

Yet while we thank God for the technological advances that result in changing the lives of the sick or injured, the best that science can do is to modify or replace. A person who receives life-saving surgery will one day die. The best a transplant recipient can hope for is a few more decades of life. Wonderful, certainly—but very much temporary.

But consider what God can do and what God will do. "We shall all be changed—in a moment, in the twinkling of an eye, at the last trumpet. For the trumpet will sound, and the dead will be raised incorruptible, and we shall be changed" (1 Corinthians 15:51, 52).

This is not a modification of the old. While modern science can do incredible things, the God of science can do so much more. One day God will raise the dead and give both the righteous dead and the righteous living new bodies. Technology could never do that!

The God who made us "fearfully and wonderfully" (Psalm 139:14) will one day wake the sleeping dead, calling forth from their final resting places all who died in faith in Jesus Christ. No artificial limbs will be needed. No reading glasses, crutches, or wheelchairs will be seen on that day. As grateful as we are for the wonders of technology, the God who gives wisdom to scientists, inventors, engineers, and doctors is going to do more than anyone has ever seen. What a day it will be when Jesus returns!

---

* Phillip Lucas, "Flesh-Eating Disease Victim Gets Prosthetic Hands," *Medical Xpress*, May 18, 2013, https://medicalxpress.com/news/2013-05-flesh-eating-disease-victim-prosthetic.html.

Winner!

Do you not know that those who run in a race all run, but one
receives the prize? Run in such a way that you may obtain it.
—1 Corinthians 9:24

It has often been said, after a sporting contest, it is regrettable there can be only one winner. When American tennis player John Isner won the longest match in professional tennis history, beating Frenchman Nicolas Mahut seventy games to sixty-eight in the fifth set of a five-set marathon, he said, "It stinks someone had to lose."* Anyone who has run all 26 miles, 385 yards of a marathon will tell you it's a grueling event, yet whenever there is a sprint to the finish of a marathon, only one athlete can get to the finish line first. The other athlete, after training and planning and competing and hurting, can do no better than second. It's a shame someone has to lose.

The citizens of the city of Corinth were very familiar with sporting contests, regularly hosting sporting events very similar to the Olympic Games. Paul referred to these ancient games in his first letter to the Corinthians. They all run, Paul said, but there's only one winner. So, run to win. It would make absolutely no sense to dedicate your life to a sporting endeavor only to fail to give your best when competing on your sport's biggest stage. Because there was only one winner, competitors gave their all as they strove to win.

But Christians can celebrate that in the Christian race, there is more than one winner. This is the difference between the sporting contests Paul referenced and the Christian faith. You need not be the fittest, fastest, or strongest Christian in town. You need not look with envy at the natural gifts or talents of another believer and wish you could have what he or she has. In the Christian "race," every believer in Jesus can be victorious. Unlike an athletic event, faith isn't a matter of being first across the line. If you can have faith in Jesus, you can be a winner—eternally.

---

* John Banks, "June 24 in Sports History: 'It Stinks Someone Had to Lose'," *MSN Sports*, June 23, 2020, https://www.msn.com/en-us/sports/more-sports/june-24-in-sports-history-it-stinks-someone-had-to-lose/ar-BB15SlEK.

Trust

"Though He slay me, yet will I trust Him. Even so,
I will defend my own ways before Him."

—Job 13:15

I t's easy to trust God on a warm day when all is well and you find a parking place in the perfect spot and people everywhere are smiling. But when things are falling apart, trusting God can be far more difficult. What happens when a tornado destroys a town, and it's your town? And your home? Tragedy usually strikes other families. What happens when it strikes yours? Even the children of the most faithful believers come down with cancer. Lifelong believers in Jesus get Alzheimer's. Committed Christians die in tragic accidents.

For some people, one of the great mysteries of a life of faith is that believers are not always exempt from life's harsh and bitter circumstances. But it must be remembered that faith in God was never intended to be a guarantee against sickness or suffering. The apostle Paul prayed three times that God would remove his "thorn in the flesh" (2 Corinthians 12:7, 8), but his prayer wasn't answered in the way he had hoped. The faithful saint Dorcas "became sick and died" (Acts 9:37), James was beheaded (Acts 12:2), and Job lost not only most of his family but also virtually all of his possessions.

The circumstances of our lives are not a measure of God's faithfulness. The extent of God's faithfulness was settled millennia ago. "In the beginning," God created the world as an expression of His heart of love. Several thousand years later, Jesus died on the cross, "while we were still sinners" (Romans 5:8). God has given to the world the gift of the Holy Spirit and the promise of everlasting life. There is no question that God is faithful.

The trials that come into our lives are opportunities for us to understand our own faithfulness. Job was able to say, "Though He slay me, yet will I trust Him" (Job 13:15). While we don't always understand why God permits certain circumstances, we can trust Him. Such a testimony not only speaks volumes to those looking on but also tells God we are not merely fair-weather Christians.

The Blown Call

And forgive us our debts,
as we forgive our debtors.

—Matthew 6:12

A Major League Baseball pitcher was one out away from pitching a perfect game. In a perfect game, the pitcher doesn't allow a single opposing batter to get to first base. A perfect game is a rare achievement. Only about two dozen perfect games have ever been recorded. In baseball, it's a big deal.

One more out, and Armando Galarraga would have become only the twenty-first pitcher ever to accomplish that feat. The pitcher pitched, the batter hit the ball, the fielder threw it to first base in time to beat the sprinting batter, and the pitcher had his perfect game. Except that the first-base umpire ruled the batter safe! That mistake—and it was a mistake—cost the pitcher his perfect game and a place in sports history. But when Galarraga saw the batter was called safe, he simply smiled, went back to the mound, and got the next batter out. A twenty-eight-out perfect game, if you would.

What would most people do if they were robbed of a place in history? Galarraga simply said of the mistaken umpire, "Nobody's perfect. Everybody's human. I understand." He met with the umpire, who admitted he made a mistake and tearfully apologized. The baseball player hugged him and forgave him, which in the emotionally charged world of professional sports is remarkable.*

God asks us to exercise forgiveness, even when the other person is wrong and denies us something precious. Jesus taught us to pray, "Forgive us our debts, as we forgive our debtors" (Matthew 6:12). In fact, Jesus said that if we refuse to forgive others, we cannot expect God to forgive us. It isn't always easy to forgive, but it's always important. When a man chose to forgive the woman who killed his seventy-five-year-old grandmother—a Bible teacher—it caused tension in his family. There were those who didn't believe he should forgive the killer. Yet he said choosing to forgive brought him "tremendous healing."

Most people have some forgiving to do. And forgiveness is always best. Forgiveness is God's way.

---

* Tom Verducci, "A Heartbreaking Call That Could Change the Course of Baseball," *Sports Illustrated*, June 2, 2010, https://www.si.com/more-sports/2010/06/03/joyces-missedcall.

The God of This World

*Whose minds the god of this age has blinded, who do not
believe, lest the light of the gospel of the glory of Christ,
who is the image of God, should shine on them.*

—2 Corinthians 4:4

The world has largely chosen its leader, and that leader is not the God of heaven. The moral trend of the world is directly opposed to the principles of the Bible. Society in general, while maintaining a superficial acknowledgment of God, has largely abandoned faith in God.

It is easy to think that the sins of this present world are worse than those of previous ages. Whatever the reality, what is beyond question is that sin is now the *prevailing* trend in the world. There appears to be a general acceptance of sin, unlike that which we have seen in recent generations. Society as a whole seems very comfortable in a world that is sinking deeper into evil and vice.

Because Satan is "the god of this world" (2 Corinthians 4:4, KJV), Christians need to be especially on guard. If those around me are serving the enemy of souls and my life is indistinguishable from theirs, I need to ask myself who my God really is. The church also must be alert. Some years ago, Ellen White wrote, "Daily the church is being converted to the world."* History demonstrates that, often, as goes the world, so goes the church.

Surrounded by ungodliness, believers need to be especially vigilant that society's worldly customs and attitudes don't become their own. You don't need to plant weeds in your own garden for weeds to take root. Seeds from your neighbor's garden can easily drift into yours. Without vigilant care and constant attention, even the best garden can be overrun by pests and weeds.

While Satan is the god of this world, he doesn't need to be the god of you. Stay close to Jesus today. When His influence in your life is strong, the influence of the world is weak. A heart that is surrendered to Christ will be kept as His fortress. As the world sinks deeper into sin, God's people can grow more and more into the likeness of Jesus.

---

* Ellen G. White, *Christ's Object Lessons* (Washington, DC: Review and Herald®, 1941), 316.

The Man in the Uniform

Your word is a lamp to my feet
and a light to my path.

—Psalm 119:105

Disoriented in the New York City subway, I didn't have a clue where to go. I knew where I was, and I knew where I wanted to go. But although I had a map, I could not find the platform where I needed to catch my next train.

Thankfully, I was able to find a man in a uniform, a man who worked for the Metropolitan Transportation Authority. A brief explanation and a couple of questions later, he had directed me to the place I needed to be. I continued on my journey, and everything worked out well.

A lost person needs directions. The same is true spiritually, and God in His goodness provides us with all the direction we need. His Word is a lamp that helps us find and keep our footing and a light that makes the pathway clear. The Bible is given by God to be used as a reliable guide.

The major issues confronting society today are all addressed in the Bible. While millions of people are struggling financially, the Bible provides solid financial advice. While marriages continue to fall apart and children continue to lose their way, the Bible counsels us regarding interpersonal relationships, marriage, and raising children. The Bible contains time-tested advice. God doesn't dispense flaky, gimmicky advice but the kind of trustworthy counsel an all-wise Father would give to His children. Governments continue to wrestle with massive health-care issues and the immense financial implications, even while the Bible provides advice that has been scientifically proven to improve health and lengthen life.

Who is informing the decisions you make? Whose wisdom provides the basis for your choices? When you're not sure which way to turn, whom do you ask for directions? The guidance provided in the Bible will never let you down. God only wants the very best for His children. Not a single person was ever disadvantaged by trusting the Word of God. As you allow God's Word to be your counselor, expect to see God bless and prosper your life.

"I'm Free Now!"

But now having been set free from sin, and having become slaves of God,
you have your fruit to holiness, and the end, everlasting life.
—Romans 6:22

I t was a horrifying story that captured the attention of the nation. Three young women were held captive in a basement in Cleveland, Ohio, for ten years, enduring treatment no person should ever be subjected to. When one of them was finally able to speak to a 911 operator, she said, "I've been kidnapped, and I've been missing for ten years. And I'm here. I'm free now." It is difficult to imagine the emotions experienced during that phone call. After ten years of misery, the young women would now be liberated.*

When a group of hostages was taken in Lebanon in the late 1980s, the news media kept the world regularly updated on their situation, and governments applied continual pressure in an effort to have the hostages freed. In contrast, these young women—prisoners, not hostages—were presumed dead and languished in horrible conditions for a decade. But now they were free!

Freedom is the gift that Jesus came to give to the world. The gift of salvation makes us free. Paul wrote, "Having been set free from sin, . . . you have your fruit to holiness, and the end, everlasting life" (Romans 6:22). John 8:36 says, "Therefore if the Son makes you free, you shall be free indeed." And Paul urged the Galatians to "stand fast therefore in the liberty by which Christ has made us free" (Galatians 5:1). Through Jesus, we are free, no longer the captive of sin, no longer the prisoner of the tyrant, self. We are no longer under the death sentence that awaits those who choose to be separate from God.

Thank God those young women were freed from such a terrible situation. While we can only imagine the joy they must have felt, we can experience a similar joy. Do you rejoice for the freedom you have through Jesus, or has the thrill of liberty lost its luster? Christ has truly liberated us from the worst sort of prison, a prison that robs us of our eternal freedom. Be grateful to God for the freedom you have through Jesus.

---

* Devika Bhat, Alexandra Frean, " 'Help Me. I've Been Kidnapped, and Missing for Ten Years. I'm Free Now'," *The Times U.K.*, May 8, 2013, https://www.thetimes.co.uk/article/help-me-ive-been-kidnapped-and -missing-for-ten-years-im-free-now-fp2pbpfqtnd.

What Do You Value?

For where your treasure is,
there your heart will be also.

—Matthew 6:21

It isn't uncommon for collectors to pay large sums of money for sporting memorabilia. A man once paid nearly $93,000 for a blood-stained sock worn in a playoff game by a big-time baseball player. Another collector paid over $650,000 for a hockey jersey worn during the famous "Miracle on Ice" hockey game.* In order to spend that kind of money on something, you have to really want it. What we spend our money on reveals where our values lie.

What does how you spend your money say about your priorities? An interesting "devotional" exercise would be to read your credit card statement. A record of your purchases will help you to see what you consider to be truly important. Compare what you read in your credit card statement with your history of giving to support the work of sharing the gospel. What you find will speak clearly to you about what you value most. Investing in reaching souls with the everlasting gospel brings a greater return on investment than investing in gold, property, or the stock market.

In the Sermon on the Mount, Jesus addressed the phenomenon of people spending their money on that which one day is going to wear away. He said, "Where your treasure is, there your heart will be also" (Matthew 6:21). The man who built the Taj Mahal did so out of love for his deceased wife. Expensive cars are bought by car lovers, not car haters. People ordinarily take vacations in places they like to be. Someone who spends a fortune on a team jersey or a baseball card is a fanatic. (The word *fan* is short for *fanatic*.)

If you are enthusiastic about faith in Christ, your spending will show it. Your offerings will reflect it. Your discretionary spending will reflect it. Your receipts should confirm that your heart is with Jesus. Your money follows what you personally value. Do your spending habits testify that you value Jesus?

---

* Associated Press, "Curt Schilling's Bloody Sock Sells for $92,613 at Auction," *USA Today*, March 24, 2013, https://www.usatoday.com/story/sports/mlb/2013/02/24/curt-schilling-bloody-sock-sells-at-auction /1942457/.

Jonah's Attitude

But it displeased Jonah exceedingly,
and he became angry.

—Jonah 4:1

The story of Jonah is one of the great stories of the Bible. Jonah ran from God's call, was swallowed by a sea creature, and then was belched upon the seashore three days later. Jonah then warned the Ninevites of impending judgment, and—incredibly—the prodigiously wicked Ninevites repented.

But Jonah wasn't happy that the Ninevites repented. He was disappointed that they came to faith in God and were spared divine punishment. It's hard to imagine someone having such a negative attitude. In fact, Jonah complained about the death of a plant while at the same time wishing the Ninevites had perished.

It has been suggested Jonah's disposition was due to fear he would appear to be a false prophet. It is also possible it was simply a matter of malice. The Assyrians were exceptionally wicked. Their cruelty was well known, and they were idol worshipers. It is possible Jonah simply felt that the Assyrians—avowed enemies of Israel—simply didn't deserve to live.

Concerning God sparing the inhabitants of Nineveh, Jonah was "displeased . . . exceedingly," and "very angry" (Jonah 4:1). He was very angry that God had chosen not to destroy a city full of people! The Ninevites repented, God spared them, and Jonah was "very angry." If Jonah's heart had been right with God, he would have instead been jumping for joy.

Humanly speaking, one could justify Jonah's attitude. But what Jonah's attitude reveals is that even God's own people—even those involved in ministry—can have hard hearts. Jonah should have remembered God's great mercy toward him. When Jonah disobediently ran from God, God saved his life, showing him mercy and grace.

It pays to remember what we really are. In dealing with others, honest recognition of our own sinfulness will infuse us with mercy and tolerance. It is easy to write off someone as too sinful to save. But if you remember that God saved you—you whose sins held Jesus on the cross—then you'll realize that God can save anyone. And you'll rejoice when He does. The last thing we want is to have an attitude like Jonah's.

The Best You Can Do

From childhood you have known the Holy Scriptures, which are able
to make you wise for salvation through faith which is in Christ Jesus.
—2 Timothy 3:15

Go into any major bookstore, and you'll find plenty of books on the subject of raising children, and some of them will contain useful advice. But the best thing you can do for a child is found in Paul's words to the young church leader Timothy.

A young mind needs the very best influences, and the best thoughts you can put into a mind are God's words. Young children are deeply impressionable, and their malleable minds are like sponges. While adults tend to struggle with learning new languages, children can learn languages with comparative ease. Their minds are open.

Impressions made on the mind of a child can last a lifetime. Solomon wrote in Proverbs 22:6, "Train up a child in the way he should go, and when he is old he will not depart from it." Research conducted by the Barna Group, a California-based Christian polling group, shows that nearly half of all Americans who accept Jesus as their personal Savior do so before the age of thirteen and that two out of three born-again Christians made their decision to accept Jesus before their eighteenth birthday.*

If children are not being educated in the things of heaven, it is certain Satan is working to program them with values opposed to the gospel. There is no time to lose when it comes to educating children spiritually. There is a vast, cosmic conspiracy engineered to separate even small children from God. Timothy grew up to be a church leader. If he had not been taught to value the Word of God as a child, it is likely that Paul would never have written the two letters to Timothy we find in the New Testament.

The very best thing for a child is to be connected to God and to know the Word of God. If there are children or grandchildren in your life, give them the best possible advantage by encouraging them to know God's Word.

---

* "Evangelism Is Most Effective Among Kids," Barna, October 11, 2004, https://www.barna.com/research /evangelism-is-most-effective-among-kids/.

Leading by Example

I call to remembrance the genuine faith that is in you,
which dwelt first in your grandmother Lois and your
mother Eunice, and I am persuaded is in you also.
—2 Timothy 1:5

As a parent, I'm mindful that my influence in the lives of my children is a powerful thing. Parents typically want to do all they can to encourage their children toward heaven.

Timothy was a significant figure in the early Christian church, and he received his example of faithfulness to God from his mother and grandmother. Lois and Eunice are mentioned in the Bible because the faith they lived guided a young man to a life in Christ.

Many people have told me they are Christians today due to the influence of a godly parent or grandparent. There are many engaged in full-time ministry who can confidently say it was a praying parent or grandparent or a family member who sacrificed to make church school possible, who was the difference between a life of faith and a life of faithlessness. It is impossible to overestimate the importance of parents and grandparents in the spiritual development of children.

Parents especially have the solemn responsibility of not only teaching children biblical principles but also modeling those principles so that Christianity becomes attractive to children. Far too many children who were raised in the church and in a Christian home have left the church and walked away from God because they failed to see Christianity demonstrated in the lives of their parents. Children aren't attracted to a Christianity that doesn't make a difference in the lives of their parents. If public Christians are private tyrants, the majority of children are going to see Christianity as the domain of hypocrites and failures.

God isn't asking anyone to be a perfect parent. Parenting is too difficult a science for anyone to master completely and consistently. But parents who humbly love God, gently share Jesus, and—as did Lois and Eunice—reveal to children the beauty of the Scriptures and the character of God are doing the greatest work ever committed to human beings.

Difficult to Resist

*"You are the salt of the earth; but if the salt loses its flavor,
how shall it be seasoned? It is then good for nothing but
to be thrown out and trampled underfoot by men."*
—Matthew 5:13

My breakfast show cohost and I were discussing what we thought were the worst tasting vegetables. And we found—to absolutely no one's surprise—that a *lot* of people *despised* brussels sprouts. I was one of the many who had them at the very top of the list of foods I dislike. I was raised in a home where we children didn't get to be picky when it came to food, but brussels sprouts were a bridge too far for me. And that morning on our radio program, it seemed that almost everyone agreed. While visiting Pike Place Market in Seattle, Washington, I noticed a sign describing brussels sprouts as "Little Green Balls of Death."

Once we had concluded the unscientific poll on our breakfast show, we were inundated with calls from defenders of the brussels sprout. "No, you're all wrong," they told us. Person after person said that while brussels sprouts have an unfortunate reputation in certain circles, the key to enjoying them is in how you prepare them. "If you just boil them to death," people said, "they'll be awful. But if you prepare them right"—and we were given myriad suggestions as to how this is properly done—"they're fantastic!"

As it happens, time has done its work on me, and I now love brussels sprouts. Evidently, something might not be as bad as it seems if you give it a chance by presenting it right. Is it possible more people would respond positively to Christianity if it was presented attractively? Ellen White said that "the strongest argument in favor of the gospel is a loving and lovable Christian."*

If Christianity is boiled to death, it isn't going to be palatable. But when the love of God is presented appropriately, it is hard not to appreciate. Jesus said, "You are the salt of the earth." Too much salt isn't palatable, but the right amount enhances the taste. When we present it in an attractive way, the gospel is difficult to resist.

---

* Ellen G. White, *The Ministry of Healing* (Mountain View, CA: Pacific Press®, 1942), 470.

What If You Really Knew?

"When you go out to battle against your enemies, and see horses and chariots and people more numerous than you, do not be afraid of them; for the LORD your God is with you, who brought you up from the land of Egypt."
—Deuteronomy 20:1

What if you really knew that God was with you in your toughest moments? When three young men found themselves in a fiery furnace, Jesus stood with them in the heat of the flames. When Daniel was cast into a lions' den, an angel sent from heaven shut the mouths of the lions. While it isn't likely many people will find themselves in a den of lions or a furnace of fire, people do lose jobs or receive bad diagnoses. It isn't uncommon for someone to have their car stolen or not be accepted to the school of their dreams.

So notice what Moses told the Israelites: "Do not be afraid of them; for the LORD your God is with you" (Deuteronomy 20:1). God assured His people He was with them in their battles. And while the danger of finding yourself targeted by horses and chariots is low, there will likely be times you will find yourself in a conflict with a neighbor, a colleague, or a fellow student. It can be uncomfortable, and it isn't always easy to see a way out. But God enters into those moments to provide you with heaven's presence and support.

Deuteronomy 20:4 says, "For the LORD your God is He who goes with you, to fight for you against your enemies, to save you." Sometimes your enemy is pride or covetousness or anger. Who fights that enemy for you? God does. He's with you in your conflict with others and with you in your battle against dishonesty, lust, or fear. The God of heaven isn't a faraway God. He is present with you, and He steps into your weak moments and contends for you. When you find yourself in a spiritual struggle, remember God fights for you. Rely on His strength. God is strong enough.

The Christian's Kryptonite

I am not ashamed of the gospel of Christ, for it is the power of God to salvation for everyone who believes, for the Jew first and also for the Greek.

—Romans 1:16

If you were the devil, what would you do if you wanted to ruin God's plans to bring salvation to the lost? How would you work to prevent people from receiving everlasting life? And how would you upset the faith of those who are committed to God? You would quickly discover that while drugs, alcohol, and immorality would work against some who have faith in God, they would not entangle most.

In 1938, a new comic book character was introduced to American readers.* By 1941, Superman was being read by twenty million newspaper readers a day. While the mythical Superman had superhuman powers, they were nullified by something called kryptonite radiation. In the face of kryptonite, Superman was powerless.

What would the Christian's kryptonite be? What would eliminate power from the life of a believer in Jesus? Romans 1:16 says that the gospel of Christ "is the power of God to salvation."

A Christian's spiritual strength is found in the Word of God and prayer. Little wonder that the devil does all he can to keep people from prayer and from reading the Bible. It seems people today are busier than ever and very often are busy with good things. But the net result is that there seems to be less time for what is really important. With more distractions than ever, the world is tilted away from faith in God. Devices mean people have less time to think because downtime isn't downtime anymore. Between distractions and the demands of daily life, it is now easier than ever for time with God to disappear into the busyness of living.

The answer to the challenge so many people face is to put God *first*. Don't give God what's left. Instead, give Him what is best. Protect your time with God. Make sure you have time set aside to read the Bible, to meditate on God's Word, and for a meaningful prayer life. Put God first, and the attacks of the devil will not be able to separate you from Him.

---

* "Superman," Library of American Comics, accessed April 1, 2021, http://libraryofamericancomics.com/product-category/loac/dccomics/superman/.

Outside Looking In

"You are the light of the world.
A city that is set on a hill cannot be hidden."
—Matthew 5:14

A business, struggling to attract customers owing to construction outside its front door, hired people to pretend to be happy shoppers. It was hoped that people who looked through the store windows would see activity inside, notice that the people in the store looked happy, and would therefore be drawn inside.

The message for Christians is obvious. What if people looked inside the church and saw happy, satisfied people? Would positivity on the inside be attractive to people on the outside? It would certainly be much more attractive than looking into a church from the outside and seeing unhappy, unkind, unloving, joyless people.

What do people see when they look into your church? Or into your heart? Jesus said, "You are the light of the world" (Matthew 5:14). While you certainly don't want to fake it, it is important that people who believe in a loving, forgiving God and a place called heaven give evidence that their relationship with God has impacted them for the better. You would want a visitor to your church to notice that the people in the church are happy. If someone knows you're a believer, but your belief in Jesus hasn't brightened your home, there's something seriously wrong. With alarming frequency, I hear from people about visiting a church for the first time and being completely ignored. Such people never fail to get the message that their presence is not valued.

A man who had been hired as a fake shopper reported that the project was successful. When people see joy, happiness, and enthusiasm, they want to be part of it. The same is true in matters of faith. No one wants to be part of something that doesn't appear to be enjoyable. The good news is that when Jesus has your heart, joy will shine out of your life. If a group of believers is committed to Jesus, it will show. And if God inhabits your home, it will affect you and will speak loudly to others.

Blessings and Challenges

Through the LORD's mercies we are not consumed,
Because His compassions fail not.
They are new every morning;
Great is Your faithfulness.
—Lamentations 3:22, 23

A thirty-eight-year-old man was diving with friends when he was caught in a rip current and swept out to sea. His friends thought he had drowned, but the man drifted in the ocean for seventy-five hours. A buoyancy compensator helped him to stay afloat, and his wetsuit provided protection from the elements. Being a big, strong man and physically fit also worked to his advantage. But it was extraordinary that he survived in an ocean for more than three days. His family presumed he was dead.

What is often puzzling for those trying to understand the providence of God is that while one person survives three days drifting in the ocean, another person gets tangled up in a far less consequential scrape and does not survive. The diver's brush with death gave him cause to reflect on his life. After he was rescued, he said, "I'm a different person now." Receiving a second chance at life had a transformative effect on him. What happens in your life when you come through a tough experience? Do life's challenges embitter you against God or work to transform you and increase your faith? The dark challenges of life can be make-or-break experiences for a believer in Jesus. When someone recovers from a serious illness, survives a car accident, or has what might be referred to as a "lucky escape," God is typically praised, and His goodness is celebrated. But when someone doesn't make it home from work, is involved in an accident caused by a drunk driver, or loses a job, the temptation is to doubt the goodness of God.

While circumstances may differ, God is the same on both days. Lamentations 3:22 says, "Through the LORD's mercies we are not consumed" and "His compassions fail not." His faithfulness is truly great! Whether there is miraculous deliverance or a difficult time of trial, God is good, and God is love. Let both blessings and challenges draw you closer to God and cause you to say, "Because of His providences, I'm a different person."

The Right Thing

*Repay no one evil for evil. Have regard
for good things in the sight of all men.*

—Romans 12:17

Roommates in New Paltz, New York, paid twenty dollars for a secondhand sofa. Noticing it felt a little lumpy, they discovered $40,000 stuffed in envelopes hidden in the sofa. At first, they started to dream about what they could do with the money. They were university students, after all! But after much discussion, they decided that the right thing to do was to find the original owner of the sofa. They learned that the woman's deceased husband had saved the cash so she would have some money when he was no longer able to provide for her, but her children—not knowing about the money—replaced the sofa with a new one and donated the original to a thrift store.*

It's always better to do the right thing. Honesty is always the best policy. When you have a chance to explain to the person at the cash register that they've given you too much money; when you realize you're not actually entitled to that tax refund; when you discover that the person who moved out of the apartment before you left something valuable behind, it's hard to feel good about yourself if you're not honest. God wants His people to be honest in all things. Opportunities to be honest (or not) are moments in which we reveal to ourselves what we're really like.

The students were under no legal obligation to return the money. When they arrived at the humble home in what they described as a "rough neighborhood," they realized returning the money would be life-changing for the woman who had lost her husband. But even if the woman lived in the nicest home in town, returning the money would still have been the right thing to do.

Romans 12:17 says, "Provide things honest in the sight of all men" (KJV), which could also be expressed as "do the right thing." The honesty or dishonesty of a believer speaks loudly about the genuineness of the person's faith. An ill-gotten advantage is no advantage at all. Nothing is worth betraying your integrity, and in the process, dishonoring God.

---

* Associated Press, "New York Roommates Find $40,000 in Sofa and Return Cash to Owner," *The Guardian*, May 15, 2014, https://www.theguardian.com/world/2014/may/16/new-york-roommates-find-cash-in-sofa -return-owner.

Rubik's Cube

*"Believe on the Lord Jesus Christ, and you
will be saved, you and your household."*

—Acts 16:31

The Rubik's Cube was invented in Hungary in 1974. Inventor Ernő Rubik studied sculpture and architecture in college. His father was an engineer. In the 1980s, his invention exploded in popularity around the world. Hundreds of millions of Rubik's Cubes have now been sold.*

If you've ever attempted to solve a Rubik's Cube, you know how challenging it can be. There are 43,252,003,274,489,856,000—43 quintillion, 252 quadrillion, 3 trillion, 274 billion, 489 million, 856 thousand—possible arrangements for a Rubik's Cube. But in 2010, a group of mathematicians and computer programmers discovered that a Rubik's Cube is never further than twenty moves away from being solved. Once you learn the method for solving the puzzle, it really isn't that complicated. But if you don't know how to arrange the cube, doing so seems impossible.

For too many people, salvation is endlessly complicated. The truth is, it really doesn't have to be. Paul and Silas told a jail keeper in Philippi, "Believe on the Lord Jesus Christ, and you will be saved, you and your household." Nothing has changed in the two thousand years or so since Paul uttered those words. If you believe in Jesus, salvation is yours. That does not mean that you need not experience a change of heart. To believe on the Lord Jesus is to *have* a change of heart. And the simplicity of salvation does not suggest that obedience is optional. Saved people obey God, serving Him out of love. But it's important not to get the cart before the horse. Obedience to God is not the basis upon which one receives salvation. Instead, obedience comes as a result of receiving the gift of salvation.

Salvation isn't as complex as a Rubik's Cube. There is one way of salvation. Anyone who ever surrendered their life to God was saved by grace through faith in Jesus Christ. Saving faith is a belief that encompasses trust and surrender.

While there are more than 43,000,000,000,000,000,000 ways of arranging a Rubik's Cube, there is just one way of salvation. Truly believe in Jesus. It will bring you salvation and change your life for eternity.

---

* "Our Heritage," Rubik's, accessed April 1, 2021, https://www.rubiks.com/en-us/about.

A Frustrated Future

So all the guests who were with Adonijah were afraid,
and arose, and each one went his way.
—1 Kings 1:49

Los Angeles is the largest city by land area in California. The second largest is San Diego. The third-largest city in California by land area is not Sacramento or San Jose, but, of all places, California City, about a hundred miles northeast of Los Angeles.* In the late 1950s, there were plans to develop California City into a city larger than Los Angeles. Lots sold like hotcakes, and homes were built, but the big plans basically came to nothing. About fourteen thousand people call California City home today, many of whom are connected with Edwards Air Force Base, less than twenty miles away.

Scottish poet Robert Burns once wrote that "the best-laid schemes of mice and men go often askew."† The Bible teaches that if God is not in your plans, your plans will come to little. When King David was nearing the end of his life, Adonijah, David's fourth son, declared himself to be the new king. His supporters gathered and exclaimed, "God save King Adonijah." If Adonijah became king, Solomon not only would not have ascended the throne but also, in all likelihood, would have been killed by his half-brother.

When word of Adonijah's insurrection reached David, he announced that Solomon would succeed him as king. "So all the guests who were with Adonijah were afraid, and arose, and each one went his way." A king without followers isn't much of a king, and before long, Adonijah's power grab was over, and he was pleading for his life.

Wise people make plans. But wise plans are made in accordance with God's plans. You might want to attend a prestigious university, marry a certain someone, retire early, buy a new home, or pursue a certain career, all of which are goals that in and of themselves are perfectly fine. But if your plans for your life are not consistent with God's plan for your life, pursuing those plans can only secure a frustrated future.

The original vision for California City didn't work out. But if your plans are connected to God's plans for you, they'll work out every time.

---

* "California Land Area City Rank," USA.com, accessed April 1, 2021, http://www.usa.com/rank/california
-state--land-area--city-rank.htm.
† Author's translation from the Robert Burns poem, "To a Mouse," 1785.

What More?

"What more could have been done to My vineyard
That I have not done in it?
Why then, when I expected it to bring forth good grapes,
Did it bring forth wild grapes?"

—Isaiah 5:4

Isaiah 5 begins with God speaking of His beloved people, comparing them to a vineyard. He calls it "a vineyard on a very fruitful hill" (verse 1). Then He asks, "What more could have been done?" (verse 4).

The same question can be asked of God's people today. God has left nothing undone in reaching every heart with heaven's greatest gifts. When Jesus returns, no one will be able to blame God if they are not saved. In most countries of the world, everyone has access to the Bible. Those who have never taken the time to read the Bible cannot blame God for their ignorance. There are churches in every town, tracts printed in every major language, and religious holidays celebrated annually that remind people of the birth and death of Jesus. God has knocked loudly on the door of the world.

Witness a sunrise, a sunset, a kitten, a monkey, a flower, a butterfly, a whale, or a bolt of lightning, and you *could* say, "That came from nowhere," or "That's all due to evolution." Or maybe you could say, "That was made by an intelligent God." There are Christians living their faith, prayers being answered, and blessings being received, and most everyone has seen something miraculous that defies rational explanation. No one will ever be able to say, "Why didn't God do more to get my attention?"

And God doesn't just advertise Christianity. He works through living, breathing Christians to show others what faith in God looks like. God wants you to be someone He can work through to reach out to those who haven't yet included heaven in their plans. While God is doing everything He can to convince people He is real, He is counting on the church to be a living embodiment of what faith in God looks like. God asks, "What more could I have done?" And while God has clearly done everything He could, we might want to ask ourselves, "Is there anything more that I could do?"

Confirmation Bias

But they shouted, saying,
"Crucify Him, crucify Him!"

—Luke 23:21

A man arrived home to discover his wife had been brutally attacked, and eventually, he was convicted of the terrible crime. An employee at the fast-food restaurant he claimed he had visited testified that he had seen the man that night. The accused husband even had warm food with him when police arrived at his home. There were no witnesses to the crime. And yet, the man served sixteen years for a crime he didn't commit before being exonerated by DNA evidence. Another man later confessed to having carried out the attack.

We can all be affected by confirmation bias. People with preconceived ideas can interpret evidence in such a way as to confirm their thinking.

This even happens in matters of faith. If someone wants to believe humans evolved, you can show them evidence that the Bible is true, and yet that evidence is rejected. Scientific evidence in favor of Creation can be dismissed as bad science. An atheist can see a sunset or a penguin or consider the development of a baby in the womb and explain it as being just the way things happen. While no one would dare believe a computer designed itself, many rational people believe that the human cell—and therefore the human being—came into existence on its own.

It is right to think critically. God would have you use your mind to weigh the evidence. When Jesus was tried, there were people in the crowd who knew He had healed the sick and raised the dead, but they shouted, "Crucify Him." It is possible some of the people in that crowd drank the wine Jesus had made from water or ate the bread and fish He multiplied from a young boy's lunch. Yet they cried for His blood because, at that moment, they wanted to believe what they wanted to believe.

It's important to think, to read the Bible, and carefully consider what it says. When you do so, allow God to lead you in the direction He has planned for your life.

Unchanging

*"For I am the LORD, I do not change; therefore you
are not consumed, O sons of Jacob."*

—Malachi 3:6

We now have cameras without film, phones that aren't attached to a wall, meatless burgers, driverless cars, and the ability to communicate with anyone, anywhere, anytime. Payphones are extremely rare, record stores basically no longer exist, few people use folding maps when they drive, and CDs are following cassette tapes into obsolescence. Today's young adults don't remember 9/11 or a time when airport security was not like it is today. Many people don't know the phone numbers of their friends or family members. A phone isn't just a phone anymore, but a GPS, a music player, a flashlight, a camera, a video camera, and a device to be used for paying for everything from groceries to gasoline. Many people don't go out to eat without first reading online reviews of the restaurant. There are now hundreds of television channels, and it seems unbelievable that there were once twenty-seven thousand video rental stores in America. We are now closer to the year 2050 than 1990. People no longer smoke in restaurants or on buses, trains, or planes.

The world has changed dramatically in the last few decades. Some of that change is undoubtedly good. Some of it is not so positive. But there is one thing that doesn't change—one Person who doesn't change. And that Person is God. God was love and still is love. God was good, and He always will be. God is patient and kind and merciful, and that is never going to change. The God who for thousands of years has offered forgiveness to the human family continues to do so. He is as relevant today as He ever has been, and after thousands of years of pleading with people to follow Him in faith, He still calls to hearts and minds and offers the gift of salvation. In a world of change, in a world where it seems nothing is constant, God is unchanging. You can rely on God to be a loving God and a good God always and forever.

Even in Painful Times

"Naked I came from my mother's womb,
And naked shall I return there.
The LORD gave, and the LORD has taken away;
Blessed be the name of the LORD."

—Job 1:21

I t isn't unusual for people who are going through serious difficulties to lash out at God. It is very human to reason that if God could have prevented a certain thing from happening, then it was unfair or unjust that He chose not to. Our limited human understanding can prevent us from understanding God's working.

Job lost his livestock and all ten of his children in one day. He did not lose his wife, who urged him to yield to the devil's temptations (see Job 2:9). And yet Job praised the Lord. The attitude of this man who lost virtually everything he had was to bless and praise God.

A man who had been falsely imprisoned for twenty-seven years, having been convicted of a crime he did not commit, was asked upon his release if he was bitter. He said, "No, I'm not bitter. I'm just happy to be free." Spending a third of his life behind bars did not cause the man to become angry, even though he had almost three decades to reflect on the injustice perpetrated against him.

There is often a very real battle that takes place in the minds of believers in Jesus when they suffer loss or hurt. Even if you are a person of faith and experience, the weight of pain or disappointment can be significant and difficult to bear. It would be wise to remember that even Jesus struggled with His circumstances, crying out to His Father from the cross, "Why have You forsaken me?" (Matthew 27:46). Even Jesus asked, "Why?" And even though the Father did not answer Jesus' question, Jesus trusted Him in the midst of great anguish.

Job demonstrated real faith. He trusted God even when circumstances didn't make sense, even while he endured severe difficulty. Despite his confusion and even desperation, Job never abandoned faith in God. He knew that somewhere beyond his ability to comprehend was a God who could be trusted.

A Box of Birds

Then Jesus said to them, "Most assuredly, I say to you, unless you eat the flesh of the Son of Man and drink His blood, you have no life in you."
—John 6:53

It's likely there are certain words or phrases you use that would confuse a person from another country. Someone from Great Britain may well enjoy a "cuppa," be "chuffed," or ask his "mate" where the "rubbish bin" is. A Canadian will ask to use the "washroom," while a "fair dinkum" Australian might spend the "arvo" with a few of his "cobbers." What is familiar and understandable to one person might not make sense to someone of another culture.

So imagine being a Jew listening to the teachings of Jesus and hearing Him say, "Unless you eat the flesh of the Son of Man and drink His blood, you have no life in you." For Jews, the drinking of blood was not only grotesque but also specifically against their law. What could this rabbi possibly mean?

To eat Jesus' flesh and drink His blood is to accept Jesus as Savior and receive His teachings as the basis for your life. Jesus wasn't suggesting cannibalism, and His hearers realized that, as far as they were willing to do so. Jesus was saying, "If you want to live a life of blessing, accept Me as Messiah and internalize My teachings to such an extent that they become a part of you." Jesus often focused on the closeness He wants to experience with us. In John 15, He spoke about abiding or dwelling in us and we in Him. In John 6, Jesus suggested a union so close He described it as becoming part of our being.

For the uninitiated, the thought of eating Jesus' flesh and eating His blood could seem shocking. But to accept Jesus so totally that He becomes part of who you are and is totally and completely your Lord and Savior is God's will for your life. And when you eat His flesh and drink His blood? If you're British, everything will be as "good as gold." Well then things are going well, a New Zealander might say that life is a "box of birds." However you express it, a life in Christ is God's plan for you today.

Watch What You Eat

"Whoever eats My flesh and drinks My blood has eternal life,
and I will raise him up at the last day."
—John 6:54

Nutritionists tell us the average man should consume around 2,500 calories a day, and the average woman, 2,000. Yet a burger restaurant in Las Vegas once sold a hamburger that contained 8,000 calories! The establishment that sold the burger in question said their food was "so bad for you it's shocking." Few truer statements have been uttered.* What you put into your body matters, as so many sick people can testify.

But what are you feeding your soul? Receiving Jesus into your life by faith is to eat His body and drink His blood. If it is important to be careful about the food you eat, it is even more important to make sure you're getting the right spiritual nourishment.

The Christian diet should be made up of plentiful amounts of God's Word. In the Bible, Jesus—and by extension, His Word—is likened to bread. But not all bread is created equal. Someone once joked that in some cases, you'd receive more nutritional benefit if you threw away the bread and ate the bag it came in! Some bread has been emptied of almost all nutritional value. Much bread is made with enriched flour, flour that has had much of its goodness removed and has then been "enriched" in an attempt to add some goodness to the depleted flour! Some bread contains little or no roughage and often contains so much sugar experts have claimed it should not be classified as bread.

And that's how some people like the Word of God. Sweet to the taste but refined and without any roughage. When you come to the Bible, remember that a little roughage is good for you. Challenge yourself to broaden your spiritual horizons and strengthen your character by digging deep into God's Word and reading widely.

Do yourself a favor and make sure your spiritual diet is what it ought to be. A healthy, balanced spiritual diet is essential for people planning to live healthy, eternal lives.

---

* Debra Kelly, "The Untold Truth of Heart Attack Grill," *Mashed*, July 15, 2020, https://www.mashed.com/210610/the-untold-truth-of-heart-attack-grill/.

Sensational

For all the Athenians and the foreigners who were there spent their time in nothing else but either to tell or to hear some new thing.

—Acts 17:21

For some, the Bible isn't interesting unless there is some special twist or unique view that differs from what others are teaching. This was true in the time of the early church. When Paul went to Athens, "All the Athenians and the foreigners who were there" wanted to discuss the latest, the newest, and the most impressive ideas (Acts 17:21).

A group of gospel ministers were discussing the traditional interpretation of one of the Bible's great prophecies when a well-known pastor spoke up and said, "I don't like that interpretation." When asked why, he simply said, "It isn't exciting enough for me."

The Bible is plenty exciting. It might not have the special effects of a Hollywood blockbuster, but it does have the heavens departing as a scroll, the sun going backward in the sky, and ten thousand times ten thousand and thousands of thousands of angels gathered around the judgment seat of God. The great truths of God's Word fortify the mind and give spiritual strength as they connect sinners with the Almighty. Nothing else can do that.

The desire for the excitement of a unique interpretation of the Bible does not build faith. God hasn't called His people to share anything other than the old, old story. Jesus Christ came into the world to save sinners. Everything in the Bible—historical, prophetic, poetic, or biographical—was inspired by God to illuminate the great plan of salvation.

Without a doubt, there are new discoveries for each person to make in the Bible. But the Bible remains the story of a loving God who gave His Son to die for the sins of the world. We mustn't get bored with the teachings of Scripture and allow ourselves to be sidetracked with a search for something novel. The Bible is the greatest story ever told. If you really want something sensational, you don't have long to wait. Jesus is soon to return in the clouds of heaven. *That* will be sensational!

On the Fence?

Then Agrippa said to Paul,
"You almost persuade me to become a Christian."

—Acts 26:28

A baseball player's swing for the fences is sometimes caught by an outfielder on the warning track. A soccer player's shot at goal might narrowly miss. A golfer's putt stops just short of the hole, or a swimmer misses a world record by the smallest fraction of a second. Nearly, but not quite. In light of eternity, a sportsperson coming up short is of no consequence, but when it comes to matters of salvation, it's an entirely different story.

The apostle Paul appealed to King Agrippa from the Word of God, urging him to surrender his heart to what he knew was the truth. Paul knew Agrippa believed the Scriptures. But Agrippa's reply to Paul in Acts 26:28 is one of the saddest statements in the Bible. "You almost persuade me to become a Christian." Almost persuaded, but totally lost. The Holy Spirit was pricking the king's conscience. He was being drawn to Jesus in a powerful way. It was decision time for King Agrippa.

It might have taken Agrippa more effort to resist the Holy Spirit than it would have to yield. Pride, self-interest, peer pressure, and likely more prevented Agrippa from surrendering to God's appeal. Agrippa came close to becoming a child of God. One day he will stand before the throne of God and bitterly regret his stubbornness. God spoke to his heart through one of the greatest Christian workers in the history of the church, yet Agrippa chose to harden his heart against God. He was almost persuaded. He came close to salvation. But not close enough.

If you are still trying to decide what to do with God and the Bible, Agrippa's experience speaks to you today. It wasn't Paul who was appealing to the heart of the Jewish king, but God. God wanted Agrippa to be saved for all eternity, and He wants the same for you. When God speaks to your heart, let nothing prevent you from yielding to the moving of the Holy Spirit. The God who appealed to Agrippa appeals to you now.

Happy Now?

"These things I have spoken to you, that My joy may
remain in you, and that your joy may be full."

—John 15:11

A recent survey found that the happiest of the United States is Hawaii. Of those surveyed, Hawaiians were most likely to say they were "thriving," that they smiled and laughed a lot. And they were the least likely to say they experienced stress. While no place on earth is perfect, warm weather and beautiful beaches in a tropical setting are the things many people only dream about. People travel to Hawaii from all over the world because of its beauty. The next happiest states, according to the Gallup-Healthways poll, were Wyoming, Alaska, Montana, and Utah, while the five least happy states were said to be West Virginia, Arkansas, Kentucky, Mississippi, and Tennessee.*

But what is it that "really" makes a person happy? No matter where you live, you still have to deal with the ups and downs of daily life. Where can a person find happiness that really lasts?

Evidently, living your life without reference to God doesn't bring true happiness, and while palm trees and balmy weather can be nice, nicer still is the peace that comes from being connected to God. God tells us that real happiness is found in a life that is hidden in Christ, where someone so abides in Jesus that he or she not only recognizes the love of God but also is moved by that love to live a life of loving obedience. Anything short of that is a life that lacks heaven's peace, assurance, and the hope of a certain future.

Jesus' desire is that our joy be "full" (John 15:11). His plan isn't that we are merely happy but happy *to the full*. Your living circumstances may change. Life will forever have its ups and downs. True happiness can only be found—and will always be found—in a life lived for the honor and glory of God. The closer you draw to God, the happier you will be.

---

* Dan Witters, "Hawaii Tops U.S. in Wellbeing for Record 7th Time," Gallup, February 27, 2019, https://news.gallup.com/poll/247034/hawaii-tops-wellbeing-record-7th-time.aspx.

Bruised

And the God of peace will crush Satan under your feet shortly.
The grace of our Lord Jesus Christ be with you. Amen.
—Romans 16:20

In 1956, then Soviet premier Nikita Khrushchev was speaking with a group of Western ambassadors at the Polish embassy in Moscow when he said, according to an interpreter, "Whether you like it or not, history is on our side. We will bury you." Khrushchev later explained his statement to mean that he believed socialism would eventually bring about the demise of capitalism, although, at the time, his comment was understood to be far more ominous. His remarks made a strong impact during those Cold War years.*

Mr. Khrushchev's prediction has not come to pass. The Soviet Union did not defeat the United States, nor did the working class bury capitalism. Instead, the Soviet Union was dismantled, and communism disintegrated.

Predicting the future is a tricky business, but back in the Garden of Eden, God made a prediction that offered enormous encouragement to a world that had just cast itself adrift. The population of the planet stood at just two, yet the sin committed by our original grandparents brought separation between humanity and God. However, assessing Adam and Eve's situation, the God of heaven said to Satan,

> "And I will put enmity
> Between you and the woman,
> And between your seed and her Seed;
> He shall bruise your head,
> And you shall bruise His heel" (Genesis 3:15).

Some Bible translations use the word *crush* in the place of *bruise*. Satan will be "crushed." Writing to the church in Rome, Paul said, "The God of peace will bruise Satan under your feet shortly" (Romans 16:20), echoing what God said in the Garden of Eden. Life presents no shortage of serious challenges, and it might appear that Satan has run away with the world, but the fact is that his time is strictly limited. The architect of all sin, the originator of every dispute and difficulty, the cause of all trials and disappointments will soon be crushed. Satan's defeat is certain. Hold on to Jesus today, and you are holding on to victory.

---

* Jamie Shea, "1956: Khrushchev Delivers His 'Secret Speech'," video lecture, March 6, 2009, North Atlantic Treaty Organization, https://www.nato.int/cps/en/natohq/opinions_139302.htm.

All That You Do

Let all that you do be done with love.
—1 Corinthians 16:14

Look in a dictionary, and you will find that the definition of the word *all* is something like "the whole of" or "the whole number of." It has been said many times that "all means all." Every single one. The whole amount. Everything.

Bible writers use words such as *all* very deliberately. When Paul wrote in 1 Corinthians 16:14, "Let all that you do be done with love," he meant exactly what he said. Everything.

That's clearly a challenge for any believer in Jesus. When Paul said "all," he must have included disciplining children, dealing with colleagues, interacting with a frazzled store employee, or reacting to an angry driver. Paul said that all of it must be done "with love." Always, and at all times.

It wouldn't take long for anyone to think of a time when Paul's encouragement was ignored. There are times when we just don't want to act in love or when it seems the person or people we're dealing with don't deserve to be treated with love. And when we start using such words as *all*—not *the majority of the time* or *under most circumstances*, but *all*—it is easy to see the enormity of what Paul is saying. And, in all honesty, the impossibility of what he is saying. In all reality, who can do *that*?

But this is why Paul's injunction is so encouraging. The God of the Bible doesn't ask us to do what we can't do. He asks us to allow Him to do in us what we can't do in ourselves. Philippians 2:13 reminds us that "it is God who works in you both to will and to do for His good pleasure." Paul wrote in Galatians 2:20 that "it is no longer I who live, but Christ lives in me." When we consent, surrender, yield our will to God, we give Him permission to work out His perfect will and do for us what we could never do.

When God says "all," He means "all." He means that if we allow Him to do so, He will do all in our lives that needs to be done.

Devoted

I urge you, brethren—you know the household of Stephanas,
that it is the firstfruits of Achaia, and that they have
devoted themselves to the ministry of the saints.
—1 Corinthians 16:15

S ix medical professionals visiting Biafra in the late 1960s were moved by what they witnessed. Biafra was a group of states in the east of Nigeria that declared independence from Nigeria. The military action against Biafra that followed its declaration of independence resulted in almost two million people dying of starvation. The small medical team was so moved by what they witnessed that Médecins Sans Frontières—Doctors Without Borders—was born. Winners of the Nobel Peace Prize in 1999, Doctors Without Borders is a major humanitarian organization active in approximately seventy countries.*

Writing to the church in Corinth, Paul mentioned the family of Stephanas, saying that "they have devoted themselves to the ministry of the saints" (1 Corinthians 16:15). What would the world be like without those who devote themselves to making a difference in the lives of others?

How would the world be different if such missionaries as Hudson Taylor, David Livingstone, and Harry Miller didn't respond to God's call to devote their lives to mission work? Although their decisions exposed them to illness and loss, they went forward in the knowledge that God would make an eternal difference through them. Missionaries today still choose to leave behind the comforts of modern life in order to reveal Jesus to others.

Romans 15:2 says, "Let each of us please his neighbor for his good, leading to edification," while Philippians 2:4 says, "Let each of you look out not only for his own interests, but also for the interests of others." God's people have been called to be channels of blessing. We have not been put in this world to think merely of ourselves but to use the time and talents given us by God to urge others toward the kingdom of heaven.

Is God calling you to devote yourself to ministry? Some are called to full-time ministry or mission work. Some are called to serve God in faraway foreign fields, while others are called by God to labor for Him in their own neighborhood. But all are called by God to work for Him. What does God want to do through you today?

---

* "Founding," Doctors Without Borders, accessed April 1, 2021, https://www.doctorswithoutborders.org /who-we-are/history/founding.

Comfort

Blessed be the God and Father of our Lord Jesus Christ,
the Father of mercies and God of all comfort.
—2 Corinthians 1:3

There are many people going through real difficulty on a personal, emotional level. There are likely people with whom you interact on a daily basis who are dealing with desperately ill loved ones or facing illness themselves. People everywhere face financial hardship, employment issues, or parents or grandparents in declining health. These gritty realities of life were not what God intended when He created the earth.

So where is God when people suffer from the challenges of life? God is present when we hurt. He is with us in our struggles. He is the God of all comfort. If you bring your burdens to God, He will ease them and provide the comfort and strength you need to navigate the troubled waters.

God knows what it's like to go through hardship. He watched while evil men condemned His Son to die. He witnessed Jesus' death by crucifixion, one of the most depraved and inhuman methods of execution ever devised.

God knows what it's like to suffer pain and therefore is qualified to provide comfort to people who are facing life's toughest challenges. When life gets hard, it is important to remember that God is with you and not against you. God knows what it's like to hurt. Knowing that makes it easier to turn toward Him and not away from Him when challenges come.

A dear lady once told me she was terminally ill. When I asked her how she felt she would be, she told me with a smile that she thought she was going to be OK. She said, "Pastor, Jesus and I will get through this together."

Even when God is with you, trouble still comes. His presence doesn't remove the challenges. Bad news is bad news no matter who receives it. Pain is painful whether you are a believer or not. But God is always with you when you need Him. He is the God of all comfort.

The Sin of Racism

*"You know how unlawful it is for a Jewish man to keep
company with or go to one of another nation. But God has
shown me that I should not call any man common or unclean."*

—Acts 10:28

In Acts chapter 10, Peter received a vision he did not understand. God showed Peter a sheet being let down from the sky containing unclean animals, and He told Peter to kill and eat the animals (Acts 10:13). Peter had never eaten anything unclean, so he was confused by what he heard.

At about that time, a group of Gentiles knocked at the door of the home where Peter was staying and invited him to go with them and share the gospel with the household of Cornelius. But Cornelius was a Gentile. It was against Jewish law for a Jew such as Peter to visit the home of a Gentile.

Later at the home of Cornelius, Peter explained, "God has shown me that I should not call any man common or unclean" (verse 28). Conditioned by his upbringing and the social and religious milieu of his day, Peter was racist. God instructed him to put aside his racism and take the gospel to people with whom he normally wouldn't associate. If God worked to remove racism two thousand years ago, there's no question He cares about the issue today.

While people generally interact positively and kindly with those of other races, racism still exists. It even exists among Christians, the last place on earth hatred and intolerance should ever be found.

After the Los Angeles riots in 1992, the late Rodney King asked, "Can't we all just get along?" Imagine if we did. Imagine if the sin of racism disappeared from Christianity, and every believer in Jesus treated all others with love, without reference to race. Philippians 2:3 says, "In lowliness of mind let each esteem others better than himself." Paul wrote those words for people of every race.

God went to great lengths to demonstrate to Peter that he shouldn't show preference to one race and unkindness to another. We can be certain God's mind hasn't changed on this. A society—or a church—that demonstrates love to all people, regardless of race, is a society or a church that is, to a considerable extent, demonstrating the love of God.

Miraculous Answers

*Peter was therefore kept in prison, but constant prayer
was offered to God for him by the church.*

—Acts 12:5

It's simply impossible to overestimate the importance of prayer. In Acts 12, we learn that James, the brother of John, was executed. Peter was imprisoned, and it seemed that he would follow James to martyrdom, and the future of the church would be jeopardized. "But constant prayer was offered to God for him by the church" (Acts 12:5).

Church members prayed, and then they prayed some more. Their hearts were stretched out toward God, and Peter was miraculously released from prison. He went on to be extremely influential in the growth of the nascent church and wrote two books in the New Testament.

Great things still happen in answer to prayer. God urges us again and again to pray, assuring us that our prayers will be heard and answered. "Now this is the confidence that we have in Him, that if we ask anything according to His will, He hears us. And if we know that He hears us, whatever we ask, we know that we have the petitions that we have asked of Him" (1 John 5:14, 15). It is true that God doesn't always see fit to answer our prayers in the way we want, but that's because God knows better than we do what is ultimately best.

It is a wonder people don't pray more. People buy lottery tickets knowing full well that there is only a minute chance they might win a prize. When lottery jackpots rise into the multiplied millions of dollars, people who wouldn't normally buy lottery tickets do so because "you just never know." The possible payout is so large that it's considered worth buying tickets. The potential benefit compels people to buy, even when their chance of winning is virtually nil.

But when you pray, you are guaranteed God will hear and answer your prayer. And better than the assurance that God will give you what you want is the assurance that God will give you what is best.

Ask yourself whether you're taking enough time in prayer with God. If not, you know what to do.

Put to the Test

*These were more fair-minded than those in Thessalonica, in that
they received the word with all readiness, and searched the
Scriptures daily to find out whether these things were so.*

—Acts 17:11

When a missing girl was found alive years after she had disappeared, the psychic who had told her parents the girl was dead was exposed as a fraud. How could she explain her failure when she had consistently claimed to possess a special "gift"? This psychic maintains her predictions have a high success rate, but an organization who checked her claims says she has a success rate of precisely 0 percent. For all that, and in spite of empirical evidence that the predictions of modern psychics almost always fail, there are many people ready to watch programs and buy magazines that promote the claims of these charlatans.

Sadly, some people will believe almost anything, and that's a problem even in religious circles. Perhaps it is because people are conditioned to trust pastors and gospel teachers that masses of people believe without question whatever they hear in church. "The pastor said so" or "that's what the church teaches" is often used as the rationale to explain why people believe what they believe.

Of course, that approach is not biblical. In Acts 17:11, Luke writes that the people of Berea "were more fair-minded than those in Thessalonica, in that they received the word with all readiness, and searched the Scriptures daily to find out whether these things were so." They used God's Word to test what they heard proclaimed. When a man asked Jesus the secret to receiving everlasting life, Jesus answered by saying, "What is written in the law? What is your reading of it?" (Luke 10:26).

What we believe must be put to the test of the Bible. While it is good to have confidence in churches or ministers or teachers, the bottom line of belief is the Word of God. No Bible teacher can possibly be right about everything. On the other hand, Jesus promised that the Holy Spirit "will guide you into all truth" (John 16:13).

Let the Bible be your final authority. When you rest your faith on the Word of God, you are trusting in something that will never let you down or lead you astray.

"Come and Die!"

I have been crucified with Christ; it is no longer I who live, but Christ
lives in me; and the life which I now live in the flesh I live by faith
in the Son of God, who loved me and gave Himself for me.
—Galatians 2:20

Twentieth-century German theologian Dietrich Bonhoeffer once said, "When Christ calls a man, He bids him come and die."* Bonhoeffer, who was executed by the Nazis at a concentration camp in Flossenburg, Germany, just days before the end of World War II, understood from experience what it meant to die for Christ. But his statement had less to do with literally dying than it had to do with spiritually living.

Bonhoeffer understood what Paul meant when he wrote, "I am crucified with Christ: nevertheless I live" (Galatians 2:20, KJV). Paul's graphic language is a potent way of expressing that when a person comes to Christ, that person surrenders his or her life to Jesus so completely that Jesus has permission to carry out His will in the person's life. Self-interest is the enemy of the Christian. Our carnal nature pits us against the will of God. In fact, Paul wrote in his letter to the church at Rome that "the carnal mind is enmity against God; for it is not subject to the law of God, nor indeed can be" (Romans 8:7). Paul never suggested that the carnal mind we are born with can ever make peace with God. There can be no deal brokered between God and the unconverted heart. The only way the carnal, unregenerate mind can be reconciled to God is through death—the death of self and self-interest.

Paul described the nature of this battle against self when he said in 1 Corinthians 15:31, "I die daily." Christianity requires constant vigilance and continual surrender. The devil is a cunning enemy, and the modern world is filled with temptations that conspire against the Christian. Society has been flooded by sin, and the church is being relentlessly attacked on many fronts. Yet the toughest foe you will ever fight is yourself.

God calls you to come to Him and die. When you do, He can then live His life in you. It is then that you will experience the joy and victory God desires for you.

---

* Dietrick Bonhoeffer, *The Cost of Discipleship*, trans. R. H. Fuller (New York: Touchstone, 1959), 89.

Making a Difference

How then shall they call on Him in whom they have not believed?
And how shall they believe in Him of whom they have not heard?
—Romans 10:14

A series of difficult events led a man to feel so devoid of hope that he believed his best option was to end his life. As Dan was driving to the location where he intended to take his life, he stopped to buy gas for his vehicle. While walking back to his vehicle, moments from driving away to his demise, a man he vaguely knew called out to him. "Hey Dan, what are you doing Tuesday night?"

"Nothing much," Dan replied.

"Why don't you come to my house?" the man asked. "We're having a group Bible study that I think you might enjoy."

Dan paused a moment and then accepted the invitation. He chose to attend and see if the Bible study might help him turn a corner in his life. He continued to attend the Bible study week after week, gave his life to Jesus, was baptized, and became active in ministry and a vital part of his local church. All because someone reached out to him.

Obviously, God prompted the man to invite Dan to his home. God saw what was going on in Dan's heart, and He knew there was not only a life hanging in the balance but also someone's eternal life. And that included the eternal life of all who would be reached through Dan's conversion. Only eternity will be able to measure the impact of that one simple invitation.

When God prompts you to encourage someone, or invite someone, or to reach out to someone, follow that prompting. It might be that you will never know the extent of how God used you. When you follow God's prompting and extend yourself to make even a small difference in someone's life, God is always honored.

Jesus said, "You are the salt of the earth" (Matthew 5:13). Every believer is called by God to add flavor, to impart a preserving quality, and to make a difference to his or her circle of influence. Expect God to make a difference through you as you make yourself available to be used by Him.

Losers and Winners

*Beloved, I pray that you may prosper in all things
and be in health, just as your soul prospers.*

—3 John 2

They don't mind being called losers. A married couple in the United States decided to do something about their excess weight. They joined a gym, and they began walking regularly together. Before long, they were running, and they lost 500 pounds (227 kilograms) between them!

Jesus came into the world to save us from our sins, and He wants to give us what He described in John 10:10 as a more abundant life. God wants us to flourish both spiritually and physically.

Thriving spiritually and physically sometimes requires tough decisions and lasting lifestyle changes, but those changes are always worth making. Jon weighed more than 350 pounds when he began to take steps to reverse the many diseases that were destroying his health. When he changed his lifestyle and began exercising, Jon lost weight, and his high blood pressure came down to very healthy levels. He no longer requires medication of any kind and is no longer diabetic. Jon's doctors are astonished. Today he regularly runs and rides his bicycle for exercise. He could do neither when he began his remarkable journey to good health.

Nick was 90 pounds overweight and tired of being out of shape. He attended a wellness program, adopted a new lifestyle, and watched the pounds fall away. He says he has more energy and is no longer plagued by the health problems that used to trouble him. Simple steps led him to a new life of good health.

It is true that for various reasons, some people are not able to see the same kinds of health benefits. However, good health itself is not the end but a means to an end. We want to honor God with our physical well-being so we can enjoy optimal spiritual well-being.

The reason the Bible speaks so much about health is that God knows a healthy body lends itself to a healthy mind. God wants us to prosper in health, physically and spiritually. God's blessing can take you to new heights.

The Safest Bet

For the love of money is a root of all kinds of evil, for
which some have strayed from the faith in their greediness,
and pierced themselves through with many sorrows.

—1 Timothy 6:10

The story has been played out many times. The man initially gambled mostly on sports and only with small sums of money. But in time, his gambling became such an obsession that he began to lie and steal in order to get money to gamble. Invariably, he would lose the money he wagered, trapping him in a cycle of more lying and more stealing in order to get more money to repay his debts and gamble still some more. Eventually, he lost more than just money. His family, his career, and virtually everything important to him slipped through his fingers.

A young lady with a single coin in her pocket visited a casino. She placed the coin in a machine and pressed the button. When alarms sounded and lights flashed, she thought she had broken the machine and apologized to casino employees for what she had done. The amused staff members told her she had, in fact, won a jackpot of $25,000! It was her very first visit to a casino. Delighted by her good fortune, she took the money home. But subsequent visits to the casino worked out differently. In just a few short months, she had gone through all her savings and was $30,000 in debt.

Many things that are legal simply aren't good for a person. Gambling stems from a violation of the tenth commandment, which says, "Thou shalt not covet" (Exodus 20:17, KJV). All too often, gambling ruins lives. This is one reason Jesus said, "Take heed and beware of covetousness, for one's life does not consist in the abundance of the things he possesses" (Luke 12:15). When you're consumed by getting, you'll have nothing but problems.

The good news is that both people mentioned above have put their lives back together, and they no longer gamble. Even when we create problems for ourselves, God is in the business of forgiveness and restoration. But it is far better to prevent a problem from developing than to experience the pain of putting a broken life back together. Covetousness is damaging in any form. Let Jesus keep you from suffering that damage.

Character Development

And not only that, but we also glory in tribulations,
knowing that tribulation produces perseverance.

—Romans 5:3

F ew people enjoy having their patience tried, which is why Romans 5:3 challenges us when it says, "We glory in tribulations also: knowing that tribulation worketh patience" (KJV).

Patience is a prerequisite for developing a Christlike character. But according to Paul, patience is developed through trials. When you get a flat tire in the rain on a dirt road, miles from home, your response should be to praise the Lord because He's developing the likeness of Christ in you. Few people would say, "The line in the post office is so long that I'm going to be late to my doctor's appointment, but praise the Lord anyway!" But, in reality, that is exactly the attitude we ought to have.

Think of the alternative. Failing to honor God in difficult, uncomfortable situations is not only choosing to manifest an un-Christlike spirit but also failing to trust Him. No one should be happy they're stuck in traffic and will be late for work, but a close connection with Jesus will allow you to keep your cool instead of getting steamed about something that is out of your control.

Seventeenth-century English philosopher John Locke is widely quoted as saying, "What worries you, masters you."* God desires to grow us, to shape us to be more like Him and less like what we are without Him. Christianity isn't merely a belief system. It's a life system. More than a foundation for our lives, faith in Jesus is to *become* our life. God continues to allow patience-building opportunities to come to us so that we will learn to consult with Him as our first resort and not as a last resort.

When we learn to see trials as opportunities to develop our character, we will learn to handle them better. In the midst of trial, it is better to say, "What is God trying to teach me here?" than to complain, asking, "Why is this happening to me?!" Tribulation works patience. When trials next confront you, look to Jesus and understand He will not only get you through, but He also is growing you to be more like Him.

---

* What Locke actually said is, "But if any extreme disturbance (as sometimes it happens) possesses our whole mind, as when the pain of the rack, an impetuous uneasiness, as of love, anger, or any other violent passion, running away with us, allows us not the liberty of thought, and we are not masters enough of our own minds to consider thoroughly and examine fairly;—God, who knows our frailty, pities our weakness, and requires of us no more than we are able to do, and sees what was and what was not in our power, will judge as a kind and merciful Father" (John Locke, *An Essay Concerning Humane Understanding*, Volume 1, Project Gutenberg e-book, https://www.gutenberg.org/files/10615/10615-h/10615-h.htm).

Dealing With the Unexpected

*So Moses made a bronze serpent, and put it on a pole; and so it was, if a
serpent had bitten anyone, when he looked at the bronze serpent, he lived.*
—Numbers 21:9

A man in Illinois was golfing with friends when he disappeared. Literally. He was
walking along a fairway when he disappeared into a sinkhole! Friends who searched
for him heard his muffled yells and rescued him. The man was fortunate to escape
serious injury and get out of the sinkhole with his life.

Sinkholes can be a serious problem. In Florida—where there are many sinkholes—a
man still in bed disappeared, never to be seen again, when a sinkhole swallowed part of
his home. Not a single person expects a bizarre incident like this to ever happen, but life
is full of the unexpected. The question is, what will you do when the unexpected strikes?

As the Israelites traveled through the wilderness, poisonous snakes entered the
camp and bit many of the people. "So Moses made a bronze serpent, and put it on a
pole" (Numbers 21:9). When someone had been bitten, there was now an antidote. It
was certainly a terrible ordeal, but those who looked at the serpent, trusting in God,
survived.

When your life is centered in Jesus, instead of falling apart or becoming discouraged,
you'll look to Him when the unexpected happens. There are Christians who turn into
devils when things don't go their way. God wants better for us than that.

When your heart is connected with the heart of Jesus, the turbulence of life isn't
going to cause you to forget your faith in God. When your default reaction is to turn to
Him rather than to blow up or get discouraged, amazing things happen. The power and
presence of God have brought many people through incredibly difficult circumstances.
It isn't possible to get so low that God cannot reach you.

An up-and-down approach to life and faith doesn't get a person past anger and
bitterness. If you maintain constant communication with God, you will look to Him
when rough experiences come. In dark moments, you can shine for Jesus.

Trustworthy!

*It is better to trust in the L*ORD
Than to put confidence in man.
*It is better to trust in the L*ORD
Than to put confidence in princes.

—Psalm 118:8, 9

Surveys consistently reveal that no group of professionals is trusted more than firefighters. In one European country, firefighters enjoy a 97 percent confidence rate. It seems the reason firefighters are so trusted is that they have proven to be concerned for the welfare of others and are prepared to sacrifice for the benefit of society. Firefighters are always there to help and rarely, if ever, make the news for unprofessional or selfish behavior.

But even the most trusted person can still let you down. Trust is essential in day-to-day life. We trust that the package we send will arrive at its destination at the appointed time. We trust a company will fix a defective product and that our money will be available when we want to withdraw it from the bank. Without this trust, life, as we know it, simply wouldn't work.

But trust can be and often is abused. In 2009, an American businessman was sentenced to 150 years in prison after his wealth management company was found to have defrauded billions of dollars from thousands of people. People trusted that the man with whom they invested their hard-earned money would act in their best interests, but that trust was betrayed.

God can be trusted. Always. Believing Him changes your attitude in the midst of challenging situations. When God says, "I will never leave you nor forsake you" (Hebrews 13:5) or you read "My God shall supply all your need" in Philippians 4:19, you can expect Him to do as He has said. God's promises of forgiveness should never be doubted.

There is someone who will never let you down. Someone you can always rely on 100 percent. You can lean on God and know that He is trustworthy. As the Bible says in Numbers 23:19, "God is not a man, that He should lie." God can be trusted!

The Faith of Abraham

Being fully convinced that what He
had promised He was also able to perform.

—Romans 4:21

When my son was young, he climbed onto the roof of a small shed in the yard of a friend's house. After enjoying the view, he asked me to help him get down. I offered to catch him if he would jump into my arms.

I coaxed, I pleaded, I cajoled, and I persuaded, but to no avail. He wasn't jumping, and that was that. My daughter—two years younger than my son—saw what was going on and asked if I would put her up onto the roof of the little building so she could jump and have me catch her. While the illustration is a little imperfect—not everyone is comfortable with jumping from heights under any circumstances—it made a point about faith. Intellectually, my son had no doubt I would try to catch him if he jumped. But there was no way he was going to jump into my arms. He was not convinced that things would work out as I insisted they would.

Paul wrote about Abraham's experience when describing the reality of faith. After God had spoken with him regarding His promise that the aged patriarch would father a child, Abraham was "fully convinced that what He had promised He was also able to perform" (Romans 4:21). God promised Abraham he would father a child in the most unlikely of circumstances, and Abraham believed God. He was convinced that God *could* do what God promised He *would* do.

When God makes you a promise, faith simply says, "God is able to do what He has promised to do." When God promises forgiveness, faith says, "I am forgiven." When God promises you a new start, faith replies by saying, "God has given me a new start." When you need strength or patience or courage or anything else, if God has promised you these things, real faith simply believes God is able to do what He has promised.

Faith is believing the promises of God and then expecting God to do exactly what His promises say He will do. You can have real faith in God today.

APRIL

A Twelve-Billion-Dollar Pen?

*The entirety of Your word is truth, and every
one of Your righteous judgments endures forever.*
—Psalm 119:160

The story goes that NASA once developed a pen that would work in zero gravity, meaning astronauts would be able to use the pen in space. Reports stated NASA spent ten years and twelve billion dollars developing such a pen, while the Russian space agency simply gave their cosmonauts pencils. Evidently, the public perception of government agencies was bad enough that the story was widely believed, despite the fact that it wasn't true. There was never a twelve-billion-dollar space pen.*

People will believe almost anything if it is said convincingly by a person in a position of authority. Especially is this true in spiritual matters. Some of the strangest claims about the Bible are made without even the slightest evidence that the claims are true. Entire denominations have come into existence as a result. No, Jesus is not going to return to earth on a certain predicted date, regardless of how many prophecies a person appeals to and how sincere they are about their belief. Jesus said that no man knows the day or hour of His return (Matthew 24:36). The law of God has not been done away with, and we can be certain of it because the Bible is clear on that topic. Sinners are not going to burn in hell forever, no matter how enthusiastically a minister of the gospel insists they shall. Again, the Bible is clear.

Christians should be certain that what they believe is actually true. In Acts 17:11, we are introduced to the people of Berea, who "received the word with all readiness, and searched the Scriptures daily to find out whether these things were so."

It is important to make sure that what you believe is actually biblical. The Holy Spirit has been promised to us so that He might guide us "into all truth." Some errors are believed because they are promoted by people in authority or repeated with such earnestness they must surely be true. The Scriptures have been given to us as a safeguard against spiritual misrepresentation. Error is never harmless. God's Word is always true.

---

* Ciara Curtin, "Fact or Fiction?: NASA Spent Millions to Develop a Pen That Would Write in Space, Whereas the Soviet Cosmonauts Used a Pencil," *Scientific American*, December 20, 2006, https://www.scientificamerican.com/article/fact-or-fiction-nasa-spen/.

No Condemnation

What then shall we say to these things?
If God is for us, who can be against us?

—Romans 8:31

If you really want to be blessed spiritually, read Romans chapter 8, a truly remarkable chapter of the Bible. It starts with Paul affirming that there is "no condemnation to those who are in Christ Jesus" (verse 1).

Guilt and condemnation are debilitating. When we hurt others, ourselves, or God, it is normal to feel remorse over what we have done. But people who don't find an appropriate way to deal with the guilt that results from sin can find it spiritually crippling.

The fact is that "all have sinned" (Romans 3:23), and "the wages of sin is death" (Romans 6:23). Sin results in separation from God (Isaiah 59:2) and brings condemnation into a person's life. But Romans 8:1 assures us that if we are surrendered to Jesus and have accepted Him as Lord and Savior, we are not under condemnation.

There is never any need to doubt that God is willing to forgive you for the sins you have committed. There is no place for wondering whether God will forgive you for your failures. God forgave Moses for murder. He forgave Peter for denying Jesus. Jesus cast seven demons out of Mary Magdalene. The woman at the well not only was forgiven for her sins but also brought an entire city to the knowledge of salvation through Jesus. Nebuchadnezzar was forgiven for sins we could scarcely imagine, while Adam and Eve were pardoned for introducing sin into the world and thereby assuring the death of Jesus.

Micah 7:18 says that God "does not retain His anger forever, because He delights in mercy." Twenty-six times in Psalm 136, we are told that "His mercy endures forever." And where sin abounds, grace abounds much more (Romans 5:20). Regardless of what you have done, what you have been in the past, or what you may be in the midst of right now, God is gracious. When your life is given to Jesus and you are surrendered to the leading of the Holy Spirit, there is no condemnation.

Died in Their Place

*For scarcely for a righteous man will one die; yet perhaps for a good man
someone would even dare to die. But God demonstrates His own love toward
us, in that while we were still sinners, Christ died for us.*
—Romans 5:7, 8

I n February 1943, an American troop transport ship was traveling as part of a naval convoy bound for Greenland. The USAT *Dorchester* was carrying nine hundred people, including military personnel, merchant seamen, and civilians. Transporting servicemen during World War II was a dangerous business. While the ship was off the coast of Newfoundland, it was torpedoed and sunk by a German submarine.

Many died in the blast, and many others were wounded. Although lots of the survivors had life jackets, there weren't enough for everyone. But the four chaplains on the ship—a Catholic, two Protestants, and a Jew—encouraged the troops, helped them off the ship, and then gave their life jackets to soldiers. Singing and praying together, they went down with the ship into the frigid water and died.

They gave their lives for others, not only for their friends, not only for those of their religious belief but also, in effect, for all of the men on that ship. Four brave men, four dedicated individuals, made the ultimate sacrifice.*

The divine Son of God, the Maker of the world (John 1:3), had such love in His heart for a fallen planet that He gave His life so that others might live. This was no small thing. This was God dying for sinful humanity, the perfect for the corrupt, the pure for the vile.

In dying for the world, Jesus didn't play favorites or show preferences. Today He says that "whoever believes" in Him may have everlasting life (John 3:16). He did not die only for others; Jesus died for you.

We can only imagine how the four men who received the chaplains' life jackets were affected, knowing that they lived because the four chaplains chose to die in their place. How is your life affected today, knowing that the Son of God chose to die for you?

---

* James H. Clifford, "No Greater Glory: The Four Chaplains and the Sinking of the USAT Dorchester," The Army Historical Foundation, accessed April 5, 2021, https://armyhistory.org/no-greater-glory-the-four -chaplains-and-the-sinking-of-the-usat-dorchester/.

Condemned

"For God did not send His Son into the world to condemn the world,
but that the world through Him might be saved."

—John 3:17

As I walked through a rough neighborhood, I passed several old houses that had the word *condemned* painted on them. *Condemned* is a strong word, but it was acknowledged that the houses in question were so far gone that repairing them was considered a hopeless task. It wasn't hard to imagine the houses as they looked when they were first built. New housing developments are usually hopeful places. Designed for families, they very often ring with the sounds of children playing. A new home is a place of promise as people look to the future and plan for what lies ahead.

But now, these houses were condemned. Workers had proudly built them, using all-new materials. But over the years, they had been neglected, and they were now dilapidated—too far gone. There was nothing left to do but demolish them. They were beyond hope. Leaving the houses standing would have been dangerous; reckless, even.

Every newborn child is filled with possibility and promise. Within every child is the prospect of growing up to be a Martin Luther or a Martin Luther King Junior. A Marie Curie or a Sojourner Truth. Every child has the potential to change the world. Even more important, that child has the opportunity to know the God of heaven and reflect His character to the world.

But people who don't look after themselves become spiritually run down. Eventually, they become spiritually dilapidated, and in time so out of harmony with heaven's plan for their lives that they do not possess everlasting life. Condemned! But the gospel is good news! Romans 8:1 says, "There is therefore now no condemnation to those who are in Christ Jesus, who do not walk according to the flesh, but according to the Spirit." No matter how far gone a person might be, if they can take hold of Jesus, there is no condemnation—whether that is you, a child, your parents, family, or friends. God is in the business of remaking lives so that the condemned might instead live forever.

Victory Instead of Failure

*The righteous requirement of the law might be fulfilled in us who
do not walk according to the flesh but according to the Spirit.*
—Romans 8:4

Even though the power of God is promised to every believer in Jesus, a lot of people battle through life feeling like failures. For as long as they can remember, they've been stuck in a rut, defeated by the same old sins again and again, feeling as though they'll never get it right.

If you follow the desires of your selfish self, you will be governed by the old you. But the promise is that God's righteousness will be manifest in those who walk "according to the spirit" (Romans 8:4).

When you walked as a small child, you put your hand in your parent's hand, and Mom or Dad kept you upright. If you now put your hand in the hand of the God of heaven, He will do exactly the same for you. Consider someone with a bad temper. Something happens that agitates that person. Walking according to the flesh, that person will follow the promptings of their carnal, fleshly self. There will be a fall into sin, which is often followed by the despairing feeling that he or she will never get it right and will continue to fall when temptation arises.

But instead of following the promptings of self, that person may call out to God when temptation strikes. Those who ask God to guide them and to keep them by the power of the Holy Spirit experience the alternative to spiritual failure. They hear the Holy Spirit say, "Take a deep breath and walk away from the situation, and don't hold a grudge." Or, "Just smile and carry on." And, miraculously, when the person surrenders to the leading of God, the power of God brings that person to victory instead of defeat.

Through God's power and blessing, the righteousness of the law may be fulfilled in you. God wants you to experience His righteousness today.

Educated?

*O Timothy! Guard what was committed to your trust, avoiding the profane
and idle babblings and contradictions of what is falsely called knowledge.*
—1 Timothy 6:20

I t is possible today to access the Bible in myriad ways. For hundreds of years, the
only way to encounter the Word of God was through the printed page. But with the
advent of modern technology, the Bible was made available as recordings on cassettes,
albums, and CDs. Now Scripture is available digitally, and people can read the Bible
on the internet with a phone, a tablet, or a personal computer.

In the time of Christ, the Scriptures were readily accessible to everyday people.
A man who asked Jesus a pointed question heard the Savior reply, "What is written
in the law? What is your reading of it?" (Luke 10:26). Jesus directed the man to the
Scriptures, trusting he would read for himself and discover the answer to his question.
But as time passed, the Word of God became increasingly difficult to access, especially
for less affluent people. Incredibly, there came a time when severe penalties were levied
against people for possessing even a portion of the Bible, penalties that were often
imposed by the church itself.

Today the Bible is ubiquitous. It is by far the best-selling book of all time. But in
many cases, the enemy of faith isn't ignorance but knowledge. Paul told Timothy to
avoid "profane and idle babblings and contradictions of what is falsely called knowledge" (1 Timothy 6:20). Some people allow their education to undermine their faith.
Fundamental teachings of the Bible are frequently ridiculed by men and women of
higher learning. The Creation account is routinely disparaged. Many theologians deny
the miracles of the Bible, including the virgin birth. There is no shortage of people who
believe Christianity is for the ignorant and deceived.

The opportunity to learn is a blessing granted by God. Many of the most influential
figures in the history of Christianity have been people of great learning. But faith can
never be eliminated from the Christian experience. Jesus prayed to His Father in John
17:17 and said, "Your word is truth." If Jesus was comfortable trusting God's Word as
truth, we can well afford to do the same.

Discovering Gold and Diamonds

Open my eyes, that I may see wondrous things from Your law.
—Psalm 119:18

In 2013, the government of South Korea approved the construction of Tower Infinity. While it will become one of the top ten tallest buildings in the world, what sets Tower Infinity apart is that when completed, it will have the ability to be "invisible." Projectors mounted on the skyscraper's exterior will project images of the surrounding area onto the building, meaning it will appear to people viewing the 1,476-feet-tall structure from a distance that they are looking right through it.*

In the same way, it is possible to read the Bible and see nothing at all. Many atheists have read the Bible cover to cover. Some passages in the Bible are challenging and don't lend themselves to easy understanding. Peter said that Paul wrote some things that are hard to understand (2 Peter 3:16). Closed eyes will never be able to discern even the plainest truths of God's Word.

When you approach the Bible with a prayerful attitude, you will begin to see the beauty and the depth of God's Word. Those who want to find gold or diamonds usually have to do a lot of digging. But the miner considers all the difficult digging worthwhile when valuable minerals are unearthed.

Although it happens infrequently, gems are occasionally found on or near the earth's surface. In 2019, a hobbyist with a metal detector located a 49-ounce (1.4-kilogram) gold nugget near Kalgoorlie in Western Australia.† In 1975, a white diamond weighing more than 16 carats was found by a visitor to the Crater of Diamonds State Park in Arkansas, where park visitors are allowed to keep any diamonds they find.‡ In the Bible, statements such as "God is love" (1 John 4:8) are easy to find. And it takes little study to understand, "You shall love your neighbor as yourself" (Matthew 22:39).

As you pray, ask God to open your eyes. Then dig into His Word, determined to see what lies beneath the surface. You will see deeper and deeper. And in doing so, you will uncover many of the Bible's priceless treasures.

---

* Karla Cripps, "Coming Soon: World's First 'Invisible' Tower," CNN, last updated September 15, 2013, https://www.cnn.com/travel/article/seoul-invisible-skyscraper-tower-infinity/index.html.

† "Australia Finds A$100,000 Gold Nuggest Using Metal Detector," *BBC News*, May 2019, bbc.com/news/world-austarlia-48331769.

‡ "Famous Finds," Crater of Diamonds State Park History, Arkansas State Parks, https://www.arkansasstateparks.com/parks/crater-diamonds-state-park/history/famous-finds#:~:text=The%20Amarillo%20Starlight%20Diamond,the%20park%20with%20his%20family.

The Question

He said to him, "What is written in the law? What is your reading of it?"
—Luke 10:26

Harry Miller was born in 1879, ten miles northwest of Dayton, Ohio. He went on to become Dr. Harry Miller—a surgeon and hospital medical director. As a Seventh-day Adventist missionary, Dr. Miller spent many years in China and was instrumental in the establishment of almost twenty Adventist hospitals. Today, Dr. Miller might be most famous for pioneering the development of soy milk.

Dr. Miller recalled one particular occurrence during his time in medical school. A certain student did not know the answer to a question asked in class. The teacher made no further comment. The next day, the lecturer asked the same student the same question. Again, the student did not know that answer. On the third day, the lecturer asked the same question of the same student, but this time the student knew the answer to the question.* Soon-to-be Doctor Miller learned a lesson. Be ready with the answer before the question is asked!

One day, a man asked Jesus a question, and Jesus answered him with a question of His own. He said, "What is written in the law? What is your reading of it?" (Luke 10:26). Jesus was urging the man to go to the Scriptures to find the answers to his questions. His lesson for the man is the same lesson He wants us to learn today. The answers to our questions are almost always found in Scripture.

Imagine if the man had answered Jesus by saying, "I have no idea what is written in the law." Peter wrote that we should be "always be ready to give a defense to everyone who asks you a reason for the hope that is in you" (1 Peter 3:15). It is imperative for believers to be acquainted with the Word of God.

There is power in the Word of God. Temptation often gets the better of people for the simple reason that they are not reading the Bible, and God's promises do not, therefore, spring readily to mind. Time spent studying God's Word is time wisely spent.

---

* Raymond S. Moore, *China Doctor: The Life Story of Harry Willis Miller* (Nampa, ID: Pacific Press®, 2012), 25.

The Spirit or the Flesh?

*For those who live according to the flesh set their minds on the things of the
flesh, but those who live according to the Spirit, the things of the Spirit.*
—Romans 8:5

A paraphrase of Paul's writings to the Corinthians states that by beholding, we
become changed (2 Corinthians 3:18). We become like that upon which we focus
our attention. What we behold, or put into our minds, molds us into its own image.
What you focus on forms you into what you will be.

In Romans 8:5, the same author tells us that the person who fills the mind with
things of an earthly or carnal nature is going to live "according to the flesh." The
old-fashioned preachers who denounced going to the theater or watching television
had a very good point. There are things that go into the mind that don't do anything
positive for a believer in Jesus in light of eternity and therefore place obstacles between
the believer and the gates of pearl.

On the other hand, those who "live according to the Spirit" will set their minds on
"the things of the Spirit." Reading the Bible develops an inclination for reading the
Bible. Habitual worship bends a life toward God. Prayer connects a heart with the heart
of God. Serving others is an antidote for selfishness.

While focusing on exterior matters is not the way to spiritual health, a desire for
holiness should be accompanied by practices that develop a love for the things of
heaven. The mind absorbs that which it is fed. Just as malnourishment can retard
physical and mental development and lead to illness, spiritual malnourishment unfits
a person for the society of heaven. A real danger with spiritual malnourishment is that,
just as poor health practices often take years to damage a body or a mind, spiritual
carelessness can often appear harmless until serious spiritual damage has been done
and it is too late to undo.

Mind the things of the Spirit today. Living "according to the Spirit" brings joy on
this earth and in the world to come.

Carnal or Spiritual?

For to be carnally minded is death,
but to be spiritually minded is life and peace.

—Romans 8:6

Residents of Belcoo in County Fermanagh, Northern Ireland, were unimpressed by some of the preparations made for a meeting of G-8 political leaders in their little town. A severe economic downturn had their region and others like it struggling financially, so in order to give the best possible impression to the visiting dignitaries, many shopfronts in Belcoo were covered with large stickers and posters. One empty shop was made to look like a thriving office supply store. A former butcher's store was altered to appear as though it boasted a packed meat counter and business was booming. The truth was, the town was in bad shape. The suggestion that all was well in Northern Ireland at that time was mere pretense.*

In the Bible, God shows us things as they really are. Reality might not always be pleasant, but God would evidently have us embrace a difficult reality rather than an attractive falsehood. Naturally, the sinful mind is attracted to the low and the sinful, but God is honest enough to tell us that to be carnally minded—interested in earthly, impure things—is death.

Many who profess faith in God are indistinguishable from those who are lost. Eternal life is given to those who are spiritually minded. Paul says that surrendering your mind to the Holy Spirit brings life and peace. As attractive as the world can be, there is no spiritual future in having your life centered on the secular. Filling the mind with low, earthly things unfits a person for heaven and renders a disciple of Jesus unsuitable for the companionship of the redeemed. Rather than being an empty Christian with a pleasing veneer, God's promise is to fill us with His presence and make His children genuine believers in Jesus.

The Holy Spirit's work in a person's life is to make the person spiritually minded. If you allow Him to do so, God will change your heart and mind. He will give you a desire for that which God loves and make you a member of the family of heaven.

---

* Cathal McNaughtan, "Fake Shop Fronts Hide N. Ireland Economic Woes Before G8," *Reuters*, June 3, 2013, https://www.reuters.com/article/us-irish-g8-fakeshops/fake-shop-fronts-hide-n-ireland-economic-woes -before-g8-idINBRE95210520130603.

Intense

Behold, you are fair, my love!
Behold, you are fair!
You have dove's eyes.
Behold, you are handsome, my beloved!
Yes, pleasant!

—Song of Solomon 1:15, 16

While the Song of Solomon is the love story of Solomon and his wife, it also describes the love of God for His church. The word *love* has come to mean many things. You can love your dog, love a bargain, love ice cream, and love your mother, each kind of love being somewhat different from the other. But the love God has for His children is a powerful, passionate love that puts concern for the one being loved ahead of the One doing the loving.

Consider the kind of love expressed in the Song of Solomon. The two protagonists in this story are absolutely head-over-heels in love with each other. God uses this love story to help us understand His great love for His children.

God loves people with intense love. And the privilege of every believer is to have a love for God that is alive and vibrant. In Revelation 2:4, God expresses His disappointment with His people in these words: "Nevertheless I have this against you, that you have left your first love." First love is the "I can't wait to see you again" love, the "I just called to hear the sound of your voice" love. It's "I'll do anything for you" love, the very sort of love God wants us to have for Him. Unfortunately, there is a tendency for that kind of love to wear off over time.

The tragedy is that a person can leave the first love experience and begin to simply go through the motions of being a Christian. This isn't to suggest that a relationship with God is all about feelings of giddiness and butterflies in the stomach. Love is not a feeling but a principle. As you daily surrender control of your life to the indwelling Holy Spirit, your love for God will grow and intensify. Your desires will be merged with God's will for your life.

Turn Again

Let us search out and examine our ways,
and turn back to the LORD.

—Lamentations 3:40

I t is well-known that most pictures we see of models in glossy advertisements are not accurate representations of what they look like in "real life." "Photoshopped" images are the norm, and many techniques are used to get the perfect picture. Today it is standard for pictures of models to be digitally enhanced—teeth are whitened or straightened, blemishes are removed, necks are lengthened, and pounds are removed by software that can literally reshape the subject of a photograph. What is seen in glossy magazines is almost never reality.

What happens when we accept falsehood in the place of reality in our spiritual life? The Bible encourages us not to Photoshop our lives or attempt to airbrush our Christian experience. It's wise to regularly carry out a moral inventory and take a good look in the spiritual mirror to see how your life compares with God's will. Doing so requires spiritual bravery because when you ask God to help you to see yourself as you truly are, you may well see some things you don't much like.

But the Bible makes clear that when you see you are falling short and identify areas where you could grow spiritually, you should not become discouraged. Jeremiah's instruction offers us a balanced hope. We must examine ourselves carefully; then, we must "turn back to the LORD" (Lamentations 3:40). Discouragement is one of the devil's most effective tools. He would like you to see your shortcomings and turn away from God. But it is when you see your weaknesses that you most need to turn to God. Don't be afraid to see yourself as you really are. And when you do, turn *to* God and not away from Him.

His!

*"Yes, I swore an oath to you and entered into a covenant
with you, and you became Mine," says the Lord God.*
—Ezekiel 16:8

A man in Utah was surprised to discover $45,000 in the attic of a home he had recently purchased. The money was sealed in a number of small metal boxes, and it was apparent to the new homeowner it had been deliberately hidden.

He then started to wonder if he could keep the money or whether he should return the money to the previous owners of the house. A question he had to answer in his own mind was, "To whom does the money rightfully belong?" Once he established that, he could move forward with confidence and without regret.*

In the Bible, God leaves no doubt as to whom the human family belongs. In Ezekiel 16, God expresses frustration with a stubborn people. After having done so much for the people of Israel, God was forced to look on as they turned away from Him and followed their own ways, ways that must ultimately lead them to ruin. But in spite of Israel's sin and stubbornness, God says, "I swore an oath to you and entered into a covenant with you, and you became Mine" (verse 8).

Consider those words: "you became Mine." God wants you to know that you are His! In spite of your weakness, in spite of your failures, in spite of your lack, you are His! There is never a reason for the child of God to doubt his or her standing with God. If your heart is yielded to Christ, if you have accepted Jesus as your Lord and Savior, if you have surrendered your life to Him, you are the property of the God of heaven. The child of God who by faith holds the hand of heaven is a child of God who is daily growing toward God's eternal kingdom.

God was very careful to remind His people, "you became Mine." Like something owned, or—better yet—as something cherished, we are His. We can look forward to the return of Jesus with hope. He will soon return for His own. And we shall be His throughout eternity.

---

* Michael Murray, "Utah Man Finds $45,000 in New House and Returns It to Rightful Owner," *ABC News*, May 20, 2011, https://abcnews.go.com/Business/utah-man-finds-45000-house-returns-rightful-owner /story?id=13648293.

"I Will Allure Her"

*"Therefore, behold, I will allure her, will bring her
into the wilderness, and speak comfort to her."*

—Hosea 2:14

One of the great questions to be considered in the entire plan of salvation is that of God's character. What is God really like? Is God kind and loving, or is God stern and grim? Or is He a combination of the two—kind to those He loves and stern toward those who choose not to accept Him? For many people, a clear answer to that question would bring an end to a lifetime of fear and doubt.

When disaster strikes, it is common for people to ask why God caused tragedy rather than stepping in to spare lives. Many people portray God as unkind and unloving because He permits suffering. The late Steve Jobs, a titan of the computer industry, wrestled with this question when he was a boy. When he was about thirteen years old, Jobs told the pastor of his church that he didn't want to have anything to do with a God who would permit people to starve in Africa. For him, God was unjust and harsh. He believed a loving God would have prevented such terrible suffering.

In the book of Hosea, God speaks of His people's lack of faithfulness. What does He say about those people who are so famously disloyal? "I will allure her," God says (Hosea 2:14). "I will attract her, entice her. I will win her affections. I'll go after her and woo her back to myself, and I will speak sweet words to her." What a picture of God!

While sin runs its course in our universe, a loving God does everything He can to draw people away from sin and attract them to His heart of great love. The presence of sin in the world is not an indictment against the character of God. Rather, it reflects the true nature of the spiritual enemy we face and is a commentary on the folly of choosing the service of sin over the service of God.

The Valley of Decision

Multitudes, multitudes in the valley of decision!
For the day of the LORD is near in the valley of decision.

—Joel 3:14

E ach of the nearly eight billion people in the world today has an eternal destiny. Stretching before every person on earth is a forever future. The decisions made on a daily basis will affect every individual's future life. Joel proclaims that multitudes are in the valley of decision, suggesting something remarkable about not only the importance of God's gift to us but also about the power of choice.

Life is simply a series of choices. We are all born into this world with others making choices for us. But as children grow and gain experience, they begin to make decisions for themselves. Life-altering decisions are made: where to attend college, what career to pursue, whom to choose as a life partner. These are weighty decisions that should not be made without careful study and earnest prayer. But no choice is as important as the choice you make regarding your relationship with God.

You are privileged to determine your own spiritual destiny. In Joshua 24:15, God said through His servant Joshua, "Choose for yourselves this day whom you will serve." Elijah addressed Israel on Mount Carmel and said, "How long will you falter between two opinions? If the LORD is God, follow Him; but if Baal, follow him" (1 Kings 18:21). When the crowds were turning away from Him, Jesus said to His disciples, "Do you also want to go away?" (John 6:67). The decision to remain with Jesus or to turn away from Him was theirs.

Not everyone has the same standard of living, educational opportunities, privileges, or talents, but every single person has the power of choice, the opportunity for eternal self-determination. Today, you have the opportunity to make the decision to belong to Jesus. If you are in the valley of decision, let your decision be for the God of heaven. While some of the decisions that confront you from day to day are small and others large, they add up together to determine your eternal destiny. Let your decisions today be for Jesus.

The Sin Remains the Same

"I will stretch out My hand against Judah,
And against all the inhabitants of Jerusalem.
I will cut off every trace of Baal from this place,
The names of the idolatrous priests with the pagan priests."
—Zephaniah 1:4

The times might change, but the sin all too often remains the same. When God speaks to Judah in the book of Zephaniah, He gives a warning often repeated throughout the Bible. God's own people were worshiping pagan deities. They were worshiping the sun, the moon, and an array of idols.

It seems incongruous that Israel would have worshiped idols after all God had done for them. These were people whose parents and grandparents had seen the Red Sea part before their eyes, who had eaten manna that miraculously appeared six mornings a week, and drank water that flowed from a rock. How do people plunge into idolatry with such clear evidence of God's grace and power?

In truth, time has changed things very little. While few church members gather on rooftops to worship the sun and the moon, there is no shortage of idolatry being practiced today. People make idols of their possessions, working hard to accumulate money that is squandered on things of no eternal value. Houses and lands can become idols. Sports teams or particular athletes are an idol for many. Even religious beliefs can become idols, as people cling to errors that place them in opposition to the teachings of the Bible.

When God said at Sinai that His people should have no other gods before Him, He wasn't referring solely to other deities. Gods can be made of almost anything at all. If there is something in your life that is more important to you than Jesus, the One who died for you, it is time to think again. God spoke very plainly about idols and other gods because He knows they can easily drain the spiritual life out of believers and destroy their faith. Judah never truly recovered from its idolatry. As we prepare for the return of Jesus, it is important we do not repeat the same mistake.

Why Did God Do *That?*

"Now go and attack Amalek, and utterly destroy all that they have, and do not spare them. But kill both man and woman, infant and nursing child, ox and sheep, camel and donkey."
—1 Samuel 15:3

One of the great challenges many people have in understanding the Bible is understanding why God at times commanded that peoples or cities be destroyed.

How, people ask, could God order the destruction of the defenseless, the very young, and the elderly? It is really not such a mystery. In this instance, God was dealing with prodigiously wicked people. In His wisdom, He knew the Amalekites had resisted His grace and were fully given over to Satan. He knew they would never repent and had only lives of sin and rebellion to look forward to. The world would be better off without the Amalekites, and they would no longer be a threat to God's people.

The Bible assures us that "God is love" (1 John 4:8). Even the destruction of the wicked and rebellious is an expression of His love. God knows what we don't know and sees what we cannot see. God knew Amalekite children would have grown up to be at least as wicked as their parents. In mercy, He brought their existence to an end.

There is no question that God's handling of the Amalekites was severe. But sin is severe. A depraved life is severe. Living apart from God not only brings eternal death but also causes the virus of sin to proliferate. The Amalekites were thoroughly corrupt. The constant threat they presented to the viability of Israel jeopardized the coming of the Messiah. God acted to protect His people and to contain the threat that evil posed to His people and the world.

God need not be charged with injustice. It is Satan who spreads misery and death. One of his greatest deceptions is to accuse God of causing the damage for which sin is responsible. As difficult as it may sometimes be to understand, the tough decisions made by God are always the right decisions.

When Bad Things Are Good

Now the LORD had prepared a great fish to swallow Jonah.
And Jonah was in the belly of the fish three days and three nights.
—Jonah 1:17

While in the military, a young man was told he was to be on a flight back from Europe to the United States. He grabbed his few possessions and reported for the flight, only to be told his name wasn't on the list. "How can that be?" he pleaded. "It has to be. I heard my name called earlier!" He explained that he desperately wanted to return home. But his name was not on the list. Someone had made a mistake, and he wouldn't be going home until later. How much later, he didn't know. He was devastated that God hadn't permitted him to make the flight.

He lay on his bunk and sulked, feeling bitter that he would have to wait to see his family. But the next morning, he received the shocking news that the plane he was determined to be aboard didn't make it to the United States. It had crashed in the Atlantic Ocean. Everyone on board perished.

It is not unusual for people to feel aggrieved when disappointments strike. But not all bad things are bad. Not being able to board a plane home is bad. Avoiding tragedy is good, and the young man—who went on to become a minister of the gospel—could not have experienced the good if he hadn't first gone through the bad. Jonah lived through a similar experience. Without a doubt, the first reaction of someone swallowed by a large fish would be, "This is really, really bad."

But God Himself had prepared that sea creature for a special purpose. What Jonah thought was a disaster was actually something magnificent in the making. He was saved in a storm, preserved in a sea creature, and transported to dry land where he could begin his journey back to the place God wanted him to be. His preaching brought salvation to an entire city. What was bad for Jonah turned out to be a phenomenal blessing.

Don't be too quick to judge God when things don't go right. Bad is often a step on the way to good.

Faithful Shepherds?

"My people have been lost sheep.
Their shepherds have led them astray;
They have turned them away on the mountains."
—Jeremiah 50:6

M any books have been written on the subject of leadership. But few books include as many important case studies on leadership as does the Bible. For forty years, Moses led God's people through the wilderness to the borders of the Promised Land, dealing, along the way, with insurrection, rebellion, and complaint. Joshua led Israel into Canaan, defeating (and being defeated by) opposing nations. David, though flawed, was a great leader of God's people. And the leadership of Solomon facilitated the construction of the magnificent temple in Jerusalem. Second Chronicles 21:11 says that King Jehoram of Judah "caused the inhabitants of Jerusalem to commit harlotry, and led Judah astray." Jehoram led an entire nation into sin.

Leaders can be hugely influential, and faithfulness to God is a key characteristic of truly effective Christian leaders. In Jeremiah 50, God addresses the unfaithfulness of His people, and what He says regarding leadership is sobering: "Their shepherds have led them astray; they have turned them away on the mountains" (verse 6).

While acknowledging that His people have wandered, God places much of the responsibility for the unfaithfulness of the people on their spiritual leaders. Those shepherding the flock of God are liable to a significant degree for the spiritual health of those they serve and are called to be faithful in exhorting, encouraging, and guiding.

Those in positions of church leadership have a responsibility to be more than wise managers and astute planners. Those God calls to lead in the church are to be spiritual, committed to God, and dedicated to the message and mission of the church. Most importantly, they must be Christian—Christlike, striving to surrender to the indwelling of the Holy Spirit. In the early Christian church, even the deacons were "full of the Holy Spirit" (Acts 6:3).

Those whom God calls into positions of leadership will be relentlessly opposed by the enemy of souls. It is important to pray for those in leadership roles. And those who accept the call to leadership must also pray that their leadership will reflect the character of Christ and encourage others to live lives of faithfulness to God.

A True Hero!

And one shall say unto him, What are these wounds in thine hands? Then he shall answer, Those with which I was wounded in the house of my friends.
—Zechariah 13:6, KJV

F ew verses illustrate the love of God toward a sinful world as vividly as Zechariah 13:6. When Jesus tells the story of His death on the cross, He speaks of the wounds He suffered having been inflicted by His "friends."

When a soldier is wounded or killed because of his or her actions in saving others in combat, that soldier typically receives awards and recognition and is considered a hero. It is not uncommon for combat personnel to be seriously injured. Such individuals deserve the respect of society. They not only volunteered to serve their nation but also paid a very significant price as a result of their decision to do so.

The greatest war hero of all is Jesus. Caught in the heat of the battle of the ages, Jesus came to earth and was tortured and killed by the enemy so that both His friends and enemies could have the opportunity to live. And yet Jesus did not have to die. He said to Peter in Matthew 26:53, "Do you think that I cannot now pray to My Father, and He will provide Me with more than twelve legions of angels?" He chose to die. Jesus could have opted to remain in heaven and leave earth to its fate. No one would have blamed Him if He had.

Jesus was committed, not to His own welfare, but to the welfare of others. Jesus was a true hero, who "did not come to be served, but to serve, and to give His life a ransom for many" (Matthew 20:28). Jesus died willingly for the sins of the world, knowing that the sacrifice He made would result in heaven being populated by men and women and boys and girls who had been redeemed because of the Cross. He wasn't awarded a Purple Heart or a Congressional Medal of Honor for what He did. But you can honor His heroism by giving Him your heart today.

Big Dividends

"Go, gather all the Jews who are present in Shushan, and fast for me; neither eat nor drink for three days, night or day. My maids and I will fast likewise."
—Esther 4:16

In the famous Bible story, Queen Esther chose, at the urging of her uncle, to advocate for her people. Owing to the evil scheming of Haman, a high-ranking official in the king's court, the Jews were threatened with extermination. Unless something decisive was done, Haman's plan would certainly be carried out. It was vital that someone would advocate with the king on behalf of the Jews. Without someone intervening on their behalf, an entire people group would be destroyed.

As strange as it seems today, even the queen could not enter the presence of the king without being first invited. Esther was confronted with the choice of doing nothing and allowing her people to perish or doing something and quite possibly losing her own life due to breaking the law of the king. This was a time of crisis.

Queen Esther was careful to prepare thoroughly for the most momentous occasion of her life. Esther asked Mordecai to gather everyone he could and have them fast. "I also and my maidens will fast likewise; and so will I go in unto the king" (Esther 4:16, KJV). Something as momentous as what Esther was about to do required serious spiritual preparation. This is a lesson for all who believe in Jesus. Momentous actions require significant time spent with God. Entering into a conflict with evil necessitates meaningful time breathing the atmosphere of heaven.

God is a prayer-answering God, and Esther would not choose to do what she did without seeking His blessing. Students preparing for final exams study diligently. Runners, preparing for a marathon, train extensively. Anyone preparing for everlasting life will spend time in fasting, prayer, and Bible study, receiving strength and blessing from God in anticipation of eternity.

Esther and her people were miraculously delivered from certain death. Deliverance did not come in the form of mounted cavalry or an invading military force. God moved in answer to the prayers of His people. Time spent in prayer and fasting is time invested for eternity.

Boldness

"I will go to the king, which is against the law; and if I perish, I perish!"
—Esther 4:16

It is a dramatic story. Esther, the Jewish queen of Persia and Media and wife of King Ahasuerus, chose to be an advocate for her people. A malicious counselor to the king was determined to destroy the Jewish people. Only Esther, the wife of the king, could help them. The culture demanded nobody enter the presence of the king uninvited, but Esther risked her life to save her people.

There are times when doing the right thing demands that you don't stop to consider the consequences to yourself. "We should choose the right because it is right, and leave consequences with God."* History is replete with examples of those who stood boldly for the Word of God. Nicholas Ridley and Thomas Cranmer were burned at the stake in Oxford, England, because they refused to renounce their faith in God's Word. Martin Luther and many others jeopardized their existence for daring to stand with the Bible against the teachings of the established church. And in being so bold as to risk all for the sake of the Cross, they gave power and impetus to Christianity and inspired countless others to live lives of faith and obedience.

If heroes of faith had not been bold enough to follow the call of God on their lives, history might have followed a very different course. It is doubtful any one of them was fully aware of the power of their example, but we who look back on their bravery and fidelity can see how one person's life can encourage multitudes to be true to Christ.

While God might not be calling you to die for Him, He is certainly calling you to live for Him. A life lived as a witness for Jesus has the potential to make the type of difference that Esther's boldness made thousands of years ago. In eternity, not one of the redeemed will regret a word spoken, a stand made, or an example given for the sake of Christ.

---

* Ellen G. White, *The Great Controversy Between Christ and Satan* (Mountain View, CA: Pacific Press®, 1950), 460.

Sink or Swim

*Jesus answered and said to him, "Most assuredly, I say to you,
unless one is born again, he cannot see the kingdom of God."*

—John 3:3

Children learn to walk gradually. Slowly. While newborn horses and giraffes normally walk within thirty minutes of being born, and newborn zebras walk within twenty minutes and are running within an hour, human children operate on a different schedule. Immobile at birth, they progress to rolling, then to crawling, and to cruising (walking while holding on to furniture). Most babies take their first tottering steps somewhere between nine and fifteen months of age. But even after learning to walk, children are not able to run right away. Neither can they hop or skip. This comes as they grow.

Something very similar happens when we come to Jesus. Jesus described the miracle of a sinner coming to faith in Him as a person being born again. The forgiven sinner surrenders his or her life to Christ. Jesus is accepted as a personal Savior, and the life of the believer comes under His leadership.

After a spiritual rebirth, growth must take place. God accepts us as His own, and we are saved instead of lost, but this is just the beginning of what God wishes to do in a person's life. Just as you are born into this world without every faculty fully developed, people who come to Jesus must grow. As they do, they learn how to live the new life Jesus offers. And it must be remembered that spiritual growth is continual. A follower of Jesus never plateaus. Far too many Christians allow their experience to settle without pressing on to learn how to master the advanced stages of faith in Christ.

Even long-time followers of Jesus have more spiritual growing to do. They have more to learn, victories to win, bad habits to overcome, and a more vibrant walk with God to experience. There is no treading water when it comes to faith in God. A follower of God has the privilege of continually growing, learning, and becoming more like Jesus. That can be your experience today.

Perspective

"For the great day of His wrath has come,
and who is able to stand?"

—Revelation 6:17

Perspective is an interesting thing. A couple once told me that the life-threatening illness that struck a member of their family turned out to be the best thing that ever happened to them, although at the time, they felt quite differently. The would-be immigrant who hurriedly arrived at the wharf in Southampton, England, too late to make the *Titanic*'s maiden voyage, saw her disappointment tempered when news came that the *Titanic* had sunk in the Atlantic. Weeks later, she safely made it to the United States, where she raised her family. One man's decision to accept Jesus into his life brought about his termination from his place of employment. Shortly afterward, a business opportunity enabled him to afford Christian education for his children. What seems bad at the time can turn out to be a blessing.

And the reverse can also be true. Something that is a blessing for one can seem to be quite the opposite for another. In Revelation 6, Jesus' second coming is described. He returns to the world, which has to be good news! Right? But when Jesus returns to the world, not everyone rejoices. Some cry out for the mountains and rocks to fall on them, saying, "Hide us from the face of Him that sits on the throne" (Revelation 6:16).

For some people, the second coming of Jesus will be very bad news. In Matthew 24:40, 41, Jesus spoke about this, saying, "Then two men will be in the field: one will be taken and the other left. Two women will be grinding at the mill: one will be taken and the other left." Which is another way of saying that when Jesus returns, some will be saved, and some will be lost. Those unprepared for Christ's return are lost for the simple reason that they did not choose to surrender to Jesus. And instead of His return being the best event they've ever experienced, His coming is, for them, a calamity.

Let Christ's return be good news for you!

Time Well Spent

But one thing is needed, and Mary has chosen
that good part, which will not be taken away from her.

—Luke 10:42

S ibling discontent arose as Jesus visited the home of Mary and Martha. Martha was busy preparing food for a meal. Even today, food preparation can be involved and time-consuming. Without the benefit of modern, labor-saving devices, Martha's task was far less simple than it would be for us.

As she prepared the food, Martha became increasingly frustrated that her sister, Mary, was not giving her any help. Instead, Mary was sitting at Jesus' feet, listening to Him teach. While food preparation methods were different in ancient times, attitudes between siblings were evidently not too far removed from what they are today. Martha complained to Jesus about Mary's failure to help her, and she urged Jesus to use His influence to rectify the situation.

Jesus' reply was interesting. He said, "One thing is needed." Jesus wasn't advocating laziness or unhelpfulness, but He was pointing out that while there are many good things that need to be done, the most important thing of all is to sit at the feet of Jesus and hear the sound of His voice.

People can be too busy to take time with Jesus. It isn't only the "bad" things that can get in the way of a relationship with God. Many a worker in Christ's cause has lost their way spiritually because they were too busy doing God's work to pause and listen to God's voice. Families suffer because the pastor or the church elder is giving so much time to *good* things that there isn't time left over for the *best* things. Personal devotional time can disappear because there are so many other "good" things that need to be done.

Don't fall into that trap. As busy as He was, Jesus made time to spend with His Father, and He urged the disciples to "come aside . . . and rest a while" (Mark 6:31). While there are many good things that must be done, time spent with Jesus is the most valuable time you can spend.

Hope for Children

"All your children shall be taught by the Lord,
and great shall be the peace of your children."

—Isaiah 54:13

One of the great sadnesses in the world is the enormous amount of suffering endured by children. While so many children are never permitted to enter the world owing to the colossal tragedy of abortion, there are millions of children in the world who are forced to carry unthinkably heavy burdens.

An enormous number of children live in abject poverty. There are those who are starving, neglected, the victims of human trafficking, and those who suffer unspeakable abuse. And God sees it all.

God has made it clear that He is not indifferent to the suffering of the younger members of the human family. Jesus said in Mark 9:42, "But whoever causes one of these little ones who believe in me to stumble, it would be better for him if a millstone were hung around his neck, and he were thrown into the sea." Jesus made time for the children His own disciples felt were not worthy of His attention. He said in Matthew 19:14, "Let the little children come to Me, and do not forbid them; for of such is the kingdom of heaven." In Isaiah 54:13, God speaks to an afflicted people, saying, "Great shall be the peace of your children."

Our heavenly Father feels keenly for children, and He does not forget them. Satan works with incredible malice, causing heartache to God by striking at the little ones He loves. As our planet sinks deeper into sin, we can look beyond this world and see a time when children won't be hungry, exploited, or abandoned. Life can be especially difficult for the young and defenseless, but, one day, children will live in a world of peace.

While sin does its terrible work and the inhabitants of this world cannot be immune to its effects, God looks forward to a time of hope for those who trust in Him. One day soon, senseless suffering will be forever over. All who call God their Father can look forward to that day with confidence.

Serious Times

"Turn to Me with all your heart,
With fasting, with weeping, and with mourning."
So rend your heart, and not your garments;
Return to the LORD your God,
For He is gracious and merciful,
Slow to anger, and of great kindness.

—Joel 2:12, 13

When the United States announced it would enter World War II, Americans knew that life was going to change and circumstances would be difficult. But for those living in Europe or Asia—in the places where the flames of war burned fiercest—people prepared as much as they could for a time they knew would be indescribably difficult. They knew bad times were ahead.

The Bible makes clear this planet is headed for difficult times. God's Word assures us that "all who desire to live godly in Christ Jesus will suffer persecution" (2 Timothy 3:12), and Daniel pointed forward to a coming "time of trouble, such as never was" (Daniel 12:1). Though it isn't possible to know what exactly that time is going to be like, it is clear that the faith of God's people will be severely tested. Revelation 13:8 says, "all who dwell on the earth will worship" an end-time spiritual counterfeit, with the exception of a group of people whose names are "written in the Book of Life of the Lamb." The coming conflict involving every inhabitant of earth will be great.

What will it take to honor God at a time when the world at large is doing exactly the opposite? Consider what God says in Joel 2:12. In calling His people to repentance, God says, "Turn to me." While no one needs to live in fear of the future, God points out that anyone planning to depart this world and dwell one day in the world to come must make a radical commitment to Him. This is no time to take faith lightly. Only those who allow God to be their everything will experience the power of God to carry them through a time of difficult trial. We face tomorrow knowing Jesus is with us, and an eternity of security and peace is just ahead.

Not Advanced Math!

"If anyone wills to do His will, he shall know concerning the doctrine, whether it is from God or whether I speak on My own authority."
—John 7:17

I do not believe advanced math is easy. While I'm grateful for the tremendous mathematical knowledge some people possess—and the great contributions to society that have consequently accrued owing to the admirable acuity of mathematicians—anything mathematical beyond a certain point is like a foreign language to me. I have friends who love math and speak almost poetically regarding what they call its beauty and science, but I have never caught the math bug. As a youngster in school, I was more than capable in basic math, but once I got to high school and was exposed to a more advanced form of the discipline, I was out of my depth.

Unfortunately, some people are like that with the Bible. "Jesus loves me, this I know" they are able to grasp and appreciate, which is important and good. But push on much past that into biblical concepts that require more insight, and Bible study becomes a journey into the unknown. Jesus shared a simple, basic, yet vitally important key that makes the Bible come alive and opens up significant stores of knowledge to Bible students.

Jesus told us that if anyone wants to do His will, "he shall know concerning the doctrine" (John 7:17). These few words indicate that a person's understanding of God's Word has everything to do with their attitude. God says that if we bring a surrendered, obedient heart to the study of the Bible, our knowledge of the Bible will grow as we are willing to do His will.

In Psalm 119:105, David described God's Word as a lamp and a light. Anyone following the light on a dark pathway knows that if the light is followed, one can stay on the pathway. Should a person neglect to follow the light, the person will be left in the dark and ultimately become hopelessly lost.

A heart that holds itself back from God is likely to find the Bible difficult to understand and insights into God's Word hard to come by. But, if you open your heart to God, His Word will come alive in your life.

Perfect Sense

For now we see in a mirror, dimly, but then face to face.
Now I know in part, but then I shall know just as I also am known.
—1 Corinthians 13:12

There are some common questions asked in relation to heaven. "Will my pets be in heaven?" "Will my spouse and I be married in heaven?" "How am I going to be able to bear eternity if some of my loved ones are not there?" These are meaningful questions, and God has very clear answers for them and others like them—and He will give them to us when we get to heaven.

The challenge we have with such questions is summed up by Paul in 1 Corinthians 13:12. We are not able to see as God sees. If we could, many of our questions would melt away. We can be absolutely certain that whatever happens to pets, spouses, children, friends, and family members, God has it all worked out. It is a very human tendency to consider the deep questions about our world and matters of eternity through a lens that is clouded by our human limitations.

"For My thoughts are not your thoughts,
Nor are your ways My ways," says the LORD.
"For as the heavens are higher than the earth,
So are My ways higher than your ways,
And My thoughts than your thoughts" (Isaiah 55:8, 9).

While people form strong attachments to family members and pets, it is perfectly reasonable to assume that God is more than able to ease the pain we might expect to feel should we be without the pets or people we have learned to love on earth.

The very best thing about eternity will not be the mansions in which the redeemed dwell or streets made of gold or the fruit that grows on the tree of life. The best thing will be that God's saved children will dwell in His presence forever and ever. Jesus will be our Friend into the unending future. Eternity will be more wonderful than we can imagine. We can be absolutely certain that heaven will be better than we can imagine, and nothing there will cause us to feel any sense of loss or dissatisfaction.

Jesus in Others

*"Assuredly, I say to you, inasmuch as you did it to one
of the least of these My brethren, you did it to Me."*

—Matthew 25:40

If Jesus stopped at your home, no doubt you would welcome Him in. If Jesus asked you for a ride to the next town or for a meal or a warm coat, surely you would do everything you could to help Him, to make Him comfortable, to provide for Him. This makes Matthew 25:40 a very sobering verse.

Jesus' comment in Matthew 25:40 has the potential to make a person feel slightly uncomfortable because the question it raises is not, "How am I treating others?" The question is, "How am I treating *Jesus* in others?"

Jesus had been speaking about some of the practical aspects of a life of faith. He said, "I was hungry and you gave Me food; I was thirsty and you gave Me drink; I was a stranger and you took Me in; I was naked and you clothed Me; I was sick and you visited Me; I was in prison and you came to Me" (Matthew 25:35, 36). Christ's followers will demonstrate their love for Jesus not simply by attending church or giving offerings but by sharing the love of Jesus in practical, tangible ways—not in an effort to win God's approval but as the result of a connection with Him that sees His love flowing into and then out of the lives of His followers.

James expressed a similar thought. Discussing genuine faith, he wrote, "If a brother or sister is naked and destitute of daily food, and one of you says to them, 'Depart in peace, be warmed and filled,' but you do not give them the things which are needed for the body, what does it profit?" (James 2:15, 16).

How might it impact the church if Christians truly took these passages to heart? And how might it impact the unbelieving world to see a demonstration of genuine Christian love and compassion? Today, Jesus might give you the opportunity to serve Him by being a blessing to someone else. When that opportunity comes, take it.

Swimming Against the Current?

"And when He has come, He will convict the world of sin,
and of righteousness, and of judgment."

—John 16:8

One of the great landmarks of my childhood was the river that flowed just a few hundred feet from the home in which I grew up. We could easily be on the banks of that major river less than thirty seconds after walking out our back door. It was in that river that I learned what it feels like to swim against the current. Swimming upstream can be tough going and takes real effort, while floating downstream with the current takes no effort whatsoever. Even dead animals floated downstream. But you had to be alive and kicking to make any progress in the other direction.

The truth is that people who turn away from God are actually swimming against the current. In one sense, they are going with the flow and being carried downstream by sin, neglect, or carelessness. While it might seem that drifting with the current that surrounds you is easygoing, anyone who swims with the current of the world is swimming *against* the current of the Holy Spirit. Speaking of the way He dealt with His own people, God said in Hosea 11:4, "I drew them with gentle cords, with bands of love." Jesus said the Holy Spirit convicts the world. Jeremiah 31:3 says, "The Lord has appeared of old to me, saying: 'Yes, I have loved you with an everlasting love; therefore with lovingkindness I have drawn you.' "

God's Spirit convicts and draws people to Himself. The lack of peace many people experience comes as a direct result of constantly resisting God's draw. In order to be lost, a person has to resist the love of God, the pleading of the Holy Spirit, and the saving grace of Jesus.

Don't resist His drawing today. A heart that is surrendered to Jesus soon realizes it is hard work resisting the invitation of heaven. You don't have to swim against the current of the Holy Spirit. Jesus wants to carry you along with Him and hold you close to His heart.

Which Way?

There is a way that seems right to a man,
but its end is the way of death.

—Proverbs 16:25

After arriving at England's Gatwick airport, I traveled by train to Victoria Station in London. I was in my early twenties and had never been to Europe, and this was by far the biggest train station I had ever seen in my life. Eighty million passengers depart and arrive at Victoria Station every year, and millions more transfer there.

But getting to Victoria Station was the easy part. Buying a ticket on the underground (subway) to where I was going next was the real challenge. The ticket machine was like nothing I had ever seen. After finally working out how to purchase a ticket, I then had to figure out how to get to my final destination. What I did not do was jump on the first train I saw. I looked at the map and followed it carefully. Without the map, I would have never made it to where I was going.

The Bible says that what may seem right can end up being anything but. You can do what seems right to you, or you can do the wise thing and do what is right in the eyes of God. The Bible is the map given to us by God to help us navigate this troubled world and make it to our heavenly home. Baseball personality Yogi Berra once said, "When you come to a fork in the road, take it."* There are times you simply have to make a choice. The goal, of course, is to make wise decisions. Thankfully, But God provides reliable directions and safe guidance for our lives, enabling us to arrive at the right location.

If you look to God and depend on His Word, you will know soon enough just what to do in a given situation. Knowing that God loves you will give you the confidence to trust His leading. Moses prayed, and God guided Israel through the wilderness. Joshua prayed, and God gave him victory over his enemies. Solomon prayed, and God answered his prayer for wisdom. It was when Solomon followed his own inclinations that his experience fell apart.

A way is not the right way unless it is God's way.

---

* Nate Scott, "The 50 Greatest Yogi Berra Quotes," For the Win, March 28, 2019, https://ftw.usatoday .com/2019/03/the-50-greatest-yogi-berra-quotes.

The Best Policy

*"And everyone who has left houses or brothers or sisters or father
or mother or wife or children or lands, for My name's sake,
shall receive a hundredfold, and inherit eternal life."*
—Matthew 19:29

A homeless man found a backpack containing more than $40,000 in cash and traveler's checks in a mall in Dorchester, just south of Boston, Massachusetts. Believing honesty is the best policy, he contacted the police and turned in the bag. The man who lost the money got his bag back, along with everything inside. Boston Police honored Glen James, the man who returned the money, for what he had done. A Virginia man, impressed by Mr. James's honesty, started an online fundraiser for him and raised over $100,000 in just three days.* Mr. James, a man with nothing, found and then returned riches, before receiving more than he could have ever imagined.

That's how the Bible's good news works. When you give your life to God, you end up with far more than you had before. Peter, never afraid to give voice to what was on his mind, asked Jesus the pointed question, "We have left all and followed You. Therefore what shall we have?" (Matthew 19:29). Jesus told him that everyone who gives up things in this life for His sake "shall receive a hundredfold, and inherit eternal life" (verse 29). No one should ever be concerned that choosing Jesus will be to their detriment. Similarly, a person should never think that being honest will cause harm. Jesus was clear. "Those who honor Me I will honor" (1 Samuel 2:30). "Humble yourselves in the sight of the Lord, and He will lift you up" (James 4:10).

Finding more than $40,000 would present a temptation for most people, especially someone who has almost nothing. When the easy thing to do would have been to keep the cash and take care of needs, it was the honest decision that brought real rewards. A decision for Jesus does the same, and whether or not you're better off in this world isn't what is most important. The greatest gift of all is eternal life, and Jesus is returning soon to bring that precious gift to His people.

---

* Christina Ng, "Donations for Honest Homeless Man Tops $100,000," *ABC News*, September 19, 2013, https://abcnews.go.com/US/donations-honest-homeless-man-tops-100k/story?id=20307038.

Guardian Angels

"Take heed that you do not despise one of these little ones, for I say to you that in heaven their angels always see the face of My Father who is in heaven."
—Matthew 18:10

Although I grew up in a churchgoing family, there came a time that I began to question some of what I had been raised to believe. I never questioned the existence of God, but certain doctrinal teachings I had been raised with caused me to wonder whether what I had been taught was true. I found that according to the Bible, much of it was not. My father had always told me I had a guardian angel, and I wondered whether that was actually true. I was relieved to discover that the Bible revealed Dad was absolutely right. I had angels watching over me!

What a comfort it was to me as a child to know that an angel had been assigned by God to watch over me. That knowledge is still a comfort. Angels that "excel in strength" (Psalm 103:20), "ministering spirits sent forth to minister for those who will inherit salvation" (Hebrews 1:14), provide protection and deliverance, and bring blessing from heaven.

The Bible often speaks of angels. God encourages us to know that heaven is nearer to us than we might know. Some of the great men and women of the Bible interacted with angels. Daniel was visited by Gabriel (Daniel 8:16, 17; 9:21), as were Zacharias (Luke 1:19) and Mary, the mother of Jesus (verses 26, 27). Angels commissioned Peter to preach the gospel to the Gentiles (Acts 10:3–6), sent Philip to a desert place to meet with an Ethiopian government official (Acts 8:26, 27), and released Peter from prison (Acts 12:7–9). The ministry of angels still brings encouragement, hope, and help to God's people today.

Children and grandchildren, as well as parents and grandparents, can be reassured by the knowledge that angels are watching over every follower of Jesus at this very moment. Heaven's helpers are always near.

In Good Company

For You have made him a little lower than the angels,
and You have crowned him with glory and honor.

—Psalm 8:5

S ome of the most encouraging stories you can read are the magnificent, miraculous stories of how angels intervene at certain times to provide protection or deliverance. A group of young people in Central America were distributing Bibles when a child in one home called to his parents and said, "Who is that tall man standing behind those people?" When the child kept repeating the question, the young people realized angels were with them in the ministry. They were encouraged and thankful for God's blessing.

In the magnificent children's book *Into the Blizzard*, written by Olivine Nadeau Bohner, intrepid colporteur Jack Zachary was traversing a hillside one dark night when a hand grabbed him from behind and prevented him from walking any further. He was incredulous to discover he had been about to walk off the edge of a cliff when one of God's special helpers prevented him from coming to harm.*

It is not uncommon to hear accounts of people who have been helped by beings who have then disappeared from view or whose footprints in the snow suddenly, inexplicably stopped. Just as angels interacted with human beings in Bible times, they do so today in ways that can surprise or even amaze us. Even though angels ordinarily cannot be seen, we have the assurance that they are among us at all times.

While it won't be until we get to heaven that we will fully understand the ministry of heaven's angels, we can know today that these powerful beings travel from heaven to earth to do the bidding of God. Most common are the instances where people were unaware at the time that God's angels had intervened to provide help. Many apparent "coincidences" or episodes of "good luck" have, in fact, been times of blessing provided by angels of heaven.

The Bible says that the human family was made "a little lower than the angels" (Psalm 8:5). Angels were made by God as an order higher than humanity. Every child of God can know that angels still minister and are willing to serve God by serving His children.

---

* Olivine Nadeau Bohner, *Into the Blizzard* (Nampa, ID: Pacific Press®, 2012).

In Good Hands!

Bless the LORD, you His angels, who excel in strength,
who do His word, heeding the voice of His word.
—Psalm 103:20

I have never knowingly seen an angel. Some people have seen glowing figures or tall beings they could only explain as being angels of heaven. I have not. But on one occasion, I thought I had met with and spoken to an angel.

My journey to Washington, DC, to catch an international flight had already been interrupted by bad weather. When our vehicle broke down at a gas station in Ohio, it was clear I was not going to make it to the airport on time.

But then I saw him, a tall, tanned, bronze-bearded good Samaritan who offered to check our vehicle. He looked just like I imagined an angel in human form would be. At that moment, I knew that God had sent an angel so the story could have a happy and miraculous ending! I fully expected this angel would touch the car, and the engine would roar back to life. Surely, he would then disappear while we all looked at each other in amazement.

But the car didn't start, and the good Samaritan admitted he didn't know much about cars. When I saw our "angel" smoking a cigarette behind the gas station, I realized I hadn't seen an angel after all.

Some people have seen angels in this day and age, while many others have likely done so without realizing it. "Do not forget to entertain strangers, for by so doing some have unwittingly entertained angels" (Hebrews 13:2).

These "ministering spirits" (Hebrews 1:14) are powerful, and God lifts our spirits by assuring us angels are on our side in the great battle between good and evil. Undoubtedly, just as angels ministered to God's people in Old Testament times, the angels of heaven are busy today on missions of mercy and help. God doesn't leave us in this world to fend for ourselves. The Holy Spirit is granted us for spiritual strength and to bring us the presence of Jesus, and angels who excel in strength are sent to help us. We are in good hands!

Help at Hand

You have come to Mount Zion and to the city of the living God,
the heavenly Jerusalem, to an innumerable company of angels.
—Hebrews 12:22

These certainly aren't the "good old days." While it's true the "good old days" were far from perfect, there's no question that society, in general, is not trending in a heavenly direction. As time continues to advance toward the return of Jesus, we are reminded that "the devil has come down to you, having great wrath, because he knows that he has a short time" (Revelation 12:12). Many church members who observe the state of the world are discouraged because it seems to them as though the devil has things all his own way. But God has other ideas.

When Satan fell from his position in the presence of God, one-third of all the angels in heaven rebelled against the government of heaven. "His tail drew a third of the stars of heaven and threw them to the earth" (Revelation 12:4). While we cannot know how many angels were in heaven at the time of Satan's fall, it was surely a very large number. This explains why we see so much evil in the world. Angels given over to wickedness, assisted by billions of people who are governed by sin, are capable of instigating a vast amount of evil.

But the good news is that as many troublesome demons as there might be, there are far more holy angels. The prophet Daniel wrote of thousands of thousands and ten thousand times ten thousand angels (Daniel 7:10). And Hebrews 12:22 describes them as "an innumerable company of angels!" An enormous number of angels watch over us.

We don't ever have to worry that God is going to find Himself short-staffed. That "innumerable company of angels" assures you that heaven has plenty of help available. While we cannot readily see what takes place outside our view, the final result of the great controversy between Christ and Satan was settled long ago. With Jesus as the commander of the angel hosts, victory for God's side is assured. Those who claim the righteousness of Christ and yield to His leading are on the winning side!

Standing Watch

*The angel of the LORD encamps all around
those who fear Him, and delivers them.*

—Psalm 34:7

Psalm 34:7 exudes encouragement and assurance. It is a promise. The preceding verse gives context to David's statement. "This poor man cried out, and the LORD heard him, and saved him out of all his troubles" (verse 6). David reminds us that God's mighty angels provide protection and deliverance. God has commissioned a guardian angel to watch over every one of His children, and that angel frequently saves us out of distress.

After being rescued from the lions' den, Daniel was able to say, "My God sent His angel and shut the lions' mouths, so that they have not hurt me" (Daniel 6:22). An angel appeared in a dream to Joseph, the father of Jesus, and warned him to take Jesus and Mary to Egypt, where they would be safe from Herod, the wicked king who wanted Jesus dead (Matthew 2:13). Jesus Himself was comforted by an angel during His time of great anguish in the Garden of Gethsemane (Luke 22:43), and the appearance of a single angel caused those guarding Jesus' tomb to become "like dead men" (Matthew 28:2–4).

The help of mighty angels has been promised to every child of God. So it would be natural for someone to ask, "Where was that protection when I crashed my car?" "Where were the angels when my family member died?" "Why didn't an angel stop that drunk driver?" There are no pithy answers to questions like that. Tragedy happens. Difficulties arise. Even followers of God get sick or hurt in accidents.

Rather than blaming God for inactive angels when trouble strikes, it would be more appropriate to thank God for the protection from injury and loss angels provide on a daily basis. Every day we safely navigate is another day in which angels provide protection and blessing. There is a spiritual battle raging. Satan and the evil angels would destroy all of God's children if they were not kept from doing so by "the angel of the Lord."

You can be encouraged today. Angels of heaven are watching over you.

May 9

The Extra Mile

*"Sir, let it alone this year also, until I dig around it and fertilize it.
And if it bears fruit, well. But if not, after that you can cut it down."*
—Luke 13:8, 9

Weighing 530 pounds, Mac realized he had to lose weight. He had tried to shed pounds some years before, but a visit to a gym resulted in two treadmills belching smoke under his considerable weight. He realized it wouldn't be easy to lose the 300 pounds he wanted to lose and that doing so would take a lot of time. Setting small, attainable goals enabled Mac to chip away at his task a pound at a time. He now runs half marathons and competes in bicycle races, which a few years ago would have been impossible.

One key to Mac's weight-loss success was that he was patient. Without patience, Mac would have given up on losing weight long before seeing any progress at all. Some things—such as losing 300 pounds—simply take time.

It is important to remember that God is patient. He bears with His children as they sometimes stumble their way toward heaven. And God is also patient with the lost. Jesus taught a parable in which a vineyard owner intended to cut down a fruitless fig tree. But a worker spoke up and asked if he could "dig around it and fertilize it" and give it one more chance.

God goes the extra mile to ready us for eternity. Instead of casting aside those who don't look like they will bear fruit for His glory, God is gracious enough to work with sinners and keep drawing them to Himself.

A gardener who noticed bugs had eaten almost an entire young tomato plant, leaving only a stalk, patiently and carefully nursed it back to health. It became the most fruitful plant in the garden.

While we don't want to abuse God's patience, it is good to know that He is with His children for the long haul. He stays with us and works with us, tenderly and patiently growing us in preparation for eternity.

Division

"Do you suppose that I came to give peace on earth?
I tell you, not at all, but rather division."

—Luke 12:51

In the Bible, Jesus is referred to in a variety of ways. He is both "the Lion of the tribe of Judah" (Revelation 5:5) and "the Lamb slain from the foundation of the world" (Revelation 13:8). Jesus is our "Advocate with the Father" (1 John 2:1), and " 'Immanuel,' which is translated, 'God with us' " (Matthew 1:23). Jesus is "gentle and lowly in heart" (Matthew 11:29), yet He cleansed the temple in Jerusalem, driving out moneychangers while wielding a "whip of cords," overturning tables, and scattering the moneychangers' ill-gotten gains (John 2:15).

And while the Bible calls Jesus the "Prince of Peace" (Isaiah 9:6), He said of Himself, "Do you suppose that I came to give peace on earth? I tell you, not at all, but rather division" (Luke 12:51). Jesus was explaining that when a person accepts the principles of heaven, that person lives from then on in opposition to the principles of the world. The gospel causes separation between a believer who walks in the Spirit and unbelievers who walk in the flesh. Just as "friendship with the world is enmity with God" (James 4:4), friendship with God is enmity with the world.

Believers make a serious mistake when they attempt to show the world just how much like the world Christians can be. While it is important not to make unbelievers feel uncomfortable in their presence, Christians should not become unlike Christ in order to win others. It is genuine love that wins unbelievers to faith in Christ, not genuine compromise. A person who yields his or her life to God may experience division on some level. It is possible a new believer's family members might experience a difficult adjustment period. Friends might misunderstand, and colleagues might find it hard to relate. Christians should not strive to be oddballs, but they should determine to be Christian.

The differentness about a new Christian's life may be a light that shines into the darkness of the lives of others. If you experience division because of your faith in Jesus, remember you are one with Him. That oneness with Jesus will draw others to know and love Him.

Excess?

Let your conduct be without covetousness;
be content with such things as you have.

—Hebrews 13:5

A company known for excess included some fascinating items in a recent catalog. Dinner for ten could be purchased for $250,000. (The four chefs who would prepare the food had stellar reputations.) His and hers watches could be had for a little under $1.1 million, and a cute chicken house with ten hens was selling for $100,000. (The catalog did not state whether or not the chickens laid golden eggs.)

While God never speaks against money, and while Paul identified "the love of money"—and not money itself—as a "root of all kinds of evil" (1 Timothy 6:10), it is clear that money brings with it a raft of temptations. Jesus said to "beware of covetousness, for one's life does not consist in the abundance of the things he possesses" (Luke 12:15). Of course, greed can be demonstrated on a much less expensive scale. And it is important to recognize that having expensive possessions is in no way evidence of greed or excess. But whatever and however a person spends, anyone—rich or poor—can be preoccupied with getting "stuff." It will eventually be discovered that such a preoccupation will ultimately cause pain.

To help us see that a self-centered, me-first, have-now approach to life has a deleterious effect on a person's spiritual health, God included a prohibition on coveting in the Ten Commandments. Society today urges consumption. Easy credit means people can have almost anything they cannot afford. Modern economies are built upon that premise. Paul reminded us that "godliness with contentment is great gain" (1 Timothy 6:6). The Bible says nothing against having goods. But when your goods become your gods, you are standing on shaky spiritual ground.

However, there is one form of covetousness the Bible recommends. Paul urged the believers in Corinth to "covet earnestly the best gifts" (1 Corinthians 12:31, KJV). You can never have too much of Jesus or too great a supply of the gifts of the Holy Spirit. If we focus on possessing the best things, we will grow *toward* the kingdom of heaven rather than away from it.

On His Tracks

And as He said these things to them, the scribes and the Pharisees
began to assail Him vehemently, and to cross-examine Him about
many things, lying in wait for Him, and seeking to catch Him in
something He might say, that they might accuse Him.

—Luke 11:53, 54

Little is written in the Bible about Jesus' early life. Although He was raised in a God-fearing home, He grew up in a rough town, surrounded by temptation. The reputation of Jesus' hometown was bad enough to cause Nathanael to ask, "Can anything good come out of Nazareth?" (John 1:46).

Jesus' biggest challenges began when He entered full-time ministry. Having not been educated in the rabbinical schools, Jesus' purity and wisdom were a constant rebuke to the religious establishment. They were so outraged that they "persecuted Jesus, and sought to kill Him" (John 5:16). Another time, a whole congregation "rose up and thrust Him out of the city; and they led Him to the brow of the hill on which their city was built, that they might throw Him down over the cliff" (Luke 4:29). Civil leaders were also offended by Jesus, who received a warning to "get out and depart from here, for Herod wants to kill you" (Luke 13:31). Jesus' life was in constant jeopardy.

But even when Jesus appeared safe from threats of physical violence, He was still the target of wicked schemes and plans. The leaders were continually "lying in wait for Him, and seeking to catch Him in something He might say, that they might accuse Him" (Luke 11:54). We can only imagine how mentally, physically, and emotionally draining that sort of existence must have been.

How would you react if you had people tracking your every move and listening to your every word to find a reason to condemn you? Jesus was constantly opposed. Yet He was also constantly triumphant, refusing to fall into sin even by a thought. Jesus endured a relentless barrage of opposition, and He did so out of love for you. Experiencing the loathing of virtually an entire society, He faced his persecutors daily because He knew that in doing so, you could have everlasting life. The constant opposition Jesus faced could not distract Him from His mission.

Hypocrites

*"Woe to you, scribes and Pharisees, hypocrites! For you cleanse the outside
of the cup and dish, but inside they are full of extortion and self-indulgence."*
—Matthew 23:25

There are few people who want to be seen in public looking unkempt or shabby.
It is normal for people to tend to their appearance before they are seen by others.
Hair is brushed, and clothes are straightened or ironed. While some people take this
to an extreme, there are few people who don't care about their appearance. But there
is a danger a person could look good on the outside without being similarly well-kept
on the inside.

Jesus condemned the hypocrisy of the Pharisees. He told them, "Woe to you, scribes
and Pharisees, hypocrites! For you are like whitewashed tombs which indeed appear
beautiful outwardly, but inside are full of dead men's bones and all uncleanness. Even
so you also outwardly appear righteous to men, but inside you are full of hypocrisy
and lawlessness" (Matthew 23:27, 28).

Putting on a show does not fool many people. The Pharisees Jesus addressed appeared
religious and holy to those looking on but were in reality full of corruption. The beauty
of Christianity is that through Jesus, you don't need to make the same mistake. God
assures us in 1 John 1:9 that "if we confess our sins, He is faithful and just to forgive
us our sins and to cleanse us from all unrighteousness." The sanctuary services of the
Old Testament illustrated that God's intention was to restore human beings to purity
and righteousness. "For on that day the priest shall make atonement for you, to cleanse
you, that you may be clean from all your sins before the LORD" (Leviticus 16:30). When
Christ abides in a human heart, He brings His holiness and righteousness. And that
righteousness is increasingly seen in the life of a disciple of Jesus.

The word *hypocrite* comes from a Greek word that means "an actor." The power of
the gospel can enable any sinner to move past "acting" the part of a Christian. The
grace of God can transform you into the genuine article.

Filled With What?

We all once conducted ourselves in the lusts of our flesh,
fulfilling the desires of the flesh and of the mind, and were
by nature children of wrath, just as the others.
—Ephesians 2:3

The duty of a believer in Jesus isn't simply to adhere to the right doctrinal beliefs. As important as biblical orthodoxy is, God wants us to move past merely professing certain beliefs to possessing a certain Savior.

It is vital for a Christian to allow God to do a complete work in his or her life. God is honored and glorified when we allow Him to be what He wants to be in our lives. Jesus came to the earth to lift up the fallen and to mend the broken. For His followers to stay stuck in an old life of sin is to call into question the power of the gospel. Writing to the Ephesians, Paul admitted that "we all once conducted ourselves in the lusts of our flesh, fulfilling the desires of the flesh and of the mind, and were by nature children of wrath, just as the others" (Ephesians 2:3). But then he went on to speak of God's great mercy, which "when we were dead in trespasses, made us alive together with Christ (by grace you have been saved), and raised us up together, and made us sit together in the heavenly places in Christ Jesus" (verses 5, 6).

But what of the believer who refuses to "press toward the goal for the prize of the upward call of God in Christ Jesus"? (Philippians 3:14). "When an unclean spirit goes out of a man, he goes through dry places, seeking rest; and finding none, he says, 'I will return to my house from which I came.' And when he comes, he finds it swept and put in order. Then he goes and takes with him seven other spirits more wicked than himself, and they enter and dwell there; and the last state of that man is worse than the first" (Luke 11:24–26).

Faith in Jesus isn't simply denying what is wrong. It is being filled up with the One who is right. God's purpose is to fill the believer's life with His presence and remake that believer by His transforming grace.

From the Inside Out

*"The kingdom of heaven is like leaven, which a woman took
and hid in three measures of meal till it was all leavened."*

—Matthew 13:33

B read makers know there is a key ingredient necessary for bread to come out just right. When the flour and salt and various other ingredients have been mixed together, the baker has a lump of dough. That dough certainly isn't going to become what you would ordinarily use to make a sandwich. A vital ingredient is needed. Add yeast to the dough, and something almost magical happens.

Jesus used this metaphor to explain how we may be ready for eternal life. He described the work of God in a person's life as being like the yeast that works in dough. A change happens within the dough because of the power of the change agent, the yeast. The dough cannot raise itself, and even when the yeast is added, the dough does nothing other than experience the change that the yeast brings. The dough is changed by the yeast working in the dough.

Jesus is telling us that when the Holy Spirit enters a life, He will completely change that life from the inside out. When the Holy Spirit comes into a person's experience, that person isn't asked to *do* anything to contribute to God's work of salvation. Both justification and sanctification come through faith by leaning entirely upon Jesus and expecting him to do His work in your life. What the believer is required to *do* (for want of a better term) is to surrender, to yield, to submit to the working of the grace of God. This is not salvation by works. Rather, it is a vital key to successful Christian living.

God has never asked His followers to do the impossible. Instead, He has promised to do the impossible in us! He will bring a complete change to every willing heart. A life that makes room for the working of the Holy Spirit is a life that will bring glory to God.

An Example Worth Following

And He went through the cities and villages,
teaching, and journeying toward Jerusalem.

—Luke 13:22

What was life like for Jesus on a day-to-day basis? Jesus was constantly on the move, meeting people wherever He could with the aim of sharing eternal life. Wherever He went, He met with constant opposition. Jesus could have been living in heaven, surrounded by beauty and glory and by beings who appreciated and served Him. He could have remained with His Father and enjoyed the respect and worship of the angelic host. But instead, He dedicated His life to serving others—in obscurity. He toiled in desert places, enduring extreme heat and dirty, harsh conditions. He labored for souls in markets, in cities, and in villages that dotted the countryside.

Jesus would not stay in heaven if coming to earth meant He could save us. He was a missionary, and His life was driven by a Spirit-inspired missionary zeal to bring salvation to as many as possible. Now that Jesus has returned to heaven, He looks to His church to manifest that same zeal and commitment to the work of soul winning. Jesus gave up all else and committed His life to sharing heaven, and He didn't regret that decision. He suffered on the cross and despised its shame "for the joy that was set before Him" (Hebrews 12:2)—the joy of seeing His people redeemed for all eternity.

Jesus calls us to enter into His work of reaching the lost. "Go therefore and make disciples of all the nations" is the commission He gave to His church (Matthew 28:19). The final gospel message to go the world is to be proclaimed to "those who dwell on the earth—to every nation, tribe, tongue, and people" (Revelation 14:6). On every street and in every city, there are people waiting to learn of Jesus and His saving grace and truth. Every follower of Jesus is invited—and will be empowered—to share God's transforming Word in preparation for the second coming of Christ. Most will not be called to share Jesus in the desert wilderness. But all are called to share Jesus.

Truth and Error

This girl followed Paul and us, and cried out, saying, "These men are the
servants of the Most High God, who proclaim to us the way of salvation."
—Acts 16:17

Paul and Silas had intended to preach God's Word. The Bible says, "They were forbidden by the Holy Spirit to preach the word in Asia" (Acts 16:6). Instead, Paul had a vision in which he saw a man from Macedonia standing before him pleading with Paul to "come over to Macedonia and help us" (verse 9). It is important to be open to God's leading when doing His work. There might be times our plans and God's plans don't match. It is wise, then, to be flexible enough to go in an alternate direction.

The missionary pair instead found themselves in Philippi, and as they were preaching the Word of God, a young woman began following them and calling out loudly, saying, "These men are the servants of the Most High God, who proclaim to us the way of salvation" (verse 17). What is curious is that although the young woman was possessed by demons, she was absolutely correct in what she was saying. Satan did not try to hinder their work by telling lies about Paul and Silas. In this case, he tried to hamper their work by telling *the truth*.

The devil will often tell you the truth. He may even tell you a lot of truth. But what sets Satan apart is that he will also lie to you. And the best lies are those that are most plausible. The book of Revelation tells us that Satan's lies are ultimately so effective that he succeeds in deceiving virtually the whole world (Revelation 13:8).

The unfortunate young woman was right in what she said, as many of Satan's agents so often are. But what we want is the whole of the sanctifying, saving truth, not just a part of it. Search the Bible to make sure that all you believe is in harmony with God's Word. If something does not line up with Scripture, let it go no matter how precious it seems to you. Allow God's Holy Spirit to grow your understanding and lead you deeper into God's will. Before Jesus returns, a lot of mostly right people are going to discover—too late—that they are completely wrong.

Dog-Eat-Dog?

Let no one seek his own,
but each one the other's well-being.
—1 Corinthians 10:24

It's a dog-eat-dog world, or so the saying goes. But that sentiment is not supported in the Bible. Instead, the Bible encourages us to think of others, to serve others, and to take an interest in helping people. Paul told the Corinthian believers to seek the well-being of others. And to the Romans, he wrote, "Be kindly affectioned one to another with brotherly love; in honour preferring one another" (Romans 12:10, KJV).

Christ's way is to put others first. The Savior of the world washed the dusty, travel-worn feet of His disciples, invested time in lifting up the fallen, and mingled with society's less-respected classes in order to shine the light of God's love into their hearts. In Romans 15:1, 2, Paul said, "We then who are strong ought to bear with the scruples of the weak, and not to please ourselves. Let each of us please his neighbor for his good, leading to edification." Christ's entire mission to this world was one of self-abnegation. The Savior left the glory of heaven in order "to be made like His brethren" (Hebrews 2:17), the ultimate example of putting others first at one's own expense. "The Son of Man did not come to be served, but to serve, and to give His life a ransom for many" (Matthew 20:28).

While the everlasting gospel will ultimately be preached to the world, the most powerful sermon a nonbeliever could ever hear is one that is demonstrated by kind words and thoughtful actions. Selflessness is an attribute that preaches loudly and clearly to those who profess no faith in God. Nothing speaks to a heart like showing another person they are actually valued and cared for. Many people fall away from faith in Christ after being discouraged by uncaring Christians or uninterested churches. Followers of God have not been called to live without regard to others. Instead, love for God will result in consideration for others and in putting others ahead of yourself. Every day God gives us opportunities to serve, and when those opportunities are taken, God is glorified, and Jesus is revealed.

For the Profit of All

*The manifestation of the Spirit is given
to each one for the profit of all.*

—1 Corinthians 12:7

I once was blessed to work very near a world-class art gallery. During my lunch break, I had only a short distance to walk to see paintings by some of the world's truly great painters. A magnificent exhibition of impressionist art meant I could enjoy the beauty of priceless works of art by Monet, Cézanne, van Gogh, and others.

Imagine if these supremely talented artists had not shared their talent with the world. Or if Shakespeare had not allowed others to see his writings. Einstein might have pursued another career and only dabbled with science.

What if people did not share their *spiritual* gifts? In 1 Corinthians 12:8–10, Paul lists a number of spiritual gifts when he speaks of wisdom, knowledge, faith, healings, miracle-working, prophecy, discerning of spirits, tongues, and interpreting tongues. He writes that "the manifestation of the Spirit is given to each one for the profit of all" (verse 7). Every believer has been granted spiritual gifts, and they are imparted so that the body may be blessed and built up.

Those with the gift of teaching should teach. Those with the gift of administration are urged by God to use that gift for His glory. Someone's God-given capacity for gaining wisdom isn't granted so that the believer can be proud of his or her wisdom. Someone with the gift of faith has been given that gift to use, not to neglect. It is not humility but disobedience that leads a person not to allow God to use his or her spiritual gift for the benefit of others.

It is important for disciples of Jesus to know that spiritual gifts aren't given by God for the recipient to hide under a bushel. Spiritual gifts are to be used to God's glory for the benefit of others. God doesn't grant spiritual gifts just for the sake of granting spiritual gifts. They are to be utilized in growing the kingdom of heaven and honoring the God of the universe. The Spirit is given so all can be blessed.

A Losing Battle

*The carnal mind is enmity against God; for it is not
subject to the law of God, nor indeed can be.*

—Romans 8:7

Air pollution has become a deadly problem in many parts of the world. In 2019, 1.6 million people in India died owing to air pollution.* One infant died every five minutes owing to dirty air.† Anyone who has landed at Los Angeles International Airport is familiar with the thick layer of brown smog that blankets the city, even though air quality has improved in Los Angeles in recent years.

Anyone wanting to fix the problem of air pollution knows better than to try to clean up the air one neighborhood at a time. In order to improve air quality, the problem must be tackled at its source (factories or automobiles, for example).

When it comes to one's spiritual life, it is vital for every believer to know that spiritual problems must be confronted at their source. Paul insists that the source of the sin problem is in the mind. An unregenerate, earthly, selfish mind is never going to be in harmony with God. The carnal mind is simply opposed to God, and it can't be any other way. A believer might try to mend himself or herself by trying to master one spiritual weakness at a time, but such an approach is doomed to fail. Every sinner needs a new mind. Advertisements can be seen offering courses to teach "self-mastery," which simply cannot be attained without the indwelling power of Christ.

The only way to master self is by surrendering self to Christ and allowing Him to live His life in you. If you are trying to improve yourself by yourself, you are fighting a losing battle. The sinner's mind is simply not subject to the way of the living God. A new mind is a gift given by God at conversion, that moment when self is renounced and Jesus is accepted as Lord. To receive a new mind is to experience a miracle of divine grace, a miracle God is willing to perform for everyone who calls on His name.

---

* "Pollution Deaths in India Rose to 1.67 million in 2019—Lancet," Reuters, December 22, 2020, https://www.reuters.com/article/us-india-pollution/pollution-deaths-in-india-rose-to-1-67-million-in-2019-lancet-idUSKBN28W158.

† Bhasker Tripathi, "Air Pollution Killed a Newborn Every 5 Minutes in 2019," Bloomberg, October 21, 2020, https://www.bloombergquint.com/politics/air-pollution-killed-a-newborn-every-5-minutes-in-2019.

Promises Kept

And be found in Him, not having my own righteousness,
which is from the law, but that which is through faith
in Christ, the righteousness which is from God by faith.
—Philippians 3:9

In 1988, presidential candidate George H. W. Bush addressed his party's national convention and said, "Read my lips, no new taxes." That was a promise, and he meant it. But promises can be hard to keep, and there are times that even the best intentions have to yield to grim reality. Later, when facing a budget deficit, the Bush administration allowed certain taxes to be raised. President Bush wasn't reelected, the broken promise being a key factor in his defeat.*

Many people make promises to God only to find that they cannot keep them. "I'll do better." "I won't do that again." "That's the last time I will ever commit that sin." While they are undoubtedly well-intentioned, such promises are doomed to fail. In Philippians 3:9, Paul got to the heart of how a person can live a successful Christian life.

Righteousness is not the result of a sinner's earnest efforts to try to do better. Paul knew that the righteousness he needed was the righteousness of Christ, the only righteousness that could open to him the gates of heaven. Paul made clear that the only way he could obtain Jesus' own righteousness was through faith, not by trying harder or by doing his best. That isn't to say there is no effort involved in being a Christian. But the greatest effort we can make in our Christian experience is the effort to surrender to God and to allow Him to make our heart His own. Temptations must be resisted, and self must be denied, but that can happen only through the indwelling presence of Jesus. Those who surrender their lives to God receive the righteousness of Christ, the only kind of righteousness that does a believer any eternal good.

A promise made to God is a promise that is not worth making. God doesn't want you to make promises to Him. He wants you to believe the promises He makes to you!

---

* Daniel J. Mitchell, "Mr. President, Keep Your Promise: No New Taxes," *The Heritage Foundation Backgrounder*, No. 769, May 18, 1990, http://s3.amazonaws.com/thf_media/1990/pdf/bg769.pdf.

Focus

Set your mind on things above,
not on things on the earth.

—Colossians 3:2

There's a profoundly simple reason more people don't experience the peace of heaven or possess a solid faith experience. They simply don't set their mind to it. Every believer has the choice as to what will be the object of his or her focus—things above or things on earth.

Too often, the mind is not where it ought to be. An hour spent mindlessly watching YouTube videos or aimlessly surfing Facebook is an hour not spent focusing on spiritual growth. No doubt downtime is necessary for any person, but too many hours spent with the earthly develops a preference for the earthly over the heavenly. A physician can recall arcane medical facts, or a lawyer can quote obscure case law because these subjects have been the focus of years of study. What a person focuses on is what they come to know and love. Paul wrote in 2 Corinthians 3:18 that by beholding, a person becomes changed into the likeness of what they focus on.

David wrote in Psalm 119:97, "Oh, how I love Your law! It is my meditation all the day." Two verses later, he said, "I have more understanding than all my teachers, for Your testimonies are my meditation." David loved God and God's Word because he chose to make it the foundation of his life. Meditating on the Bible, the character of Jesus, and the love of God will have a transforming effect. Filling the mind with cheap things will also have a transforming effect but in the opposite direction. The person who waits until he or she loves exercise before beginning to exercise will likely never exercise. But many are the people who have learned to love exercise after they made the decision to get active.

Instead of being dictated to by your environment, decide today that with God's help, you will focus on heavenly things. When we focus more on Jesus, we become more like Jesus.

The Strongest of All Warriors

*Here is the patience of the saints; here are those who keep
the commandments of God and the faith of Jesus.*
—Revelation 14:12

In his acclaimed novel *War and Peace*, Leo Tolstoy wrote that "the strongest of all warriors are these two—time and patience."* Describing His last-day people, Jesus says, "This calls for patient endurance" (Revelation 14:12, NIV)—time and patience—on the part of the saints.

Sometimes the road of faith seems long and the journey arduous. It isn't uncommon to find people who are ready to give up on faith in God. But people need to remember that God won't quit on them. The enemy of souls would love to see you throw in the towel and give up on eternity. But if you will hang on to Jesus today and continue to have faith in Him in spite of what you might be facing, God will get His work done in your life.

Ellen White once wrote that "sanctification is not the work of a moment, an hour, a day, but of a lifetime."† This helps us understand that becoming the finished Christian product is not something that happens overnight. It takes many years for an acorn to develop into a mighty oak tree. The seed of the majestic redwood is tiny, yet over time it produces one of the great wonders of creation. Trees grow slowly. But they grow surely.

People who encounter hardship in life and hold on to their faith in God invariably find that God is faithful and true. Faith in God doesn't always remove the pain of loss or grief, but it does provide comfort and a context in which to better understand the challenges of life. When it seems as though the sun of hope might never break through the dark clouds of despair, faith clings to God even when He cannot be seen. David wrote with certainty in Psalm 27:14,

> Wait on the LORD;
> Be of good courage,
> And He shall strengthen your heart;
> Wait, I say, on the LORD!

---

* Leo Tolstoy, *War and Peace* (1869), translated by Constance Garnett, (Mineola, NY: Dover Publications, 2017), 703.
† Ellen G. White, *The Acts of the Apostles* (Mountain View, CA: Pacific Press®, 1911), 560.

Legacy

*"Those who are wise shall shine
Like the brightness of the firmament,
And those who turn many to righteousness
Like the stars forever and ever."*

—Daniel 12:3

Over the years, I've visited the graves of many notable people. John Wesley and John Bunyan are buried about 150 yards (137 meters) from each other just north of the old city of London. I have seen the final resting places of Abraham Lincoln, David Livingstone, and various kings, queens, and popes. But far more often, I have walked among the graves of people nobody remembers. They came into the world, lived and loved, played and worked, and died. Now they are gone, and virtually nobody remembers them. But God remembers the dead, and He notices some in a very special way.

What really matters in the long run? Not everyone can sign the emancipation proclamation, walk on the moon, or climb Mount Everest. But notice what Daniel wrote: "Those who turn many to righteousness" are the ones who will shine "forever and ever" (Daniel 12:3).

The tomb of Karl Marx, author of *The Communist Manifesto*, is in Highgate Cemetery, just outside London, England. Since its construction, it has been a destination for adherents of Marx's theories. The grave of Jim Morrison attracts tourists in Paris decades after the singer's death. Vladimir Lenin's body is still on display in Red Square in Moscow. People file past it almost every day to see the grave of the man who once led a powerful nation. These are the people—the dead people—who command attention and are remembered by the world. But in unremarkable graveyards all around the world lie the remains of humble men and women who were never household names but who will shine forever because they did what was truly valuable in God's sight. Running a country? Fronting a rock band? God says the person who will shine forever is the one who turns many to righteousness—who leads people to faith in Christ.

Winning souls is truly valuable in God's sight. It is a legacy that endures. If you want to make an eternal difference, share Jesus with someone. That's what matters. And you will shine like the stars forever.

Worth Remembering

The righteous will be in everlasting remembrance.

—Psalm 112:6

Who won last year's Super Bowl? Even someone who is not a fan of sports might know because, at the time, that one game was the biggest thing in the news. The media hype during the build-up to the game was intense. Advertisers paid millions of dollars to run a thirty-second ad during television breaks, and an enormous television audience is said to have viewed the extravaganza. Of the 30 most-watched television broadcasts of all time, 29 have been Super Bowls.

But who won the Super Bowl two years ago? What about five years ago? Only real sports fans are likely to remember. At the time, it was the only thing some people were talking about. The passage of time reveals that the result of a football game will be of great importance to a few, for a moment. Afterward, in spite of the marketing and the mania, the result is largely forgotten.

So what is really important? A group of men playing with a ball is here today and gone tomorrow and of zero lasting importance. It is the very sort of thing Solomon would have described as "vanity" or "futility." The Bible helps us to understand what is truly important.

Super Bowl MVPs, Academy Award winners, Olympic gold medalists, and even Nobel Prize winners are typically forgotten not long after their moment of glory. What is really important to God—the achievement He recognizes—is a life lived for Him, especially a life that results in turning people toward heaven. The missionary who toils in obscurity, the faithful single mom raising her children to love Jesus, and the church school teacher turning young minds toward Jesus are truly making an eternal difference. They won't receive adulation, fame, or glory in this world. But a soul won for Jesus is something we will celebrate forever.

Royalty!

And because you are sons, God has sent forth the Spirit of His Son into your hearts, crying out, "Abba, Father!" Therefore you are no longer a slave but a son, and if a son, then an heir of God through Christ.
—Galatians 4:6, 7

S he thought it was a prank call. "We want you to be the new king!" someone was telling her at three o'clock in the morning. But it was not a hoax. The king of her tribe back in West Africa had died. As his niece, she was considered by some to be the sort of person who would make an ideal king if she took his place. One day she was working as a secretary in Washington, DC, and the next—to her great surprise—she was king of a tribe of seven thousand people. (That is not a typo. She was to be the king, not the queen.)

Several sudden transformations are mentioned in the Bible. Betrayed by his brothers, sold into slavery, falsely accused, unjustly imprisoned, and forgotten by those he had helped, Joseph was in desperate straits as he languished in an Egyptian jail. But literally, overnight, Joseph went from utter disenfranchisement to being one of the most powerful figures in the government of a great nation. He was a farmhand when he was chosen to be the spokesperson for the God of heaven.

What's more incredible is that when you accept Jesus as your Savior, you go from being a slave of sin to being a child of the heavenly King. Paul told the Galatians, "You are no longer a slave but a son, and if a son, then an heir of God through Christ" (Galatians 4:7). When you have faith in Jesus, a miraculous transformation takes place. No longer a sinner, you become a saint. No longer guilty of sin, you are forgiven and acquitted. No longer a "commoner," you become royalty!

This remarkable transaction takes place by faith. When you choose to believe God's promises, those promises become true in your life. At that moment, you become royalty, the child of the Majesty of the universe.

Resistant

Because the sentence against an evil work is not executed speedily,
therefore the heart of the sons of men is fully set in them to do evil.
—Ecclesiastes 8:11

The advent of antibiotics meant that many common illnesses could be treated simply and effectively. Ailments that had plagued humanity were now easily conquered. But over time, it became apparent that some diseases were becoming resistant to antibiotics. MRSA (methicillin-resistant *Staphylococcus aureus*), one of the most common hospital-acquired strains of staph infections, has become resistant to many antibiotics that once provided successful treatment.

A very similar thing happens with sin. Those who become familiar with sin develop a certain resistance to its effects. That first glass of wine leaves many people swearing they will never drink wine again, but the person who persists with wine drinking often becomes a committed drinker. Many a youngster was physically ill after smoking their first cigarette but went on to become a dedicated smoker after learning how to tolerate what once had been literally sickening. The first lie told may make the pulse quicken, but in time, lies are told without a second thought.

It is natural to become accustomed to sin, especially because the consequences are most often not quickly discerned. It is likely that when Judas, described by John as "a thief" (John 12:6), began practicing dishonesty, he would never have dreamed he would betray Israel's Messiah to His death. But his sin led him down a slippery slope to full-blown rebellion against the God of heaven.

Sins such as adultery, murder, and theft begin with much less serious thoughts. But a continued focus on sin and a continued acceptance of its presence can bring a person to the point where sin no longer appears sinful.

The solution is simple. "Through an appreciation of the character of Christ, through communion with God, sin will become hateful to us."* The power of temptation is very real, but the power of God to create new, holy inclinations in a person's life is far greater.

---

* Ellen G. White, *The Desire of Ages* (Mountain View, CA: Pacific Press®, 1940), 668.

What Spirit?

But He turned and rebuked them, and said,
"You do not know what manner of spirit you are of."

—Luke 9:55

C hurches are usually peaceful places. But in one church in a city in the United States, a fight broke out during which a woman was stabbed, and the minister of music tased the pastor! People are capable of surprising behavior.

A delegation sent by Jesus into a Samaritan village was rejected by the local people. James and John—revealing they were not called the "Sons of Thunder" without reason—were so incensed by this slight that they asked Jesus if He would permit them to call fire down from heaven so that the offending locals would be incinerated!

The request was made by the man who would go on to write five New Testament books, including one of the gospels and the book of Revelation. "Lord, do You want us to command fire to come down from heaven and consume them, just as Elijah did?" (Luke 9:54). Both James and John were disciples of the Prince of Peace. John wrote the following words of Jesus in John 13:34: "A new commandment I give to you, that you love one another; as I have loved you, that you also love one another." And yet, along with James, John asked Jesus if it would be permissible to burn to death a town full of people!

If you are not surrendered to Jesus, you are capable of absolutely anything. Often it is people who are considered perfectly respectable that commit the most heinous crimes or the most outrageous acts. The fact that a person claims to be a Christian or goes to church or takes up the offering doesn't really prove a lot. What are you like under provocation? "It is in a crisis that character is revealed."* What are you like when someone steps on your toes or you don't get your own way? Do you know "what manner of spirit you are of?" (Luke 9:55). If God reveals to you that the wrong spirit is governing your life, see that as an invitation from Him to make room for more of His presence in your life. Only His Spirit at work in our lives can truly change us. As the old saying goes, "There, but for the grace of God, go I."†

---

* Ellen G. White, *Christ's Object Lessons* (Washington, DC: Review and Herald®, 1941), 412.
† Often attributed to John Bradford (1510–1555).

Only Good

"But let him who glories glory in this,
That he understands and knows Me,
That I am the LORD, exercising lovingkindness,
judgment, and righteousness in the earth.
For in these I delight," says the LORD.

—Jeremiah 9:24

Justice is necessary for the smooth running of any society. The Pledge of Allegiance affirms that the United States is "one nation, under God, with liberty and justice for all." God's message to His people in Zechariah 7:9 was that they "execute true justice, show mercy and compassion everyone to his brother," while Micah 6:8 exhorts all to "do justly."

Anyone who read the news story about the fourteen-year-old girl who was executed for adultery might have been thankful that Jesus doesn't mete out justice the way some societies do. God is frequently depicted as a God who majors in justice, and while it is true that God is just, He is incredibly merciful. The Monarch of the universe—who has a perfect right to dispense stern justice in the case of every human being—prefers to win us with love rather than fear. He delights in "exercising lovingkindness, judgment, and righteousness in the earth" (Jeremiah 9:24).

This does not suggest that God is not a God of justice. But heaven's justice is tempered with mercy and goodness. God deals graciously with His people. He is patient and merciful toward sinners, and instead of looking to do away with sinners, He does all He can to win the fallen and demonstrate that He is good.

The Ten Commandments—the standard of justice—were in the Most Holy Place of the sanctuary in the wilderness (Exodus 25:21) and are in the Most Holy Place of the sanctuary in heaven (Hebrews 8:5; 9:5). But on top of the ark of the covenant rested the solid gold mercy seat, demonstrating that in God, "mercy and truth have met together; righteousness and peace have kissed" (Psalm 85:10).

Before God looks to administer justice, He looks to exercise mercy. While human beings often engage in a rush to justice, God's character is to rush to mercy.

Faith Healing

So when He saw them, He said to them, "Go, show yourselves to the priests."
And so it was that as they went, they were cleansed.

—Luke 17:14

As they approached Jesus, ten men suffering from leprosy cried out, "Have mercy on us" (Luke 17:13). Leprosy was a feared disease, a terminal illness in the time of Christ. But Jesus did indeed have mercy on them. When He saw them, He simply said, "Go, show yourselves to the priests" (verse 14). He did not tell them to wash their eyes in a pool. He did not apply a healing solution. He didn't so much as spend time interviewing them. He simply told them to go and see the priests, whose job it was to declare a leprosy sufferer officially healed of their illness.

On another occasion, a leper approached Jesus and said, "Lord, if You are willing, You can make me clean" (Matthew 8:2). Jesus' response to the lone leper differed from His response to the ten. "Jesus put out His hand and touched him, saying, 'I am willing; be cleansed.' Immediately his leprosy was cleansed" (verse 3.) The touch of Jesus' hand accompanied by His Word was all that was necessary to effect healing for the suffering man.

In the case of the ten, the Bible says, they were healed "as they went." Jesus didn't heal them and then send them on their way. He sent them on their way, and then they were healed as they went believing His Word. This is an example of how real faith works. Acting on the Word of God and expecting it to do what God says it will do—as in the case of the ten lepers—is faith in action.

You can possess that same faith and expect to see the same results. When you claim the promises of God and expect them to do what they say in accordance with God's will, you can expect to see God work. Jesus invites us to take Him at His word and trust that He will act on our behalf. The Word of God will do what it says it will do.

Where Are the Nine?

Jesus answered and said,
"Were there not ten cleansed? But where are the nine?"

—Luke 17:17

You would expect that a person who had been treated especially graciously would be especially thankful. If someone were to pay for your education, fix your car, pay your rent, or give you a ride to where you wanted to go, you would no doubt be appreciative. And if someone saved your life? Surely you would be thankful for as long as you lived.

One day Jesus, the Great Healer, healed ten men of leprosy. To heal one leper (as Jesus had done on another occasion) was a great miracle. But ten healed lepers? It was a miracle of immense proportions. Yet, of the ten who were healed, only one returned to Jesus to express his gratitude. And this man was a Samaritan, predisposed by nationalistic distinctions to harbor hatred for Jesus, a Jew. The Samaritan man put aside his racial prejudice to seek out Jesus and intentionally thank Him for what He had done.

The other nine men returned to their families that day, rejoicing that they were healed of their life-threatening illness. They enjoyed the gift but forgot the Giver.

What has God done for you for which you can say "thank You"? Gratitude toward God keeps His blessings fixed in our minds and causes us to remember His goodness.

After Israel won a decisive victory over the Philistines, the prophet Samuel erected a memorial, an "Ebenezer," to testify of God's goodness and faithfulness and to keep God's special blessing before the people (1 Samuel 7:12). When Israel passed over the Jordan River into the Promised Land, Joshua had a pillar of stones erected as a reminder that "the waters of the Jordan were cut off before the ark of the covenant of the LORD; when it crossed over the Jordan, the waters of the Jordan were cut off" (Joshua 4:7). God's blessings are to be remembered.

We should thank God frequently for His many gifts. Every child of God has much to be thankful for. Cultivating an attitude of thankfulness toward God is essential to maintaining a healthy Christian experience.

JUNE

Rich Toward God

"So is he who lays up treasure for himself,
and is not rich toward God."

—Luke 12:21

Having an abundance of possessions can give rise to challenging questions. For whose benefit are your possessions, anyway? And what will happen to them when your time on this mortal coil is over? Some people leave vast sums of money to educational institutions. Business magnate T. Boone Pickens donated more than $650 million to his alma mater, Oklahoma State University, two-thirds of that to the school's sports programs.* I heard of a woman in Italy who left $13 million to an alley cat she had rescued, and a German man who left $372 million to his dog.

Jesus told the story of a wealthy man whose crops were so productive he tore down his barns and built bigger barns so he could store all he harvested. The man intended to "eat, drink, and be merry" (Luke 12:19). When he died unexpectedly, the question was, "Whose will those things be?" (verse 20). Jesus said, "So is he who lays up treasure for himself, and is not rich toward God" (verse 21). Jesus taught that what we possess should be dedicated to God. Rather than being bent on acquiring more simply for the purpose of acquiring more, we receive in order that we may give.

This isn't to suggest that God is against wealth. He is not. In the vast majority of cases, people are wealthy because they have worked hard and made wise decisions. After all, "it is He who gives you power to get wealth" (Deuteronomy 8:18).

But in an age where the emphasis is on getting and having, we need to remember that our wealth isn't given to us only for selfish reasons. Someone once said, "We make a living by what we earn. We make a life by what we give."† It's a principle that applies to all people irrespective of their bank balance. The best investment you can make is in the bank of heaven. Money retained may buy a car or a house, or it may swell an investment account. Money given to God will win souls and grow His kingdom. If you are rich toward God, you will deepen your experience with Him.

---

* Jacob Unruh, "A Look at T. Boone Pickens' Donations to OSU Athletics Throughout the Years," *The Oklahoman*, September 12, 2019, https://www.oklahoman.com/article/5641056/a-look-at-t-boone-pickens-donations-to-osu-athletics-throughout-the-years.

† Often attributed to Sir Winston Churchill.

Financially Faithful

*"And I say to you, make friends for yourselves by unrighteous mammon,
that when you fail, they may receive you into an everlasting home."*
—Luke 16:9

When a wealthy man asked his corrupt manager for an account of his work, the employee realized that, owing to his poor work, he would soon be without a job. So, he said to his employer's clients, "You owe my boss a hundred measures of oil? Pay fifty. You owe a hundred measures of wheat? Here's a deal. Pay eighty!" The Bible says that "the master commended the unjust steward" for the reason that "he had dealt shrewdly" (Luke 16:8).

The business owner was not affirming the man for his dishonesty or in any way countenancing unethical business practices. He simply recognized that his soon-to-be former employee had been wise enough to use his position to secure his future. He had not done so honestly, but he had done so cleverly. The dishonest steward had entangled others in his deceptive scheme. Those he had helped were now obliged to help him in return. They were bound together by their common dishonesty.

Jesus was certainly not sanctioning embezzlement or fraud. It was the rich man in the story who spoke favorably of his steward's duplicity, not Jesus. Jesus was pointing out that as worldly, dishonest people use their means and position to get ahead in this world, the child of God should employ his or her means and position to lay up blessings in heaven.

In contrast to the dishonest steward, God's children are to use their means to honor God and to advance His cause. Selfishness inspires us to build bigger barns for the purpose of eating, drinking, and being merry. Surrendering to God places God first in our stewardship. Unlike the dishonest steward who used the property of others to feather his own nest, a disciple of Christ will faithfully dedicate all he or she has to God. When God is put first, He will be honored and His kingdom advanced, and the faithful steward will be blessed in this world and in the world to come.

The Power of Music

Sing to Him, sing psalms to Him;
talk of all His wondrous works!

—1 Chronicles 16:9

N o doubt you have noticed there are times when a song can become stuck in your mind. An earworm, or involuntary musical imagery, can be almost impossible to get rid of, no matter how hard you try. A song you haven't heard in decades can come flooding back, bringing with it memories of every word, every key change, and every harmony.

God understands how music works, which is why the Scriptures repeatedly encourage us to sing of God's goodness. In the Psalms, we read, "Oh come, let us sing to the LORD!" "Oh, sing to the LORD a new song! Sing to the LORD, all the earth." "I will sing of mercy and justice; to You, O LORD, I will sing praises." "I will sing to the LORD as long as I live; I will sing praise to my God while I have my being" (Psalms 95:1; 96:1; 101:1; 104:33).

Music is powerful. It has the ability to elicit strong emotional responses. Sometimes these responses can be positive, while at other times, they are negative. A concerto by Brahms or a symphony by Mozart can evoke deep feelings, as can a funeral hymn, a power ballad, a rock song, or a bluegrass tune. But one would be hard-pressed to make the case that all music evokes emotions of value in the sight of God.

Songs that tell of God's goodness and encourage devotion and gratitude toward Him should be a key part of the soundtrack to a believer's life. Singing hymns or songs of praise or learning Scripture songs—Bible verses put to music—will see the Word of God take deep root in your mind. Once a sacred song is learned, it might never be forgotten. If you have filled your mind with secular music, you will be blessed if you reprogram your mind with songs of God. Let the power of music work *for* you and not against you.

New Again

He who sat on the throne said, "Behold, I make all things new."
And He said to me, "Write, for these words are true and faithful."
—Revelation 21:5

Decades ago, a magnificent hotel was built in the coastal city of Beira in Mozambique. After operating for a short time, it closed for financial reasons. During Mozambique's civil war, it was used as an army base and a prison for political prisoners. Today it is a sad-looking shell occupied by 3,500 squatters. It will never be returned to its former glory, and today it testifies mutely to the glory of a bygone era.

The run-down hotel is a lot like our planet. Shortly after it was created, this world fell into deep trouble, and today it is a shell of its former self. While there is still a lot in this world that reminds us of God's goodness, greatness, and creative power, what we see now is just a shadow of what this world once was. Sin has wrought havoc on what was once a perfect planet.

But there is good news to be found in Revelation 21:5: God is going to remake everything about our planet. This decrepit world will once again shine in the beauty of perfection. Human beings have fouled the world God made for them. Oceans and rivers are horribly polluted, power plants belch deadly toxins into the air we breathe, and massive holes dug in the ground in the search for minerals, in many cases, created environmental problems.

But when Jesus returns, there will be no greenhouse gases, no carbon monoxide poisoning, no landfills, and no arid deserts. We will not freeze in the winter and bake in the summer. Sin has had devastating consequences on our world, but out of love for His children, God will one day remake this old world. We can only imagine how beautiful it will then be. "The inhabitant will not say, 'I am sick' " (Isaiah 33:24), and "there shall be no more death" (Revelation 21:4). God's new world will be a perfect world. And He wants you to be part of it.

No Regrets

"I also will keep you from the hour of trial which shall come upon the whole world, to test those who dwell on the earth."

—Revelation 3:10

When someone tattoos the word *skinhead* on his forehead, there's a good chance he will one day regret doing so. While running with entirely the wrong crowd, one young man got such a tattoo and soon afterward felt bad about what he had done. Tattoos can be inexpensive and relatively painless. Tattoo removal—as our man found out—is neither.

Before getting a tattoo, many people have been told, "You're going to regret this!" And sure enough, many do—like the young man who tattooed his girlfriend's name on his chest in large letters. After he broke up with her, he found a new girlfriend with a different name. He wasn't the only one who wished he had never visited a tattoo artist.

Not everyone has the same regrets. But something that *always* causes regret is sin. Sooner or later, the effects of sin catch up with a person, and what may have seemed like a good idea at the time is eventually seen for what it truly is. Sin is never harmless, and it always has negative consequences, no matter how small it may have seemed at the time. Resisting sin is not a matter of will power; it is a matter of the will. Choosing not to engage in sin is a matter of choice. The choice to side with God and be kept by His power is a matter of surrendering the will to God, of praying the prayer Jesus prayed when He said the night before He died: "Nevertheless, not as I will, but as You will" (Matthew 26:39).

In Revelation 3:10, Jesus made a promise to the church of Philadelphia that anyone can claim. "I also will keep thee from the hour of temptation" (KJV). God says in Jude 24 that He "is able to keep you from falling" (KJV). While we are comforted to know God extends grace to any repentant sinner, we will experience a lot less regret when we take God at His word and choose to stand in His power.

Done to Him

"I was naked and you clothed Me; I was sick and you
visited Me; I was in prison and you came to Me."
—Matthew 25:36

New York City police officer Larry DePrimo noticed large blisters on the bare feet of a homeless man. It was a cold night in Times Square, and Officer DePrimo was moved by the plight of the man with no shoes. While onlookers laughed at the homeless man, Officer DePrimo went to a nearby shoe store and bought the man thermal socks and a pair of insulated winter boots. The surprised man received the gift gratefully.* Officer Larry DePrimo was invited to appear on television programs to discuss the kind deed he had performed.

Officer DePrimo was prompted by compassion and didn't hesitate to be the solution to a problem facing a complete stranger. From time to time, God gives us opportunities to impact someone in a significant, practical way. In blessing our fellow humans, we not only show kindness to Jesus in the person of His children but also demonstrate that our faith in God impacts us to the very core of our being.

The questioners in Jesus' parable were told they showed kindness to the King when they provided food and drink to "the least of these"—when they welcomed strangers into their homes, provided clothing as did Officer DePrimo, or visited the sick and imprisoned (Matthew 25:40). Jesus' earthly ministry was marked by compassion. Allowing God's love to call compassion from the heart is to allow the work of Jesus. Not everyone will listen to a sermon or appreciate a Bible study, but almost everyone responds to acts of kindness carried out unselfishly.

Whether it is providing warm boots to a homeless man or sharing a loaf of bread with a neighbor, God is waiting to show His love for others through you. Deeds of kindness that spring from a loving heart speak loudly of the love of Jesus and the existence of the God of heaven.

---

* J. David Goodman, "Photo of Officer Giving Boots to Barefoot Man Warms Hearts Online," *New York Times*, November 28, 2012, https://www.nytimes.com/2012/11/29/nyregion/photo-of-officer-giving-boots -to-barefoot-man-warms-hearts-online.html.

Offered Free

The free gift is not like the offense. For if by the one man's
offense many died, much more the grace of God and the gift
by the grace of the one Man, Jesus Christ, abounded to many.
—Romans 5:15

The manner in which a person receives the gift of salvation has been energetically debated down through the years. Sometimes that debate has become pointed, hostile, and even deadly. Thankfully, the Bible is clear on the subject.

As Paul wrote, the gift of salvation cannot be purchased or earned. It will never be deserved but is given freely to those who have faith in the Savior. Those who possess saving faith believe not only that Jesus is the Savior of the world who died for the sins of humanity but also that He will certainly give the gift of salvation to any and all who genuinely ask to receive it.

There is little a person can get for free. It is commonly believed that if something *seems* too good to be true, then it is too good to be true. Many "free" offers are free until you read the fine print. But the greatest things in this life—forgiveness, pardon, and eternal life—are offered totally free with no strings attached. Jesus died for all "while we were still sinners" (Romans 5:8). Jesus died so that "whoever" wants salvation might be saved and not lost (John 3:16), and still today, He is "able to save to the uttermost those who come to God through Him" (Hebrews 7:25).

Although the gift of salvation is entirely free, a person does give something in order to receive it. Jesus gives His perfect righteousness to all who surrender their heart to Him. Salvation is a transaction. God says in Ezekiel 36:26, "I will give you a new heart and put a new spirit within you; I will take the heart of stone out of your flesh and give you a heart of flesh."

Surrender to Jesus allows Him to take possession of your heart and give you the assurance of eternal salvation. When you yield your heart to Him, He becomes its rightful owner and remakes your life in His image.

Power Available

He would grant you, according to the riches of His glory,
to be strengthened with might through His Spirit in the inner man.
—Ephesians 3:16

B eneath the hood of a large truck is an engine that has been designed to deliver a lot of power when it is needed. A motorcycle, a blender, a flashlight, or a clock on a wall all rely on a source of power to keep them operational. Without a source of power, many things will not function.

The gospel is described in Romans 1:16 as "the power of God to salvation for everyone who believes," while Hebrews 1:3 says that Jesus upholds "all things by the word of His power." Eternal life depends upon God's power working in every life that is surrendered to Him. Our own power is good for nothing.

Today, God's power is made available to all in the Person of the Holy Spirit. Paul tells us that God will strengthen us with His might "through His Spirit in the inner man" (Ephesians 3:16). Having been told that the Holy Spirit is given to those who ask for the gift (Luke 11:13), we have heaven's assurance that God is willing to give us exactly what we need so He can do all that needs to be done in our lives.

Far too many believers continue to labor under the mistaken impression that if they try harder, or do better, or struggle more bravely, spiritual breakthroughs will be experienced, and victories will be won. There is something in the human psyche that is attracted to the idea of salvation by works. The truth is that as sinners yield to Jesus, His power will work in broken lives to bring not only the assurance of salvation but also transformation and re-creation. Without the power of God at work, a sinner cannot possibly experience victory or reflect the character of Jesus. But yielded to heaven's power, any sinner may shine brightly to the glory of God. The power of God can achieve everything God wills to do.

The power of God makes all the difference. Surrender to Jesus unleashes God's power in your life.

Love Beyond Measure

To know the love of Christ which passes knowledge;
that you may be filled with all the fullness of God.

—Ephesians 3:19

In the 1800s, poet Elizabeth Barrett Browning wrote,

> How do I love thee? Let me count the ways.
> I love thee to the depth and breadth and height
> My soul can reach, when feeling out of sight
> For the ends of being and ideal grace.*

In her most famous poem, Browning expressed her love for her husband in a lyrical and somewhat elaborate fashion.

Paul wrote that he wanted the Ephesians "to know the love of Christ which passes knowledge" (Ephesian 3:19)—a love beyond knowledge, beyond our ability to truly comprehend. God's love for a fallen world is so dramatic that John was moved to say, "Behold what manner of love the Father has bestowed on us, that we should be called children of God!" (1 John 3:1). He asked his readers to "behold" God's love because that would be the best possible way for them to comprehend a love "which passes knowledge."

Pause to consider that God loves you *that* much. God's love for you is not dependent upon how much you deserve that love or on your performance as a Christian. John wrote that God "first loved us" (1 John 4:19). After sin, God pursued Adam and Eve in the Garden of Eden, not to threaten or censure them, but to offer them eternal life at infinite cost to Himself.

There isn't anything you can do to stop God from loving you. That is not to say God approves of everything a person might do. Love is not license, and love is not blind to eternal realities. But God's love is certain and constant. There is something almost incomprehensible about a love that moves God to create the world, give life to the human family, and allow Jesus to die in the place of sinful beings. It is doubtful that the love of God can be truly understood this side of Jesus' return, but we can accept God's love and know it to the best of our capability. One thing that can be known with certainty is that you are loved by God with perfect love.

---

* Elizabeth Barrett Browning, "How Do I Love Thee? (Sonnet 43)," public domain, Poets.org, accessed February 4, 2021, https://poets.org/poem/how-do-i-love-thee-sonnet-43.

Always There

Where can I go from Your Spirit?
Or where can I flee from Your presence?

—Psalm 139:7

As a young British woman tended cabbages in a communal garden, her wedding ring slipped off her finger. After several days of searching, she and her husband concluded the ring would never be found and bought a replacement. Forty-one years later, the woman's husband noticed a neighbor with a metal detector in the same village garden and jokingly asked him to look for the lost ring. After a brief search, the ring was found in almost the exact spot where it had been dropped and returned to its owner—who slipped it right back on her finger. The ring wasn't really lost. It was in the garden all that time, exactly where it had been left.

Many people wonder where God is during certain times. "Where was God when I was going through that trial?" "Where was God when my child was ill?" Perhaps God knew those questions would frequently be asked when He inspired David to write these beautiful words:

Where can I go from Your Spirit?
Or where can I flee from Your presence?
If I ascend into heaven, You are there;
If I make my bed in hell, behold, You are there.
If I take the wings of the morning,
And dwell in the uttermost parts of the sea,
Even there Your hand shall lead me,
And Your right hand shall hold me.
If I say, "Surely the darkness shall fall on me,"
Even the night shall be light about me;
Indeed, the darkness shall not hide from You,
But the night shines as the day;
The darkness and the light are both alike to You (Psalm 139:7–12).

It might be that circumstances obscure our view, but when we cannot see God's love, we can be certain it is still present with us. The love of God is as certain as God Himself. When God's love cannot be seen, it can be believed. We remember Paul wrote "we walk by faith, not by sight" (2 Corinthians 5:7). God has given us an almost infinite number of reasons to trust His love for us. Circumstances never change the fact that God is love.

Priceless

*Jesus said to His disciples, "If anyone desires to come after Me,
let him deny himself, and take up his cross, and follow Me."*
—Matthew 16:24

On average, a rhinoceros is killed every ten hours in southern Africa. Because of poaching—the illegal killing of these majestic animals—rhino numbers have been plummeting in recent years. Rhinos are easy targets because they are creatures of habit. Once a sign of recent rhino activity is spotted, all an unscrupulous hunter must do is wait. The rhinoceros will be back and will be easy prey for a well-armed poacher.

Although the precipitous decline in rhino numbers has slowed, it is still at a crisis point. Much of the poaching has occurred in Kruger National Park, a vast preserve almost as big as New Jersey. Between 2007 and 2014, rhino killings in South Africa surged by more than 9,200 percent. At $60,000 a kilogram, rhino horn is more valuable on the Asian black market than both gold and cocaine. Believed by some to have medicinal properties, it is one of the most valuable commodities in the world.* However, rhino horn is made primarily of keratin, the same protein that makes up hair and nails. From a medicinal point of view, you would derive as much benefit from chewing your nails as you would from consuming rhino horn.

The most valuable "commodity" of all is salvation. Yet comparatively few people invest any amount of effort in securing everlasting life. Anyone may have it. Yet, instead of striving to enter in at the narrow gate, masses are taking the broad road to destruction.

That which stands between a sinner and salvation is the sinner's will. Denying oneself and taking up the cross of Christ is neither pleasant nor easy. The drive to indulge one's selfish self is very real and can be very strong. Saying no to one's own desires can be challenging. But it definitely isn't impossible.

The Bible promises God will make a way of escape from any temptation. A plea for grace, a prayer for divine assistance, or an appeal for the righteousness of Christ will never be turned down. Faith in Jesus unleashes the power of God in your life and lays hold on something truly priceless.

---

* Hannah Ellis-Petersen, "Vietnam Seizes 125 kg of Smuggled Rhino Horns Worth $7.5m," *The Guardian*, July 29, 2019, https://www.theguardian.com/world/2019/jul/29/vietnam-seizes-125kg-of-smuggled-rhino-tusks-worth-75m.

A Sick World

"If you diligently heed the voice of the LORD your God and do what is right in His sight, give ear to His commandments and keep all His statutes, I will put none of the diseases on you which I have brought on the Egyptians. For I am the LORD who heals you."

—Exodus 15:26

The headline said, "How Western Diets are Making the World Sick." Canadian physician Dr. Kevin Patterson discovered, while working in Kandahar, Afghanistan, that Afghan adults undergoing surgery typically weighed around 140 pounds and had no fat under their skin. But the internal organs of Westerners who were operated on were typically encased in fat. Dr. Patterson could literally see the difference. Discussing type 2 diabetes, which was rare just 70 or 80 years ago but has risen dramatically with the rise in obesity, Dr. Patterson noted that indigenous populations in such places as the Arctic Circle and the Marianas Islands in the Pacific are contracting Western diseases as a result of consuming the unhealthy Western diet.*

When God led His people out of Egypt, He promised to keep them safe from the diseases of the Egyptians if they followed His instructions. The Egyptians of that time were dying of many of the lifestyle diseases we suffer from today. Tests on mummies have revealed that ancient Egyptians had heart disease and cancer and suffered strokes, often the result of lifestyle choices. But the Israelites, who followed God's plan, were healthy for the forty years they wandered in the wilderness. Why would we choose to be ill when God says that if we follow His plan, we are going to be healthier?

This is not to say Christian believers are exempt from getting sick. But people thrive when they get with God's program and take care of their health. Good health is often simply a matter of choice. The Bible urges you to make choices that honor God.

In cases where poor health practices are deeply ingrained, God can be looked to as the source of power to change. Some illnesses cannot be avoided. Cancer, stroke, and other diseases often strike randomly. But honoring God with your body gives you a far greater chance of living a long, healthy life.

---

* "How Western Diets Are Making the World Sick," *Fresh Air*, NPR, March 24, 2011, https://www.npr.org/2011/03/24/132745785/how-western-diets-are-making-the-world-sick.

Without Consent

My son, if sinners entice you, do not consent.

—Proverbs 1:10

The young man grew up in a rough neighborhood. There was a very good chance he would become yet another statistic. When a friend stopped at his house, determined to teach another boy a lesson, he was tempted to go with him. But he remembered a simple Bible verse his mother had taught him in his childhood: "My son, if sinners entice you, do not consent" (Proverbs 1:10). With those words burning in his mind, he was able to tell his visitor that, no, he wouldn't be joining him. You can guess how the story ends. The tough guy ended up serving time, while the subject of this story went on to become an internationally known figure who has made an enormous contribution to the betterment of the world.

If the Bible verse had not flashed into his mind at that time, things almost certainly would have been very different. Proverbs 1:10 teaches us something. When sin comes knocking at your door, you have a choice to make. Our friend chose not to go with sin. He did not consent. Sin doesn't happen without your approval. It is certainly true that people can consent to sin without even really thinking about it, largely because they are on autopilot. The reason you don't think about God at that time is that you are not surrendered to God at that moment. You blew up before you considered your rising blood pressure, or you cheated on an exam before stopping to really think about the consequences because that's the kind of person you have let yourself become.

When temptation comes, do not consent. God does not ask you to fight in your own strength. When temptation comes, when you are enticed to sin, if you will choose not to consent and choose instead to surrender to God and allow Him to work in you, you will discover that the power of God will work in your life. When you are tempted, choose to yield to God rather than consent to sin. The devil has plans for your future. Yielding to God gives Him permission to alter those plans and ensure your eternal future.

Messing With Your Mind

But we all, with unveiled face, beholding as in a mirror
the glory of the Lord, are being transformed into the same
image from glory to glory, just as by the Spirit of the Lord.
—2 Corinthians 3:18

A recent study revealed that four-year-old children who watched nine minutes of a certain popular television cartoon show demonstrated what one writer called "less self-control, a reduced ability to delay gratification, and poorer working memory skills than their peers who had engaged in 'calmer' activities." While one group of children was shown the fast-paced cartoon show, another watched something educational and slower-paced, or they colored with markers and crayons. The children who took the calmer route did much better than those who experienced input overload.*

It shouldn't surprise us to find out that what children watch on television affects the way their minds work. Paul wrote to the Corinthians long ago and said we are transformed as we look at Jesus. Looking to Jesus, we become like Him.

What you put into your mind affects what plays out in your life. Just as a programmer programs a computer, believers in Jesus program their minds one way or another. Focusing on images or content that plants disturbing messages in your mind will affect you negatively. Programming your mind in a positive way will grow you in a healthy direction.

What are you beholding? Reading the Word of God puts you in touch with the God of eternity, enabling you to hear His counsel and know His character. Prayer has a transformational effect on the whole person. Time in nature has a calming, restoring effect on human physiology. If you make heaven your focus, the Bible your guide, and prayer your link with heaven, you will be transformed into Christ's image. Today, think about where your focus is. If you want to be like Jesus, if you want to be the person God wants you to be, make the things of heaven your focus. By beholding, you will be changed.

---

* Esther Entin, "The SpongeBob Squarepants Story: Cartoons Harm Higher Cognition," *Atlantic*, October 22, 2011, https://www.theatlantic.com/health/archive/2011/10/the-spongebob-squarepants-story-cartoons -harm-higher-cognition/247138/.

Temptation and Sin

*But each one is tempted when he is drawn away by his own
desires and enticed. Then, when desire has conceived, it gives
birth to sin; and sin, when it is full-grown, brings forth death.*

—James 1:14, 15

t is important to understand the difference between temptation and sin. James spoke
to this distinction in James 1:14, 15.

It is not a sin to be tempted. When someone cuts you off in traffic, and the impulse
rises to shake your fist and shout something inappropriate, that is not sin. That is
temptation. When you see an attractive person and something within you suggests you
take a lingering look, that is temptation and not sin. You may wish to ask yourself why
certain temptations seem to be so persistent, but temptation and sin are two different
things.

Having been tempted does not mean you have fallen into sin. But it is important to
tread carefully in this area. If you fail to flee that temptation, you may well fall prey to
it. There is a reason Jesus taught us to pray, "Lead us not into temptation" (Matthew
6:13, KJV). Yielding to temptation leads directly to sin and ultimately brings death.

But living a life in connection with Jesus will bring you to the place where temptation will not present any kind of moral predicament. As you continue to grow your
relationship with Jesus, you will mature in your experience to the extent that you won't
respond to temptation. When Jesus has your will and is allowed to blend it with His
own will, His purposes can be carried out in your life.

As you grow in the grace of God, keep in mind that there is a significant difference
between temptation and sin. Even Jesus "was in all points tempted as we are, yet without
sin" (Hebrews 4:15). Peter wrote that "when He was reviled, [He] did not revile in
return; when He suffered, He did not threaten, but committed Himself to Him who
judges righteously" (1 Peter 2:23).

Thank God that He is able to keep you in the hour of temptation. You are not
doomed to be trapped in sin without escape.

Natural Disasters

"And there will be signs in the sun, in the moon, and in the stars; and on the earth distress of nations, with perplexity, the sea and the waves roaring."
—Luke 21:25

A 2011 survey revealed that almost 40 percent of Americans agree or mostly agree that natural disasters are a sign from God.[*] While it is important not to read too much into a cold winter or a destructive hurricane, one publication described the weather several years ago by saying, "It was a disaster."[†] The country had just been through the deadliest tornado season on record. Weather events that year cost the country $52 billion. A once-in-five-hundred-year flood had inundated the Mississippi River Valley.[‡]

Does this mean Jesus is coming back soon? Yes, it does. But we have to be extremely careful how we allow natural disasters to inform our theology. It is impossible to know how much time remains before the return of Jesus, and it is important to resist the temptation to speculate. Unlike mileage signs that tell us how far we are from our destination, the signs of Jesus' coming are more like the highway markers informing us which road we are on. Other than knowing we are close and getting closer to the return of Jesus, it isn't possible to know exactly when He will return. However, we can know we are on the right road, and the signs we see in the world today tell us that we are definitely journeying rapidly in the direction of the return of Jesus.

Social, environmental, religious, and political developments alert us that time is short. While we are encouraged that we can expect to see Jesus return soon, we are prompted to do all we can to reach as many as possible with the saving good news. One day the last sermon will have been preached. The last Bible study will have been given. There is no need to speculate as to how much time we have, but we can know that Jesus is coming back soon.

---

[*] Eric Marrapodi, "Poll: Few Americans Believe Natural Disasters Are Signs From God," Belief Blog, CNN, March 24, 2011, https://religion.blogs.cnn.com/2011/03/24/most-americans-think-god-is-in-control-for-better-or-worse/.

[†] Brian Resnick, "The Year in Weather: It Was a Disaster," *Atlantic*, December 22, 2011, https://www.the atlantic.com/national/archive/2011/12/the-year-in-weather-it-was-a-disaster/250371/.

[‡] Resnick.

The Defeated Serpent

"And I will put enmity
Between you and the woman,
And between your seed and her Seed;
He shall bruise your head,
And you shall bruise His heel."

—Genesis 3:15

Two hundred fifty miles northwest of São Paolo, Brazil, a brave sixty-six-year-old man saved his eight-year-old grandson from certain death. An anaconda had coiled itself around the boy and was attempting to suffocate him. It is said that it takes one man for every three feet (one meter) of snake to be able to subdue a creature of that size, but the determined grandfather did battle with the sixteen-foot-long (five-meter-long) snake for over an hour on his own. He managed to fight off the snake using rocks and a knife and save his grandson's life. "When I saw the snake wrapped around my grandson's neck, I thought it was going to kill him," the heroic grandfather said.*

A spiritual parallel isn't hard to see. In the Garden of Eden, a serpent tempted Eve to eat the fruit growing on the tree of the knowledge of good and evil. Paul wrote that "the serpent deceived Eve by his craftiness" (2 Corinthians 11:3), and in so doing, plunged the human family into defeat, despair, and disarray.

There are approximately six hundred different venomous snakes in the world. The deadliest include the inland taipan, Dubois' sea snake, and the eastern brown snake, all of which are found in or near Australia. The deadliest serpent of all, however, is the one that led Adam and Eve away from obedience to God, opened up the floodgates of sin, and unleashed misery upon the world.

But the deadliest serpent is also a defeated serpent. Jesus came into the world "that through death He might destroy him who had the power of death, that is, the devil" (Hebrews 2:14). Christ's death on the cross ensured that the enemy of souls would not succeed in forever separating the human family from a loving God. Although the serpent bruised Jesus' heel, the Savior secured salvation for the entire human family.

---

* The Associated Press, "Man Saves Grandson From 16-Foot-Long Snake," NBC News, February 8, 2007, https://www.nbcnews.com/id/wbna17052967.

The Power of Forgiveness

"If you do not forgive men their trespasses,
neither will your Father forgive your trespasses."

—Matthew 6:15

An Iranian man was so angry when a woman rejected his marriage proposal that he viciously threw acid into her face. Under Islamic law, eye-for-an-eye retribution is permissible. By order of the court, a physician was about to put several drops of acid into the man's right eye when the now-blind woman stated that she had forgiven her attacker and didn't want him to be disfigured. She said, "It is best to pardon when you are in a position of power."*

Those are powerful words, and they are very true. It takes no moral strength to hold a grudge, but it can take a tremendous amount of fortitude to forgive someone who has wronged you. Virtually everyone has issues of some kind with forgiveness. People carry grudges against friends, neighbors, family members, parents, former teachers, former spouses, or ex-boyfriends or ex-girlfriends. Every grudge chains the one carrying the grudge to the person who committed the act that triggered the grudge. It is not uncommon for people to feel bitterness or hatred years after a wrong has been inflicted. Often, people still refuse to forgive even after the person who wronged them has died.

In the Lord's prayer, Jesus taught us to pray, "Forgive us our debts, as we forgive our debtors" (Matthew 6:12). Sometimes forgiveness is difficult, but forgiveness is God's way. God understands how challenging forgiveness can be. As He hung on a cross dying for the sins of the world, Jesus prayed, "Father, forgive them, for they do not know what they do" (Luke 23:34). As difficult as it was to forgive His murderers, Jesus demonstrated the power of divine love and gave us an example, emphasizing the importance of forgiveness.

Unforgiveness does not harm the person who perpetrated the wrong. Instead, it hurts the person refusing to forgive. Forgiveness liberates the forgiver. Jesus said, just as God forgives, His children are to manifest the same spirit of forgiveness. Though it may sometimes seem impossible, the grace of God is able to lead people to forgive as Jesus did.

---

* Nasser Karimi, "Iranian Blinded by Acid Pardons Her Attacker," NBC News, July 31, 2011, https://www.nbcnews.com/id/wbna43961877.

What Matters Most

And we have known and believed the love that God has for us. God is love,
and he who abides in love abides in God, and God in him.
—1 John 4:16

While Father's Day tends to focus on food and gifts and fun, it also reminds us about the importance of being a father. Fatherhood is a big responsibility. And because no perfect father has ever lived, it's very hard to find the perfect father role model.

If you're looking for the model dad, you'll find Him in the Bible. The key to being a successful father is found in 1 John 4:16, which states simply, "God is love."

A father might be a fun dad, a disciplinarian dad, a genius dad, a creative dad, a hard-working dad, but that's not even getting close to the main quality a father should possess. The key question for fathers everywhere is this: "Is Dad a loving dad?" That question gets to the essence of fatherhood. What children need above all else is love, and love is what they most remember.

This is illustrated by a story I once heard. At a family reunion, a group of siblings connected for the first time in many years. Naturally, they discussed their childhood. The sisters reminded their brother about his habit of playing with his friends until well after the time he was supposed to be home and how, when he got home, he'd be in big trouble with his father. Yet try as he might, the brother could not remember his father punishing him for staying out late. He told his sisters that as he looked back, all he could remember was how much his father loved him.

It is wonderful for a father to be a high-achieving dad, a never-make-a-fuss-dad, or an always-at-the-game dad. But as important as those things may be, they're not the *most* important thing. Father's Day is a good time for fathers to consider how they are representing the love of God to their children. If a dad is missing the mark, he can remember that it isn't too late to redeem the time and show his children the genuine love that flows out of a converted heart. Love costs nothing, and it's the most important gift any father can give.

The Golden Lie

"And I said to them, 'Whoever has any gold, let them break it off.'
So they gave it to me, and I cast it into the fire, and this calf came out."
—Exodus 32:24

I t is one of the most absurd exchanges in the entire Bible. Moses came down from the mountain after communing with God and receiving the Ten Commandments, which had been written with God's own finger. He discovered to his horror that the children of Israel had been worshiping a golden calf. His brother, Aaron, had been left in charge of the people, and during the several weeks of Moses' absence, they constructed an idol and began to worship it. Aaron explained by telling Moses that he told the people to take off their jewelry, and when he threw it into the fire, the golden calf miraculously appeared!

Something inside Aaron evidently suggested to him that his story was believable. For some reason, he expected Moses to believe he threw jewelry into a fire, and, lo and behold, a golden calf emerged from the flames! The story demonstrates that people will say the most preposterous things in the heat of the moment. It is a sadly natural trait for people to go so far as to make themselves look ridiculous in the hope of diverting blame or responsibility from themselves. Aaron was like the child with chocolate around his mouth, telling his mother he hadn't taken the cookies. Aaron had done something egregious. He had boldly violated the commandments and had led God's people into terrible sin.

How should a Christian react when caught in violation of God's commandments? God tells us He is a loving God, a forgiving God, and incredibly patient. Aaron's best course of action would have been to admit his wrong, but sin does strange things to people. One sin leads to another, and in Aaron's case, sin prevented him from thinking straight. Aaron could have and should have avoided his shame and embarrassment by humbly turning to God after he had exercised poor judgment.

When you fall, trust that God will forgive you. Own your missteps, and trust God to set you on a new path.

Selling the Birthright

And Jacob gave Esau bread and stew of lentils; then he ate
and drank, arose, and went his way. Thus Esau despised his birthright.
—Genesis 25:34

It is as perplexing a Bible story as virtually any you will read. A grown man sold his birthright for the princely sum of . . . a bowl of lentil stew. And for the simple reason that he was hungry.

Esau came in from his wearying work in the fields to find his brother had food ready to eat. "Please feed me with that same red stew, for I am weary" (Genesis 25:30), he said to his sibling. Jacob cynically seized the opportunity, saying, "Sell me your birthright as of this day" (verse 31). Esau "swore to him, and sold his birthright to Jacob" (verse 33). For a bowl of stew, Esau forfeited the double portion of the inheritance he would receive from his father, along with family leadership and authority. They were valued by him as nothing in comparison to the opportunity to satisfy his hunger.

But every day, people sell more for less. Jesus offers everlasting life to everyone. At an inestimable cost to Himself, Jesus bore the sins of the world as He died on the cross. He came forth from the grave triumphant over sin and death, and all who choose Jesus' death in the place of their own sinful heart receive the gift of salvation. It seems incredible that anyone would reflect on this and choose their three-score and ten years on this world over the opportunity to live forever in happiness, without sin, in a land that is fairer than day.

Jesus offers everlasting life. In exchange, we surrender our will and allow Him authority in our lives. To reject salvation, someone must say, "I would rather have my pride than Jesus." "I would sooner have lust than life everlasting." "I prefer anger, dishonesty, racism, and a bad temper to the love of Jesus in my life."

Esau could have walked the short distance to his parents' home to find food without discarding the blessing that belonged to him as his father's firstborn son. He failed to value the privileges that were his. Esau's experience reminds us of the folly of trading everything for nothing, of exchanging everlasting life for the short time we have on this earth.

Radium Girls

Through one man sin entered the world,
and death through sin, and thus death spread to all men.
—Romans 5:12

Not long after Marie Curie and her husband, Pierre, discovered radium, it was found that the element could be used in producing paint that glowed in the dark. Before long, manufacturers were producing glow-in-the-dark watch dials, painted by young women and girls who were encouraged by their employers to lick the paintbrush or twirl it between their lips in order to get a more precise brushstroke. Told the paint was harmless, many painted their fingernails and teeth with radium paint. The radium dust in the workplace caused many of the women to glow in the dark from head to toe.

As time passed, the women who worked with radium paint began to get sick. Many were still only in their twenties when they became seriously ill and died slow, painful deaths. It wasn't understood at the time that radium was radioactive and extremely hazardous to a person's health. Young women ingesting the substance were hastening their own death.*

The problem with sin is that its dark side is not always easily discernible. Paul wrote that "the wages of sin is death" (Romans 6:23), but many people treat sin like a plaything, failing to realize that it is always doing its deadly work. While radium has proven to be capable of taking a life in this world, sin destroys people for eternity. Those who die connected to sin will ultimately perish in the "second death" (Revelation 21:8).

The Radium Girls could all have been saved if someone had warned them about the danger of what they were handling. In the same way, not one soul needs to be lost because of sin. Although sin pays the wage of death, God's gift through Jesus is eternal life. While sin may seem fun, in the long term, it isn't to be trifled with. Sin is deadly. But Jesus came into the world to save us from sin. God is able to remake every person who comes to Jesus in faith. If we remember how harmful sin is, we will be far less likely to treat it casually. God wants to save us from the poisonous effects of sin.

---

* Don Vaughan, "Radium Girls: The Women Who Fought for Their Lives in a Killer Workplace," Brittanica .com, accessed April 5, 2021, https://www.britannica.com/story/radium-girls-the-women-who-fought-for -their-lives-in-a-killer-workplace.

When Discouragement Threatens

*So Moses said this to the sons of Israel, but they did not listen
to Moses on account of their despondency and cruel bondage.*
—Exodus 6:9, NASB

Discouragement is one of the greatest enemies of faith. It is often irrational and frequently ignores clear evidence that things are not always as they seem.

The children of Israel were masters of discouragement. It could be said they had a good reason for their disposition. Driven by famine to a foreign land, they were pressed into slavery and forced into hard labor following the death of Joseph, who had saved Egypt from ruin. Their bitter experience was made even more bitter when the Egyptian Pharaoh decreed the Israelites must gather straw for the bricks they were being compelled to manufacture.

In this trying time, God encouraged Moses by reminding him He was the God who "appeared to Abraham, to Isaac, and to Jacob, as God Almighty." God spoke to Moses of the covenant He had made to give His people "the land of Canaan," and He reassured Moses He had "heard the groaning of the children of Israel" (Exodus 6:3–5). He then instructed Moses to tell the people He would indeed bring them out of Egypt, free them from slavery, and return them to the Promised Land (verses 6–8).

Moses passed God's message on to the children of Israel, but they were too discouraged to listen. They had seen Moses perform miraculous signs. Joseph had given instruction that his bones not be buried in Egypt, stating his belief that Israel would be liberated from Egypt. But in the heat of their trial, the children of Israel could not see with eyes of faith. Refusing to listen to Moses, they succumbed to their despondency.

Discouragement is a very human characteristic. But when discouragement threatens, it is important to look beyond extreme circumstances, and by faith, view the Almighty God seated on heaven's throne. Life is filled with situations designed to crush hopes and shatter dreams. But faith sees beyond the seen and believes that in the realm of the unseen, there is a God who has solutions for our problems and a bright tomorrow ahead.

The Toledo War

*"The kingdom of heaven is like a merchant seeking
beautiful pearls, who, when he had found one pearl of
great price, went and sold all that he had and bought it."*
—Matthew 13:45, 46

A couple hundred years ago, a dispute between Ohio and Michigan saw both states claim a strip of land along their shared border. The dispute became known as the Toledo War, even though it was a tame affair as far as disputes go and no lives were lost. Both Michigan and Ohio insisted their cause was just, but Ohio legislators pledged to block Michigan's path to statehood if Michigan didn't relinquish its claim to the 468 square miles (1,212 square kilometers) of disputed borderland. Eager to be recognized as a state, Michigan backed down and accepted thousands of square miles of land from the federal government—an area known today as Michigan's Upper Peninsula. At the time, it was believed the agreement was a bad deal for Michigan. But within ten years, minerals were found in the Upper Peninsula, and copper and iron ore mines soon produced more mineral wealth than the California Gold Rush.*

It isn't always easy to see the value of something. Salvation may well be the most undervalued commodity in the universe. God offers everlasting life to "whoever believes" in Jesus as Lord and Savior (John 3:16). Life without end in a world without sin or illness is almost impossible to comprehend. But even before that time, God offers us abundant life here in this world (see John 10:10). A life without guilt, a life where every sin is forgiven, a life filled with meaning as fallen human beings recognize their place as sons and daughters of God and members of the family of heaven.

Jesus told a parable about a merchant "who, when he had found one pearl of great price, went and sold all that he had and bought it" (Matthew 13:46). The man in the story knew what the pearl was worth, and he gave all he had for it. Jesus gave all He had for you. If you're willing, you may have all heaven offers. Nothing in this world is worth a fraction of what God gives you today in Jesus.

---

* Evan Andrews, "The Toledo War: When Michigan and Ohio Nearly Came to Blows," History, accessed April 5, 2021, https://www.history.com/news/the-toledo-war-when-michigan-and-ohio-nearly-came-to-blows.

Unseen

*"So the servants of the owner came and said to him, 'Sir, did
you not sow good seed in your field? How then does it have tares?'
He said to them, 'An enemy has done this.' The servants said
to him, 'Do you want us then to go and gather them up?' "*
—Matthew 13:27, 28

As a microbiologist, Louis Pasteur believed many diseases were spread by tiny organisms invisible to the naked eye. In the 1860s, he conducted a series of experiments on the relationship between these "germs" and disease. Through his discoveries, he became known as one of the fathers of germ theory. While not the first to propose the idea, Pasteur brought germ theory into general acceptance. He was convinced that bacteria—which cannot be seen—cause disease.*

Much of what is wrong in the world today is caused by that which we cannot see. Sin exists because a fallen angel came to this planet six thousand years ago and tempted our original grandparents to depart from faith in God's Word. Today, a spiritual battle rages. Behind the veil that separates us from the unseen world, "spiritual hosts of wickedness" tempt us to fall as they tempted Adam and Eve (Ephesians 6:12). Although unseen, the great controversy is real, manifesting itself in illness, death, violence, and pain. Satan knows that those who choose darkness over light will be lost and not saved.

It is this spiritual war that provides answers for some of the most commonly asked questions about God. Why does suffering exist? Why do people experience loss? Why is there death and disease, and why do the innocent seem to suffer so much? Jesus answered this question clearly. When a landowner's servants asked him how there came to be noxious weeds growing in a field of wheat, he simply said, "An enemy has done this" (Matthew 13:28).

Why did the accident happen? "An enemy has done this." Why did the young mother of three get cancer? "An enemy has done this." Why did a tornado devastate the subdivision? "An enemy has done this."

Life's hardships remind us again and again that we are involved in a spiritual war. The fact that we cannot see the main protagonists at work does not lessen the reality of what is happening around us. Something we cannot see is trying to lead us away from faith in Christ. Faith in Jesus will always keep us in God's hands.

---

* "Louis Pasteur," Science History Institute, accessed April 5, 2021, https://www.sciencehistory.org/historical-profile/louis-pasteur.

Preparing the Soil

"Behold, a sower went out to sow."

—Matthew 13:3

For many people, summer means time spent in the garden. Nature's provisions brighten dining room tables and promote good health in those blessed to eat and enjoy.

Jesus used gardening and farming to describe the work of the kingdom of God and the process of growth in the grace of God. He likened the Word of God to seed. He equated the maturing of a Christian believer with the ripening of grain, and He compared His return to earth to gather His saints with an agricultural harvest.

Witnessing and soul winning are much like the process of gardening or farming. Jesus said, "Behold, a sower went forth to sow" (Matthew 13:3). He explained that "the seed is the word of God" (Luke 8:11). The sower sowed the Word of God in anticipation of realizing a harvest of those who would "bear fruit with patience" (verse 15).

A vital part of gardening is soil preparation. Instead of picking and eating beans or tomatoes, the gardener may end up with nothing simply because the soil had not been prepared. Soil that is too rocky, too sandy, lacks nutrients, or does not drain well can be impossible to successfully work.

One reason more souls are not won to faith in Christ is that spiritual harvesting often takes place where there has been little or no soil preparation. Few gardeners would plant seeds in unprepared soil and expect a harvest. But churches and church members frequently expect to harvest where there has been no work done to prepare the soil. Time spent in a community "building the soil" before planting takes place is time well spent. Developing friendships makes it more likely that the seed of the Word of God will take root. Acceptance of Bible studies or an invitation to church or a church program is much more likely when preparation has taken place beforehand. As important as it is in agriculture, soil preparation is even more important in evangelism. Prepared soil is far more likely to be fruitful soil.

Successful Methods

There are diversities of gifts, but the same Spirit.
There are differences of ministries, but the same Lord.
—1 Corinthians 12:4, 5

Among the final words He spoke to His disciples, Jesus instructed them to go make disciples of every nation. This instruction is also for us today. Personal evangelism should characterize the life of every believer.

My father planted a vegetable garden every year. He seemed to approach gardening in the same way our neighbors did—nothing out of the ordinary. The garden would be dug, seeds planted, the garden watered—the usual. But today, gardening takes on many forms. While some people plant seeds or seedlings directly into the ground, others use raised beds. Hydroponics grows plants in water, without the use of soil, while straw-bale gardeners plant directly into bales of straw. Each of these gardening methods can bring great success.

Reaching people with the gospel is much the same. There are many ways of sharing God's offer of the gift of salvation. Sharing literature can be a simple, inexpensive, and extremely effective way of sharing Jesus with others. Sharing videos via DVD or the internet brings many people to faith in Christ. An invitation to a small group meeting or a prayer meeting, a kind act of disinterested service, or an invitation to a Bible study or a church program can lead to a saving relationship with God. Great numbers of people have become followers of Jesus, whose first contact with the church was health ministry.

The person who doesn't feel he or she can give a Bible study might be able to make and share a loaf of bread or offer to go shopping for a sick neighbor. A person who enjoys knocking on doors might not feel suited to leading a small group. God gifts people in varying ways. If one method of sharing Jesus doesn't seem to work for you, another may. Just as a person finds a gardening method that works best for a certain situation, there are witnessing methods that work better for different people in different places. In Jesus' commission to go and make disciples is the assurance that He who sends also equips. Everyone may share Jesus. If everyone did, the church and the world would be very different.

Nurture

"Are not two sparrows sold for a copper coin? And not one
of them falls to the ground apart from your Father's will."
"Do not fear therefore; you are of more value than many sparrows."
—Matthew 10:29, 31

Anyone who grows a garden learns very quickly that putting a seed into the soil is far from the end of the process. Small plants are delicate and vulnerable, and they require a lot of nurture if they are ever going to be ready to harvest.

Plants need attention and care. They need to be watered regularly (but not over-watered). A garden must be weeded, and plants often need to be fertilized. Plants require sunlight, but the gardener must ensure plants do not get too much sun.

The same principles hold true in soul winning. People coming to faith in Christ must be carefully nurtured. They must be cared for in a way that speaks to their hearts and encourages growth toward Jesus. New believers must be watered and fed. Just as young plants need to be protected from the elements, new believers must be protected from the destructive elements that can exist in the church. A critical church member can easily discourage a new believer. Just as a young plant can be damaged by too much water or fertilizer, a baby Christian can sometimes be given too much information too quickly, with deleterious effects.

The church is to be a safe place for those who are growing in their faith in God. It is important that the church show a genuine interest in visitors to the church, kindly follow up on Bible study interests, and invest itself in encouraging those who are learning to leave the world behind to follow Jesus.

Jesus tells us we are of great value, and He wants us to show others the same care He shows us. Many people have turned away from faith in God simply due to neglect. Taking time to show you care can be the difference between an inexperienced believer succeeding or failing as a Christian.

Pests

*The Lord is faithful, who will establish you
and guard you from the evil one.*

—2 Thessalonians 3:3

It becomes painfully obvious when gardening that care must be taken to deal with pests. A day of inattention can result in a devastated garden. My wife and I were horrified to discover several of our tomato plants had been savaged by plump, green, very well-camouflaged hornworms, intent on complete destruction. All the effort we had put into growing our tomato plants would have been undone if we had not acted swiftly and decisively.

If it isn't hornworms, it might be flea beetles, cutworms, caterpillars, or cabbage worms. Or rabbits or raccoons or groundhogs. Or deer. Animals can devastate a garden, undo untold hours of hard work, and deprive a family of fresh, healthful food.

In evangelism and soul winning, the devil has invented innumerable "pests" that must be carefully dealt with lest new believers are consumed. Just as a plant cannot defend itself against a caterpillar or a rabbit and must be cared for by the gardener, new believers cannot always defend themselves against temptation. Christians of experience are needed to provide a safe environment in which young Christians can grow. Critics, conspiracy theorists, and mean-spirited people do the devil's work by causing offense and hurt and creating confusion.

Plants in a garden are naturally defenseless. On their own, they don't stand a chance against bugs or animals. Many gardeners surround their gardens with fences—sometimes electric fences—to keep out deer and other creatures. The battle against garden pests is serious. The battle against spiritual pests is much more serious.

While the best defense against garden pests may be spray or a fence, the best defense for new believers is prayer and love. When the church makes a concerted effort to provide a safe place for new believers to grow, they have a much better chance of surviving the attacks of the enemy of souls.

Paul assured us that the Lord is faithful to protect us from the enemy. God works through His people to defend the vulnerable from spiritual attack. God may want to use you to protect a new Christian finding his or her way to faith in God.

Don't Count Your Chickens

I planted, Apollos watered,
but God gave the increase.

—1 Corinthians 3:6

A person growing a garden learns quickly that it isn't wise to count one's horticultural chickens before they are hatched. Tiny plants poking their heads above the surface of the ground promise a harvest, but that promise—for a variety of reasons—is not always kept. A flowering plant may suggest prolific production, but that suggestion doesn't always become a reality. Soil, weather, carelessness, bugs, deer, or sometimes the inexplicable can conspire to cause a flowering plant to be all flower, no fruit. A mass of flowers can convince a gardener that a harvest is guaranteed, but a mass of flowers guarantees only a mass of flowers. While a thriving plant usually develops into a productive plant, such is not always the case.

This is yet another area where gardening illustrates evangelism. Many visitors to church promise to return—never to be seen again. The person who begins a series of Bible studies and attends church enthusiastically may appear to be a baptism in the making, but disappointment is sometimes the result. A meaningful conversation, a responsive neighbor or friend, or an invitation to a church event can give the impression that the journey to discipleship is beginning for the person concerned. But it does not always work out that way.

It is imperative that we remember when sharing our faith with others, the agent of transformation is never us but is always the Holy Spirit. The uncertainty of outcomes suggests we must continue to pray for those with whom we share the gospel and do all we can to lead a soul to surrender to Jesus. But Paul made it clear, when he wrote to the Corinthian church, that ours is to work, to pray, to share, to invite, to let our light shine. But it is God who wins a heart. We cannot see the end from the beginning, so we share our faith as intelligently and prayerfully as we are able and trust God with the results.

The Harvest

He shall see the labor of His soul, and be satisfied.
—Isaiah 53:11

Jesus commonly used agricultural metaphors to describe the work of the kingdom of God. The Bible frequently speaks of a coming harvest when Jesus returns to the world to gather the saved and take them to heaven (see Revelation 14:14–16).

Just as in gardening, the harvest makes soul winning worth all the time and effort invested. When a sunflower opens and brightens up a yard or when garden-fresh vegetables are served to eat, the energy that went into growing your food is recognized as being well worth it. Although evangelism can be challenging at times, seeing someone give their life to Jesus or rise up out of the waters of baptism beaming with joy reminds you that sharing Jesus with others is what life is really all about.

Winning souls can take time, and it demands care and resources that not everyone is willing to invest in. Love for others and the hope of the harvest kept Jesus on the front lines of evangelistic outreach. He came to this world "to seek and to save that which was lost" (Luke 19:10). He was familiar with Isaiah's statements that He would be "despised and rejected by men, a Man of sorrows and acquainted with grief" (Isaiah 53:3). The Holy Spirit had inspired the gospel prophet to write,

> But He was wounded for our transgressions,
> He was bruised for our iniquities;
> The chastisement for our peace was upon Him,
> And by His stripes we are healed (verse 5).

But the same chapter of Isaiah explains what kept Jesus going. Verse 11 tells us Jesus always remembered that people would be saved because He came to earth. That same thought motivates people today to share their faith. Not everyone will respond to the gospel as you might wish. Not every Bible study leads to conversion. But the harvest inspires us to keep sowing, keep watering, keep nurturing—to keep laboring in God's vineyard, knowing that one soon day there will be people in heaven who might otherwise have never had the opportunity to know Jesus as Lord and Savior.

Good for You

*"But you shall receive power when the Holy Spirit has come
upon you; and you shall be witnesses to Me in Jerusalem,
and in all Judea and Samaria, and to the end of the earth."*

—Acts 1:8

There are many good reasons to spend time working in a garden. Time invested in gardening typically means healthy, home-grown produce served for family and shared with friends. But even if there was no harvest, gardening would still be profitable.

Gardening is good for you. Time spent caring for plants is time not spent focusing on one's own problems or the problems of the world. Growing plants is an exercise in cooperating with the creative power of the Creator. The beauty of nature exerts a calming and healing influence. Gardening is good exercise, with time spent in a garden being good for both mind and body. And gardening comes with rewards. Fresh vegetables bring health and healing and promote a more abundant life.

In the same way, being involved in evangelism is simply good for you. Whether or not a person is won to Christ, the exercise of participating in outreach is good for the soul. Many an unhealthy church would enjoy vastly improved spiritual well-being if church members worried less about smaller issues and focused on the most important matters. And the most important issues of all are living to glorify God and sharing Jesus with those who do not know Him.

Fractured churches are almost always churches that do little outreach. The devil works to sidetrack churches because he knows how powerful a congregation could be if it focused on the Great Commission. And Satan knows how good ministry is for an individual's spiritual well-being, so he does all he can to distract people from growing spiritually through involvement in mission.

Jesus promised the power of the Holy Spirit for witnessing in Acts 1:8. One reason we see less of the power of the Holy Spirit in our lives and in our churches is that we often do little that requires the Holy Spirit's presence.

Although we strive for success, we labor for the Lord knowing that whatever the result, evangelism is simply good for you.

Green Thumbs?

"Return to your own house, and tell what great things God has done for you." And he went his way and proclaimed throughout the whole city what great things Jesus had done for him.

—Luke 8:39

I once hosted a weekly radio program that featured a gardening expert. This man was a long-time television presenter and the author of twenty books on gardening, so there was little he did not know about the subject. He took questions live, with no opportunity to prepare or research in advance, and provided reliable advice whether being asked about vegetables, potted plants, trees, or decorative bushes.

While knowledge certainly helps, you don't have to be an expert to successfully grow a garden. Anyone with a little space and sufficient time can grow a garden and produce fresh vegetables. A seed, soil, water, and sunshine are all that even the least experienced gardener needs to have success. Green thumbs are not necessary.

The same is true for evangelism. While we thank God that there are people who have great experience in sharing the Bible and for the experts among us who can answer every question, the fact is that anyone can share their faith. There is no need to wait until you reach a certain level of proficiency before you point someone to Christ.

Jesus was once confronted by a naked, demon-possessed man who for some time had been living among tombs. Even though the man had been bound with chains and kept under guard, he broke the chains and struck fear into the people nearby. According to the Bible, "many demons had entered him" (Luke 8:30).

When Jesus had cast the demons out of the man, he begged Jesus to be allowed to stay with Him. But Jesus told him to go home and tell people about the great things that God had done for him. And that's exactly what he did.

Jesus didn't tell him to read certain books or attend a certain class. He simply instructed him to tell others what Jesus had done for him. Training is good, but you don't need to be an expert to share your testimony or to point people to Jesus in some way. Jesus commissioned a man who moments before was demon-possessed. If He could use a man like that, He can definitely use you.

Patience

*Therefore be patient, brethren, until the coming of the Lord.
See how the farmer waits for the precious fruit of the earth,
waiting patiently for it until it receives the early and latter rain.*

—James 5:7

One quality every gardener must possess is patience. Plants do not grow or produce on anyone's schedule other than their own.

After planting seeds, time must pass before they spring up above the soil and develop into seedlings. Then they must develop further: they must grow and then flower. Waiting is an important part of the process, and even after fruit appears, one must wait yet longer for the fruit to ripen. The simple truth is that cucumbers are going to take fifty to seventy days until they are ready to be harvested. In most cases, tomatoes will take seventy to eighty days. Corn takes a minimum of sixty days. Lettuce may be ready in as little as forty-five days, while peas take ten or more days longer. And that's just how it is. Eggplant won't be ready to pick in thirty days, cabbages cannot be harvested in six weeks, and you can hope all you want that a pumpkin will be ready in two months or less, but they simply won't. Some things can't be hurried.

Evangelism is like that. Souls will be ready when they are ready, and they can't be hurried or rushed. At least, not healthily or successfully. Just as a plant needs time to absorb nutrients, a person needs time to absorb the Word of God. As some plants mature more quickly than others, some people come to a saving knowledge of Jesus more rapidly than others. While radishes can be picked for eating just twenty-five days after seeds are sown, Brussels sprouts can take six months and garlic eight. In the same way, some people come to faith quickly, while others take considerably longer.

Just as garden plants cannot be forced to mature early, saved disciples of Jesus can grow only as fast as they can grow. Patience is required to allow people to mature in faith according to God's timetable.

What's the Plan?

Then those who gladly received his word were baptized;
and that day about three thousand souls were added to them.

—Acts 2:41

Discovering we had planted far too many jalapeño plants in our garden, my wife and I had to figure out what we were going to do with all of them—especially as we don't typically eat jalapeños! The solution for an abundance of garden vegetables is usually to share your blessings. But it isn't always easy to give away a large number of jalapeños. The plants themselves were a lot of fun to grow, and we figured that the problem of overabundance of garden-grown food would be one of life's better problems. But it would have been better if we had planned ahead when we first planted the seeds.

When it comes to soul winning and evangelism, a similar question needs to be answered. How will you deal with an abundance of souls? What is the plan if you end up with more Bible studies, more visitors to the church, or more baptisms than you were expecting?

One church received a large number of Bible study interest cards as the result of a mailing to their community. Faced with an abundance of names to follow up as part of their evangelism prework, the church simply decided to do nothing. Many months after the cards came back to the church, several frustrated church members followed up on the leads only to discover that no one wanted to study the Bible. "We were waiting for someone to contact us," they were frequently told, "but seeing as no one did, we started studies with another church." Others said that so much time had passed that they were now simply not interested.

What do you do if an outreach event generates more interest than expected, or if a series of evangelistic meetings results in a larger number of baptisms than were anticipated? It is vital to have a plan to preserve the harvest. Otherwise, souls—like garden-grown vegetables—can go to waste.

Having a plan and sufficient people to carry it out ensures the gains won't be lost. It can be a challenge to win a lost person to Christ. Letting them slip away due to a lack of preparation or commitment should be strenuously guarded against.

Fake

"Not everyone who says to Me, 'Lord, Lord,' shall enter the kingdom of heaven, but he who does the will of My Father in heaven."

—Matthew 7:21

In the late 1980s, a German pop group raced to the top of the music charts around the world. Milli Vanilli sold seven million albums and won a Grammy Award for best new artist. The problem was that Milli Vanilli was not Milli Vanilli.

When producer Frank Farian met Rob Pilatus and Fabrice Morvan, he was convinced they could provide him with the "look" he needed to make the music of his group of session musicians attractive to the record-buying public. Although they appealed to music buyers and concertgoers, no one realized that Pilatus and Morvan never sang, either in the studio or during live appearances. But when they demanded to sing on the next Milli Vanilli album, Farian admitted the ruse to journalists, and the show was over. Milli Vanilli plummeted from fame to infamy.*

Fakery is everywhere. In the 1980s, the Getty Center in Los Angeles paid almost $10 million (close to $25 million today) for a *kouros*, an ancient sculpture of a young Greek male. The statue is no longer on display at the Getty as it is believed to be a fake.† Magazine covers routinely feature electronically enhanced models who have had their teeth whitened and straightened, their necks lengthened, their thighs and hips narrowed, and skin blemishes removed. Not even the models themselves look like their magazine portrayals.

But what happens when the fakery extends to the church? The problem is serious enough that Jesus spoke to it when He said, "Not everyone who says to Me, 'Lord, Lord,' shall enter the kingdom of heaven, but he who does the will of My Father in heaven" (Matthew 7:21). He went on to say, "Many will say to Me in that day, 'Lord, Lord, have we not prophesied in Your name, cast out demons in Your name, and done many wonders in Your name?' And then I will declare to them, 'I never knew you; depart from Me, you who practice lawlessness!' " (verses 22, 23).

God is willing to give every believer a truly genuine Christian experience. When Jesus lives His life in you, your experience will be real. Anything less than a life connected to Christ is less than what God wants for you.

---

* Brianne Tracy, "A Look Back at the Rise and Fall of Milli Vanilli 30 Years After Their Lip-Syncing Scandal," *People*, March 7, 2019, https://people.com/music/milli-vanilli-lip-sync-scandal-anniversary/.

† Isaac Kaplan, "The 'Getty Kouros' Was Removed From View at the Museum After It Was Officially Deemed to Be a Forgery," Artsy.net News via *The New York Times*, April 16, 2018, https://www.artsy.net/news.

The Ignored Memorial

The fruit of the righteous is a tree of life,
and he who wins souls is wise.

—Proverbs 11:30

The great Reformer and Bible translator William Tyndale died a martyr's death just outside Brussels in Belgium, half a mile (0.8 kilometer) away from a memorial erected in his honor in a city park. Today, that memorial is essentially ignored. William Tyndale is one of the most significant Christian figures of the last five hundred years, and the vast majority of people who walk past his memorial have no idea who or what the memorial is for. I met people living in the tiny English village where Tyndale ministered half a millennium ago who have no idea he ever lived there.

In 2002, Tyndale was ranked twenty-sixth in a BBC poll of the hundred greatest Britons to have lived.* That may seem like quite an honor, but the man who translated the Bible into English and irrevocably changed the English-speaking world placed behind John Lennon, Paul McCartney, Princess Diana, and Charles Darwin. Tyndale's scholarship influenced the King James Bible, which in turn had a huge impact on the English language. It is estimated that 83 percent of the content of the New Testament in the King James Bible was originally the work of William Tyndale and that 76 percent of what is found in the Old Testament translation in the KJV also came from the English Bible translator. "Passover," "scapegoat," "my brother's keeper," "the salt of the Earth," "it came to pass," "the signs of the times," "let there be light," "a law unto themselves" and many other phrases come to us from Tyndale's pen. His faithful work for God continues to bless people all over the world.

A life lived for God's glory lives on in other lives touched. Whether remembered or forgotten, William Tyndale's life still influences our world. And your life, whether widely known or quietly lived, can make a difference forever. Submit your heart to God today, and you can know that like William Tyndale, your influence will tell for eternity.

---

* "100 Greatest Britons (BBC Poll, 2002)," Geni, accessed April 5, 2021, https://www.geni.com/projects
/100-Greatest-Britons-BBC-Poll-2002/15375.

An Occasion for Testimony

*"But before all these things, they will lay their hands on you
and persecute you, delivering you up to the synagogues and prisons.
You will be brought before kings and rulers for My name's sake.
But it will turn out for you as an occasion for testimony."*

—Luke 21:12, 13

St. Andrews in Scotland is known the world over as the home of golf. The famous golf course hosts the British Open every five years or so. But St. Andrews is significant for far more important reasons. If you were to visit St. Andrews University—the school Prince William attended—you would see "P.H." set into the paving stones in the sidewalk outside St. Salvator's Chapel. In 1528, Patrick Hamilton was burned at the stake on that spot. He was twenty-four years old.*

Less than a quarter of a mile from St. Andrews University are the ruins of the old St. Andrews castle. Outside St. Andrews castle, the initials "G.W." are written in paving stones a couple of feet out into the street. In 1546, eighteen years and one day after Hamilton was martyred, George Wishart was burned at the stake on that spot. He was thirty-three. He brought the Reformation teachings of Zwingli and Calvin to Scotland and paid the highest price possible for doing so. Wishart knew all about what happened to Hamilton less than twenty years earlier, but that knowledge did not discourage him from preaching the Word of God.†

In an age when the gospel could rarely be heard, there were men and women who dedicated themselves to the proclamation of the Word of God, fearless of the consequences.

Jesus said that hardship and persecution would be "an occasion for testimony." If Hamilton and Wishart had lived regular lives, they would be long forgotten. But their faith and courage inspire us today to let God use us to make a difference for His glory. Wherever providence leads you, following God's leading in your life will make a difference for the kingdom of heaven.

---

* "A Brief History of St. Salvator's Chapel," St. Andrews University, accessed April 5, 2021, https://www.st-andrews.ac.uk/about/history/st-salvators/brief/.

† "George Wishart, 1513–1546," Wishart Society, accessed April 5, 2021, https://www.wishart.org/Legacy/george_wishart.html.

Gifted!

Having then gifts differing according to
the grace that is given to us, let us use them.
—Romans 12:6

I t often appears that the spiritual gifts that get people most excited are the more demonstrative gifts such as healing, miracles, or tongues. But every gift given by the Holy Spirit is as important as another.

Romans 12:6–8 says, "Having then gifts differing according to the grace that is given to us, let us use them: if prophecy, let us prophesy in proportion to our faith; or ministry, let us use it in our ministering; he who teaches, in teaching; he who exhorts, in exhortation; he who gives, with liberality; he who leads, with diligence; he who shows mercy, with cheerfulness."

Among the spiritual gifts mentioned by Paul is prophecy. John, the author of the book of Revelation, had the gift of prophecy, as did Noah and Elijah. Teaching is an important spiritual gift. The apostle Paul—who also had the gift of prophecy—certainly had the gift of teaching, as did Priscilla and Aquila. When Paul wrote to the Romans about spiritual gifts, he mentioned the gift of exhortation. Exhortation is "encouragement." Someone who thought they might simply have had a sunny personality may well be missing the point that they have been specially gifted by God. Some people have that special way about them. After speaking with them, you're ready to climb a mountain, or you feel as though you have faith like Abraham.

If you have accepted Jesus as your Lord and Savior and been baptized, God has endowed you with spiritual gifts. The Holy Spirit has come into your life, bringing not only the personal presence of Jesus but also heaven-given abilities that enable you to represent Him and share His love and light with others. It isn't humility that says, "I don't have any spiritual gifts." It's a serious misunderstanding of the Bible. Use your talents and your God-given gifts for the Lord. He has equipped you to make a difference for His glory.

Spiritual gifts are given by God for the upbuilding of the church and for effectively representing Jesus to the world. You have been privileged by God to be used of heaven to draw people to Him.

The City That Changed the World

"We ought to obey God rather than men."

—Acts 5:29

Sixty miles or so southwest of Frankfurt, Germany, is a city with a population of about fifty thousand. While it doesn't often make the news today, what happened almost five hundred years ago at Speyer—or Spires—inexorably changed the world and bequeathed to us the word *Protestant*.

The emperor of the Holy Roman Empire was determined to crush the Reformers and end their work, to return society to where it was before Martin Luther started speaking in favor of the Bible and against the abuses and false teachings of the ruling church. A council in Speyer in 1526 had given German states full religious liberty, permitting people to believe and teach as they pleased. But in 1529, another council was convened for the purpose of undoing the decree of 1526. There was to be no religious liberty. People—and certainly states—would be compelled to follow and accept the teachings of the church.

There was intense pressure on the princes to vote in favor of this directive. Would they acquiesce to the wishes of the emperor? Would they surrender to the demands of the church of Rome? They did not and instead gave to the world the two great principles of Protestantism: conscience is above the magistrate, and the Word of God is above the dictates of the visible church. In other words, a person should have the right to follow God as she or he sees fit.*

The Reformers were advocating a biblical principle. Many hundreds of years before, a council in Jerusalem instructed the apostles that they should not teach in the name of Jesus. Peter responded by saying, "We ought to obey God rather than men" (Acts 5:29). That biblical principle holds today, and things would be very different if not for what happened in Speyer almost five hundred years ago. One's faith must never be subject to the dictates of government or another person. Freedom of faith is a God-given right. It is imperative that religious liberty be valued. Remember the bold stand made long ago by the Reformers, which enables us to believe and worship freely today.

---

* Ellen G. White, *The Great Controversy Between Christ and Satan* (Mountain View, CA: Pacific Press®, 1950), 197–204.

Fast and Loose

*The name of the L*ORD *is a strong tower;*
the righteous run to it and are safe.

—Proverbs 18:10

An Indian magician attempting a trick made famous by Harry Houdini was lowered bound by a chain and six locks into a river in Kolkata. He had successfully performed similar tricks many times, but on this occasion, the stunt didn't go as planned. The magician's lifeless body was recovered more than half a mile (a kilometer) downstream. The selfie generation has produced story after story of people who have taken risks in the pursuit of a memorable photo, only for things to go terribly wrong. Three American teenagers were killed by a train as they took a selfie beside a railroad track. The last photo they uploaded to Facebook before they died showed the train that killed them in the background. The caption read, "Standing right by a train hahaha, this is awesome!!!!"

In September 2020, a British woman fell from a moving car onto a freeway. She was filming a video while hanging from the open passenger door of the car. Police were astonished she survived.

We hear stories like these and marvel at the reckless behavior, but people do the same thing spiritually all the time. "I'll leave the church and go my own way." "I'll dabble with this sin." "I'll take this spiritual risk." "I know I shouldn't, but I'll do it just this once." It's easy to forget that as long as we are in this world, we are in a life-and-death battle. It's unwise to play fast and loose with salvation.

I lived for some years in a volcanic zone well known for its geothermal activity. Hot water bubbled up out of the ground, and steam escaped from subterranean vents. Signs warned people to stay on the marked trails under any and all circumstances. To do otherwise would be to invite serious injury or death. There is spiritual safety only in Jesus. To take unnecessary risks is to gamble with your salvation. It is always wisest to stay close to the Lord.

Got Milk?

*Love one another fervently with a pure heart, having
been born again, not of corruptible seed but incorruptible,
through the word of God which lives and abides forever.*
—1 Peter 1:22, 23

Founded in the 1960s, the community of Findhorn, thirty-five miles (fifty-six kilometers) northeast of Loch Ness in the north of Scotland, became well-known globally as a New Age enclave. It attracted attention because of the giant vegetables that were grown there. It was claimed early in Findhorn's existence that the vegetables grew so large owing to the intervention of spirits.*

With as many as twenty hours of sunshine a day, the state of Alaska has produced some monster veggies. A man in Palmer, Alaska, set a record in 2012 when he grew a cabbage weighing more than 138 pounds. Before he installed an electric fence, he would stay up all night to guard his garden against hungry moose.†

God wants His children to grow into strong believers with firm faith and unshakable trust in Him. Peter wrote in 1 Peter 2:2 that we should "desire the pure milk of the word, that you may grow thereby." There is life-giving power in the Word of God. Just as milk nourishes babies and gives them the strength they need to grow healthy and strong, the Word of God contains all we need to grow in the grace of God.

The person who feeds on the Word of God will be strengthened spiritually. Reading the Word of God will fortify the mind, uniting the human with the divine. Studying the Word of God not only develops a taste for the things of heaven but also serves to wean a believer off the empty things that don't represent Christ or trend in His direction. While gardeners have their secrets for growing prize-winning vegetables, the secret for the believer is not a secret at all.

Jesus described Himself as "the bread of life" (John 6:35). We receive Jesus as we receive Him in His Word. A person with an inconsistent Christian experience may find that he or she is neglecting the Word of God. God grows and strengthens us through His Word.

---

* "About the Findhorn Foundation," Findhorn Foundation, accessed April 5, 2021, https://www.findhorn.org/about-us/.

† "Alaska Man Rolls Record Cabbage Out of the Patch," NPR Interview with Melissa Block, accessed April 5, 2021, https://www.npr.org/2012/09/04/160562400/alaska-man-rolls-record-cabbage-out-of-the-patch.

John Huss

So shall I have an answer for him who
reproaches me, for I trust in Your word.

—Psalm 119:42

John Huss (Jan Hus) was born in 1369 in what we know today as the Czech Republic. Influenced by the teachings of John Wycliffe, in a time without Bible's when tradition had caused deep spiritual darkness to descend upon the world, Huss believed a person's faith ought to be founded on the Word of God. His opposition to the established church led him to be burned at the stake, and as the flames consumed him, he sang praises to God.

Completed in 1391, Huss's church, the Bethlehem chapel, still stands in Prague today, a memorial to the Reformer's faithful service to God. Huss ministered in the church from 1402 until his execution in 1415. A statue of Huss still stands in Prague's Old Town Square, just a quarter of a mile from the church where he faithfully labored. While the Czech Republic today has perhaps the highest percentage of nonbelievers in Europe, the statue of the Bohemian martyr testifies that great men and women of God have answered God's call and stood up to change the world. Like Huss, many have paid a huge price for their faith.*

Even in today's relatively peaceful times, God is looking for men and women willing to live with the focus and commitment of John Huss. David wrote that God's Word "is a lamp unto my feet, and a light unto my path" (Psalm 119:105, KJV). Our dark world is in desperate need of divine light.

The decline of Christianity is an opportunity for the church. While research indicates there are currently fewer believers, more atheists, and more who are religiously unaffiliated than ever before, the Bible promises us that "this gospel of the kingdom will be preached in all the world as a witness to all the nations" (Matthew 24:14). The task given to the church includes the promise that God is going to reach every last person on the planet with the good news. His people have the privilege of being used to share Jesus with a needy world. Earth stands on the brink of something truly spectacular. All who are willing can join with His Spirit in God's great, final work.

---

* "Jan Hus," New World Encyclopedia, accessed April 5, 2021, https://www.newworldencyclopedia.org /entry/Jan_Hus.

The Morning Star

The entrance of Your words gives light;
it gives understanding to the simple.

—Psalm 119:130

Year after year, the Bible is the best-selling book in the world. But until the Reformers stood up and reintroduced the world to the Word of God, people were unable to access the teachings of Jesus and the writings of the prophets.

England's John Wycliffe has been called the Morning Star of the Reformation. His ministry as a theology professor and pastor was strenuously opposed by the church of Rome, which did all it could to silence Wycliffe forever. But God had other plans for Wycliffe, who produced the very first English translation of the Bible. In the late 1300s, producing a Bible was difficult and expensive, so the creation of Wycliffe's translation did not mean English Christians could now access the Word of God at will. But the Bible did reach people who otherwise would never have been exposed to Scripture and paved the way for later translations.*

The world of Wycliffe did not immediately change owing to his work as a Bible translator. Almost 150 years after Wycliffe's death, bitter hostility toward the Bible was still leading people to martyrdom. In Coventry, England, a monument stands today as a memorial to a group known as the Coventry Martyrs. One of them was a Mistress Smith, who was found to be in possession of handwritten copies of the Lord's Prayer, the Ten Commandments, and the Apostles' Creed. Mistress Smith was burned at the stake for her "crime."†

Religious freedom came slowly in Britain, but it eventually did come. Wycliffe's work in bringing the Bible to the nation was an integral and important part of that change.

David wrote, "The entrance of Your words gives light" (Psalm 119:130). The world still needs light, a revelation of Jesus, a demonstration of the power of God's Word. Political reforms cannot do for society what the Word of God can do. Scripture brought about change in the time of the Reformers. The light of God's Word is still the change needed by the human heart.

---

* Ellen G. White, *The Great Controversy Between Christ and Satan* (Mountain View, CA: Pacific Press®, 1950), 79–96.

† John Foxe, *Foxe's Book of Martyrs: The Actes and Movements of the Church* (United Kingdom: G. Virtue, 1851), 247–248.

With an Old Man?

"The grass withers, the flower fades,
but the word of our God stands forever."

—Isaiah 40:8

I t hasn't always been the case that the Bible is freely available. And those who worked to make it so were often persecuted ruthlessly by the church of their day. The ruling church of his day tried to have Bible translator John Wycliffe condemned to the stake. During one of the several occasions he was put on trial for his beliefs, he said to his accusers, "With whom are you contending? With an old man on the brink of the grave? No! With truth—truth which is stronger than you and will overcome you."*

Wycliffe wasn't burned at the stake while he was alive, but forty years after he died, his body was exhumed by the church, and his remains were burned. His ashes were cast into the River Swift, which flows a little more than a quarter mile south of St. Mary's church in Lutterworth—where Wycliffe ministered—before emptying into the Avon River.† Wycliffe made a powerful point. God's Word is truth, and God's truth will triumph.

Critics of the Bible have many times proclaimed its imminent demise. German philosopher and atheist Friedrich Nietzsche famously declared that "*Gott ist tot*" (God is dead). While a philosophical statement rather than a theological position, Nietzsche's 1882 proclamation expressed his view that philosophy had demonstrated not that a living God had died but that governments no longer needed to be organized around the idea of the existence of God. Nietzsche claimed God was no longer needed as the source of morality or order.‡

The famous English scientist Stephen Hawking had an IQ of 160, yet he was an avowed atheist. He said belief in heaven was a "fairy story for people afraid of the dark."§ Hawking died in 2018. While he believed there is no God, what is incontrovertible is that there is now no Stephen Hawking.

As Isaiah wrote, God's Word stands forever. Stand on the Bible, and you will stand forever too.

---

* James A. Wylie, *The History of Protestantism*, book 2, chapter 3, quoted in Ellen G. White, *The Great Controversy Between Christ and Satan* (Mountain View, CA: Pacific Press®, 1950), 90.

† Ellen G. White, *The Great Controversy Between Christ and Satan* (Mountain View, CA: Pacific Press®, 1950), 95, 96.

‡ Friedrich Nietzsche, *The Gay Science*, quoted in Scotty Hendricks, " 'God Is Dead': What Nietzsche Really Meant," Big Think, August 12, 2016, https://bigthink.com/scotty-hendricks/what-nietzsche-really-meant-by -god-is-dead.

§ Lydia Warren, "Stephen Hawking: 'Heaven Is a Fairy Story for People Afraid of the Dark,' " *The Daily Mail* (UK), last updated May 17, 2011.

Fanaticism

"He who touches you touches the apple of His eye."

—Zechariah 2:8

F anaticism never helps the work of the gospel. While Martin Luther was teaching people to base their faith on the Word of God, certain ones rose up, claiming people need not follow the Bible but instead rely on personal revelations from God. They claimed it was sufficient for a believer to rely on feelings, on what they individually felt or thought to be right.*

Lest we think such ideas disappeared into the annals of history, similar ideas still permeate Christianity. I recently spoke with a young lady attending an evangelistic series I was conducting who agreed with the messages being presented, but she told me that she needed to wait until she felt impressed within herself that the Bible's teachings were for her. "The Spirit speaks to me about these things," she told me. "When that happens, then I can believe."

In the church, we witness a similar dynamic. With alarming frequency, people choose not to adhere to a certain doctrinal position taught by the Bible but instead go their own way in opposition to the body. While we recognize that the church is not the final arbiter of truth—that role is filled by the Holy Spirit—an immense amount of damage is done when individuals gather a group after their own teaching and lead that group in opposition to biblical truth.

While disagreements among Christians seeking a deeper understanding of the Bible are inevitable, there can be no place for disunity in the church. Iron sharpens iron, and a differing viewpoint need not be harmful. But disagreement and disagreeability are two starkly different things. When factions splinter away from the body to promote doctrines counter to the church's understanding of the Bible, great damage is done. This is modern fanaticism. Those who draw people away from the church to establish rival groups are not doing the work of God. God said, "He who touches you touches the apple of His eye." Fanaticism in the church is an attack on God Himself.

---

* Ellen G. White, *The Great Controversy Between Christ and Satan* (Mountain View, CA: Pacific Press®, 1950), 186.

Captured!

For we can do nothing against the truth, but for the truth.
—2 Corinthians 13:8

It can take some time for God to work out His plans. And the passage of time can cause discouragement if we allow it to do so. The church has been proclaiming the imminent return of Jesus for more than 150 years. For some, this seems to be evidence that there is something faulty about the message. But consider: In Genesis 12, God promised Abram that He would make of him a great nation. The book of Genesis continues with the stories of Abraham, Isaac, and Jacob. The story of Joseph covers the final eleven chapters of Genesis, and at the time of Joseph's death—three hundred or so years after the promise was made to Abraham—Israel is not a great nation and has not arrived in "a land that I will show you" (Genesis 12:1).

An enslaved Israelite suffering under the oppressive hand of a tyrannical Egyptian taskmaster as he or she made bricks without straw may well have concluded that Abraham was mistaken and that God would never make a great, free nation out of Israel. But that discouraged laborer could not have known deliverance was only days or weeks away, a deliverance so remarkable that we would be talking about it almost four thousand years later.

On his way from the Diet of Worms to his home in Wittenberg, Martin Luther was captured. A disaster! He was spirited through the forest and locked up in a castle. Luther's enemies were thrilled that he was out of their hair. But even though he didn't realize it at the time, Luther had been captured by friends. And while in that castle, he not only wrote tracts but also translated the New Testament into German. Luther was physically out of circulation, but through his pen, he was preaching perhaps louder and more clearly than ever before. God's hand was over Luther's situation, and He was working it out for the furthering of the gospel.*

"We can do nothing against the truth." You can trust that no matter what your circumstances may be at present, God ultimately has it all worked out for the best.

---

* Ellen G. White, *The Great Controversy Between Christ and Satan* (Mountain View, CA: Pacific Press®, 1950), 168, 169.

"I Can Do No Other"

Therefore take up the whole armor of God, that you may be able to withstand in the evil day, and having done all, to stand.
—Ephesians 6:13

When Martin Luther stood before an important council of religious and political leaders in the town of Worms in Germany in the year 1521, representatives of the Holy Roman Empire demanded that he retract what he had written about the Bible. In particular, they were incensed by what he had said about justification by faith and the Bible's teaching on the subject of salvation.

To press on would almost certainly mean death for Luther, while to retract would be to severely damage the cause of God. Luther is said to have spoken to that august assembly and stated, "I cannot, and I will not retract, for it is unsafe for a Christian to speak against his conscience. Here I stand, I can do no other; may God help me. Amen."*

On a daily basis, Christians are confronted by the same temptation that assailed Martin Luther at the Diet. In reality, the stakes were no higher for Luther than for anyone facing temptation today. While Luther appeared before a conclave determined to take his life, believers today are assailed by an enemy committed to separating us from *eternal* life. Paul wrote that "the wages of sin is death" (Romans 6:23). When temptation comes, no person is really choosing between sobriety and alcohol, violence and calmness, dishonesty and honesty, or immorality and purity. Temptation brings us the choice between life and death, between surrender to Jesus and selfishness.

The decisions we make daily to either resist temptation or to yield to temptation ultimately form the character. They set us on a pathway to either cooperation with the Holy Spirit or enmity against God. When temptation comes, God is calling every believer to stand in the face of temptation in the same way Martin Luther stood in the face of his bitter accusers at the Diet of Worms. Strengthened by the indwelling presence of the Spirit of God, we are enabled to stand boldly for Christ in the face of any opposition.

---

* J. H. Merle D'Aubigne, *History of the Reformation of the Sixteenth Century,* quoted in Ellen G. White, *The Great Controversy Between Christ and Satan* (Mountain View, CA: Pacific Press®, 1950), 160.

Faulty People

All have sinned and fall short of the glory of God.
—Romans 3:23

The Protestant Reformation was led by some of the truly great figures of history: men such as the Bohemian Reformer John Huss; John Wycliffe, the Morning Star of the Reformation; and John Knox, the Scottish Reformer, who famously prayed, "Give me Scotland, or I die." Mary Queen of Scots said, "I fear the prayers of John Knox more than all the assembled armies of Europe."* There were also John Wesley, founder of the Methodist movement, and William Farel and John Calvin, who championed the Bible in Geneva, Switzerland.

It is not an exaggeration to say these individuals changed the world. But it would be an exaggeration to say they were perfect people. When the Anabaptist Felix Manz was sentenced to death for the crime of baptizing by immersion, Ulrich Zwingli approved of his execution. While Zwingli is considered a giant of the Reformation, it is clear he was a faulty giant. Many people are rightly troubled by anti-Semitic statements made by Martin Luther, who is undeniably one of history's most influential figures. So how is it that people as flawed as Zwingli and Luther were used by God to do such an important work?

The answer is found in the history of the great figures of Scripture. David's catalog of sins includes adultery and murder. Moses was a murderer who hid the body of his victim in a callous attempt to cover up his crime. Solomon had serious moral issues, while James and John were willing to incinerate the inhabitants of a Samaritan village. That God chose to use these individuals in a way that altered history offers us encouragement today.

The Bible is clear that we have all sinned and fall short of reflecting God's glory. But God uses faulty people, which means He can use you. No one who hears the voice of God has gone too far that he or she cannot do a great work for God. If you are weak, commit both your weaknesses and strengths to God. God is both willing and able to use you for His glory.

---

* Burk Parsons, " 'Give Me Scotland, or I Die'," Ligonier Ministries, accessed April 6, 2021, https://www.ligonier.org/learn/articles/give-me-scotland-or-i-die/.

Indulgences

What do you have that you did not receive? Now if you did
indeed receive it, why do you boast as if you had not received it?
—1 Corinthians 4:7

The question of indulgences was one of the major issues that sparked the Protestant Reformation. The Roman Catholic church taught that indulgences reduced the amount of punishment a person must endure on account of his or her sins. Venerating a statue, observing a certain holy day, visiting a church or cathedral on a certain date, or giving money to the church were among the ways people could procure indulgences. Each was a means of lessening suffering for sins.

The cynical selling of indulgences in Wittenberg by churchmen raising money for the construction of Saint Peter's Basilica so incensed Martin Luther that he boldly challenged the church to reform. Of the Ninety-Five Theses that Martin Luther nailed to the door of the castle church in Wittenberg, Germany, more than one-third referenced indulgences.* Thesis twenty-one states, "Hence those who preach indulgences are in error when they say that a man is absolved and saved from every penalty by the pope's indulgences."† Luther was clear that the blessings of God cannot be bought, earned, or in any way bargained for.

While the Roman Catholic church still grants indulgences today, it is worth pondering whether a subtle, yet no-less-deadly, form of indulgences exists in Christianity. The person who believes he or she will receive favor from God based on this act or that good deed is surely seeking to earn an indulgence. The Christian who thinks eating certain foods or making a particular lifestyle change will earn the blessing of God is perhaps not a disciple at all, but rather a customer, hoping to purchase salvation from a god who sells it.

While it is true that positive dietary choices and appropriate lifestyle changes should characterize the Christian life, it is imperative to remember that receiving the gift of salvation is not dependent upon good deeds. Salvation is received by grace through faith in Jesus Christ. After coming to faith in Christ, a believer will undoubtedly grow in his or her experience. While few Protestants would admit to believing in righteousness by works, carefully examining one's relationship with God might reveal that some of us are not as far out of Babylon as we might think.

---

* Ellen G. White, *The Great Controversy Between Christ and Satan* (Mountain View, CA: Pacific Press®, 1950), 126–130

† Martin Luther, *Ninety-Five Theses*, no. 21, quoted by Mark Gstohl, Xavier University of Louisiana, accessed April 6, 2021, https://cat.xula.edu/tpr/works/95/.

Imprudent

"Behold, I send you out as sheep in the midst of wolves.
Therefore be wise as serpents and harmless as doves."
—Matthew 10:16

During the Reformation, a group of French Protestants posted placards in certain locations across France criticizing the Catholic Mass. It isn't difficult to understand why Protestants couldn't accept the Mass as being consistent with the Word of God. But the result of this protest demonstrates that imprudence in sharing one's point of view can have calamitous results.

One of the placards was placed on the door of the bedchamber of the French king, Francis I. Unsurprisingly, the king was furious. In response, he ordered the extermination of anyone suspected of being sympathetic to Martin Luther's teachings. While the Protestants were on the right side of the theological issues, the *Affaire des Placards* was on the wrong side of wisdom and tact.*

So how does one balance the need to speak the truth with the responsibility of exercising decorum and grace? The answer is, prayerfully. God frequently prescribes a certain course of action. King David was directed by God not to build a temple (1 Chronicles 17:4). God told Joshua not only to attack the city of Ai but also the manner in which he should attack (Joshua 8:1, 2). Paul was forbidden to preach the Word of God in Asia (Acts 16:6) but was instead instructed by God to go to Macedonia (Acts 16:9). Many a mistaken believer has acted "because God told me to," when God issued no such instructions.

There is much in the world that is out of harmony with the Word of God. Even in the church, we find that which falls short of God's standard. How are we to address such situations? Paul recommended "speaking the truth in love" (Ephesians 4:15).

Peter cut off an ear while intending to cut off a head! James and John wanted to burn down a village. But Jesus' way is different. The zeal that inspired French Protestants to attack the king's deeply held beliefs was misplaced and resulted in ruin. While fear of consequences should not be our guide, concern for appropriately representing Jesus should. Stand for Jesus all you can, but always share the truth in love.

---

* Ellen G. White, *The Great Controversy Between Christ and Satan* (Mountain View, CA: Pacific Press®, 1950), 224, 225.

God's Detour

"It was not you who sent me here, but God; and He has made me a father to Pharaoh, and lord of all his house, and a ruler throughout all the land of Egypt."

—Genesis 45:8

John Calvin had been educated for the priesthood. When first confronted with Reformation theology, he bristled at the suggestion that he had been living in error. But conviction gripped his heart the day he witnessed a condemned heretic being burned at the stake in a public square. Calvin marveled at the peace and courage demonstrated by the victim while he himself was living in despair and darkness. A cousin of Calvin had once told him, "There are but two religions in the world. . . . The one class of religions are those which men have invented, in all of which man saves himself by ceremonies and good works; the other is that one religion which is revealed in the Bible, and which teaches man to look for salvation solely from the free grace of God."* Calvin found hope in the atoning sacrifice of Christ, accepting that the blood of Jesus alone could wash away his sins.

In 1536, John Calvin—now won to Protestantism but driven from his native France—was traveling to his home in Basel, Switzerland, when circumstances caused him to detour through Geneva. William Farel met Calvin and convinced him that the Reformation needed Calvin's help, and another Reformation leader was begotten by the Spirit of God. The detour through Geneva was an inconvenience to Calvin, but it was ordered by God and resulted in advancing faith in the Bible as the Word of God.

There might be occasions when your life meets with unforeseen detours. After visiting his brothers as they worked, Joseph found himself transported to Egypt and sold as a slave. A detour. But when Joseph met his brothers in Egypt, he said, "It was not you who sent me here, but God" (Genesis 45:8). Being separated from his family and his home was a tragedy, but God was working through those unfortunate circumstances to save His people.

It might be that God is working through your misfortune. Where we see problems, God sees something greater. Learn to see the hand of God in your circumstances. What you see for evil, God might see for good.

---

* Ellen White, *The Great Controversy Between Christ and Satan* (Mountain View, CA: Pacific Press®, 1950), 220.

The Reformation Wall

To him who does not work but believes on Him who
justifies the ungodly, his faith is accounted for righteousness.
—Romans 4:5

The International Monument to the Reformation, or "Reformation Wall," in Geneva, Switzerland, stretches for 110 yards (101 meters) and features ten major Reformation figures. William the Silent was a Dutch Reformer whose son became the king of England in the late seventeenth century. Roger Williams advocated for religious liberty and the separation of church and state and founded the colony of Rhode Island. The four main figures represented on the wall are William Farel, John Knox, John Calvin, and Theodore Beza, who succeeded Calvin following his death. The statues of each man stand sixteen and a half feet (five meters) tall.

The statue of Farel is unique in that Farel—who once described himself as "more popish than popery"—is depicted with his fist clenched, a reference to his uncompromising manner. Farel incited people to destroy idols, statues, and images found in churches in Geneva, and the Mass itself was abolished. In another city, he snatched an image of Saint Anthony out of the hand of a priest and threw it off a bridge into a river. He was fortunate to escape with his life.

Farel was run out of the city of Basel for his strident criticism of the Catholic Church, and along with Calvin, was banished from Geneva. His preaching has been described as "full of fire and fury." Theodore Beza said that Farel's words were "like thunder."

The man with the clenched fist was a man who wasn't afraid of swimming upstream. While the church was putting people to death, Farel stood boldly in defense of the Bible as the only rule of faith and practice, proclaiming the righteousness of Christ, received by faith, as the hope of the believer. Earlier in his life, a mentor told him, "It is God who gives us, by faith, that righteousness which by grace alone justifies to eternal life."* Farel's mentor was banished from his country owing to his views, but his counsel made an impact on Farel, who would not remain silent. May God give His people today the wisdom to know when it is time to speak.

---

* Ellen G. White, *The Great Controversy Between Christ and Satan* (Mountain View, CA: Pacific Press®, 1950), 212.

Punishable by Death

So shall My word be that goes forth from My mouth;
It shall not return to Me void,
But it shall accomplish what I please,
And it shall prosper in the thing for which I sent it.

—Isaiah 55:11

In many countries that today are considered civilized and advanced, it was once illegal to read the Bible. In some cases, it was illegal to hear the Bible being read, to preach the Word of God, to talk about the Bible, or even to pray to God in secret. Such "offenses" were punishable by death.* But in spite of bitter persecution, the truth flourished. It was said that the blood of the Christian martyrs was seed.† The early Christian church thrived in the midst of tremendous opposition.

There is something about difficult times that calls the best from the hearts of believers. Peter spoke to this when he wrote in 1 Peter 4:12, 13, "Beloved, do not think it strange concerning the fiery trial which is to try you, as though some strange thing happened to you; but rejoice to the extent that you partake of Christ's sufferings, that when His glory is revealed, you may also be glad with exceeding joy." James wrote, "My brethren, count it all joy when you fall into various trials, knowing that the testing of your faith produces patience. But let patience have its perfect work, that you may be perfect and complete, lacking nothing" (James 1:2–4).

In the book *Thoughts From the Mount of Blessing*, we read on page 10, "The trials of life are God's workmen, to remove the impurities and roughness from our character. Their hewing, squaring, and chiseling, their burnishing and polishing, is a painful process; it is hard to be pressed down to the grinding wheel. But the stone is brought forth prepared to fill its place in the heavenly temple. Upon no useless material does the Master bestow such careful, thorough work. Only His precious stones are polished after the similitude of a palace."‡

It is fascinating that it is the "precious stones" that are polished. As difficult as trials may be to endure, God knows that the challenges that confront the church are ultimately for the good of the church. God may be glorified, even in life's most bitter challenges. He is always present. Trials, which often push people away from God, are designed to draw us to Him.

---

* Ellen G. White, *The Great Controversy Between Christ and Satan* (Mountain View, CA: Pacific Press®, 1950), 239, 240.

† Tertullian, *Apology*, paragraph 50, quoted in White, 42.

‡ Ellen G. White, *Thoughts From the Mount of Blessing* (Mountain View, CA: Pacific Press®, 1955), 10.

How Long?

*"That evil servant says in his heart,
'My master is delaying his coming.' "*

—Matthew 24:48

G od promised Abram that his descendants would be a great nation and occupy the promised land. Yet four hundred years later, Israel had not yet entered Canaan. For more than two hundred years, God's people were in Egypt, and for much of that time were pressed into slavery. Ultimately, God's people escaped Egypt, but for hundreds of years, the promise of entering a land that flowed with milk and honey was nothing more than a dream.

An enslaved Hebrew struggling to find straw to use in the manufacture of bricks may well have wondered whether God's promise would ever be fulfilled. That Hebrew undoubtedly heard his grandparents tell him that *their* grandparents lived in the hope of entering the Promised Land. But all those years later, Israel's prospects seemed bleaker than ever. Although God kept His promise and Israel was liberated from captivity, for generations, the promise made to Abram may have seemed an impossibility.

Today, people may be tempted to feel the same way. An elderly friend told me about a letter he came across, written by his father to his mother during World War II. "I am convinced there is little time left until Jesus returns," the man wrote, "for I have seen man's inhumanity to man, and it is great." The better part of a century later, we are still here on earth and very much not in heaven. But the fact that Jesus has not yet returned does not mean He will never return. Jesus said it was the "evil servant" who said, "My master is delaying his coming" (Matthew 24:48).

The waiting time on this side of the second coming of Jesus is, in reality, a manifestation of the mercy and goodness of God. If Jesus had returned a generation ago, not one of today's younger generation would be saved. If Jesus returned yesterday, there would be no more tomorrows in which we could share the gospel with others. For now, Jesus waits. This tarrying time is a time for personal preparation and for sharing Jesus with those who do not yet have the assurance of salvation. The promise is certain. Let us not lose heart as we wait for Jesus' return.

Now!

*And this is the testimony: that God has given us eternal life,
and this life is in His Son. He who has the Son has life;
he who does not have the Son of God does not have life.*

—1 John 5:11, 12

While shaking hands after the early service one Sabbath morning, I remarked to a dear lady, "And the good news is that Jesus is coming soon!"

She replied, "Pastor, I just hope I'm ready."

Holding on to her hand, I looked into her eyes and asked, "What was that you just said?"

She could tell I was concerned. "I said, I hope I'm ready when Jesus comes back. Did I say something wrong?"

"Yes, I really think you did," I said, shepherding her to the side of the church foyer. "Did you say you 'hope' to be ready when Jesus comes back?" I asked her. She answered in the affirmative.

"Now, why would you say such a thing?" She paused, so I went on. "Let me ask you this. Are you a Christian?" She told me she most certainly was.

"Do you love the Lord?" She assured me she did.

"Have you surrendered your life to Jesus?" She said she had, first doing so when she was a little girl.

"Do you have a drinking problem?" I enquired. Her eyes opened wide.

"No! I surely don't!"

"Boyfriends?" I asked. "Is it boyfriends?"

"Pastor!" she answered, a shy smile on her face.

"So what you're saying is you've accepted Jesus as your Lord and Savior, and you've never changed your mind?"

"That's right," she said.

"Well, neither has He," I said. "So from now on, let's not 'hope' to be ready for Jesus' return. Instead, 'believe' you're ready and thank Him that salvation is yours. What do you think?" She thought that would be a good idea.

Salvation is a gift that we have the moment we accept it. There is no need to "hope" to receive a gift you have already received. John says, "You may know that you have eternal life" (1 John 5:13). There is nothing more important than knowing you have salvation. If you have yielded your life to Jesus, salvation is yours. Now.

Converted?

"He who believes in the Son has everlasting life;
and he who does not believe the Son shall not see life."

—John 3:36

Every time I have asked a congregation whether or not they believe they have been converted, the response has been muted. One person might say "Amen"; another person coughs and half-says "Amen," while most people look like deer caught in the headlights, unsure what to say or where to look. There might be several reasons for this. It could be that someone knows that should he or she say, "Amen, I'm converted," they will be asked by their spouse after church why a converted person doesn't act with more kindness. Some people manifest what they feel is humility and say, "Well, I wouldn't want to go so far as to say I'm converted, but . . ." The same holds true when one asks a group of people whether they are saved and have everlasting life.

While my experience may be anomalous to that of others, I have found it is uniformly the case that when asked if they are saved, the vast majority of people *in the church* will not state that, yes, they possess the gift of everlasting life.

It is not humility that prevents a person from confidently claiming they have everlasting life but bad theology. Ephesians 2:8 could not be clearer: "For by grace you have been saved through faith." While the King James Version says, "For by grace are ye saved through faith," this refers not to a manner of process but to a state of being. By grace, you are saved—or "have been saved"—"through faith." Paul was not undecided on the subject of salvation. He categorically stated that those who have accepted Jesus as Lord and Savior possess the gift of salvation and "have been saved."

Believing one has possession of the gift of salvation does not lead a person to laxity in spiritual matters. The knowledge of salvation instead produces in the believer gratitude and confidence. There is no place for uncertainty in salvation. God does not want His children to wonder whether they might ever go to heaven. If you have accepted Jesus, you have everlasting life.

God Hears

In my distress I called upon the LORD,
And cried out to my God;
He heard my voice from His temple,
And my cry came before Him, even to His ears.

—Psalm 18:6

There were times during the life of David when he found himself in difficult places. David fled from King Saul, met rebellions and insurrections, resisted enemies, and waged battles. Consider David's prayer, "In my distress I called upon the LORD, and cried out to my God; He heard my voice" (Psalm 18:6). Notice what David says and what he doesn't say. He was in distress. He called upon God. God heard him. But David says nothing about God answering his prayer. God is not heard saying, "David, I've got your back." Yet David is not swayed. He tells us he cried to God, and God heard him. That was all the assurance David needed. God heard him.

You pray for Grandma to get well or to retain your job or that your child arrives home safely. It might be that you get what you ask for, and it might be that you do not. We don't always understand why God permits one thing while not permitting another, but we can know that God hears. Every single prayer, God hears. Pray for a friend or for your children to come to faith in Christ, and you can know God heard that prayer. Pray for someone who is gravely ill, and you have the assurance God heard that prayer. You can trust God and leave your petitions and concerns with Him. When you pray, God hears your prayer.

Were there prayers David prayed that were not answered in the way he desired? Of course. There is no doubt David prayed for Absalom, but Absalom was killed in battle and died a rebel. David spent a week praying for his sick child, but the child did not recover and died. Ours is to pray. God's is to hear—which He always does—and to answer according to His perfect will. Knowing that God hears is enough. We can trust His heart and know that in every situation, He will do what is best.

Warning Signs

"So you also, when you see all these things,
know that it is near—at the doors!"

—Matthew 24:33

One Christmas Day in the Southern Hemisphere, I walked to the beach along with a group of my vacationing family members. It was a warm, sunny day, and the azure-blue water was beckoning. But we were confronted by a large sign that said, "Marine stingers are dangerous. Do not swim in these waters between October and April." Box jellyfish are a major problem in the warmer waters off the Australian coast. Their many tentacles are covered with half a million or so little cells that can each inject venom. We read the sign thoughtfully, recognizing that December 25 very definitely falls between October and April.

My brother's father-in-law had an idea. "I heard on the radio just this morning that the box jellyfish haven't arrived in the area yet," he said, "so I think we should be OK." We looked at the water, felt the day getting warmer, noticing windsurfers and boats on the shore, and reasoned we were not the only ones who had entertained the same idea. We made a decision. We would ignore the sign.

I windsurfed while my brother and his children swam. Suddenly, my five-year-old nephew let out a blood-curdling scream. He was paddling in shallow water close to the beach when a box jellyfish attached itself to the back of his hand. As my brother rushed him to an aid station, my nephew said in desperation, "Daddy, I don't want to die!"

My nephew survived the experience with a minimum of drama, although, for years afterward, he had a scar on the back of his hand that reminded all of us of the importance of not ignoring signs. In Matthew 24, Jesus gave us signs of His return and said that when we see them fulfilling, we can know that His return is near, "even at the doors" (verse 33).

The signs Jesus gave us are not to be ignored. They are invitations to take Christ's offer of salvation seriously and to share that same offer with others. The signs speak to us clearly. Jesus is coming back soon. Now is the time to surrender your heart to Him and be ready for history's greatest event.

Clickbait?

Then Jesus said to those Jews who believed Him, "If you abide in My word, you are My disciples indeed. And you shall know the truth, and the truth shall make you free."
—John 8:31, 32

This fascinating age in which we live has presented us with challenges we didn't face a generation ago. Because the business model for internet news involves convincing readers to click on stories, news websites often run headlines you wouldn't have seen years ago. Fewer clicks mean less revenue, so outrageous, provocative, and sensational headlines vie for your attention. Clickbait has become a way of life, as news sites do whatever they can to induce you to consume their content and keep your attention for as long as possible.

This phenomenon of style over substance has forced society to navigate a confusing and often misleading maze of truth, half-truths, and mistruths. News and entertainment have blended to become infotainment, which grabs the attention but often fills a person's head with the intellectual equivalent of junk food.

A cynic might say internet news agencies learned this trick from the church, which for years has in many quarters been more about the butter and less about the bread. "It's a miracle!" attracts worshipers while the Word of God is too often little more than an accessory after the fact. "God is going to shower you with blessings, and the money is going to flow" is often heard, when in reality, Jesus never promised that everyone would be wealthy. The Bible warns about the love of money while big-name preachers solicit donations for private jets. Churches strive to have excellent music, while excellent Bible teaching may be unfortunately absent. Pleasing interpretations of Scripture are popular without necessarily being biblical. Popular churches will be full for an hour a week, but Christians are often indistinguishable from non-Christians.

Jesus said that knowing the truth and its freedom comes from abiding in His Word (John 8:31, 32). Christianity isn't about clickbait. Christianity has substance. God wants to do more than excite our attention. Discipleship is surrender to Christ, not selfishness masquerading as morality. You don't want to confuse the frosting for the cake in matters of faith. Real faith in God is never superficial.

Pride

"He must increase, but I must decrease."

—John 3:30

You can't usually see it, and by the time you do, it has often done great damage. The Bible speaks strongly when it says in Proverbs 16:5, "Everyone proud in heart is an abomination to the LORD." Self-centered pride—as opposed to pride in the accomplishments of your children, for example—is rarely the subject of sermons, and few books or articles are written on the subject. Yet it was pride that brought sin to earth after a prideful angel said in his heart,

"I will ascend into heaven,
I will exalt my throne above the stars of God;
I will also sit on the mount of the congregation
On the farthest sides of the north;
I will ascend above the heights of the clouds,
I will be like the Most High" (Isaiah 14:13, 14).

Pride in the heart of Lucifer led to rebellion, and that rebellion ultimately caused the death of Jesus and the ruin of the world.

Pride is satisfaction at one's own accomplishments, an inflated opinion of one's own importance. Pride is bound up with self-centeredness, ego, conceit, and self-sufficiency, and it is destructive. In other words, pride is antithetical to the gospel of Jesus, who "did not come to be served, but to serve, and to give His life a ransom for many" (Matthew 20:28). Pride is self-seeking, and when led by a desire for self-elevation, recognition, or praise, people can be led into some unfortunate places. Pride says, "Me first. I want it my way. My thoughts are best. I am right. I won't back down."

In the book *Early Writings*, Ellen White said, "If pride and selfishness were laid aside, five minutes would remove most difficulties."* Fortunately, the statement implies that pride *may* be laid aside. Focusing on the life, ministry, and death of Jesus is the cure for pride. Studying the life of One who came to serve rather than to be served will change a heart. It is by beholding that we become changed. Looking to Jesus will cause us to echo the thoughts of John the Baptist, who said, "He must increase, but I must decrease" (John 3:30).

---

* Ellen G. White, *Early Writings* (Washington, DC: Review and Herald®, 1945), 119.

AUGUST

On Vacation

Every day I will bless You, and I will
praise Your name forever and ever.

—Psalm 145:2

This is a time of year when many people are on vacation, visiting family or friends, enjoying the beauty of nature, or recharging before heading back to school. A sign outside a church during one holiday season said, "Did you take your Bible on vacation, or are you on vacation from your Bible?"

It is easy to get caught up in the busyness of life and allow the most important things to be squeezed out. David didn't contemplate missing a day of prayer. He didn't take time off from his spiritual life because his faith in God *was* his life.

One thing Satan has masterfully accomplished over the last six thousand years is the invention of distractions to keep us from prayer and reading and studying the Bible. Interestingly, people are actually working less and sleeping more today than they were fifty years ago. But the proliferation of mobile phones, high-speed internet access, streaming movies, video games, and so much more means that people have never been so distracted. Downtime often isn't downtime.

Life is demanding. If you have to cut something, the last place you should cut is your devotional life. It is worth squeezing some other area of life to make sure you have time to connect with God every day. Jesus said in John 15:5, "Without Me you can do nothing." A branch or stem connected to a vine can be healthy and thriving, but after it is severed from the vine, it takes no time at all to wither and dry out. Disconnected from Jesus, we do the same.

Vacations are good for the body and soul. But time off should never be time off from Jesus. If we're careful to bless God "every day" as David did, we will surely praise His name "forever and ever."

August 2

Love Makes a Difference

"By this all will know that you are My disciples,
if you have love for one another."

—John 13:35

S hortly after I met her for the first time, streams of tears flowed down her face. She wiped them away with the palms of her hands. And she said something I will never forget.

Evelyn was raised by a physically abusive father, who once kicked her so hard she was permanently injured. His death made life no easier for Evelyn because she was left to be raised by her abusive mother. Following her husband's death in a tragic accident, Evelyn had no family support and felt as though she had nothing to live for. She decided to end her life and meticulously planned her last day on earth.

Then the doorbell rang. Two young ladies were conducting a community survey, and Evelyn was happy to answer their questions. Yes, she believed in God. Yes, she was raised going to church. And . . . yes, she would be interested in Bible studies. The women returned and opened the Bible with Evelyn and introduced her to the Savior they knew so well. She saw what her life could be through faith in Jesus. She attended church and accepted an invitation to an evangelistic series that was soon to begin.

When I met Evelyn toward the end of the series, she told me she would "love to be baptized and become part of God's remnant church." She said, "I had nothing and no one, and felt as though there was no good reason to live. But you people loved me." It might have been the best thing anyone has ever said about a church family. "You people loved me." Love made the difference in Evelyn's experience. I wondered to myself how much the church could do if it pleaded with God for opportunities to demonstrate the love of Jesus.

The last time I saw Evelyn, she came up out of the waters of baptism with her arms raised above her head in triumph. Evelyn had planned to take her life. Instead, Jesus took her life and made it His own.

Brand New

*Therefore, if anyone is in Christ, he is a new creation; old things
have passed away; behold, all things have become new.*
—2 Corinthians 5:17

Although the evangelistic series had only been running for four nights, Jason was insistent. "I need to be baptized. And I don't want to wait. I can't wait. Will you baptize me?" Jason had begun to study the Bible and had accepted Jesus as his Lord and personal Savior. His wife had helped him understand the teachings of Scripture, and he was ready to make a decision. The baptistry was in place and filled with water. And in two days, Jason was going to jail.

He said he had made some unwise decisions in the past and had been sentenced to four months in the county jail. "I have to pay my debt to society," Jason told me. "But I want to go in there as a Christian, having given my life to Jesus." The next night, Jason was baptized. He spoke from the baptistry about how his life spiraled downward after his brother died young. He urged people not to delay but to make a decision for Jesus. And twelve hours later, Jason was in jail.

Twelve months passed, and I was sent a photo of a young man I didn't recognize. He was clean-cut, wore glasses, a shirt, and tie; and looked like a model in an ad for a mortgage brokerage or an insurance company. Knowing I was supposed to know who this was, I looked and looked again. "No way!" I said. "It can't be. Can it?!" It was Jason, out of jail eight months and now the pastor's right-hand man at his local church. Jason was active, involved, and doing all he could to serve the Lord and the church.

It seems Paul was writing about Jason's situation when he wrote, "If anyone is in Christ, he is a new creation" (2 Corinthians 5:17). Jason and countless others like him are evidence that God is truly able. Don't give up on those who make bad decisions. God can turn lives around, just like He turned around Jason.

Growing Pains

For the earth yields crops by itself: first the blade,
then the head, after that the full grain in the head.

—Mark 4:28

P astor," the young man said earnestly, "I don't think I can go to heaven. I don't think I can be saved." He explained to me that he loved God, was very much a part of his local church, and read his Bible. "But there are still sins in my life, and I've been told that I won't be ready for salvation until I have put every sin out of my life."

"You still sin?" I asked. He nodded.

"Welcome to the human family," I said warmly.

Sin should never be taken lightly. The wages of sin is death. And the Bible is clear that there is power in Jesus to "keep [us] from falling" (Jude 24, KJV). As Ellen White wrote in *The Desire of Ages*, "The plan of redemption contemplates our complete recovery from the power of Satan. Christ always separates the contrite soul from sin. He came to destroy the works of the devil, and He has made provision that the Holy Spirit shall be imparted to every repentant soul, to keep him from sinning."*

But as I explained to the young man, coming to faith in Jesus does not make you the finished article. A baby isn't born walking, tying her shoelaces, or riding a bicycle. These things come with *growth*. I suggested to my friend that, when he accepted Jesus as his personal Savior, he was clothed with the perfect righteousness of Jesus. Growing through one's weaknesses does not mean a believer is not a child of God, any more than a child is not cut off from his or her parents because he mistook yellow for orange or called an apple a pear. Understanding and accepting that Christians must grow just as trees grow does not minimize the devastating effects of sin. But failing to understand the principles of Christian growth can devastate a believer wrestling with his or her inadequacies.

Jesus explained that Christian growth is a process, just as a plant starts as a seed, then sprouts to a seedling that ultimately reaches maturity as a grown plant. Even if you are experiencing growing pains, keep your eyes on Jesus, and grow.

---

* Ellen G. White, *The Desire of Ages* (Mountain View, CA: Pacific Press®, 1940), 311.

Receiving Righteousness

And I said, "Let them put a clean turban on his head."
So they put a clean turban on his head, and they put
the clothes on him. And the Angel of the LORD stood by.
—Zechariah 3:5

A remarkable passage in the book of Zechariah presents important details regarding the plan of salvation. Satan stands at the right hand of Joshua, the high priest, accusing him on account of his sin when God does a fascinating thing.

Joshua was "clothed with filthy garments." God said, "Take away the filthy garments from him." Then God spoke to Joshua himself. "See, I have removed your iniquity from you, and I will clothe you with rich robes" (Zechariah 3:3, 4). The symbolism is obvious. Joshua's dirty clothing represented his own sinfulness, his own righteousness. As Isaiah the prophet wrote in Isaiah 64:6, "All our righteousnesses are like filthy rags."

The unrighteous man stands before God, and God removes the man's iniquity, represented by the filthy garments. Next, the following order was issued. "Let them put a clean turban on his head." And the command is obeyed. "So they put a clean turban on his head, and they put the clothes on him. And the Angel of the LORD stood by" (Zechariah 3:5).

Joshua stood before God as a sinner, covered in "filthy robes." When Joshua's inter-action with God was completed, Joshua stood before God with clean garments—representing the righteousness of Christ—and a clean head covering indicating he had experienced a change of mind. The question we must ask is, "What did Joshua do to receive the righteousness of Christ?" The answer is, nothing at all. In fact, it was what Joshua did *not* do that is instructive. Joshua did not resist. Joshua did not put up a fight. Nor did he say, "I'm not deserving of this great blessing. I'm too great a sinner." Joshua yielded to the will of God, and when he did, God took away his sin and clothed him in His own righteousness.

God is willing to do the same today for every sinner. Salvation is received as we surrender to the will of God. It is God's will that we shall be saved and not lost. God is waiting to clothe any willing sinner with His righteousness. We will never deserve it, we can never earn it, but we may receive it. God extends to us the most precious gift we could ever receive.

Four Key Words

Let this mind be in you which was also in Christ Jesus.
—Philippians 2:5

The plan of salvation offers hope to all of humanity. At least, it should. Sadly, even many Christians are uncertain as to whether or not they actually have the gift of salvation. A powerful passage from the book *The Desire of Ages* helps us understand how to view this correctly. And everything hinges on just four words.

> All true obedience comes from the heart. It was heart work with Christ. And if we consent, He will so identify Himself with our thoughts and aims, so blend our hearts and minds into conformity to His will, that when obeying Him we shall be but carrying out our own impulses. The will, refined and sanctified, will find its highest delight in doing His service. When we know God as it is our privilege to know Him, our life will be a life of continual obedience. Through an appreciation of the character of Christ, through communion with God, sin will become hateful to us.*

We notice several things. God calls for "true obedience." But how to render that "true obedience" is where many believers come unglued. Four key words reveal how "true obedience" can be experienced in a Christian's life. The author writes, "And if we consent." *Consent* means "to allow" or "to give permission." If we give God permission, the following happens. He will "identify Himself with our thoughts and aims." He will "blend our hearts and minds into conformity to His will." And He will do that to such an extent that obedience will simply be the result of "carrying out our own impulses." We will find our "highest delight in doing His service," and "our life will be a life of continual obedience." Further, "sin will become hateful to us."

What incredible promises! And how does this come about? "If we consent." When we allow God to do so, He does all that we just read. If we give God permission, He will continue to change us so that we grow more and more into the image of Christ.

God does the work. We grant the permission. As we surrender to Jesus, our lives become what they could never be without Him living His life in us.

---

* Ellen G. White, *The Desire of Ages* (Mountain View, CA: Pacific Press®, 1940), 668.

Yield

Know ye not, that to whom ye yield yourselves servants
to obey, his servants ye are to whom ye obey; whether
of sin unto death, or of obedience unto righteousness?
—Romans 6:16, KJV

On April 9, 1865, the Civil War effectively ended when General Robert E. Lee and the Army of Northern Virginia surrendered at the McLean House in the village of Appomattox Court House, twenty miles east of Lynchburg, Virginia.[*]

Perhaps the most famous surrender ceremony in history was the Japanese surrender on September 2, 1945. It took place in Tokyo Bay on the deck of the battleship USS *Missouri*. Representatives from Japan and the Allied nations signed a formal document of surrender, and World War II was over.[†]

There is a war that rages in every human heart, and it continues to rage until surrender is made. According to Paul, every person is the servant of one of two powers—sin or obedience. Serving sin leads to eternal death, but serving obedience leads to righteousness and everlasting life. An individual gets to choose which master he or she wishes to serve.

Paul stated a person is the servant of the one to whom he or she "yields," or surrenders. There is no compulsion to serve Christ. We are free to choose to serve Him or not. In entertaining the temptation of the serpent, Adam and Eve yielded to his suggestion and chose the path that leads to death. Every person who ever chose the service of sin made a decision to surrender to sin. Choosing to surrender to Jesus brings about a very different outcome.

Every time you are assailed by temptation, the Spirit of God calls you to yield to Jesus instead of sin. Temptation presents us with a choice. When we yield our hearts to Jesus, He fills us with His presence and leads us in His way. If we choose not to yield to Jesus, another power takes possession of our lives. To surrender to Jesus is to choose everlasting life.

---

[*] "McLean House," National Park Service, accessed April 6, 2021, https://www.nps.gov/apco/learn/education/mclean-house.htm.

[†] "Surrender," Battleship Missouri Memorial, accessed April 6, 2021, https://ussmissouri.org/learn-the-history/surrender#.

Eyes Wide Open

Then the word of God spread, and the number of the disciples multiplied greatly in Jerusalem, and a great many of the priests were obedient to the faith.
—Acts 6:7

As I shared the message, I noticed a man in the congregation looking at me intently. It was clear he was thinking hard about what he was hearing. I could almost see the wheels turning in his mind. I was a young evangelist, speaking in a high school auditorium in the Pacific Northwest, and that night I was sharing what the Bible says about the judgment and the 2,300-day/year prophecy. Emmett was sitting forward, listening carefully, taking in and weighing every word. Toward the end of the presentation, his demeanor changed noticeably. His eyes opened wide. It looked as though he had made a discovery. He smiled, sat back in his seat, looked at his wife, and nodded.

He later told me he had never before heard anything like what he heard that night—a prophecy about Jesus, anchored in history, connecting the Old Testament with the New, pointing to the baptism, death, and high-priestly ministry of Jesus Christ—all in harmony with a divine timeline. The message changed him. His whole family deepened their understanding of the Bible and their relationship with Christ and were baptized. Emmett told me it was the truth of the Word of God that made the difference. "How could we do anything else?" he said. "We want to serve and honor God, so we want to follow the Bible."

When the message of the Bible is proclaimed, it is inevitable that lives will be touched. The great English preacher Charles Spurgeon likened the Word of God to a lion. He said that those who wished to defend a lion "should kindly stand back, and open the door, and let the lion out! I believe that would be the best way of defending him, for he would take care of himself; and the best 'apology' for the gospel is to let the gospel out."*

Share the gospel, and lives will be changed. Proclaim the Word of God, and people will respond to the drawing of the Holy Spirit.

---

* Charles Spurgeon, "Christ and His Co-Workers," sermon from *Metropolitan Tabernacle Pulpit*, vol. 42, The Spurgeon Center, accessed March 14, 2021, https://www.spurgeon.org/resource-library/sermons/christ-and-his-co-workers/#flipbook/.

The Search for Meaning

For I consider that the sufferings of this present time are not worthy
to be compared with the glory which shall be revealed in us.
—Romans 8:18

When evangelist Jason Morgan was conducting meetings in the southwestern United States, a well-to-do man began attending the nightly series. Don was highly educated and had a very demanding role with a major multinational company. But his success did not prepare him for the challenge he was now facing. Don had been diagnosed with colon cancer and had begun to look for real meaning in his life.

As the meetings progressed, Don found assurance in the Bible, and he found meaning through faith in Jesus. Don was anointed during the meetings, and when the series concluded, he gave his heart fully to Jesus and was baptized. Not long after his baptism, Don received word from his physicians. To their surprise, Don was cancer-free. No trace of the disease could be found in his body. Don had not only received a new lease on his physical life but also received the gift of everlasting life. Regardless of what happened with Don's health, he had the assurance that he was going to live forever.

Major changes in a person's life often lead them to reconsider their life's direction and to reorder their priorities. A friend told me that during the last days of his brother's life, his brother found great comfort in reading the Bible, even though he had kept God at arm's length for much of his life. Illness, loss, financial pressures, and a whole host of challenges we would rather not be confronted with can bring us to the place where we allow God into our lives. No one wishes for hardship, but hardship will draw us to Jesus if we seek God in life's challenging times.

Paul said that our present suffering isn't even worthy of being compared with the glory that will be revealed in us. In eternity, no one will find fault with God for what afflicted us while on earth. If we look for God in life's trying times, we will find He is near and willing to uphold and bless us.

With You

*"And lo, I am with you always,
even to the end of the age."*

—Matthew 28:20

Life-altering challenges can have one of two effects. A difficult trial can cause a person to become angry with God. It isn't unusual for someone to say, "Why would God do this to me? Why has God allowed this?" For someone who thinks it is God's role to prevent all hardships from occurring, a bad diagnosis or a family tragedy can be tremendously destabilizing.

Margaret was a young mother when her daughter Shona died at just a few days old. Margaret, a church member, was devastated. She couldn't understand why God—who could have prevented the death of her baby—allowed her precious child to fall asleep in death. Margaret turned her back on God. Consumed by anger toward God, she left the church, stopped reading the Bible, and made her way in the world without God in her life.

Forty years later, Margaret buried another child. Daryl was thirty-eight years old and a committed Christian when he died of cancer. This time, Margaret spoke to God. She said, "It's OK. I understand. He's going to be with You throughout eternity." She thought about how she would like to see both of her children again.

When Margaret watched *Hope Awakens*, an online It Is Written evangelistic series, her heart was touched. "I decided it wasn't worth staying away from God for even another day, and I made the decision to surrender my life to Jesus." Margaret was baptized and immediately became active in her church. She became involved in service projects and shared her testimony with others.

Margaret allowed her first devastating trial to pull her away from God. When disaster struck a second time, she realized that staying away from God was only hurting her. She believed God could carry her through her trial, and she experienced His comfort, strength, and healing. Margaret is now ready to meet Jesus as well as Shona and Daryl.

God is with us even when we hurt. Jesus said, "I am with you always" (Matthew 28:20). Even when life's road seems too difficult to walk, Jesus is with you.

Differing Outcomes

Trust in the LORD with all your heart,
and lean not on your own understanding.

—Proverbs 3:5

In Acts 12, the fledgling Christian church was under relentless attack. Not only was hatred of the religious establishment directed against the followers of Jesus, but also the state had also begun to persecute Christians. The chapter begins by saying, "Now about that time Herod the king stretched out his hand to harass some from the church." Verse 2 states that "he killed James the brother of John with the sword." Realizing that his actions "pleased the Jews, he proceeded further to seize Peter also" (verse 3). "But constant prayer was offered to God for him by the church" (verse 5), and in answer to those prayers, an angel led Peter out of prison to freedom. James was executed, but Peter walked free. The question is often asked, "Why does God protect, or heal, or help one person but not another?" The answer is that there is no perfect answer, at least not one that truly satisfies the questioning of the human heart.

In spite of being shot in the leg, Patience Carter survived the mass shooting at the Pulse nightclub in Orlando, Florida, in 2016. In a poem she wrote after the attack, she said, "The guilt of feeling lucky to be alive is heavy. It's like the weight of the ocean's walls crushing, uncontrolled by levees."* Patience Carter could easily have died in the sickening attack that left fifty others dead—that she didn't seems almost random.

Such is often the case. A car is hit by a drunk driver. One child miraculously survives the accident while the rest of the family perish. Can we accuse God of injustice or unfairness? Two cancer patients, one funeral. Same illness, but different eventualities.

It isn't possible to unravel the mystery of differing outcomes. But it is possible to trust God in all things. The philosophers in our midst might hypothesize that James was spared an even worse fate or that he may have turned from God had his life been prolonged. The truth is, we cannot know. And we can choose to trust God and believe that eternity will reveal that He always made the right decisions.

---

* Katie Zezima and Kevin Sullivan, " 'The Guilt of Being Alive Is Heavy,' Survivor of Nightclub Shooting Says," *Washington Post*, June 14, 2016, https://www.washingtonpost.com/politics/the-guilt-of-being-alive-is-heavy-survivor-of-nightclub-shooting-says/2016/06/14/ac366268-3251-11e6-8ff7-7b6c1998b7a0_story.html

Why Me?

You do not know what will happen tomorrow. For what is your life?
It is even a vapor that appears for a little time and then vanishes away.
—James 4:14

When Alvin was diagnosed with cancer, he and his family were told by doctors there was a very real chance he might not survive. With a wife and three young children, cancer seemed to be an extremely cruel blow. The dreams he and his wife had of traveling together, of raising their children and pursuing their promising careers, were in serious danger of coming to naught. But where some may have been discouraged, Alvin and Lisa were not. Instead, they prayed that whatever happened to Alvin, God would be glorified.

Alvin never once asked, Why me? "It seemed like an inappropriate question," Alvin told me. "If I was to ask why something bad was happening to me, then surely I would have to ask why so many good things have happened to me. Why did I marry such a wonderful woman? Why me? Why were we given three beautiful, healthy children? Why was I never badly injured in an accident, and why have I never been to jail? I've been healthy all my life, I have had wonderful friends, I was raised by loving parents who stayed with each other all their married lives. If I'm going to ask why I got this disease, as though God is at fault, surely I would have to ask why I was blessed to live such a charmed life."

James says life is "a vapor that appears for a little time and then vanishes away" (James 4:14). I have asked many people who have lived to the age of one hundred how long it took them to get there. Every one of them has said, "Not long." Life is short. Eternity, on the other hand, is a very long time. Charging God with unfairness because of the circumstances of our brief sojourn on this planet is to ignore the incredible blessings He bestows upon us. There is no question that life can present some overwhelming challenges. It is in moments like those that we can lean on God, trust in His faithfulness, and look forward to an eternity without sickness or death.

The Dentist Knew

*"The LORD does not see as man sees; for man looks at
the outward appearance, but the LORD looks at the heart."*
—1 Samuel 16:7

Calvin enlisted to serve his country during World War II. He joined the navy, completed basic training in San Diego, and headed to the Pacific to join the fight against Japan. Calvin saw heavy fighting at Guadalcanal in the Solomon Islands. He was injured when his ship, the *South Dakota*, took more than forty direct hits.

While manning a gun, shrapnel from an exploding bomb tore through his jaw, knocking out his front teeth. He fell three stories onto a cold steel deck but staggered to his feet to attend to some of the thirty-eight men who had been killed and the sixty who were wounded. But Calvin wasn't like all the other servicemen on the *South Dakota*. He was different. Calvin Graham was twelve years old.

He had lied about his age in order to enlist in the military. While he managed to fool the navy recruiters, there was one person he couldn't trick—the dentist. As Calvin attempted to pass himself off for seventeen, the dentist looked into his mouth and said, "You're only twelve years old!" But Calvin had stood in line behind a boy who was fifteen years old and another who was fourteen. Because the dentist let them through without protest, Calvin argued that he too should be permitted to serve. Tired of arguing, the dentist waved Calvin on.

It wasn't his mother's forged signature that gave Calvin away. Nor was it his youthful looks. Many a baby-faced serviceman has looked younger than his age. The dentist could see what others could not, and when he looked at Calvin's teeth, he knew the truth about Calvin.

It isn't hard to hide the "real" you from others. A congregation that sees you praying up front in church, singing in the choir, or taking up the offering might believe you are ready for translation. But God doesn't see only what others see. He is able to look into the heart and see the real you. You can't fool God. And there isn't any need to. God accepts you as you are, loves you as you are, and by His grace can make you what you can never make yourself.

Miracles

"Ask, and it will be given to you; seek, and you will find;
knock, and it will be opened to you."

—Matthew 7:7

Finances and family issues were crushing Natasha. So when she saw a billboard inviting people to call and request Bible studies, she wondered whether this was an opportunity to find clarity in her life. When she called the number, a pastor answered. She told him she was calling about the Bible studies being advertised on the billboard. "What billboard?" the pastor blurted out before catching himself and saying, "Oh yes, the billboard." The church had never rented a billboard, nor had the pastor ever publicized his number. It was clearly a miracle. Before long, Natasha was studying the Bible with the pastor, and Jesus was bringing peace and clarity into her life.

God says, if we call, He will answer. And He promises to show us "great and mighty things" (Jeremiah 33:3). Miracles really should not surprise us. The God of heaven opened the Red Sea, carpeted the ground with manna, and caused water to flow from a rock. The same God still lives and still works miracles of divine grace. The sick are still healed. Financial blessings are still received. What you might call coincidence is, in reality, God's providence. He brings together circumstances and details in a way that could never be orchestrated by human wisdom. Someone once said that coincidence is God's way of remaining anonymous.

It is right to expect much from God. John Knox asked God to bring an entire country to faith in Jesus.* George Müller once asked the blessing on food he did not have, while three hundred hungry children bowed their heads. Minutes after Müller said "amen" at the conclusion of his prayer, there was a knock on the door. A baker delivered bread for the orphans—bread he felt impressed to bake the night before. Then there was another knock. This time, it was a milkman whose cart had broken down outside the orphanage. He wondered if Mr. Müller could use the milk for the orphans.†

God is still the God of miracles. He still performs miracles to draw human hearts to His own.

---

* Burk Parsons, " 'Give Me Scotland, or I Die'," Ligonier Ministries, accessed April 6, 2021, https://www.ligonier.org/learn/articles/give-me-scotland-or-i-die/.

† "George Müller, Did You Know?" Christian History Institute, accessed April 6, 2021, https://christianhistoryinstitute.org/magazine/article/did-you-know-mueller.

Patient

The longsuffering of our Lord is salvation.
—2 Peter 3:15

D on received a flyer in the mail advertising a series of Bible meetings. When he attended and discovered the meetings were presented by It Is Written, he remembered that forty years earlier, he had attended It Is Written meetings conducted by an evangelist named George Vandeman. At that time, he didn't make the decision to surrender his life to Jesus. But, this time, he yielded his heart to Christ, was baptized, and joined the church. Forty years is a long time, but God patiently waited for Don to come to faith in Jesus.

Pat prayed for her husband, a faithful Roman Catholic, for thirty-seven years. Pat was hopeful Sal would choose to follow the teachings of the Bible and trust in Jesus alone for his salvation. For many years he attended church with Pat and their children on the Sabbath and still attended Mass on Sunday. After his retirement, Sal began volunteering at It Is Written. After attending an evangelistic series, Sal told Pat he wanted to talk with her. "I can't do this anymore," he said. Pat was concerned. Did Sal no longer want to go to church with her? She held her breath. "I'm going to stop going to Mass on Sundays." Sal was baptized a few months later.

Peter wrote that "the longsuffering of our Lord is salvation." God could have turned His back on the human family after Adam and Eve fell in the Garden of Eden. If He had done so, not a single being in the entire universe could have found fault with His decision. Yet God continues to work on the hearts of those who have not yet come to Him. God is gracious and, in His mercy, appeals to the lost to respond to the pleading of the Holy Spirit.

God is patient. We don't want to presume upon that patience, but God's longsuffering should encourage us to continue working for the salvation of our friends and family. He is still drawing them to come to Him in faith.

August 16

Worth It

Behold, now is the accepted time;
behold, now is the day of salvation.

—2 Corinthians 6:2

The Crawfords were happy to have someone come to their home each week and study the Bible with them. Roy was an elder in his church and patiently opened God's Word, explaining passages and answering questions. Bill, Kath, and their seven children enjoyed the film strips he showed.

Roy's church family prayed for his weekly Bible study, and Roy reported periodically about how things were progressing. Roy was hopeful the Crawfords would choose to follow Jesus and become a part of the church family.

But it wasn't to be. Bill explained to Roy one night that while they all appreciated the studies very much, there was no need for Roy to return. Bill was clear that the Crawford family had made their decision. Roy was heartbroken. There was nothing anyone could do.

Almost forty years later, when Bill was confined to his home owing to emphysema, Kath was driving into town with her daughter, Dawn, who by now was close to fifty years old. As a radio station faded in and out, they heard an advertisement for a series of public meetings dealing with Bible prophecy and decided they would attend. They noticed the opening night message had a familiar ring to it. Before long, they were convinced. These people *must* be from the same church as that nice man, Roy, with whom they had studied the Bible four decades earlier.

When I spoke to Kath, Dawn, and Dawn's sister, Judy, they told me they had accepted Jesus as their Lord and Savior and were serious about following Him. They began keeping the Sabbath as soon as they heard it mentioned in the meetings. "And we want to be part of God's remnant church," they told me emphatically.

Kath and her two daughters were baptized, while Bill—by now in very poor health—joined the church by profession of faith. I can't wait to be there at the resurrection when Roy realizes several of the Crawfords accepted Jesus as their Lord and Savior. He will have waited a long time to have learned of their decision. I'm sure he'll consider that the wait was worth it.

Don't Give Up

*And after the earthquake a fire, but the LORD was not
in the fire; and after the fire a still small voice.*
—1 Kings 19:12

Volunteers from the church were following up on Bible study interest cards. The church had mailed them to their community, and people who were interested in studying the Bible mailed them back. Church members then went to the homes and dropped off Bible studies. At their weekly meeting, two church members explained that they had twice tried to reach a man at a certain address. They let the group know that they didn't plan to go back, which is when Deion and Lillian stepped in.

Deion and Lillian recognized the address as being near where they lived. They went to the home of a Mr. Betts, knocked on the door, and waited. Mr. Betts didn't come to the door, so they decided they would try to reach him on another day.

Deion and Lillian visited Mr. Betts's home six times without reaching him. On their seventh visit, they were about to leave when the door opened. It was Mr. Betts! On the first four visits, they dropped off Bible studies for Mr. Betts, but on the fifth visit to his home, Mr. Betts asked them to come inside. "If you wouldn't mind," he said, "I have some questions I would like to ask you." The three became good friends, and when the It Is Written evangelistic team arrived in town, Mr. Betts was eager to attend. After attending almost the entire series of meetings, Mr. Betts only had one question for me. "Before I join the church," he said, "do you think I ought to be rebaptized?" He was ready. He had given his life to Jesus, accepted the teachings of the Bible, and was growing with God every day.

I have often wondered what would have happened if Deion and Lillian had given up on Mr. Betts after their first attempt to reach him. Or after their second. Or after their sixth! I am grateful they persisted. And we can be grateful God persists with us. Even though we often might not have listened, God continues to call to us. God doesn't easily give up on us. We shouldn't give up on others who are not yet surrendered to Him.

The Prodigal Son

"But when he came to himself, he said, 'How many of my father's hired servants have bread enough and to spare, and I perish with hunger!' "
—Luke 15:17

The story of the prodigal son is one of the great stories of the Bible. A son is desperate to receive his share of his father's wealth, so he asks for his inheritance while his father is still living. The son then goes to a far country and squanders all he has before deciding to return home and throw himself upon his father's mercy. Most recitations of the story explain that the father in the story represents our heavenly Father, who patiently waited for his beloved son to return after he walked away from the family farm. Which, of course, cannot possibly be true.

While undoubtedly well-intentioned, this version of the famous Bible story portrays God as waiting back at the family farm while His children are lost out in the world. An accurate retelling of this story would have the son leaving for the bright lights of the big city while the Holy Spirit appealed to the boy every step of the way. Through the agency of the Holy Spirit, heaven did all it could to persuade the prodigal to remember the God of his youth. The Holy Spirit was present every time the young man woke up with a pounding headache after a night of partying and every time he squandered his money on yet another wasteful purchase. And the Spirit of God urged the young man to return home.

Feeding swine in order to eke out a living, the young man "came to himself." That is, the voice of the Holy Spirit finally broke through the young man's tough exterior. While mud squeezed up between the toes of the reluctant pig farmer, the Holy Spirit impressed upon him the claims of the love of God, and finally, he relented and repented.

If you are burdened for unsaved family or friends, know that God is at this moment doing all He can to reach them for eternity. You can be grateful today that God doesn't leave anyone alone to come to their senses. Instead, He pleads with sinners through the agency of the Holy Spirit. And if you have not given your life to Him, the Holy Spirit is pleading with you.

The Searcher

*"However, when He, the Spirit of truth, has come, He will guide you
into all truth; for He will not speak on His own authority, but
whatever He hears He will speak; and He will tell you things to come."*
—John 16:13

As he sat in the pastor's Bible study class, people wondered who the man was. It was his first time visiting the church. It turned out Aaron lived just five blocks away and had come under conviction as a result of his own personal study that the seventh day was the Sabbath. He returned to church again and again and made it clear he believed God was leading in his Christian growth.

Eventually, he was joined at church by his wife, Leonie. Leonie was distant and unfriendly and carried a notebook in which she wrote furiously. When the pastor asked Aaron about Leonie's notebook, he said, "She is trying to prove me wrong. She writes down what she hears being taught and then goes home to study to find the flaws."

Week after week, Aaron and Leonie attended church together. Slowly, Leonie's demeanor and attitude began to change. One week, Leonie came to church without her notebook. The pastor asked Leonie where it was. "I've heard enough," she said. "I can't find any fault in what is being taught. You are Christians who follow Jesus, and you're basing your faith on nothing but the Bible. I want to be baptized with Aaron and become part of the church family."

There is power in the truth of God's Word. It is important to expose people to the teachings of the Bible and the Christ of God's Word. Those who study the Bible with a true heart and a desire to find the truth will be guided by the Holy Spirit. Jesus said when the Spirit of Truth comes, "He will guide you into all truth" (John 16:13). An important function of the Holy Spirit is to guide people into truth—*all* truth. He seeks to lead us deeper in our understanding of the Word of God, which leads us deeper in our relationship with Jesus.

Many a person has been like Leonie, trying to prove someone wrong and, in the process, has come to a deeper understanding of the Bible. When a person has a genuine desire to know the truth, they will find it. And they will find Him.

Great Results

Now an angel of the Lord spoke to Philip, saying, "Arise and go toward the south along the road which goes down from Jerusalem to Gaza." This is desert.
—Acts 8:26

Pastor Donavon Kack was studying the Bible with a husband and wife when the wife's phone rang. It was a friend. "Why don't you join me in the Bible study?" she asked. "I'm sure you would enjoy it." The friend wasn't able to make it but asked to speak to the pastor. "Would you be able to come to our home and study the Bible with my husband and me?" she asked. It was an offer the pastor couldn't refuse! They set a date and time, and when Pastor Kack arrived, he was amazed to find there were thirty-five people waiting to study the Bible! The Bible study continued for many weeks, and before long, fourteen people were baptized.

There are times when it might seem that few are interested in Bible study or knowing more about God. But that is never true. Ellen White wrote in *The Acts of the Apostles*, "All over the world men and women are looking wistfully to heaven. Prayers and tears and inquiries go up from souls longing for light, for grace, for the Holy Spirit. Many are on the verge of the kingdom, waiting only to be gathered in."* She wrote those words with reference to the Ethiopian man to whom God guided the deacon Philip. The Bible says an angel gave Philip explicit directions to an exact location. When he got there, Phillip saw a man from Ethiopia riding in a chariot. "The Spirit said to Philip, 'Go near and overtake this chariot' " (Acts 8:29).

Philip found an earnest Bible student in the desert. A pastor found thirty-five willing to study the Bible. The people are there. Jesus said that "the harvest truly is great" (Luke 10:2). When the church rises up to meet the challenge of a lost, sinful world and is prepared to share the Christ of Scripture with those who are seeking Him, great will be the results, and eternal the effect.

---

* Ellen G. White, *The Acts of the Apostles* (Mountain View, CA: Pacific Press®, 1911), 109.

Life-Changing

"You are My witnesses," says the LORD.

—Isaiah 43:10

Kenneth and Letitia had held virtually every office in the church. They had taught Sabbath School to children and adults. They had served as deacon and deaconess; they had served on the board and assisted with every kind of program their church had conducted. But they had never given a Bible study. When the church mailed out Bible study request cards and dozens were returned from people wanting to study the Bible, they knew it was time to get involved in outreach in a way they had never done before.

"We were scared to death!" they both admitted. Yet, the Holy Spirit nudged them to step forward. Wanting to serve God, assist the church in this important outreach initiative, and grow spiritually, they agreed to help when their pastor asked for volunteers. The experience was unlike anything they were expecting.

They knocked on a door, anticipating that they would leave Bible studies with the person who had requested them. Instead, they were greeted at the door by a young woman with a bright smile. Kenneth and Letitia were invited in, and they quickly got acquainted with a family of five. "We've been waiting for you to come," they said.

They had the first Bible study right then and there, and a close friendship quickly developed. The family often texted Kenneth and Letitia with questions about the Bible, and they appreciated that every answer was found in Scripture. Several months after they first met, the family of five were baptized. Kenneth and Letitia were overjoyed. "If only we had done this sooner!" they said.

There is no shortage of people wanting to increase their understanding of God. In this unstable age, people are looking for answers to their questions, and they are looking for someone to provide those answers. God has called every one of His children to be the light of the world. But ours is not to merely be a silent witness. There are times we are called to speak and to share. Pray that God will give you opportunities to share Jesus with others. It will change someone's life—especially yours.

Christ Our Life

When Christ who is our life appears,
then you also will appear with Him in glory.

—Colossians 3:4

I was raised in a churchgoing family, but we didn't have much of anything to do with the Bible. We were undoubtedly committed to our church and to our faith. But if we were committed to Jesus, it didn't really show. When one of my brothers accepted Jesus as his Lord and Savior, what bothered us most was that he took it all so *seriously.* He went to church for much of an entire day. He wouldn't do anything on Friday night or Saturday that didn't relate to his religion and certainly wouldn't do anything secular. His diet changed. He stopped using drugs and alcohol and even changed the way he used his spare time. His faith impacted his entire life.

For many people, faith in God is only a *part* of their life. Christianity is simply a thing to do, much like joining a service organization or a club. But faith in God was never designed to be an appendage attached to the life—an option, like leather seats or a sunroof for a new car buyer. The apostle Paul was clear that Jesus *is* life.

Jesus is Creator and Redeemer. He is our High Priest in heaven, giving aid to all who come to Him by faith. He described our connection with Him as being like a branch joined to a vine and urged us to "abide" in Him. Only Jesus living His life in a believer can bring spiritual growth and victory; as He said, "Without Me you can do nothing" (John 15:5).

Attending church is to be the icing on the cake for disciples of Jesus. Those who follow Him every day follow Him to church on the Sabbath to join in corporate worship. Faith in Jesus impacts every facet of life because Christianity is a surrender to the will of God for the entire life. Faith is not a philosophy or an extracurricular activity. The Spirit of God is striving to bring us to the place where Christ "is our life."

Occupy

"So he called ten of his servants, delivered to them ten minas,
and said to them, 'Do business till I come.' "

—Luke 19:13

Wayne was convinced he was one of the last people who would be saved before Jesus returned. He had studied the Bible, was aware of the signs of the times, and believed the Second Coming was imminent. The year Wayne was baptized, Arthur Ashe won Wimbledon, the Vietnam War ended, a gallon of gas cost fifty-seven cents, and Gerald Ford was President of the United States. It was 1975. Clearly, my brother was wrong about the timing of the return of Jesus.

Although Jesus has given us signs so we may know His return is near, He hasn't asked us to know precisely when His return shall be. Rather than focusing on the *timing* of His return, Jesus focused instead on how we should live in preparation for His return.

In Luke 19, Jesus spoke a parable "because they thought the kingdom of God would appear immediately" (verse 11). Jesus told of a nobleman who gave his servants ten pounds and instructed them to "occupy till I come" (verse 13, KJV). The word translated "occupy" essentially means "do business." Jesus was clear that whenever He returns to the earth, our role is to be about our Father's business until that time. If Jesus is to return in a year, or a decade, or a century from now, our mandate remains the same: "Occupy till I come." "Be about My Father's business until I return." If we are young, old, black, white, professional, or uneducated, our purpose in these last days of earth's history is the same. We are to occupy—to be about the work of God—until Jesus returns.

God is looking to His people to be busy in the field in preparation for the harvest. There are people to reach. Large cities with their vast populations still remain virtually untouched by the gospel, even in first-world countries that have a long and rich Christian heritage. There is much we can find to occupy our time, but the urgent need today is for individuals who will occupy until He comes and be about their Father's business of sharing Jesus with the world.

A Great Mistake

*"And this gospel of the kingdom will be preached in all the world as
a witness to all the nations, and then the end will come."*

—Matthew 24:14

K im and her outreach partner knocked on the door. A woman at this address had requested Bible studies. This was the first time they had ever been involved in this kind of outreach, and while they wanted to do their very best, there was a part of each of them that hoped no one would answer the door. They knocked several times, and when no one answered, they turned to walk back to their car, partly disappointed and partly relieved.

Upon reaching the curb, they heard the door of the house open and a voice asking what they wanted. Kim replied that they were there to deliver a Bible lesson. What they heard next amazed them both. The lady who came to the door explained that the reason she was so slow to respond to their knocking was that she was in her back room asking God to send someone to help her to better understand the Bible! She was delighted that Kim and her outreach partner were there, and she gratefully accepted the Bible study they were there to deliver.

We make a great mistake when we think people will not respond to the gospel. It is true; we live in a very secular age. A generation ago, most people identified in some way with a church. More and more people today have been raised without a church connection, meaning they don't approach faith in God with a series of predetermined ideas.

Of course, not everyone is going to respond positively to the Christ of the Bible. But God isn't asking us to be successful. He is asking us to be faithful and to work alongside the Holy Spirit in reaching out to those in whose lives He has already been working. We cannot see God speaking to hearts or intervening in people's lives. We cannot tell when someone is crying out to God or experiencing circumstances where God is reaching or impressing them with their need for a Savior. But Jesus has assured us that the "gospel of the kingdom will be preached in all the world as a witness to all the nations" (Matthew 24:14).

Like a Hand in a Glove

*Therefore we were buried with Him through baptism into
death, that just as Christ was raised from the dead by the glory
of the Father, even so we also should walk in newness of life.*
—Romans 6:4

The first time I experienced cold weather—really cold weather—I gained a greater appreciation for gloves. My family and I were conducting an evangelistic series in Grand Forks, North Dakota. The sign outside said the temperature was -29°F (-34°C), and with the wind blowing at ten miles per hour, the wind chill factor was -52°F (-46°C)! Before the meeting began that night, I went outside to get something from our vehicle. In just moments, my ears and nose were hurting, and I wished I was wearing gloves. I had them with me at the meeting hall but didn't put them on before I went outside. Gloves that are not worn are gloves that cannot protect you from the elements.

Now consider Philippians 2:13. "For it is God who works in you both to will and to do for His good pleasure." Notice that the text says God "works in you." It is God's wish to dwell in the lives of His people. Christians who have not truly invited Jesus to live His life in them are like the person who has gloves but doesn't wear them. Gloves that aren't worn cannot provide warmth. A Savior who doesn't occupy your heart cannot transform your life, lift you out of sin, or give you the assurance of salvation.

If you invite Him to do so, Jesus will live His life in you. Instead of asking God to help you to do right, live right, or "be good," acknowledge your complete inability to live a Christian life and ask Jesus to live in your heart. For many people who call themselves Christian, this is the missing piece of the puzzle. They want to live a Christian life, they happily identify with the church, and they believe the teachings of the Bible, but they don't experience assurance. Instead, they stay stuck in the old life, unable to "walk in newness of life." Jesus is willing to fill your heart with His presence. You will find that your life and the life of Jesus go together like a hand in a glove.

August 26

"Our Eyes Are on You"

"For we have no power against this great multitude that is coming against us; nor do we know what to do, but our eyes are upon You."

—2 Chronicles 20:12

D escribed as "a great multitude," this enemy would surely lay waste to the armies of Jehoshaphat and bring the nation under foreign domination. The king called people together from throughout his realm and proclaimed a national fast before he approached God and asked for deliverance from what was a powerful enemy. Against this backdrop Jehoshaphat, king of Judah, prayed a powerful prayer.

In 2 Chronicles 20, the desperate king called on God and said, "O LORD God of our fathers, are You not God in heaven, and do You not rule over all the kingdoms of the nations, and in Your hand is there not power and might, so that no one is able to withstand You?" (verse 6). Jehoshaphat knew precisely who God was. Jehoshaphat believed God was all-powerful and ruled over all kingdoms of the earth. In other words, defeat was not certain, no matter how bleak things looked.

He continued, "Are You not our God, who drove out the inhabitants of this land before Your people Israel, and gave it to the descendants of Abraham Your friend forever?" (verse 7). In other words, "You have done great things for us in the past. You promised us this land. I am only asking You to keep Your promise and do for us now what You have done for us in the past." Then he made an honest admission. "For we have no power against this great multitude that is coming against us; nor do we know what to do" (verse 12). He acknowledged that they were incapable of defeating this enemy and that they did not know what they should do. And then came the real power of his prayer. He said, "But our eyes are upon You" (verse 12). In other words, "We are looking toward heaven. We are looking to You. And we are expecting great things."

When you pray, no matter how apparently mighty your enemy, remember God is all-powerful. He has done great things for you in the past. If your eyes are on God, they are focused in the right direction. Jehoshaphat was delivered. His people were saved. Like Jehoshaphat, you can expect deliverance when you pray and keep your eyes on God.

The Response

*"If My people who are called by My name will humble themselves,
and pray and seek My face, and turn from their wicked ways, then I
will hear from heaven, and will forgive their sin and heal their land."*
—2 Chronicles 7:14

It was a fearful time. Made up of just two tribes since the rebellion of Jeroboam and the ten northern tribes during the reign of Rehoboam, Judah was especially vulnerable. Judah was surrounded by a mighty enemy, a confederacy made up of nations from east of the Dead Sea. The Ammonites, from northeast of the Dead Sea (Amman, Jordan, was originally named "Rabbath Ammon"*), the Moabites, who lived to the south, and the inhabitants of Mount Seir, who were Edomites, were bent on destroying Judah. From a human standpoint, things were hopeless for the king of Judah.

But Jehoshaphat knew what to do. "And Jehoshaphat feared, and set himself to seek the LORD, and proclaimed a fast throughout all Judah. So Judah gathered together to ask help from the LORD; and from all the cities of Judah they came to seek the LORD" (2 Chronicles 20:3, 4). Jehoshaphat was the son of Asa, one of the rare kings who "did what was good and right in the eyes of the LORD his God" (2 Chronicles 14:2). He rallied Judah to pray and seek God in their hour of need.

Perhaps even more remarkable than Jehoshaphat's leadership is the manner in which the people reacted to his appeal. When the nation was plunged into a crisis, the people all responded to Jehoshaphat's plea to seek God. They came "out of all the cities of Judah . . . to seek the LORD" (2 Chronicles 20:4, KJV). The story ends with God miraculously delivering Judah, leaving us to wonder what the church or the world would look like if God's people took His call to pray seriously. In the same book, we read this mighty promise: "If My people who are called by My name will humble themselves, and pray and seek My face, and turn from their wicked ways, then I will hear from heaven, and will forgive their sin and heal their land" (2 Chronicles 7:14).

God can work just as powerfully today as He worked for Judah during Jehoshaphat's reign. When the church rises up as one to seek God in prayer and repentance, we will undoubtedly see God do remarkable things.

---

* "Amman," Britannica, accessed April 6, 2021, https://www.britannica.com/place/Amman.

Able

"O LORD God of our fathers, are You not God in heaven, and do
You not rule over all the kingdoms of the nations, and in Your hand
is there not power and might, so that no one is able to withstand You?"
—2 Chronicles 20:6

Jehoshaphat was in trouble. Judah was facing destruction and death. A confederacy of Ammonites, Moabites, and Edomites was closing in on the southern kingdom with malice on their minds. Unless God intervened, there would be death on a frightening scale.

Although Jehoshaphat had acted imprudently in going to war alongside the wicked Ahab and would have died owing to the cowardice and deception of Israel's king if God had not intervened (see 2 Chronicles 18:31), he had been a faithful king. He had "removed the high places and wooden images from Judah" and "his heart took delight in the ways of the LORD" (2 Chronicles 17:6). At his direction, religious reforms had been carried out throughout the land. The book of the law had been taught in cities all across the land. "The fear of the LORD fell on all the kingdoms of the lands that were around Judah, so that they did not make war against Jehoshaphat" (verse 10). But now, Judah's future was very much in jeopardy. So Jehoshaphat prayed.

Jehoshaphat said, in effect, "We know who You are. You are so powerful no one can stand before You." Jehoshaphat expressed absolute confidence that God was able to deliver His people, even in a time when deliverance seemed humanly impossible. He said, "You have driven out the inhabitants of this land, and You gave this land to Abraham. We are only asking You to keep us in possession of what You already gave us."

When you pray, pray with the confidence of Jehoshaphat. You are praying to the one true God, the Architect of the cosmos. You need never pray with doubt about God's ability to answer your prayer. As Jehoshaphat believed, *God is able.*

Guilt

Let the wicked forsake his way,
And the unrighteous man his thoughts;
Let him return to the LORD,
And He will have mercy on him;
And to our God,
For He will abundantly pardon.

—Isaiah 55:7

D id you ever feel bad about something you had done? No doubt you did. Did you ever feel *really* bad about something? There's no question about it. But a little guilt is good for the soul. People who feel no guilt at all when they harm others are sociopaths. The question isn't, "Guilt or no guilt?" but, "What do you do with guilt?"

Judas was wracked with guilt after selling Jesus for thirty pieces of silver—the traditional price of a slave—and "went and hanged himself" (Matthew 27:5). Peter also sold out Jesus that night, denying three times that he even knew Him. After the rooster crowed, Peter "went out and wept bitterly" (Luke 22:62). One man was consumed by guilt, and the guilt killed him. But guilt didn't destroy Peter. Instead, he built on his failure and became one of the very few people who wrote two or more books of the Bible.

What do you do with your guilt? You can let it eat you alive, or you can confess it to your loving and forgiving Savior. You could ruin your entire day right now by reflecting on something terrible you have done and spend the rest of the day in the viselike grip of condemnation. But there's another way. When tempted to condemn yourself, remember Isaiah 55:7. Forsake your wickedness and unrighteous thoughts and return to the Lord. He *will* pardon. And He will *abundantly* pardon!

It is never a question of whether you deserve forgiveness. The fact is, Jesus died for your sins. He forgives you. He takes away your guilt, which frees you to be able to let it go. When that same guilt rears its ugly head, remind yourself of Isaiah 55:7 and the many other Bible promises that reassure you of God's forgiveness. Allow God to free you from the chains that bind you to your past mistakes, and accept that you are forgiven and made new. Your mistakes do not have to define you. Let guilt go. Jesus died so that you could do just that.

The Nightclub Owner

Create in me a clean heart, O God,
and renew a steadfast spirit within me.

—Psalm 51:10

James approached me as soon as church was over. "John, I'd love you to meet a friend of mine and invite him to the evangelistic meetings starting Friday." The name sounded familiar, but at that moment, I couldn't place it. "This is Sam McKenzie," James said. When I shook Sam's hand, the penny finally dropped. Sam had been a successful nightclub owner. As a teenager, I used to visit his nightclubs with friends. Sam drove an expensive European car, and whenever he arrived at the club, a buzz would ripple through the crowd. He would ascend the staircase to his private booth with glamorous-looking women at his side.

But life had taken a turn for Sam. He told me that at the height of his business success, he went twenty years without being sober a single day but had since lost everything except for his children and his friendship with James. James shared hope with Sam, who had begun attending church and was considering attending the evangelistic meetings I would be holding. When I saw him opening night, it was apparent that God was working in Sam's life and I prayed that Sam would surrender his life to Jesus.

During the meetings, Sam made decision after decision. When the series was over, I was privileged to baptize the man whose nightclubs I had frequented before either of us were Christians. I baptized Sam about a quarter of a mile from the nightclub he used to own. He came out of the water with his arms raised in victory.

Several years later, I met Sam again, and it was clear he was different. He seemed nervous and barely spoke. I learned he was suffering from dementia and now lived in a group home for his own safety. James was the only person Sam recognized, and church was his only outing. Sam died shortly after. But we knew that Sam—the nightclub owner who was drunk for twenty years—had died a new man. A changed man. A saved man. Sam found hope in Jesus and had accepted Him as his Lord and Savior. I'm looking forward to seeing Sam again. Soon.

The Impossible Work

*Being confident of this very thing, that He who has begun
a good work in you will complete it until the day of Jesus Christ.*
—Philippians 1:6

In our home, if we don't make peanut butter ourselves, we buy natural peanut butter. But one drawback with natural peanut butter is that because the oil and the peanuts separate, they have to be mixed together. I don't know anyone who enjoys that job. My shortcut is to empty the contents of the jar into a bowl, mix it in the bowl and return it mixed into the jar. It's much easier than mixing it in the jar.

While visiting my wife's parents, I saw something that could be a peanut butter game changer. My mother-in-law was using a device that screws onto the top of the peanut butter jar and mixes the peanut butter while it is still in the jar. The hard work is done by the device. A difficult task is made simple.

There is some hard work involved in Christianity. Denying self isn't an easy matter. There is a reason Jesus encouraged us to "strive to enter through the narrow gate" (Luke 13:24). Revelation says we are in a war against the devil himself (Revelation 12:17), while Paul used military imagery when urging us to "put on the whole armor of God" (Ephesians 6:11). The work of resisting temptation and living a new life in Christ is not a work that we alone can successfully accomplish. What is needed is the presence and power of God. Knowing this, Paul reminded the Philippian church "that He who has begun a good work in you will complete it until the day of Jesus Christ."

The hard work—the humanly impossible work—of changing the heart and of successfully repelling temptation is done by Jesus. You are promised that the One who began the work—who called you to repentance and touched your heart with the love of God—will carry the life-changing work being done in you through to completion. We have been provided with unlimited spiritual power in Jesus. Surrendering to His presence assures you of a finished work in your life.

SEPTEMBER

Working for God

*"It is like a man going to a far country, who left his house
and gave authority to his servants, and to each his work,
and commanded the doorkeeper to watch."*

—Mark 13:34

Jason felt as though he didn't belong in the student colporteur program. He had been with the group for two weeks, and sales were slow. He wasn't confident knocking on doors and felt he didn't think quickly enough to be able to meet objections and answer questions. Knocking on another door, he looked down at his shoes with an uneasy feeling in his heart. Would he get many books out today? When he got back together with his fellow literature evangelists and heard their success stories, would he feel as though he belonged? He knew he was doing important work, but it just wasn't working out for him as he wished.

When no one came to the door, Jason knocked again. As He turned to walk away, he heard a voice. "Excuse me," a woman said. "Can I help you?" He started his canvass, explaining that he was a student working his way through college and was in the neighborhood offering life-changing resources. But there was something different about this woman. Jason wasn't sure what it was. She was clearly interested but stopped him mid-canvass.

"There's something I have to tell you," she announced. His heart sank. All Jason wanted was to see people take the books he knew could change their lives. "I've been feeling so low lately. You might not believe this," she said, "but when you knocked on the door, I was literally on my knees, praying that God would send someone to my home to help me understand the Bible."

She bought every one of the Bible-based books in Jason's carry bag. And at that moment, Jason's summer changed completely. He walked with a spring in his step, knowing by experience that he was doing God's work. His sales were never spectacular, but his enthusiasm was. He knew he was working for Jesus and that God was using him to make a difference. God has a work for everyone. Don't let discouragement prevent you from doing the work He has for you.

"Great News!"

Oh, taste and see that the LORD is good;
blessed is the man who trusts in Him!

—Psalm 34:8

A young college student began attending a series of meetings held by the evangelist Eric Flickinger. Amy was excited about what she was learning from the Bible and occasionally would bring one of her roommates to the meetings with her. When the series concluded, she wasn't ready to surrender her life entirely to Jesus, but her view of God and of the Bible was changing. She said, "I used to look at the Bible as a list of dos and don'ts, but now I look at it as God's cookbook of love!"

After the meetings finished, church members continued to study with her. Several months later, she made a decision to be baptized. But that's not where the story ends. Sometime later, Eric received the following message from the church: "Great news! Toni was baptized yesterday! It was a beautiful ceremony and a high day for the church."

Toni was Amy's friend and had recently graduated from university. She had come to the United States from an Asian country, and just one year before didn't believe in God, didn't own a Bible, and had never prayed. Toni was fascinated with the health food that church members made for the meetings she attended with Amy, and when Amy posted a picture online of some of the food she had made, Toni asked her if she would like to get together and cook. They became good friends, and Amy invited Toni to a cooking school at the church. Toni loved it and began attending church with Amy. Amy gave her a Bible and a box of It Is Written Bible studies, and Toni's life began to change. She attended another series of meetings and came forward when an altar call was made. Toni not only yielded her life to Jesus but also began bringing her friends to church.

Amy met Jesus and introduced Him to Toni, who then shared her new faith with others. Our privilege as followers of Jesus is to not only know Him ourselves but also to introduce Him to those who do not yet have the assurance of salvation.

The Shy Evangelist

Then Jesus said to them, "Follow Me,
and I will make you become fishers of men."

—Mark 1:17

K endra had no idea that a visit to a dentist's office would change her life. While her young daughter was seeing the dentist, Kendra noticed a small display in the waiting room that offered free Bible studies. She took the free lesson and mailed in a request for Bible studies. Before long, Tom and Sharon knocked on her door, Bible studies began, and a friendship developed.

Kendra began attending church. She enjoyed growing in her understanding of the Bible and seeing God become a bigger part of her life. Kendra surrendered her life to Jesus and was baptized, and she became a part of the church family.

A few weeks later, she heard her pastor announce that an It Is Written mission team would be heading to the Philippines and was inviting people to join the mission trip and preach a series of evangelistic meetings. Kendra was naturally shy and had no experience with public speaking, but she sensed God urging her to find out more about the mission trip. Without the needed funding, she couldn't understand how it could all work out. Nevertheless, before long, Kendra was in Manila, standing before a group of interested listeners, confidently teaching the three angels' messages. As Kendra made appeals, people responded by filling out decision cards or coming to the front on altar calls. Quiet Kendra had become Kendra the soul winner.

The dentist that her daughter saw that day could not have known a future evangelist was about to enter his practice. But that silent invitation printed on the back of an It Is Written Bible study was used by the Holy Spirit to draw Kendra into becoming a disciple of Jesus and then a disciple maker. To those who followed Him, Jesus said, "I will make you become fishers of men" (Mark 1:17). In *The Desire of Ages*, we read, "No sooner is one converted than there is born within him a desire to make known to others what a precious friend he has found in Jesus."* Kendra returned from the mission trip and began studying the Bible with a friend, who was then baptized.

God calls us to Himself so that He can use us to call others to follow Him.

---

* Ellen G. White, *The Desire of Ages* (Mountain View, CA: Pacific Press®, 1940), 141.

September 4

Unlikely

So when the centurion and those with him, who were guarding
Jesus, saw the earthquake and the things that had happened,
they feared greatly, saying, "Truly this was the Son of God!"
—Matthew 27:54

The city of Prague, in the Czech Republic, is renowned as one of the most atheistic cities in Europe, yet God works even in the most challenging of locations.

The evangelistic meeting I held there several years ago was streamed online, and unbeknownst to anyone on our team, Anna had stumbled onto the livestream and began watching. She watched every night and was being touched by what she was hearing. When I invited people to fill out a decision card during the meetings, Anna, realizing she did not have a decision card, was undeterred. She wrote down the decision questions and made a decision card of her own. She filled it out, found an address online, and mailed in the card. Anna was determined to make a decision and wanted us to know she had done so.

Jessica worked as a Bible worker on an evangelistic series in a large city in the United States. Her husband, Kent, was not a practicing Christian. Jessica was disappointed Kent wasn't able to attend more than a handful of meetings owing to the long distance from their home to the meeting hall. During one of the final appeals of the series, Jessica's phone rang. It was Kent. He had been watching the livestream and wanted to make a decision for baptism! "Jessica," he began, "would you mind filling out a decision card for me? Say that 'Yes, I want to follow Jesus.' Check 'Yes, I would like to be baptized.' And please write on the card that 'Yes, I would like to join the church!' " Jessica was overjoyed. Kent's baptism was truly memorable.

We must remember that although we can't always see what God is doing in hearts, He is at work. In unlikely cities, in unlikely lives, and through unlikely circumstances, God is appealing to hearts everywhere. When Jesus died on the cross, a Roman centurion, perhaps the least likely person to express belief in Jesus as Lord, said, "Truly this was the Son of God!" (Matthew 27:54).

We must not limit God's ability to reach a lost soul. God's Spirit is working to bring the most unlikely to faith in Jesus.

When in Rome

"Behold, I am the LORD, the God of all flesh.
Is there anything too hard for Me?"

—Jeremiah 32:27

We had been planning an evangelistic series in Rome, Italy, for several years. But a few months before the meetings began, we realized that someone did not want to see the three angels' messages proclaimed in the Eternal City.

The mother of our local evangelism coordinator became gravely ill and required her full attention. An arson attack damaged the largest church involved in the series, meaning an entire congregation would not be able to participate actively. Certain individuals began verbalizing their antagonism not only to public evangelism but also to evangelism of all kinds, and several very supportive church leaders became ill. It was clear the devil did not want these meetings to take place, meetings that would be held just three-quarters of a mile from the Vatican.

But God *did* want the series to take place. People of all backgrounds came out to the church night after night. One man drove across Italy to attend, traveling 130 miles from his home on the Adriatic coast before driving the same distance home again. He would let nothing prevent him from learning the truth of God's Word.

A radio station operated by the church broadcast the presentations to all of Rome, and the series concluded with more than forty people requesting baptism. People streamed to the front of the church when altar calls were made, pressing their way out of the crowded balcony and finding their way to the platform. In the weeks following the meetings, numerous people approached the pastor and stated that they wanted to study the Bible in preparation for baptism.

The Bible makes it clear that, even in challenging circumstances, God can reach people with the gospel. A young slave girl influenced a Syrian army captain when she suggested Naaman should visit the prophet Elisha in Samaria. Nebuchadnezzar was moved by the witness of Daniel and his friends. No city or territory is outside the reach of God. He says, "I am the LORD, the God of all flesh. Is there anything too hard for me?" (Jeremiah 2:27).

He Knows

For He knows our frame; He remembers that we are dust.
—Psalm 103:14

In his book *The Treasury of David*, nineteenth-century British preacher Charles Spurgeon said the following about Psalm 103: "As in the lofty Alps some peaks rise above all others, so among even the inspired psalms there are heights of song which overtop the rest."*

Psalm 103 is one of those towering peaks of Scripture and contains this unforgettable passage:

> The LORD is merciful and gracious,
> Slow to anger, and abounding in mercy.
> He will not always strive with us,
> Nor will He keep His anger forever.
> He has not dealt with us according to our sins,
> Nor punished us according to our iniquities.
>
> For as the heavens are high above the earth,
> So great is His mercy toward those who fear Him;
> As far as the east is from the west,
> So far has He removed our transgressions from us.
> As a father pities his children,
> So the LORD pities those who fear Him (Psalm 103:8–13).

In one brief cluster of verses, David impresses upon us the beauty of God's mercy, forgiveness, and tender, paternal care. And then he adds a verse that gives life to the reality of the Father's love and grace: "For He knows our frame; He remembers that we are dust" (verse 14).

In other words, God knows what you're made of. When the battle against your fallen nature gets the better of you, God remembers that you are dust. Your loving heavenly Father is no more ready to cast you aside when you fail than a parent is willing to abandon a growing child learning how to tie his or her shoelaces.

This is not to suggest God is unconcerned about sin. God seeks to correct us when we need to be corrected. But His feelings toward His children are feelings of pity, patience, kindness, and love. He will never give up on you. He loves you too much to give up on you. He understands your struggles. God knows what you're made of.

---

* C. H. Spurgeon, *The Treasury of David*, vol. 4, 2nd ed. (New York: Funk and Wagnalls, 1883), 447, https://www.google.com/books/edition/The_Treasury_of_David/cIcXAAAAYAAJ?hl=en.

Compel Them!

*"Go out into the highways and hedges, and compel them
to come in, that my house may be filled."*
—Luke 14:23

N ot all attempts to witness are successful. At least, not immediately. Not all church outreach projects seem to accomplish a great amount of good. One person who understands this is Jesus. He made it clear that when initial attempts are not immediately successful, we are to respond to apparent failure with energy and perseverance.

In Luke 14, Jesus told a parable in which a man invited many people to a "great supper." After invitations had been sent out, a servant was dispatched to let the invitees know that the banquet was ready. Their presence was requested.

Person after person made excuses. "I have recently married," said one. "I just bought some land," said another. A third excused himself on the basis of having recently bought some oxen.

The invitation was received but rejected. So the man instructed his servant to "go out quickly into the streets and lanes of the city, and bring in here the poor and the maimed and the lame and the blind" (Luke 14:21). When it was found there was still room for more guests to attend, the master sent his servant out again, this time into the "highways and hedges," to "compel them to come in, that my house may be filled" (verse 23).

While primarily spoken with reference to the Israel of Jesus' day, this story is also given for God's people today. Jesus shows us what our attitude should be when invitations to know Him are spurned. If an outreach event isn't successful, we are to try again like the man in the story. If the evangelistic series seems to yield smaller results than hoped, we forge ahead and "compel them to come in."

We have little time to waste. Discouraging results should not prevent us from letting our light shine. Rejection did not prevent the apostles from sharing their faith in Jesus in unpromising areas. Instead of dialing back our evangelistic fervor, we must continue to share Christ and make it harder than ever for people to resist His offer of everlasting life.

Baby Jessica

He saved them from the hand of him who hated them,
and redeemed them from the hand of the enemy.

—Psalm 106:10

In 1987, the eyes of the world were on Midland, Texas, after an eighteen-month-old girl fell into a well in her aunt's backyard. The well was just eight inches wide, and Jessica McClure became wedged in the well shaft twenty-two feet below the surface of the ground. The drama was perfect for cable news, which at the time wasn't yet ten years old. The story received wall-to-wall media coverage as an anxious nation watched. Getting baby Jessica out of the well was a race against time. President Ronald Reagan said, "Everybody in America became godmothers and godfathers of Jessica while this was going on." She was often referred to as "Everyone's baby."

The rescue was fraught with difficulty. Rescuing a twenty-pound girl from a pipe more than twenty feet below ground, surrounded by rock described as "nearly impregnable" and "as hard as steel," was as difficult as it sounds. Workers who labored to near exhaustion said that thinking of little Jessica kept them going.

It seemed that everyone remotely close to the situation was asked to comment. The physician who delivered Jessica was interviewed by the Odessa American newspaper and said she was praying for the child. She had a baby about the same age.

Baby Jessica was stuck in the well for fifty-eight hours before being rescued. After the ordeal, she continued to live in Midland, and as an adult, lives less than two miles from the well where she almost lost her life. While unable to remember the event, Jessica is acutely aware she was saved. A scar on her forehead serves as a visible reminder of what happened back in 1987. It tells her that when she was hopelessly stuck and couldn't save herself, she was rescued. Now a mother of two children, Jessica Morales was saved by people who cared.*

Scars on Jesus' hands and feet remind us that when we were hopelessly stuck in sin and unable to save ourselves, Jesus gave His life so we might live. Like baby Jessica, you have been saved by Someone. This Someone paid the ultimate price to give you everlasting life.

---

* "October 16, 1987, Everybody's Baby," This Day in History, October 26, 2018, https://todayinhistory.blog/2018/10/16/october-16-1987-everybodys-baby/.

Pinball

Do not be deceived: "Evil company
corrupts good habits."
—1 Corinthians 15:33

You may be surprised to learn that pinball was once outlawed in many major American cities. Elected in 1933, New York City Mayor Fiorella LaGuardia made his crusade against pinball a major issue of his mayoral campaign. He believed that the millions of dollars being earned each year by the pinball industry came out of the "pockets of school children in the form of nickels and dimes given them as lunch money."* At the time, playing pinball was considered gambling. In its early days, pinball was a game of chance, and prizes—ranging from free games to gum, jewelry, and dinner plates—were awarded to winners. The first coin-operated pinball machines were manufactured in 1931, but it wasn't until 1947, when flippers were added, that pinball became a "game of skill." For decades, pinball machines were associated with vice, dishonesty, and bad behavior among school-aged children. Schools argued that pupils were skipping school to play and were wasting money that would otherwise be used for much-needed food.

It would be easy to look at this as a sign of the nation's puritanical past, a relic of a narrow-minded, old-fashioned age. But if we think again, we might recognize that not only was Mayor LaGuardia right to be concerned about gambling, but also his misgivings—intentional or otherwise—were actually based upon solid biblical principles. Paul's direct counsel to the Corinthian church was, "Do not be deceived: 'Evil company corrupts good habits' " (1 Corinthians 15:33).

It is imperative for Christians to remember the power of influence and association. Some activities serve as gateways to other, less savory enterprises. Children and adults are strongly influenced by those with whom they associate. It might be that many seemingly innocuous activities are not as inconsequential as society believes. A spiritual enemy has been diligently studying human behavior for six thousand years and has by now succeeded in causing us to see sin as being much less serious than it is. While the dangers of pinball can be debated, what isn't debatable is the need for believers to live lives that are committed to Christ, lives in which temptation is avoided rather than courted.

---

* Christopher Klein, "That Time America Outlawed Pinball," History, last updated August 22, 2018, https://history.com/news/that-time-america-outlawed-pinball.

Trivial Pursuit?

Depart from evil and do good;
Seek peace and pursue it.
The eyes of the LORD are on the righteous,
And His ears are open to their cry.

—Psalm 34:14, 15

In 1979, upon finding that several of their Scrabble pieces were missing, two Canadian men invented their own board game. Trivial Pursuit was released in 1981 and by 2014 had sold more than 100 million games.*

Christianity is anything but a trivial pursuit. Christianity is the unfolding experience of a person who has chosen Jesus as Lord and Savior. The nuances of the Christian life are learned over time by a connection with God through prayer and Bible study. Having the correct understanding of what it takes to make Christianity work is essential to a believer's satisfaction with his or her Christian life and that person's success as a follower of Jesus.

In the book *Steps to Christ*, the following advice is given:

Consecrate yourself to God in the morning; make this your very first work. Let your prayer be, "Take me, O Lord, as wholly Thine. I lay all my plans at Thy feet. Use me today in Thy service. Abide with me, and let all my work be wrought in Thee." This is a daily matter. Each morning consecrate yourself to God for that day. Surrender all your plans to Him, to be carried out or given up as His providence shall indicate. Thus day by day you may be giving your life into the hands of God, and thus your life will be molded more and more after the life of Christ.†

We are called to total consecration to God, complete dependence upon Him in the Christian experience. Faith in God is a daily matter, not a one-and-done approach to religion. When we surrender our plans to God, we turn our lives over to Him and declare our desire that God would not only guide our lives but also make us progressively more like Jesus.

Christianity is no trivial matter. God asks for an entire surrender of the will to Him. Nothing less than the power of God is needed to guide and lead in every aspect of our being. Christianity is a matter of eternal life and death and demands an entire heart commitment to God.

---

* Morgan Cutolo, "10 Fun Facts You Never Knew About Trivial Pursuit," *Reader's Digest*, updated December 4, 2019, https://www.rd.com/article/trivial-pursuit-facts/.

† Ellen G. White, *Steps to Christ* (Washington, DC: Review and Herald®, 1956), 70.

Take My Heart

"The heart is deceitful above all things,
and desperately wicked; who can know it?"

—Jeremiah 17:9

Another model prayer shines a bright light on the Christian experience, giving a clear picture of the heart commitment necessary for Christianity to be successful in the life of an individual.

In *Christ's Object Lessons*, Ellen White wrote, "No outward observances can take the place of simple faith and entire renunciation of self. But no man can empty himself of self. We can only consent for Christ to accomplish the work. Then the language of the soul will be, Lord, take my heart; for I cannot give it. It is Thy property. Keep it pure, for I cannot keep it for Thee. Save me in spite of myself, my weak, unchristlike self. Mold me, fashion me, raise me into a pure and holy atmosphere, where the rich current of Thy love can flow through my soul."*

Reliance on self is the fatal flaw in the Christianity of many professed followers of Christ. The path of Christ is the path not only of self-renunciation but also of total dependence on Jesus. The God who has promised to freely give His children the precious gift of the Holy Spirit neither asks nor expects that they would work their way to heaven in their own strength. Humans are irretrievably broken. Every person alive is unfitted for the eternal company of Christ and of angels. Knowing this, God has made every provision for even the weakest sinner to receive the righteousness of Christ and live a life of victory and growth in Jesus.

While we cannot empty ourselves of self, we can "consent for Christ to accomplish the work." You cannot give your heart to Jesus, but you can allow God to take it. You cannot keep your heart pure, but you can trust God to keep it pure for you. It is God who saves you in spite of your un-Christlike self. God is willing and able to do for the believer what the believer cannot do. God can change your life. God can give you a new heart. God can give you a victorious Christian experience. And He will do so as you surrender to Him and grow daily in His grace.

---

* Ellen G. White, *Christ's Object Lessons* (Washington, DC: Review and Herald®, 1941), 159.

Submit

*Therefore submit to God. Resist the devil
and he will flee from you.*

—James 4:7

Not a single person alive needs to believe that the power of temptation is too great to overcome. Although temptation can be extremely trying, the power of God is always able to deliver a believer from the power of sin.

James wrote a remarkable promise for every Christian when he said, "Resist the devil and he will flee from you" (James 4:7). James made a statement of fact. When you resist the devil, the devil will flee from you. Therefore, the devil need not defeat you. You need not be overcome in the hour of your trial. James said it plainly, "He will flee from you."

But lest we get the impression the Bible is urging us to fight in our own strength, we notice what James said immediately preceding his emphatic statement. "Submit to God." Then he said, "Resist the devil, and he will flee from you."

You can fight against the enemy of souls in your own strength as energetically as you wish, but you will ultimately meet with discouraging failure. He is described in the Bible as a "roaring lion" (1 Peter 5:8). Precious few people have ever defeated a roaring lion single-handedly. Of those who did, far fewer did so more than once.

When we submit ourselves to Jesus, His power and presence work miraculously on our behalf. The Christ of the Bible is able to vanquish all spiritual enemies. Success in spiritual warfare depends entirely on submission to Jesus. Spiritual defeat is only ever the result of failure to surrender to Jesus in the moment of temptation.

Habitual submission to God is learned over time. Lessons are often impressed upon us due to missteps and failure. The more you surrender to Jesus, the more of His presence you welcome into your life, and the more you will surrender at each advance step in your experience. This is the process of spiritual growth.

Temptation doesn't have to end in defeat and discouragement. Satan can be resisted in the strength of Jesus. James promises that when you submit to God, the devil will flee from you.

A Way of Escape

No temptation has overtaken you except such as is common
to man; but God is faithful, who will not allow you to
be tempted beyond what you are able, but with the temptation
will also make the way of escape, that you may be able to bear it.
—1 Corinthians 10:13

There are 31,102 verses in the Bible. Temptation first appears in the fifty-seventh verse. It is an ever-present part of life. Temptation exists on supermarket shelves and magazine covers. It affects us through family, friends, and enemies. Temptation accesses us through television, radio, music, and the internet. Temptation is everywhere, calling us to loosen our hold on God and abandon faith in Christ.

But temptation does not have to get the better of you. The apostle Paul made a remarkable statement to the Corinthians. In *every* temptation, there is a way of escape. When you are tempted to be angry, there is a way of escape. When lust rears its ugly head, there is a way of escape. Even though the temptation to engage in racism, dishonesty, covetousness, or theft assails you, you need not be overcome. God makes a way of escape available to you.

The evening we filmed an *It Is Written* Christmas program was especially cold. A persistent wind cut right through us as we hurried to finish and escape to warmth. The next day or even the next week weren't viable options for filming, so we soldiered on—and shivered on. We hadn't expected such cold weather. My wife, Melissa, wrapped herself in a shawl and a blanket in a futile attempt to keep warm.

The next morning, she discovered that her down jacket had been in our car the entire time! She was fighting cold weather while warmth was less than fifty yards away. She lost a battle she would have won if she had remembered her warm jacket was nearby.

The way of escape from temptation is Jesus. When you remember He is near and call on Him in faith, He will deliver you from temptation. Every time! Remember that there is a way of escape from *every* temptation.

"Do You Really Think . . ."

"Remember the Sabbath day, to keep it holy."

—Exodus 20:8

I was about nine years old when one of my brothers joined a new church. He surprised our family by going to church on Saturday. In fact, he believed the entire seventh day of the week should be kept holy, from sundown Friday to sundown Saturday. Having never heard of such a thing, I asked him why he believed the way he did.

He opened his Bible and had me read from Exodus 20:8–11. It clarified nothing. "Which day is the seventh day of the week?" he asked me.

I knew the answer. "Sunday!"

He suggested I take a look at the calendar hanging on the wall about ten feet away, a calendar my father had purchased from our church. "One, two, three, four, five, six, Saturday?" He wasn't surprised by the confused look on my face. I turned to my mother. "Is Saturday the seventh day of the week?"

She confirmed that yes, it indeed was. I turned back to my brother. "So why do we think of Sunday as the Sabbath day?"

"Because hundreds of years ago, your church changed it from Saturday to Sunday," he answered.

I felt a wave of relief wash over me. "Well, if the church changed it, it has to be right!"

He asked me one more question. "Do you really think any church has the right to change what God wrote in the Ten Commandments?"

The answer was obvious to me, but I don't recall responding to him. I never forgot my brother's question. Years later, when I sensed God calling me to commit my life to Him, I knew I would keep the seventh-day Sabbath. How could I not? I knew little about keeping the Sabbath and had never visited a church that worshiped on Saturday. What would it be like? And what would people think of my decision?

None of that mattered. Before my first Bible study, before attending church, I was committed. I had decided to follow God's Word. I learned a lesson that has stayed with me ever since. You will never regret a decision to follow Jesus and allow the Bible to be the guide for your life.

Too High a Price

"Those who honor Me I will honor, and those
who despise Me shall be lightly esteemed."
—1 Samuel 2:30

As a brand-new Christian, I was blessed to have several friends who acted as role models. Having traveled to London from my home country of New Zealand, intending to see the world, my world was turned upside down when I accepted Jesus as my Lord and Savior. Twelve thousand miles from home, I knew virtually no one in what was at the time a city of seven million people.

But I met people at church who were especially gracious toward me. They not only became friends but also modeled faith in God and helped me understand and grow in my new faith.

Douglas had traveled from his home country in Africa to study actuarial science at a London university. Something he said to me one day struck me and stayed with me. I had asked him how he was able to keep up with his very demanding studies while not studying on Sabbaths. "Many of my fellow students have asked me that," he said. "They told me I was crazy not to study on Friday nights and Saturdays. They said I would never be able to keep up if I didn't use that time for study. I told them I believed that if I honored God, He would honor me and give me the ability to keep up my grades. I told them I never study from sunset Friday to sunset Saturday, as well as Wednesday nights so I can attend prayer meetings."

It was easy to see why other students would think he was at a disadvantage, so I asked him how it was working out. "I am second in my class," he told me. "My classmates can't believe it."

As God told Eli the priest, "Those who honor Me I will honor" (1 Samuel 2:30). There are times when a decision to be faithful to God may seem to be a disadvantage. Sacrificing principle could promise prosperity, status, or opportunity. But God's promise is that those who put Him first and surrender to His will shall experience the blessing of heaven. Compromising your faith to gain an advantage in worldly affairs is too high a price for any Christian to pay.

A Step of Faith

"If you turn away your foot from the Sabbath,
From doing your pleasure on My holy day,
And call the Sabbath a delight, . . .
Then you shall delight yourself in the LORD."

—Isaiah 58:13, 14

They had emigrated from Switzerland. Selling everything they had, they chose to relocate to the United States. After studying potential locations, the husband and wife chose to move to Oregon, where they established a successful tourism venture.

Intrigued by a brochure that they received in the mail, they decided to attend a Bible seminar focusing on the prophecies of the Bible. They were eager to learn. They were Christians but would readily admit they had never really taken their faith seriously. They felt this might be a good opportunity to learn more about the Bible.

They loved what they learned and opened up their hearts to receive Jesus as they had never done before. They would practice their faith and allow the Bible to be their guide. However, there was one challenge. The seventh-day Sabbath was very clearly the will of God for their lives, but what would they do about their business? Saturdays were by far their most profitable day. There was just no way they could operate their business successfully if they were not open on Saturdays.

Or was there? They wondered what would happen if they simply chose to trust God and allow Him to work it out one way or another. They prayed and decided that God was able to bless their business, even if it was closed on the busiest day of the week. And if He chose not to, they would take that as a sign that He had better plans for them.

Late one Friday afternoon, they closed their business, planning to reopen early Sunday morning. When Sunday came, they couldn't believe what happened. They experienced their busiest day since opening their venture. And with each passing week, they found that they were now doing more business in six days than they had previously done in seven.

God asks followers of Jesus to "turn away your foot from the Sabbath, from doing your pleasure on My holy day" (Isaiah 58:13). A lack of faith may see challenges and obstacles. Faith knows that God is able and claims and experiences the blessing of heaven.

Farewell, Beautiful Sabbath!

"You shall delight yourself in the LORD;
And I will cause you to ride on the high hills of the earth,
And feed you with the heritage of Jacob your father.
The mouth of the LORD has spoken."

—Isaiah 58:14

We were walking along a gravel road. It was a Saturday evening, and I had not noticed the sun was setting. My friend, Jairus, stopped, looked toward the horizon, waved his arm as if saying goodbye to someone he knew, and said, "Farewell, beautiful Sabbath!" I had been a Christian for only a couple of years and had never witnessed anyone relate to the Sabbath in that way. I was deeply impressed.

Yes, the Sabbath *was* a beautiful day, and yes, this was farewell. The Sabbath wouldn't be back for almost another week. I realized again what a special experience the Sabbath was. It was a release valve. Work stopped. All secular cares were set to one side. There was time for unhurried worship, for fellowship, and for enjoying nature and the companionship and encouragement of friends.

Before making room for Sabbath observance in my life, my churchgoing experience had included an hour each week at church. In fact, it was usually a little less than an hour a week, especially if I "had to" leave the worship service a little early. That day wasn't any sort of Sabbath at all. There was no rest in the sense God intended. It was an hour at most of churchgoing squeezed into the business of my life. Keeping the Sabbath called a halt to the busyness of what Ezekiel referred to as "the six working days" (Ezekiel 46:1). It placed the focus of my week on my relationship with not just any god, but with the Creator God, the One who formed me, redeemed me, and sustains me and whose Son, Jesus, is soon returning for me.

My friend helped me to see that the Sabbath isn't simply a matter of one day being more right than another. Rather, the Sabbath is the capstone of a close, personal relationship with the Majesty of the heavens. It is recognition of God's ownership of a life and, therefore, of God's pledge to sustain and prosper that life. The Sabbath directs the believer to the heart of God and works to open the heart to heaven's blessing.

One Miraculous Hour

No one can say that Jesus is Lord except by the Holy Spirit.
—1 Corinthians 12:3

Robbie had been relentless in his ridicule of his father. Charles had been attending an Adventist church for several years. He had never been baptized or joined the church, but his relationship with Geri had drawn him into church fellowship. He attended every week and was a much-loved part of the church family.

But Robbie never let up. So it was surprising that when he visited his father for Thanksgiving, he accepted an invitation to attend the evangelistic series the church was conducting. No one expected too much from Robbie's visit to the church. I was going to be speaking that night about the gift of prophecy, not the presentation to which one would typically invite an antagonistic, first-time visitor.

Robbie sat with his father and Geri on the second row. He was attentive throughout the entire presentation. But after the meeting was over, I was surprised to notice Robbie was in tears. Wiping tears from his eyes, Robbie said, "This is what I've been looking for my whole life. I have to be part of this. What do I have to do to be baptized and be part of this church?"

No one anticipated Robbie's reaction. His father was stunned. Just that day, Robbie had been ribbing Charles about attending the church. There was no malice in what Robbie was saying. He simply couldn't understand how his father could be so wrong. But in one evening, his entire attitude had reversed. It couldn't possibly have been the preaching that left Robbie feeling his unanswered questions had been resolved. The Holy Spirit had spoken to him that night, he had surrendered his will to the will of God, and God had touched his life and changed his heart in one miraculous hour.

The Holy Spirit is able to reach a human heart in ways that we can only imagine. Objections are often only resistance in disguise. Conviction frequently manifests itself as argument or disagreement. Before long, Robbie was baptized. He yielded to the convicting power of the Holy Spirit. A moment of surrender allowed God to overcome years of resistance.

Thus Saith the Lord

"Sanctify them by Your truth. Your word is truth."

—John 17:17

In the 1970s, mysterious patterns started showing up in fields across Great Britain. Crops had been flattened into strange patterns, and even though many experts said the designs were not the result of anything supernatural, there were those who believed they were the work of aliens from outer space. In 1991, after men claimed responsibility for the creation of the circles, many people continued to believe the crop circles were part of some wider phenomenon.*

Mysterious patterns appeared, people were intrigued, and in the rush to assign a far-fetched origin to the crop circles, many people were convinced by unlikely explanations. Even when the creators of the patterns themselves raised their hands and said, "It was us," and gave demonstrations showing how they created the mysterious circles, people didn't believe them. When my team produced programs that discussed certain conspiracy theories—in which we were clear we did not agree the earth was flat or that the moon landing was faked—I was assailed by people who questioned my judgment and others who told me I was a danger to society.

How does a mind get to the place where it is prepared to believe the unbelievable? Psychologists say people who are prone to believe off-the-wall ideas are urged on by paranoia, among other things. I was told many times, "You simply can't believe anything they tell you," even when no one was sure who "they" were.

A more important question might be, How does a person get to the place where they will believe the strangest ideas about God and the Bible? Although faith is not merely an intellectual pursuit, it *is* important a person searches for the truth of what the Bible says. Jesus prayed to His Father and said, "Sanctify them by Your truth. Your word is truth."

God's Word prepares us for eternity. While there is certainly room for differing opinions on matters of faith, it is important not to be led into doubt and skepticism. It is important to stand on the Bible, on what may still be referred to as a "thus saith the Lord."

---

* William E. Schmidt, "2 'Jovial Con Men' Demystify Those Crop Circles in Britain," *New York Times*, September 10, 1991, https://www.nytimes.com/1991/09/10/world/2-jovial-con-men-demystify-those-crop-circles-in-britain.html.

Generational Drift

And they forsook the Lord God of their fathers, who had brought
them out of the land of Egypt; and they followed other gods
from among the gods of the people who were all around them.

—Judges 2:12

N o demographic is challenged more by the times in which we live than young
people. Every church on the planet struggles to retain its youth. Judges 2:10, 11
speaks to this when it says,

When all that generation had been gathered to their fathers, another generation
arose after them who did not know the Lord nor the work which He had done
for Israel.

Then the children of Israel did evil in the sight of the Lord, and served the
Baals.

The generation that had not had the experience of their parents or grandparents
drifted catastrophically from God.

History repeats, and today we face the same challenge as that faced by God's people
in earlier times. Raising children in a "good Christian home" simply isn't enough. In
order to maintain faith in God, children must have an experience of their own in the
things of heaven. It is imperative that they are led to develop a personal relationship
with God.

It has often been the case that Grandma and Grandpa chose to follow God and were
faithful believers. Their children were educated in good schools and became successful
in their chosen fields, but *their* children ended up far from where faith led Grandma
and Grandpa. The difference wasn't that Grandma and Grandpa were old-fashioned and
their grandchildren were worldly. Grandma and Grandpa were involved in church life,
took part in mission work, and valued their faith so much they shared it with others.

If we want to see our children stay connected to God, we must teach them to
have a personal relationship with God and give them opportunities to experience and
share their faith. No young person ever turned away from faith in God while having
a meaningful daily devotional experience. The tendency of the world is to drag our
children downstream and away from faith in Christ. If we are intentional, proactive,
and prayerful, our children can be successful Christians who love and live for God.

The Challenge With Having Enough

"Beware that you do not forget the LORD your God by
not keeping His commandments, His judgments,
and His statutes which I command you today."
—Deuteronomy 8:11

Living in a prosperous country brings with it a raft of temptations. It is imperative that people guard against their wealth or possessions overtaking them and compromising their faith in God.

Moses said this in Deuteronomy 8:11–17: "Beware that you do not forget the LORD your God . . . lest—when you have eaten and are full, and have built beautiful houses and dwell in them; and when your herds and your flocks multiply, and your silver and your gold are multiplied, and all that you have is multiplied; when your heart is lifted up, and you forget the Lord your God who brought you out of the land of Egypt, from the house of bondage. . . . then you say in your heart, 'My power and the might of my hand have gained me this wealth.' "

A person who works hard, spends carefully, and invests wisely will typically enjoy a measure of comfort or even prosperity in life. But that prosperity could end up being your undoing. You can become so enamored with your goods that you forget your God.

There is nothing inherently wrong with wealth. God is certainly not against it. Again and again, in the Bible, He blessed certain individuals with fabulous material wealth. But He reminds us that we need to be careful that our prosperity doesn't cause us to forget Him. When your secular needs are being met, it is easier to forget that you have spiritual needs. And you don't have to be wealthy for this to be a challenge. Forgetting God is Lord of all of your life can result in worldly cares becoming much greater than spiritual cares.

It is possible that getting ahead in the world can lead a person to forget that it is God who truly provides for you. Everyone needs possessions to one degree or another. It is appropriate to want to do well in life. But it is necessary to acknowledge that abundance can lead to forgetfulness of God. Abundance is given to us so we might remember God and be supportive of His work.

Remember that it is God who gives you all you have. Let your possessions cause you to turn toward God, not turn away from Him.

Hopeless Cases

He received his entreaty, heard his supplication, and brought him back to
Jerusalem into his kingdom. Then Manasseh knew that the LORD was God.
—2 Chronicles 33:13

M y dad was a hard drinker," Peter told me. "When I was younger, I used to drink
with him. I became a Christian, and my life changed, but Dad never showed
any interest in the Bible."

Anyone who has seen a family member continue on a self-destructive course understands Peter's anguish. But Peter prayed for his father, believing that God could and
one day would reach his father's heart.

When his father was diagnosed with cirrhosis of the liver, Peter knew time was
running out for his dad. "When I held a Daniel seminar in our little hometown, my
father said he wanted to attend," said Peter. "He never missed a night, and when we
began a class for people who wanted to prepare for baptism, my father joined the class."

A week after his baptism, Peter's father was hospitalized and died soon after. But
toward the very end of his life, he surrendered his heart to Jesus and died in the blessed
hope of the Second Coming.

There are many people who might be considered hopeless cases: people who have
been antagonistic to the gospel, who have shown no inclination to know anything
about the Bible, or whose lifestyle has been in opposition to the principles of heaven.
But God sees what we cannot. Would anyone in the ancient world have thought King
Nebuchadnezzar of Babylon would have become a follower of the true God? Yet the
Spirit of God worked upon Nebuchadnezzar's heart. The witness of Daniel and his
friends spoke to the king when argument could not. King Manasseh of Judah lived in
open rebellion against God for decades. The Bible says he "made his son pass through
the fire, practiced soothsaying, used witchcraft, and consulted spiritists and mediums.
He did much evil in the sight of the LORD, to provoke Him to anger" (2 Kings 21:6).
However, "when he was in affliction, he implored the LORD his God, and humbled
himself greatly before the God of his fathers, and prayed to Him" (2 Chronicles 33:12,
13). And God "received his entreaty, heard his supplication, and brought him back to
Jerusalem into his kingdom" (verse 13).

Saul of Tarsus went from merciless persecutor of Christian believers to apostle,
missionary, defender of the faith, and author of the majority of New Testament books.

No case is too tough for God. Peter will see his father in heaven. Who are you praying
you will see there?

Northern Lights

Then God saw everything that He had made,
and indeed it was very good.

—Genesis 1:31

I was concerned, worried even. The pastor and I were in the parking lot of the church after an evangelistic meeting, and it was apparent a major fire had broken out in the mountains above us. The orange-red glow in the distance slowly got bigger, growing in proportion to our anxiety. But after studying the glow a little longer, we realized the mountains were not on fire at all. What we were looking at were the northern lights!

The aurora borealis and their cousins, the southern lights—the aurora australis—are formed when electrically charged particles from the sun collide with gaseous particles in the earth's atmosphere.* The resulting, stunning light show is almost impossible to imagine. I alerted my wife, and we scooped up our baby son and drove out into the country, hoping to get a better view of this amazing phenomenon.

We weren't disappointed. We drove into valley, got out of our car, and watched in awe as shafts of red and green light knifed their way through the valley and passed us on their way to some other place. It was our first time seeing the northern lights, and we have never forgotten that night in Northern California.

It has been said that nature is God's second book. While there is a very sound scientific reason the northern lights appear, their origin goes beyond science to the God of science. The northern lights suggest to us that God is a God of beauty, of phenomenal creativity, and that He loves to amaze us with evidence of His power and brilliance. At the end of the sixth day of Creation week, "God saw everything that He had made, and indeed it was very good" (Genesis 1:31). While six thousand years of sin have marred creation and have obscured our view of the Creator Himself, there is evidence everywhere in creation of the existence of a loving God who delights to amaze His children. Let the marvels of creation point you to the marvelous God of creation.

---

* "Northern Lights," Northern Lights Centre, accessed April 6, 2021, https://www.northernlightscentre.ca /northernlights.html.

Inexplicable Mysteries

For since the creation of the world His invisible attributes are
clearly seen, being understood by the things that are made, even
His eternal power and Godhead, so that they are without excuse.
—Romans 1:20

'll never forget the first time I saw salmon making their way up a stream to spawn. That stream in Washington State was absolutely crowded with the beautiful, large fish and resembled a freeway in rush hour. Somehow, salmon navigate back to the very stream in which they were born in order to spawn. Scientists believe salmon use the earth's magnetic field to guide them, and being euryhaline creatures, they are able to thrive in both salt water and fresh water.

But perhaps even more amazing is the experience of the longfin eel, which leaves its home in the waters of New Zealand to travel almost 1,500 miles (2,414 kilometers) to the ocean surrounding the Pacific Island nation of Tonga. Once there, the longfin eel lays its eggs, which are then carried for many months by ocean currents back to New Zealand, where baby eels are born. Unlike the salmon, which travels back to the place it was born in order to spawn, the longfin eel swims great distances to a place it has never been so it can reproduce. Year after year, this process continues. Longfin eels may live for more than one hundred years, their life cycle challenging scientists to provide an explanation for their incredible behavior.

The inexplicable mysteries of nature direct us to nature's Designer, the one true God whose creativity reveals much about His character. If the only flowers in the world were roses and tulips, it would still be a very beautiful world, and we would see in those flowers unmistakable evidence of God's love of beauty and His desire to enrich our lives. But along with roses and tulips is an almost endless variety of flowers and plants. Trees of every kind, dogs of different shapes and sizes, and people of varied colors who speak different languages all tell us that God is the God of creation. He intentionally made this world, and He beautifies it to draw our attention to Himself.

Speak the Word Only

The centurion answered and said, "Lord, I am not worthy that You should come under my roof. But only speak a word, and my servant will be healed."
—Matthew 8:8

Certain things in the Bible we are forced to accept by faith. There is no logical explanation for God's ability to create the universe out of nothing. One day God spoke into the darkness and said, "Let there be light" (Genesis 1:3). Light appeared. Each day for six days, God simply spoke, and the world was created. He spoke the firmament into existence, as well as water, plants, animals, and more. Psalm 33:6, 9 says,

By the word of the LORD the heavens were made,
And all the host of them by the breath of His mouth.

For He spoke, and it was done;
He commanded, and it stood fast.

But equally important as the objective fact that God made something out of nothing is the reality that there is still creative power in the Word of God—and *re*-creative power. The same Word that called worlds into existence still brings the power of God into our lives. In Matthew, chapter eight, we read about a centurion that pled with Jesus to heal his servant. When Jesus offered to visit his home and heal the servant, the centurion explained his unworthiness and told Jesus to "only speak a word" (Matthew 8:8). He was certain that a word from Jesus would heal his servant. He explained to Jesus that he was also "a man under authority, having soldiers under me. And I say to this one, 'Go,' and he goes; and to another, 'Come,' and he comes; and to my servant, 'Do this,' and he does it" (verse 9).

Recognizing that people acted in accordance with his own word, the centurion believed the word of Jesus possessed power to do infinitely more. Even diseases would obey Jesus' command. Jesus remarked that He had never before seen such faith in all of Israel, and here it was being exercised by a Gentile.

The centurion simply believed that there was power in Christ's word. There was then, and there still is. The same word that called the universe into existence speaks today, with no less power than it manifested then. Bring the creative power of God's Word into your life, and you will experience God's re-creative power at work.

Great and Precious Promises

By which have been given to us exceedingly great and precious promises,
that through these you may be partakers of the divine nature,
having escaped the corruption that is in the world through lust.
—2 Peter 1:4

There is a world of difference between a promise and a good intention. Any child who is told that there is a chance they will have ice cream that evening is wise not to get their hopes too high. But *promise* a child ice cream, and the child understands that ice cream is a certainty. A promise is something definite. You know something is going to happen because a promise has been made.

The Bible is filled with promises made by God. Peter says that God has made promises to you by which you may be restored into the image of God. God's promises make it possible for us to be delivered from the corruption of this broken world.

God's promises are to be believed, and they are to be claimed. The one who claims the promises of God must expect that what God has said will necessarily be so. When God says, "I will never leave you nor forsake you" (Hebrews 13:5), we have His word—His promise—that it is so. When Paul writes that "He who has begun a good work in you will complete it until the day of Jesus Christ" (Philippians 1:6), we confidently anticipate that the God of heaven will work in our lives. There is no doubt there. When God assures the believer who tithes that He will "open for you the windows of heaven and pour out for you such blessing that there will not be room enough to receive it" (Malachi 3:10), there is no place for uncertainty. The promise of forgiveness made in 1 John 1:9 is a life-changing, empowering guarantee that your sins will be forgiven and that you may live before God without guilt or condemnation.

The promises found in the Bible are given to God's people today. You can believe them and claim them to realize the powerful, transformational blessing of God in your daily experience.

Failsafe

*I will instruct you and teach you in the way
you should go; I will guide you with My eye.*

—Psalm 32:8

Emma was desperate. The poison ivy was driving her mad, and now that it was on her face, it was affecting the way she looked. She wanted to get rid of it quickly. A woman she met had a suggestion. Find a certain root, boil it, and apply the brew to the poison ivy. She assured Emma she had done this over many years, and it was a remedy used with great success back in her home country in Europe.

Emma figured she had nothing to lose. She found the root growing in her backyard, dug it up, and placed it in boiling water. After a few minutes, she had a saucepan full of bubbling brown liquid, just as the woman said. When it cooled, she applied it to her face. It smelled awful, but she was prepared to do it if it meant relief from the poison ivy plaguing her. In spite of the odor, she splashed it on her face several times, as directed by the kind woman.

But before long, Emma realized the woman's potion was useless. She felt embarrassed for having listened to a stranger and for following her questionable advice.

When you face challenging situations, whose instructions do you follow? There is no shortage of advice available today. Social media, the internet as a whole, television, friends, family, and colleagues are all ready to offer their opinions. But the counsel you most need is that which God offers, the guidance of Scripture and the leading of the Holy Spirit.

God says He will instruct us, teach us, and guide us. The Bible is far more than a rule book filled with dos and don'ts. The Bible is God seeking to lead and bless your life. He is a loving God looking to prepare His children for eternity. God provides guidance for relationships, health, finances, and so much more. A Bible that isn't read is a Bible that can't affect your life.

Advice comes in many forms, but only God's guidance is failsafe.

Uncommon

I can do all things through Christ who strengthens me.
—Philippians 4:13

Peter, James, and John were fishermen. While Paul was well educated and Luke was a physician, Matthew was a tax collector, both David and the prophet Amos were shepherds, and Elisha was a farmer. Rahab was a prostitute, Gideon came from a poor family, and Moses was a fugitive from justice.

Another who rose from humble beginnings to greatness in God's service was Nehemiah. Nehemiah was the cupbearer (butler) to Artaxerxes, the king of Persia. His access to the world's most powerful monarch placed him where God could use him to effect revival in Judah.

As prophesied by Jeremiah, God's people had spent seventy years in Babylonian captivity. When given the opportunity to appeal to the king on behalf of his nation, Nehemiah said, "If it pleases the king, and if your servant has found favor in your sight, I ask that you send me to Judah, to the city of my fathers' tombs, that I may rebuild it" (Nehemiah 2:5). It was a bold request, but having been granted the king's favor, Nehemiah returned to Jerusalem and set about not only rebuilding the ruined city but also establishing far-reaching reforms that would turn Judah in God's direction in spite of threats, treason, opposition, and overwhelming odds.

Nehemiah was a common man who had made an uncommon commitment to God's service. Although he was not an architect, he rebuilt a wall. While not a military leader, he readied God's people for battle. Despite being neither a priest nor a prophet, he instituted religious reforms in Jerusalem and throughout Judah.

Nehemiah was committed, and his life stands as a shining example of what God can do through the person who makes himself or herself available to the moving of the Holy Spirit. "There is no limit to the usefulness of one who, putting self aside, makes room for the working of the Holy Spirit upon his heart and lives a life wholly consecrated to God."*

As you surrender your life to God, expect Him to use you powerfully for His glory.

---

* Ellen G. White, *The Ministry of Healing* (Mountain View, CA: Pacific Press®, 1942), 159.

A Finished Work

And next to them Meremoth the son of Urijah, the son of Koz, made repairs.
Next to them Meshullam the son of Berechiah, the son of Meshezabel, made
repairs. Next to them Zadok the son of Baana made repairs.
—Nehemiah 3:4

Nehemiah quickly realized the situation in Jerusalem was desperate. The walls of the once-great city had been broken down, and fire had devoured the city gates. It was clear to Nehemiah that immediate action was required, so he appealed to the people of the city to join him in what would be an enormous undertaking.

Their response was dramatic. Nehemiah chapter three begins with an account of the work carried out by Eliashib, the high priest. Then, "next to Eliashib the men of Jericho built. And next to them Zaccur the son of Imri built" (Nehemiah 3:2). The chapter recounts the remarkable cooperation that existed between the people of Jerusalem. Almost thirty times, the phrase "next to them" or "after them" is used in Nehemiah chapter three, demonstrating a profound unity of purpose that achieved extraordinary results. But against this backdrop of unity, there were still those who refused to participate in the work God was doing. "Next to them the Tekoites made repairs; but their nobles did not put their shoulders to the work of their Lord" (verse 5). Their unwillingness to labor was recorded as a lesson for future generations.

God is calling His people today to join together in a similar fashion to fulfill the gospel commission. In great cities, small towns, and villages, there exists a real need for the three angels' messages to be proclaimed. "And this gospel of the kingdom will be preached in all the world as a witness to all the nations, and then the end will come" (Matthew 24:14). God's people will one day band together to herald the glad tidings of a crucified, risen, and soon-coming Savior. May God grant us the grace to unite as did the workers in Nehemiah's day, that we might see a finished work in our time.

A Mind to Work

*So we built the wall, and the entire wall was joined together
up to half its height, for the people had a mind to work.*
—Nehemiah 4:6

When Nehemiah arrived in Jerusalem, he found the city in ruins. His audacious plan to rebuild the city could have been viewed as overly optimistic. This was not the flourishing Jerusalem of King David or King Hezekiah. The city had been destroyed by invading Babylonian armies, and the remaining inhabitants had been demoralized. Nehemiah encouraged the people to rebuild the city wall, an enormous task made more difficult by the opposition of those committed to hinder any progress.

Tobiah, an Ammonite, mocked Nehemiah's people, saying, "Whatever they build, if even a fox goes up on it, he will break down their stone wall" (Nehemiah 4:3). Nehemiah responded by pleading with God for deliverance. "Hear, O our God, for we are despised; turn their reproach on their own heads, and give them as plunder to a land of captivity!" (verse 4).

The ultimate success of the building project can be traced to a single telling factor. Verse 6 says, "The people had a mind to work." One translation says, "The people worked with all their heart" (NIV). Against overwhelming odds, against real enemies committed to their demise, the people of Judah worked enthusiastically to achieve a goal that others may have found impossible. The difference was that they "had a mind to work"; they were committed to carrying out the task God had placed on their hearts.

Church growth is frequently limited or disadvantaged for the same reason. Churches that have "a mind to work" undertake outreach and are involved in the community for the purpose of inviting people to accept Jesus as Lord and Savior. When churches are not growing, it is almost always because the members do not have "a mind to work." Evangelism takes effort, involvement, and investment, but the returns make the effort worthwhile. A ministry mindset transforms a church into a soul-winning center. When the church has "a mind to work," church health and church growth are inevitable.

OCTOBER

October 1

As Safe as a Sparrow

Even the sparrow has found a home,
And the swallow a nest for herself,
Where she may lay her young—
Even Your altars, O LORD of hosts,
My King and my God.

—Psalm 84:3

Passer domesticus, the house sparrow, is the most common bird in the world. Sparrows are typically about six inches long and weigh about an ounce. And they are adaptable. They have been seen feeding eighty floors up on the Empire State Building and spotted breeding in an English coal mine two thousand feet below ground. They thrive around people, but they are vulnerable—to cats, birds of prey, rodents, and humans. Only one in five hatchlings make it to their first breeding season.

The picture painted of the sparrow in Psalms is especially poignant—a beautiful picture: a vulnerable, defenseless, tiny bird, finding refuge in God's house. The psalm begins,

> How lovely is Your tabernacle,
> O LORD of hosts!
> My soul longs, yes, even faints
> For the courts of the LORD;
> My heart and my flesh cry out for the living God (Psalm 84:1, 2).

It goes on to say, "Blessed are those who dwell in your house" (verse 4). Even a little bird is safe, protected, and secure in God's house.

Where do you look when you're worried or concerned, when you feel vulnerable? Where do you find hope? To whom do you turn in those moments when life is squeezing you, when the world seems to be against you, or when you need to feel safe, secure, and sheltered? God has shown us that He offers us safety even in the storms of life. He protected Noah and his family in an ark while floodwaters covered the earth. Moses was cradled in a basket boat when a royal decree threatened his life. Three young Hebrews were shielded by Jesus Himself in a fiery furnace, and Daniel was protected from certain death in a den of lions. Like a mother bird sheltering her young in God's house, you're safe when you're in God's heart. The tiny bird, safe in God's presence, is heaven's assurance that you may find a safe haven in the heart of God.

Just a Little

A little leaven leavens the whole lump.

—Galatians 5:9

She did everything right—until she didn't. And that's when things began to go very wrong.

Anna, a physician, was enjoying an oceanside walk when she spotted some mushrooms growing beneath an oak tree. She took the mushrooms home, planning to cook and eat them. As a doctor, Anna knew she should first check to make sure the mushrooms were safe to eat. But when she saw the mushrooms the next day, she completely forgot about her concerns and cooked the mushrooms and ate them. She woke early the following morning, violently ill. Looking on the internet, she discovered she had eaten death cap mushrooms. Just half of one death cap mushroom contains enough toxins to kill a human being. Those who survive might need a liver transplant.

Fortunately for Anna, she did survive after a period of serious illness.

Although not nearly as serious as what Anna endured, her experience reminds me of a time I was in Africa conducting evangelistic meetings. Drinking water had to be boiled, and all the water I drank had a strong smoky taste. On one occasion, I was given a glass of unboiled water to use for brushing my teeth. I was told it would be fine to use as long as I did not swallow the water. But it tasted so good! I wondered if it would be OK to drink the small amount of water that remained. *What harm could just a little water possibly do?* I wondered. I soon found out. Drinking that water—even though it was only a small amount—was not a good decision. I became violently ill.

I reflected on my decision to drink the water. *It's only a little bit*, I had thought. *Surely I'll be OK.* And I realized that's the same attitude some people have toward sin. "This isn't too serious." "Just this once." "What harm could it possibly do?" But such an attitude ignores the clear statements of the Bible. "The wages of sin is death" (Romans 6:23). Even a little is too much. A moment of carelessness can do great damage. Far better to remain surrendered to God and allow His Spirit to keep you in the right way.

Identity Theft

"Many will say to Me in that day, 'Lord, Lord, have we not prophesied
in Your name, cast out demons in Your name, and done many
wonders in Your name?' And then I will declare to them,
'I never knew you; depart from Me, you who practice lawlessness!' "
—Matthew 7:22, 23

Identity theft occurs when a dishonest person uses the personal information of another individual to assume that person's identity. Identity theft is usually perpetrated for financial gain, and those affected by the practice can suffer significant loss, credit history damage, and enormous inconvenience. Identity thieves fraudulently claim to be someone they are not.

People who claim to be Christians assume another identity. That is, before a person comes to faith in Christ, that person is a lost sinner. Surrendering one's life to Jesus results in that sinner identifying so completely that he or she takes Jesus' name—a Christian identified as a follower of Christ. Jesus is invited into the heart. The entire life is surrendered to Him.

It may be that some who call themselves Christians are, in fact, guilty of identity theft. While a person who fraudulently uses a social security number or driver's license claims to be someone else, they are not. It is a ruse, an act carried out for dishonest gain. The one who names the name of Jesus but does not surrender the heart to the indwelling of the Holy Spirit is not, in reality, a follower of Jesus. He or she has assumed Jesus' identity—taken His name as his or her own—but has not yielded to Jesus.

There are benefits that accrue from being called or considered Christian. Often, there is built-in respect from family, friends, and church family. There is forgiveness of sin and acceptance into the family of God and the very real promise of everlasting life. Life for the Christian believer is a thing of hope. The return of Jesus promises streets of gold, the earth made new, and the companionship of the saved throughout eternity.

But this form of identity theft is as unnecessary as it is futile. Rather than pretending to be a follower of Jesus, every person made in the image of God can experience the reality of true union with Jesus. A prayer for a new heart is always answered in the affirmative. The Spirit of God will gladly reside within the one who invites Him to do so. Jesus identified with the human family when He came to the earth two thousand years ago. It is our privilege to identify with Him now and to do so in sincerity.

Open Wide!

"I am the LORD your God, who brought you out of the land
of Egypt; open your mouth wide, and I will fill it."
—Psalm 81:10

The last act of Elisha the prophet was to impress upon his people God's desire that we pray big prayers and make significant demands upon heaven. Fearing the advancing Syrian army, the young king Joash came to Elisha in a moment of crisis. Shooting an arrow in the direction of his enemies, his hands in the hands of the prophet, he was told by Elisha that he "must strike the Syrians at Aphek till you have destroyed them" (2 Kings 13:17).

The prophet then tested the faith of King Joash. "He said, 'Take the arrows'; so he took them. And he said to the king of Israel, 'Strike the ground'; so he struck three times, and stopped. And the man of God was angry with him, and said, 'You should have struck five or six times; then you would have struck Syria till you had destroyed it! But now you will strike Syria only three times' " (verses 18, 19).

The prophet's displeasure was a reflection of God's disapproval of the king's faithlessness. Knowing that the prophet was encouraging him to press back against Israel's enemies, Joash asked God for little. Striking the ground just three times placed little demand on the grace of God. Pounding the ground repeatedly would have demonstrated a determination and dedication worthy of the leader of God's people. God was dishonored by the king's indifference.

The same is true when God's people ask Him for little rather than much. When you pray for the salvation of a family member, remember that John Knox prayed for an entire nation. When you pray about a medical challenge, remember that blind Bartimaeus requested that he might have his sight restored. The God who fed a nation in a desert and brought forth water from a rock, who opened up a highway through an ocean and troubled Egypt with an unprecedented outpouring of plagues, has ways to provide for you of which you know nothing.

God spoke to His people and said, "Open your mouth wide, and I will fill it" (Psalm 81:10). The God of heaven is the God of great gifts, miracles, and deliverance. Expect God to work on your behalf. Expect Him to do great things.

October 5

Fueling the Fire

Therefore we do not lose heart. Even though our outward man
is perishing, yet the inward man is being renewed day by day.
—2 Corinthians 4:16

The water in the home in which I grew up was heated by a fire that burned in a firebox in our kitchen. Every day, summer or winter, we fed the fire with wood or coal, ensuring we had hot water for our family's needs. If the fire had not been lit, there was no hot water. We made sure we always had newspaper and kindling wood on hand, and a steady supply of coal was delivered to our home. It was a part of our everyday lives. Light the fire, keep it going, make sure we have hot water. It happened every single day. If it didn't, the water was stone cold.

A relationship with God is very similar. The fires of faith have to be kindled every day. Without coming to God to heat your faith, you'll be surviving on whatever faith you have left in the tank. It doesn't take long for hot water—or faith—to cool and eventually become cold.

Ellen White's counsel in *Steps to Christ* is as important today as it has ever been. She wrote, "Consecrate yourself to God in the morning; make this your very first work. Let your prayer be, 'Take me, O Lord, as wholly Thine. I lay all my plans at Thy feet. Use me today in Thy service. Abide with me, and let all my work be wrought in Thee.' This is a daily matter."*

These important words spell out how the mechanics of Christianity operate. Every day we are granted the privilege of inviting God into our lives. Our prayer is to be one of complete surrender: "Take me as *wholly* Thine. I lay all my plans at Your feet. Use me today as You see fit. Dwell in me, and let my actions be guided by Your Spirit."

This is the life of faith, the life of a Christian believer—total surrender to God, permitting His will to be done in one's daily life. The person who follows this divine plan will possess a faith that will never run cold.

---

* Ellen G. White, *Steps to Christ* (Washington, DC: Review and Herald®, 1956), 70.

When We Submit

Who can bring a clean thing out of an unclean? No one!
—Job 14:4

The first book of the Bible to be written presents us with timeless questions, questions that must be answered if we are to experience eternal closeness with God.

As Job wrestled with questions of life, death, and suffering, he asked, "Who can bring a clean thing out of an unclean?" (Job 14:4). Elsewhere, the Bible tells us that "all our righteousnesses are like filthy rags" (Isaiah 64:6) and that we are "wretched, miserable, poor, blind, and naked" (Revelation 3:17). How, then, may we possess the purity needed to enter into eternal life?

Christ's Object Lessons tells us:

By His perfect obedience He has made it possible for every human being to obey God's commandments. When we submit ourselves to Christ, the heart is united with His heart, the will is merged in His will, the mind becomes one with His mind, the thoughts are brought into captivity to Him; we live His life. This is what it means to be clothed with the garment of His righteousness. Then as the Lord looks upon us He sees, not the fig-leaf garment, not the nakedness and deformity of sin, but His own robe of righteousness, which is perfect obedience to the law of Jehovah.*

Salvation is contingent upon what Jesus has done for us. "By His perfect obedience" we may obey God's commandments. The only appropriate response to Jesus' death for us is to submit ourselves to Him. When we do, heaven works to unite our heart, will, mind, and thoughts with His own. It is a work Jesus does when we submit to Him, a work we can never do for ourselves but that must be done if we are to inherit eternal life.

We need not think this work is completed in a moment. The work of growing in Christ is a work that continues for a lifetime, as we yield more and more to the presence of Jesus. Jesus died so that we may live. Without the Cross, salvation would be an impossibility. Daily submission on the part of the believer brings the presence of God into the life, as the Holy Spirit restores in the sinner the character of God.

---

* Ellen G. White, *Christ's Object Lessons* (Washington, DC: Review and Herald®, 1941), 312.

Challenging Questions

"Can you search out the deep things of God?
Can you find out the limits of the Almighty?"

—Job 11:7

I t is important for a follower of Jesus to know something about his or her limits.

God is vast. He is eternal. The Bible says, "The heaven of heavens cannot contain Him" (2 Chronicles 2:6). He created the world out of nothing, hung the planets in space, opened the Red Sea, healed the sick, and raised the dead. Human beings, on the other hand, are finite and prone to err. Perhaps that is why Zophar the Naamathite asked, "Can you search out the deep things of God? Can you find out the limits of the Almighty?" (Job 11:7).

Human understanding is very limited, yet there exists a temptation to assume we may know more than God has revealed. While God has given great light concerning His Word, we must guard against placing our wisdom above that of God.

With some regularity, voices are heard predicting when Jesus will return to the earth. These prognostications are usually presented something like this: "I'm not saying exactly when Jesus is going to return, but if you look at this prophecy, it seems to me that it could possibly be . . ." Forecasts of that nature are never helpful. Jesus said we do not know the day or the hour of His return (Matthew 24:36). His statement should settle the question.

The Bible provides us with no shortage of challenging questions. How can three Persons be one God? How can the Father, the Son, and the Holy Spirit be separate, eternal, and yet one? While there is more than enough in the Bible to answer most questions, there is not enough to remove every possible query or objection.

While we strive to enter through the strait gate, it is important that we are not distracted by questions for which there are no answers. Far better to content ourselves with what God has clearly revealed than to become sidetracked and waylaid by questions we cannot yet hope to resolve.

Viewing God

"For My thoughts are not your thoughts,
nor are your ways My ways," says the LORD.

—Isaiah 55:8

It is possible to view God through a human lens without taking time to better understand Him as He wishes to be understood. It is a very human trait to choose not to forgive. People have often been heard to say, "I will never forgive that person for what they did to me." We can understand that. Pain is painful. Hurts hurt. It isn't easy to see through our crises to a place of grace and peace.

This may be why some people find it hard to accept God's forgiveness. In spite of God repeatedly telling us He is willing to forgive our sins, some people have a hard time believing God could forgive them. The Bible says in Psalm 86:5, "For You, Lord, are good, and ready to forgive, and abundant in mercy to all those who call upon You." David, who had been in desperate need of God's forgiveness, wrote in Psalm 103:12, "As far as the east is from the west, so far has He removed our transgressions from us."

A woman once asked me if God could forgive her for a terrible thing she had done. Whatever it was, she had committed a certain sin more than fifty years before. She told me she had confessed her sin to God many times a day, every day, during those fifty-plus years. A quick calculation revealed to me she had confessed that one sin at least fifty thousand times. I told her that her problem was not sin but that she didn't believe God. When she protested my assertion, I had her read 1 John 1:9: "If we confess our sins, He is faithful and just to forgive us our sins and to cleanse us from all unrighteousness."

God sees things from heaven's perspective. After promising He will forgive repentant sinners (Isaiah 55:7), God says,

> "For My thoughts are not your thoughts,
> Nor are your ways My ways," says the LORD.
> "For as the heavens are higher than the earth,
> So are My ways higher than your ways,
> And My thoughts than your thoughts" (verses 8, 9).

Viewing God through the lens of Scripture gives us an accurate picture of who God really is.

All Scripture

All Scripture is given by inspiration of God, and is profitable for doctrine,
for reproof, for correction, for instruction in righteousness.
— 2 Timothy 3:16

Look at many Bibles, and you'll typically see that the pages of the Gospels are a little worn. The paper has become slightly discolored around the edges, and some of the pages may even have become dog-eared. The same might be true for the Psalms, the book of Acts, and maybe Romans or Revelation. Those books of the Bible are usually well read. But look at the rest of the Bible, and you'll more often than not notice that those other pages are pristine—virtually untouched. While some books of the Bible are read again and again, other parts of those same Bibles appear as new as they did on the day the Bible was purchased!

On the one hand, it is not at all surprising. Few people read the "begats" over and over again. Even though the book of Zechariah is frequently quoted in the New Testament, it is tougher to digest than the Gospel of John. But Paul, writing to Timothy, said that "all Scripture is given by inspiration of God, and is profitable." While most people have their favorite Bible passages, books, and stories, much is missed if parts of the Bible are neglected or ignored. There's a blessing in reading the book of Amos, the story of Hosea, the wisdom of Ecclesiastes, and the prophecies of Jeremiah. While the book of Acts reads rather easily, the book of Hebrews takes a little more diligence but contains no less blessing. The gripping stories of First and Second Kings and First and Second Samuel are powerful reading, while the books of Ezra, Nehemiah, Esther, and Jude, for example, contain beautiful insights into the character of God and the plan of salvation. As you come to the Bible, read broadly. Let as much of God's Word speak to your heart as possible, and get the fullest picture you can of the Word of God. All of the inspired Word of God is given for our eternal good!

Hopeful

*These things I have written to you who believe in the name of the
Son of God, that you may know that you have eternal life, and
that you may continue to believe in the name of the Son of God.*
—1 John 5:13

He had waited to speak with me. It was obvious something was weighing heavily on his heart. "Pastor, I don't think I'm ever going to be able to go to heaven," he began. He had been told that in order to be ready for heaven, he had to stop sinning and lead a morally perfect life. He would have to completely stop sinning before he could be sure he would be saved.

"And I take it you're not able to do that?" I inquired.

"No. I can't. There's no way."

"Here's what I want you to do," I continued. He listened intently. "I want you to look at this from a biblical perspective."

I explained to the young man that when we come to Him in faith, Jesus saves us absolutely and completely just as we are. "Like Zacchaeus, the thief on the cross, and the woman taken in adultery. Were they forgiven and saved right then and there?" He had to agree that, yes, they were.

"Do you think they had gained the victory over every sin in their lives?" The answer was obvious. They had not. We agreed that as these individuals maintained their surrender to Jesus, they would continue to grow more and more in the image of God, all the while possessing the righteousness of Christ. It was clear that if people had to wait until they had overcome every known sin before they received the gift of salvation, one could never have the assurance of salvation. And yet John wrote that "you may know that you have eternal life" (1 John 5:13).

The one who chooses Jesus as Lord and Savior surrenders his or her life to Jesus and grows more and more into the image of God. Our primary focus need not be our sins or our moral imperfection. Our focus must be on Jesus, who died so that we might be saved. The one who looks to Jesus is clothed with the righteousness of Christ and, denying self, is "renewed day by day" (2 Corinthians 4:16).

The young man went away hopeful. He could surrender his life to Jesus, believe he is accepted by heaven, and grow each day in the grace of God.

October 11

Invite Them to Come In

"Therefore go into the highways, and as
many as you find, invite to the wedding."

—Matthew 22:9

When it was constructed in 2005, the South China Mall in Dongguan was the largest mall in the world. It covered an area of almost ten million square feet, or 230 acres, with over seven million square feet of leasable space. There were 2,350 retail outlets, and the seven zones in the mall were modeled on iconic international cities or regions, such as Paris, Rome, and the Caribbean. It boasted a 1.3-mile-long canal and such features as a giant Egyptian sphinx and an 82-foot-tall replica of the Arc de Triomphe. But owing to its location and because most people who lived near the mall were factory workers with little time or disposable income, the shoppers simply didn't show up. One hundred thousand visitors a day were expected, but years later, only one percent of the retail spaces were in use.*

Many churches today are nearly empty when they really should be bursting at the seams. Sometimes it is a matter of changing economics or shifting demographics, but the reality is that people need Jesus today as much as they ever have. The church has the answers to the problems being faced by the world today.

In the parable of the wedding feast in Matthew 22, Jesus said, "Go into the highways, and as many as you find, invite to the wedding" (verse 9). People don't typically invite themselves to church or wake up one morning and suddenly decide to become Christian. If we want to see people come to Jesus, it's important we share with them, minister to them, invite them, and help them to see the character of Jesus.

Too often, the church concedes defeat, believing that church growth is impossible. But as long as church members are satisfied with small things, they are disqualified to receive the great things of God. Is there someone with whom you could share your faith in Jesus or encourage to connect with your church family? The church will grow. God wills that His kingdom expands. Do His people share that burden?

---

* Matthew Keegan, "World's Biggest Shopping Mall in China Is No Longer a 'Ghost Mall'," The Culture Trip, January 31, 2018, https://theculturetrip.com/asia/china/articles/worlds-biggest-shopping-mall-china-no-longer-ghost-mall/.

The Greatest Battle

*Let us therefore come boldly to the throne of grace, that we
may obtain mercy and find grace to help in time of need.*
—Hebrews 4:16

Millions of people died, and millions more were injured during World War I. The death toll from World War II ran into the tens of millions. Yet, it has been said that "the warfare against self is the greatest battle that was ever fought."*

It isn't uncommon to hear this warfare described as a battle against a bad temper or the desire for chocolate cake. But the battle against self is more insidious than many people realize.

Those who believe they have gone too far to be forgiven by God are, in reality, losing the battle against self. The Bible plainly states that if we confess our sins, God will not only forgive our sins but will also cleanse us from all unrighteousness (1 John 1:9). That is the Word of God. Confronted by this truth, a sinner has two options: either to believe that what the Bible says is true and that the sinner can indeed be forgiven or to look at one's self and focus on sin rather than the Savior.

A Christian who has wandered from God may be tempted to believe that he or she has strayed so far that return is impossible. But the experiences of the prodigal son, King Manasseh, and others provide emphatic assurance that God welcomes back those who have wandered far from home. The Bible is clear that God accepts faulty human beings. Discouragement or distrust of that fact is simply a manifestation of self.

The book of Hebrews is abundantly clear that Jesus is our heavenly High Priest, and those who come to Him in faith "may obtain mercy, and find grace to help in time of need" (Hebrews 4:16). Confronted by this evidence, it can only be self that chooses to turn from the forgiveness Jesus offers and focus instead on human weakness and failure.

The one who chooses to look at sin instead of the Savior and chooses to reject God's grace and love is choosing self over salvation. The battle against self is truly a great battle. Making one's sin bigger than God's grace and mercy is a form of self-centeredness that has entangled far too many.

---

* Ellen G. White, *Steps to Christ* (Washington, DC: Review and Herald®, 1956), 43.

Look and Live

Then the LORD said to Moses, "Make a fiery serpent, and set it on a pole; and it shall be that everyone who is bitten, when he looks at it, shall live."

—Numbers 21:8

Jesus' explanation to Nicodemus of the plan of salvation contains what is likely the most well-known verse in the entire Bible. But on the way to John 3:16, Jesus pointed Nicodemus to a curious passage of the Bible in an attempt to help the respected Pharisee understand how a person is saved.

When Jesus told Nicodemus it was essential that he be born again, Nicodemus appeared confused as to what Jesus meant. So Jesus directed him to Numbers 21 and recounted a story that was so clear Nicodemus could not possibly fail to understand. Jesus said, "As Moses lifted up the serpent in the wilderness, even so must the Son of Man be lifted up, that whoever believes in Him should not perish but have eternal life" (John 3:14, 15).

Journeying through the wilderness and overtaken by discouragement, the children of Israel complained bitterly, even expressing contempt for the very means God was employing to keep them alive. "There is no food and no water, and our soul loathes this worthless bread" (Numbers 21:5). When venomous snakes moved among them and people began to die, God instructed Moses to make a serpent of brass and place it on a pole, "and it shall be that everyone who is bitten, when he looks at it, shall live" (verse 8).

It required no pilgrimages, no penance, no money given, and there was no distinction between one person or another. In order to live, all a person had to do was look at the snake on the pole. God asked them to look and live. And this is how Jesus explained the plan of salvation to Nicodemus.

We are to look to Jesus and live. The one who beholds Jesus, who looks upon the Savior, is looking upon life itself. While sin ends in death, eternal life is found in looking away from sin and self and looking to the One who died for the sins of the world. By beholding Jesus, we are changed into His image. Old things pass away, and Jesus remakes the life in His image. We are to look to Jesus and live.

The Pulling Horse

Now the purpose of the commandment is love from a pure heart, from a good conscience, and from sincere faith, from which some, having strayed, have turned aside to idle talk.
—1 Timothy 1:5, 6

A wise pastor once gave me a powerful lesson in church unity in just six words. "What I have found in my ministry," he said to me, "is that a pulling horse does not kick."

If the old saying is true and idle hands are indeed the devil's workshop, one can only imagine the potential trouble that exists in a congregation that is not active in mission and ministry. Little wonder that entire churches get bogged down in matters of little importance when church members are not engaged in service and the church does not have a clearly defined outreach plan.

The person who is opening up the Bible with those who are searching for meaning and truth or is otherwise sharing the love of Jesus with others has neither the time nor the inclination to engage in petty politics or inconsequential church squabbles. One who prays for the opportunity and ability to share Jesus with the lost will have patience with young people and compassion toward the erring. If half of the people who attended any one church were receiving a daily baptism of the Holy Spirit, that same Spirit would develop in them grace and forbearance that would enable them to turn the other cheek and work for solutions rather than perpetuate problems. One can only imagine what would happen if the entire church was praying that prayer!

When Jesus commissioned His disciples to go and "make disciples of all the nations" (Matthew 28:19), He undoubtedly intended that a believer would start nearest where they were. Our families, our communities, and our places of education or work are all venues where followers of Jesus are able to let their light shine for the glory of God. As we take personal ministry seriously, the important things—church growth, soul winning, evangelism, and mission—take the primary place in our lives, while less important things—the color of the carpet in church, who gets to be a deacon or an elder—are treated with appropriate emphasis. When mission is our focus, church members unite on what is truly important in God's eyes. The horse pulls and doesn't kick.

October 15

The Immortal Woman

"This is the bread which came down from heaven—not as your fathers
ate the manna and are dead. He who eats this bread will live forever."
—John 6:58

Henrietta was raised by her grandfather in rural Virginia in a small cabin that was once slaves' quarters. She knew she was not well when she moved to Baltimore, Maryland, with her husband and children in search of work. In 1951, Henrietta was diagnosed with cervical cancer. She was dead before the year was over.

But a medical marvel occurred. It was discovered that, unlike normal human cells, cells taken from the body of Henrietta Lacks lived on in a laboratory, making them invaluable for medical research. In her death, with her cells still living, HeLa cells became world-famous as they were used to develop the polio vaccine, HIV and AIDS treatments, and numerous other treatments and research projects. This unassuming woman who died at the age of just thirty-one, treated at a segregated hospital during the height of Jim Crow laws, has influenced medicine more than almost any other woman in history. Her cells still live more than seventy years after her death. She has often been referred to as The Immortal Woman.

God promises everlasting life to all who believe in Jesus. Life on earth is painfully short. Someone born in India can expect to live to about 70 years. Life expectancy in Jamaica is 75; Puerto Rico, 80; and Japan, 85, even though God created human beings to live forever! The book of Genesis tells us that Adam lived to be 930, Jared lived to be 962, and Noah died at the age of 950, still pitifully short of God's ideal. Today it is rightfully considered to be an achievement to live to be 100. In British Commonwealth countries, centenarians may receive a congratulatory birthday card from the reigning monarch.

In referring to Himself as the Bread of Life, Jesus promised that "he who eats this bread will live forever." Eternity brings with it the promise of life without end, life in the presence of Jesus, the angels, and the redeemed. Tales of the legendary Fountain of Youth have captivated people for centuries. But for much longer, God has promised much more. Eternal life is granted in Jesus to all who believe.

No Limit

By the grace of God I am what I am, and His grace toward
me was not in vain; but I labored more abundantly than they
all, yet not I, but the grace of God which was with me.
—1 Corinthians 15:10

Neil Armstrong walked on the moon. Rosa Parks refused to sit in the back of the bus. Johannes Gutenberg invented the movable-type printing press. Alexander Graham Bell invented the telephone. And Florence Nightingale was the founder of modern nursing. Each person made a monumental, lasting impact on the world.

There are only so many people who will invent, develop, create, or pioneer, but any single person can have a greater influence than the most prominent inventor or titan of industry.

Consider this statement: "There is no limit to the usefulness of one who, putting self aside, makes room for the working of the Holy Spirit upon his heart and lives a life wholly consecrated to God."* King David was a young shepherd before he led Israel to power and prosperity. Gideon described himself as "the least in my father's house" (Judges 6:15) but went on to deliver Israel from its enemies and restore peace to the beleaguered nation. James and John were fishermen, and Naaman was led to faith in God owing to the humble witness of an enslaved young girl. None seemed likely candidates to do great things for God, but as has often been stated, God does not necessarily call the equipped; God equips the called.

When Jesus called Simon and Andrew to be His disciples, He said that *He* would make them fishers of men. The qualifications needed by the two brothers in order to be effective gospel ministers would be granted them of heaven. Jesus Himself would make them fishers of men.

If we want to live life with no limit, we must notice there is a caveat. It is as self is put aside, as room is made for the Holy Spirit, and as one's life is lived in complete surrender to God that there is "no limit to the usefulness of one." As good as training, education, and experience may be, it is surrender to God that truly qualifies a person to be used for His glory. When one's life is given to Jesus to do as He wills, there is truly no limit to what God can do.

---

* Ellen G. White, *The Ministry of Healing* (Mountain View, CA: Pacific Press®, 1942), 159.

Working in You

Therefore, my beloved, as you have always obeyed, not as in
my presence only, but now much more in my absence, work
out your own salvation with fear and trembling; for it is God
who works in you both to will and to do for His good pleasure.
—Philippians 2:12, 13

I t often isn't until you need a flashlight that you realize the importance of working batteries! A flashlight without working batteries is useless. The difference between a useful flashlight and a useless flashlight is often a matter of what is inside. The same is true for disciples of Jesus Christ. The key to a successful Christian experience is what—or who—is at work inside the believer.

Paul underscored this when he wrote to the church at Philippi. We are tempted to question why Paul would tell his readers, "Work out your own salvation" (Philippians 2:12). But clearly, Paul isn't even hinting at righteousness by works. He explains his instruction in the very next verse, where he says, "It is God who works in you both to will and to do for His good pleasure" (verse 13).

Genuine Christianity shows God's working in the life. A believer without Jesus in the heart is like a flashlight without batteries. People may try to compensate for the absence of Jesus in their lives by doing good deeds, saying the right things, or eating the right foods. But without Jesus in the heart, our good deeds are as useless as a flashlight without batteries. They are no better than the fig-leaf garments worn by Adam and Eve after their cataclysmic fall into sin.

When God enters your life, He brings His power, His purity, and His presence. He works in you, transforming your life into a theater of His mighty grace. Day-to-day Christianity becomes a matter of surrendering one's life to God. As we learn to do so more and more, the God who dwells in us will transform us and prepare us for eternity. Without Jesus dwelling in the heart, eternity will only ever be an illusion. Jesus in the heart brings faith alive.

Free Indeed

"If the Son makes you free, you shall be free indeed."
—John 8:36

The nineteen men who died in the Tuckasegee River in western North Carolina were facing abother day of forced labor when tragedy struck. They were part of a prison chain gang digging the Cowee Tunnel for the railroad that was opening up the area for logging and mining.

As they crossed the river in a boat being pulled by a cable line, water that had pooled in the bottom of the boat caused some of the men to believe the boat was sinking. They surged forward, causing the boat to capsize. Thirty men went into the river. Eleven came out alive. Nineteen men drowned that day, December 30, 1882.*

The tragedy was an accident, but an accident that never should have happened. The men were convicts who, like so many African Americans at that time, were being leased by the state to business enterprises. Convict leasing addressed the labor shortage that arose when slavery was abolished and provided states with enormous revenues. Men were frequently arrested on the flimsiest of pretexts and, unable to pay their fines, were forced into a grossly unjust system that was in reality slavery by another name in reality.

Slavery had long ended, but free men had their freedom stripped away. Power and profits were valued over justice and humanity. Leased convicts were free men who were anything but free.

Both the world and the church are today filled with people who are free in name only. When Jesus died on Calvary's cross, He opened heaven's gates to all who are willing to go. He offered eternity to all who would choose the gift of everlasting life. But rather than serving Jesus and enjoying the freedom He brings, countless millions of people ignore freedom and remain enslaved to sin. We are the servants of the one we choose to serve. Jesus came to the world to break the chains that bind us to the old life of sin and guilt and give us new hearts and lives.

Real freedom is found through faith in Jesus. "If the Son makes you free, you shall be free indeed" (John 8:36).

---

* Gary Carden, "All of the Passengers Were Cast Into the Icy Waters Where They Struggled in Vain," *Appalachian History*, May 22, 2013, https://www.appalachianhistory.net/2013/05/all-of-the-passengers-were-cast-into-the-icy-waters.html.

Chains

For when you were slaves of sin,
you were free in regard to righteousness.

—Romans 6:20

Among the nineteen who drowned in the Cowee Tunnel near Dillsboro, North Carolina, in December 1882 were Charles Eason—who was just fifteen years old—and Allen Tillman, James Fisher, and Jim McCallum, who were eighteen. They should never have been fed into a system designed to control them, prevent their advancement, and strip away their freedom.

They were convicts who had been leased to work on the railroad as part of a chain gang. Not only could they not swim, but having been chained together, it also was impossible for them to survive what otherwise would have been a simple mishap.*

Jesus came to the world to break the chains that bind us to the old life. "You were slaves of sin." "But now having been set free from sin, and having become slaves of God, you have your fruit to holiness, and the end, everlasting life" (Romans 6:20, 22).

One who is controlled by lust cannot claim to be free but is held captive by desire. Many are held in chains by temper, dishonesty, or addiction and are not experiencing the freedom that Jesus came to give. God is able to free any soul from the grasp of sin. It is not necessary to be held captive by the old life.

While he was being held in prison, "Peter was sleeping, bound with two chains between two soldiers; and the guards before the door were keeping the prison. Now behold, an angel of the Lord stood by him, and a light shone in the prison; and he struck Peter on the side and raised him up, saying, 'Arise quickly!' And his chains fell off his hands" (Acts 12:6, 7).

Peter's experience was echoed in Charles Wesley's classic hymn, "And Can It Be": "My chains fell off, my heart was free." If you allow Him to do so, Jesus will break the chains that connect you to the old life of sin, and *your* heart will be free.

---

* Gary Carden, "All of the Passengers Were Cast Into the Icy Waters Where They Struggled in Vain," *Appalachian History*, May 22, 2013, https://www.appalachianhistory.net/2013/05/all-of-the-passengers-were-cast-into-the-icy-waters.html.

Purified

*Who gave Himself for us, that He might redeem us from every lawless deed
and purify for Himself His own special people, zealous for good works.*
—Titus 2:14

Purified water doesn't always look different from water that has not been purified. Unfiltered tap water, for example, looks much the same as filtered water.

In order to purify drinking water, a reverse osmosis process, a carbon filter, or a sand filter might be used. Even then, filtered water might not *look* much different. But close examination would reveal it is not the same as it once was. And it will certainly taste different.

Growing up, I often swam in a river where the water was a kind of green color. It wasn't possible to see our hands underwater unless we held them close to our face, and yet our town's drinking water came from that river. But between the river and the faucets in our home, that water was purified, meaning it could be safely used and consumed.

That purification process is what God wants to achieve in your life. Titus says Jesus "gave himself for us, that he might redeem us from all iniquity, and purify unto himself a peculiar people, zealous of good works" (Titus 2:14, KJV). God wishes to purify His people and remove what should not be within them. When that work is done, and even while it is being done, it might not be easy to tell the difference from the outside. But the work God wants to do in the life of His children is such a complete work that He removes the impurities from within, from inside the heart—inside the mind.

Purifying sinners speaks to the grace and power of God. Some people are so aware of their shortcomings and failings they think that not even God can clean them up. But this is what God seeks to do in every life. Through the power of the Holy Spirit, God works in lives to whatever extent He is permitted to do so.

Those who yield to the work of the Holy Spirit will be purified by God and prepared for everlasting life.

The Apology Line

I will cleanse them from all their iniquity by which they have sinned against Me, and I will pardon all their iniquities by which they have sinned and by which they have transgressed against Me.

—Jeremiah 33:8

In the early 1980s, an artist in New York City began Apology Line, an answering service that allowed people to call and leave a confidential, recorded apology for misdeeds they had committed. Some people called to apologize for small matters, such as petty theft and lying, while some phoned the Apology Line to ask forgiveness for marital infidelity, violent assault, and murder.

But what came as a surprise was the sheer volume of calls that were received. More than a hundred thousand people apologized—to no one in particular—and in many cases expressed their gratitude that the service had been made available. People felt a burden was lifted when they were able to apologize and ask forgiveness for things that had burdened them for years in many cases.*

God set up an Apology Line millennia ago. While calling a phone number and leaving a message of apology doesn't achieve anything meaningful in terms of actual experience, those who come to God in sorrow for sin are assured God will not only pardon but also will "abundantly pardon" (Isaiah 55:7).

There isn't a single reason that a person should not come to God to ask for forgiveness for sin. Sin causes guilt, shame, regret, and sorrow. Unconfessed sin—the burden of sin carried and not released—frequently manifests itself as dysfunction. Carrying a sense of responsibility for actions that have caused pain or loss in the lives of others can be debilitating. But God assures sinners that He is a God of forgiveness. Those who bring their burdens to Him, willing to relinquish their sinful past, can know God will forgive, cleanse, and restore them to oneness with Himself.

The Apology Line in New York City was an art project that took on a life of its own, a gimmick that spawned a television movie before coming to an end in 1995. Divine pardon has been available to sinners since the Garden of Eden. God offers pardon—*abundantly.*

---

* Michael Kaplan, "The True Story of Allen 'Mr. Apology' Bridge, Founder of an Apology Hotline," *New York Post*, January 16, 2021, https://nypost.com/article/true-story-of-allan-bridge-mr-apology/.

Extravagant Forgiveness

"For as the heavens are higher than the earth, so are My ways higher than your ways, and My thoughts than your thoughts."
—Isaiah 55:9

The prophet Isaiah appealed to a rebellious people who were steeped in idolatry, immersed in sin, and in great need of God's grace and mercy. Through the prophet, God said, "Let the wicked forsake his way, and the unrighteous man his thoughts: and let him return unto the LORD, and He will have mercy upon him; and to our God, for He will abundantly pardon" (Isaiah 55:7).

Such extravagant forgiveness challenges selfish, sinful human beings. We are programmed from childhood to believe that people get what they deserve. "If you are good, we'll have ice cream when we get home." "You exceeded the speed limit, so you are receiving a ticket." It's perfectly understandable in human terms, but it can often jaundice our view of God—who operates in a completely different manner.

Following the assurance that God will abundantly pardon the repentant sinner, Isaiah explains that God doesn't think like we do, " 'For My thoughts are not your thoughts, nor are your ways My ways,' says the LORD" (verse 8).

While Moses was receiving the Ten Commandments from the hand of God, his brother, Aaron, led the children of Israel into gross apostasy, crafting a golden calf to be the centerpiece of worship. Yet God not only forgave Aaron but also appointed him to be the high priest (Exodus 40:13). A Gentile prostitute not only was accepted by God and His people, but Rahab also became an ancestor of Jesus (Matthew 1:1–16). Although religious men lined up to stone a woman taken in adultery to death, Jesus told her that He did not condemn her (John 8:11). And not long after Peter had denied Jesus the night He was betrayed, Jesus commissioned Peter to be a leader of His people (John 21:15–17).

None of this is to suggest the God of heaven treats sin lightly. He does not. But God is gracious and meets sinners with patience, sympathy, and forgiving love. His ways are not our ways, but by God's grace, our ways may be His ways.

Lightened With His Glory

After these things I saw another angel coming down from heaven,
having great authority, and the earth was illuminated with his glory.
—Revelation 18:1

Where would you turn were you to try to locate yourself in a passage of the Bible? First Thessalonians 4 speaks of the resurrection of the righteous and the catching up of the saved of all ages when Jesus returns. That's one place you might see yourself. In Revelation 14, the everlasting gospel goes to "every nation, tribe, tongue, and people" (verse 6), which clearly includes everyone living on the earth in the final days of history. "Here are they that keep the commandments of God, and the faith of Jesus" (verse 12, KJV). That's another place you might see yourself in the Bible, somewhere God sees you.

Revelation 18:1 is a picture of the earth illuminated with a manifestation of the character of God. An angel in Revelation typifies a messenger. In this case, a messenger shares a heavenly message with the world, and the result is that the earth is lit up with a revelation of the glory of God, which will be witnessed in His people. Revelation 18:1 is where God tells His people that His plan for them is that they are so filled with the presence of Jesus that they reveal His character to the world.

Undoubtedly, that is an extremely high calling. But God calls us to great heights. "God's ideal for His children is higher than the highest human thought can reach. . . . The plan of redemption contemplates our complete recovery from the power of Satan. Christ always separates the contrite soul from sin."*

To the person struggling with addiction or seemingly unable to shake off old habits or overcome certain weaknesses, such thoughts could seem almost impossible. But the power of the gospel is found in what God does in a sinner's life, things that the sinner cannot do for himself or herself. Even in our weakness—perhaps especially in our weakness—we must never doubt God's ability to do in us that which we could never do for ourselves.

---

* Ellen G. White, *The Desire of Ages* (Mountain View, CA: Pacific Press®, 1940), 311.

In Their Midst

*"As many as I love, I rebuke and chasten.
Therefore be zealous and repent."*
—Revelation 3:19

Since virtually the beginning of time, the "church" has had a great many problems to contend with. Adam and Eve were cast out of the Garden of Eden. The father of the faithful was duplicitous. Israel wandered in the wilderness for forty years.

The early Christian church was hampered by a corrosive theology that attempted to enforce Jewish traditions upon Christian believers. And today, there is no shortage of voices prepared to proclaim that the church falls woefully short of God's ideal. Which, of course, would have to be true. The church is made up of humans. Humans are faulty. Therefore, the church will reflect the faultiness of those who comprise the church. Church leaders are frequently the target of the wrath of God's children, and their actions are often misrepresented by church members bent more on reprimand than redemption.

Jesus leaves us in no doubt as to how He feels about the church. In Revelation 3, He declares that Laodicea—His church in earth's last days—is "wretched, miserable, poor, blind, and naked" (Revelation 3:17). But before imploring His people to repent, He identifies with them. John writes that he "saw seven golden lampstands, and in the midst of the seven lampstands One like the Son of Man" (Revelation 1:12, 13). "The seven lampstands which [John] saw are the seven churches" (verse 20).

Jesus is depicted as being in the midst of the churches! The following chapters reveal these churches to be faulty and in need of correction, yet Jesus is in their midst. He is with His church today. "The church of Christ, enfeebled and defective as it may be, is the only object on earth on which He bestows His supreme regard."*

If the church was prayed for as much as it is criticized; if church leaders were interceded for as much as they are condemned; if critics channeled their zeal into service and outreach rather than censure and denunciation, the church—and the world—would be a different place.

---

* Ellen G. White, *Testimonies to Ministers and Gospel Workers* (Mountain View, CA: Pacific Press®, 1944), 15.

October 25

Lost Time

"The Lord Himself will give you a sign: Behold, the virgin shall conceive and bear a Son, and shall call His name Immanuel."

—Isaiah 7:14

Pauline was just fourteen years old when she became pregnant. When she was fifteen, she gave birth to a daughter she named Louise, and at the insistence of family members, she placed her little girl up for adoption. Pauline went on to marry and have four more children, but she and her husband often talked about the baby she never knew. She longed to be able to see her again.*

"Louise" was named Carol by her adoptive family. They were not supportive of her desire to find her birth mother, and local authorities told Carol that the papers relating to her adoption were lost in a fire. With a heavy heart, Carol accepted she would never be able to locate her birth mother.†

When a television program reunited the women, fifty years after Carol was born, they discovered they had spent many years living just ten minutes from each other. Both women regretted they had lived in such close proximity without being able to spend time together.‡

It is not uncommon for people who come to faith in Jesus to say that their greatest regret is that they had not done so sooner. Every minute disconnected from Jesus is a minute that cannot be retrieved. Yet God is always near. He is not a distant God who cannot be reached. He is not an inaccessible Being who chooses to remain aloof. When He gave Moses directions to build the sanctuary, God said, "Let them make Me a sanctuary, that I may dwell among them" (Exodus 25:8). Jesus is portrayed as walking in the midst of His church (Revelation 1:12, 13). The prophet Isaiah promised King Ahaz that "the virgin shall conceive and bear a Son, and shall call His name Immanuel" (Isaiah 7:14), which means "God is with us" (Matthew 1:32). Speaking of His people, Jesus lamented, "You are not willing to come to Me that you may have life" (John 5:40).

A woman and her biological daughter would naturally rue their missed opportunities to spend time together. How important it is that we waste no opportunities to spend time in the presence of the God of heaven. If God is calling you to spend more time in His presence, accept His gracious invitation and draw near to Him.

---

* Jessica Green, "Woman Renunites With Firstborn She was Forced to Give up as a Teenage Mother on Long Lost Family, and Finds Out Her Daughter Has Followed Her on Facebook for Three Years but Didn't Contact Her for Fear of Rejection," *DailyMail.com*, January 25, 2021, https://www.dailymail.co.uk/femail /article-9184583/Mother-forced-baby-away-aged-15-reunited-50-years-later-Long-Lost-Family.html

† Green

‡ Green

His Presence

"Take these things away! Do not make
My Father's house a house of merchandise!"

—John 2:16

People came from all over Israel to celebrate the Passover in Jerusalem. Some came from even farther afield. Many of the assembled worshipers were not able to bring sacrifices, so a brisk trade was conducted in the outer court as people bought and sold animals. Offerings of money were brought to the temple, and foreign money was exchanged for the local temple currency. Much of the trade being conducted was poisoned with dishonesty. Greed was given the opportunity to rear its ugly head.

Against this backdrop of trade and merchandising, Jesus "found in the temple those who sold oxen and sheep and doves, and the money changers doing business. When He had made a whip of cords, He drove them all out of the temple, with the sheep and the oxen, and poured out the changers' money and overturned the tables. And He said to those who sold doves, 'Take these things away! Do not make My Father's house a house of merchandise!' " (John 2:14–16).

Jesus was not yet a figure of major importance in Jerusalem. He had not yet raised the dead or caused the blind to see. So how was it that any individual—even Jesus—could drive moneychangers and animal traders out of the temple, end their avaricious trade, and disrupt the biggest season on the Jewish calendar? A person who replicated Jesus' actions in the casinos of Las Vegas or Atlantic City would not be tolerated. Security would be called, and the offender would be escorted from the premises and into the hands of law enforcement.

The people in the temple that day did not escape the presence of an angry man. It was not the whip in Jesus' hand that drove men from the temple. Ellen White writes in *The Desire of Ages* that people rushed from the temple "with the one thought of escaping from the condemnation of His presence."*

Sin flees from the presence of Divinity. In the same way that the presence of Jesus drove sinners from the holy precincts of the temple, the presence of Jesus in the life of the believer will drive sin from the heart.

---

* Ellen G. White, *The Desire of Ages* (Mountain View, CA: Pacific Press®, 1940), 158.

Expert Testimony

The law of the LORD is perfect, converting the soul;
the testimony of the LORD is sure, making wise the simple.
—Psalm 19:7

When Cameron Todd Willingham was executed in 2004 at the age of thirty-six, there were serious misgivings regarding his alleged guilt. No one could identify a motive for torching his home and murdering his three young daughters. He had prior run-ins with the law, and prosecutors suggested that the tattoo on his arm and a poster of a heavy-metal rock band on the wall of his home indicated he was a psychopath. But it was expert testimony that convinced a jury Willingham had intentionally taken the lives of his little girls. Arson investigators pointed to patterns found in the charred ruins of the Willingham home that they claimed proved accelerants were used to deliberately start the deadly blaze.

However, just weeks before Willingham was scheduled to be executed, a renowned scientist and fire investigator reviewed the scientific evidence used to secure the condemned man's conviction. Dr. Gerald Hurst concluded that the fire was accidental and that the report that had placed a man on death row was based on "junk science." Dr. Hurst and others were convinced the expert testimony that had convicted Mr. Willingham was not so expert after all.*

It isn't always easy to know who to believe, and both sides in a court trial have a vested interest in the outcome. It might appear that in religious matters, little is different. Many people say they are confused by the multiplicity of voices within Christianity and do not know how to determine which opinion is right. A similar situation may exist within the church, where people can struggle to find the truth on an issue over which two or more viewpoints are proffered.

The only truly reliable voice in matters of faith is the voice of God. Jesus once answered a question with this question: "What is written in the law? What is your reading of it?" (Luke 10:26). Paul wrote that "all Scripture is given by inspiration of God, and is profitable for doctrine, for reproof, for correction, for instruction in righteousness" (2 Timothy 3:16).

Opinions are as varied as are the people that hold to them. The follower of Jesus looks to the Bible as the foundation of faith. God's Word is true expert testimony.

---

* "Cameron Todd Willingham: Wrongfully Convicted and Executed in Texas," Innocence Project, September 13, 2010, https://innocenceproject.org/cameron-todd-willingham-wrongfully-convicted-and-executed-in-texas/.

Independent

Train up a child in the way he should go,
and when he is old he will not depart from it.

—Proverbs 22:6

It is a problem faced by every Christian denomination. Keeping our young people in the church is an age-old, never-ending challenge. Today's world has more distractions calculated to draw young people away from God than ever before. Years ago, people dreamed of sports and movies on demand, of instantaneous communication, and of vast resources of knowledge at our fingertips. The future has arrived.

The solution for the challenge of keeping our young people connected to Christ often appears to be the church doing more for young people—more programs, more events, more weekends away, more productions. All these years later, "more" does not seem to have been especially effective.

Young children soon get to the place where they wish to feed themselves. No longer content to be spoon-fed by mother or father, children will take the spoon into their hands and attempt self-sufficency. Before long, the same children are trying to tie their shoelaces and wanting to ride a bike. As the child grows, he or she—no longer satisfied with being chauffeured—wants to drive, then get a part-time job in order to have spending money, and stay out late with friends. Children naturally want to do these things as they get older. They wish to experience a certain level of independence.

Children who feed themselves, get jobs, drive cars, and stay out after dark should also be encouraged to take responsibility for their spiritual well-being. While the church must always strive to be relevant, engaging, and welcoming for young people, it has never been the church's responsibility to make sure children are biblically literate or reading their Bibles and praying daily. This is to be taught in the home. No child ever walked away from faith in Jesus while having a meaningful daily devotional experience.

If we want our children to *stay with* Jesus, we must first lead them *to* Jesus. Children who are old enough to go to high school or college, responsible enough to handle money, and old enough to spend time away from home are old enough to understand the gospel and maintain a personal relationship with the God of heaven.

Bread?

"Why do you spend money for what is not bread,
and your wages for what does not satisfy?"

—Isaiah 55:2

There are numerous good sources of personal devotional reading: the Bible, other inspirational books, devotional books, . . . and credit card statements! In Isaiah 55, God issued a gracious invitation through the gospel prophet:

"Ho! Everyone who thirsts,
Come to the waters;
And you who have no money,
Come, buy and eat.
Yes, come, buy wine and milk
Without money and without price" (Isaiah 55:1).

The inference is clear. The one who comes to God can freely receive grace and mercy.

Then Isaiah issues a challenge, asking a very pointed question: "Why do you spend money for what is not bread, and your wages for what does not satisfy?" (verse 2). While certainly talking about more than one's finances, Isaiah is also speaking to what we are doing with the means entrusted us by God. This is where reading a credit card statement or reviewing receipts can be such an effective exercise. Are we spending our money on "bread," or are we frittering it away carelessly, investing it in that which has no eternal value?

God's admonition is, "Listen carefully to Me, and eat what is good, and let your soul delight itself in abundance" (verse 2). There is a balance that must be found: vacations should be taken, vehicles must be purchased, clothing must be worn, and food must be consumed. But do all vacations need to be expensive? Should all vehicles be purchased new? Do the latest fashions really need to be adopted? The answers to these questions will rightly vary from person to person. But with Americans owing nearly a trillion dollars in credit card debt and credit card delinquency on the rise, it is clear people are spending money they don't have—often for things they don't need.

One's lifestyle can be a tyrannical taskmaster. If we are honest about our needs and wants, we may well find our money going further and our stewardship of God's resources coming into closer alignment with His plans for us.

Go

*"Go therefore and make disciples of all the nations, baptizing them in
the name of the Father and of the Son and of the Holy Spirit."*
—Matthew 28:19

At just one word, it is the shortest complete sentence in the English language. "Go." For the Christian, it is a word brimming with importance.

In some of the last words Jesus spoke to His disciples, He encouraged them to be directly involved in the great work of sharing the gospel with others.

The Ethiopian government official would never have been baptized if Philip did not go. Paul is famous for his missionary journeys, traveling to reach people he had never before met. Yet the church today must wrestle with the fact that the vast majority of people alive have no functional knowledge of Jesus Christ or the Bible. There are still great cities with large populations where few, if any, have accepted Jesus as Lord and Savior. While technology gives us opportunities we once did not have, it is still necessary for God's people to go, to get out of their comfort zones, and actually take the gospel to people living in darkness.

Not everyone is called to leave their home and travel to a foreign land to share the gospel. Missionaries are needed close to home and are often needed in the home. The number of people in the United States who claim no religious affiliation is on the rise. The same is true in other Western countries. While it used to be true that the majority was in some way connected to a church, things have definitely changed.

And perhaps that is for our own good. Decades ago, it was possible for a church to secure the services of a professional evangelist and expect a crowd of people to come out to hear a Bible-based lecture series. While there are still many who are attracted to the preaching of God's Word, we have discovered it is necessary to pray, to sow seeds prior to the harvest time, and to engage in personal evangelism in preparation for public evangelism. As we do this work, God will bless His church with success.

Power Outage

"For everyone who asks receives, and he who seeks finds,
and to him who knocks it will be opened."

—Matthew 7:8

Greg realized that being in Africa and preaching an evangelistic series was itself a miracle. Not everyone thought he was the best candidate for public speaking, but he loved to share his faith. He wanted to believe that working with members of a congregation to try to reach their community with the love of Jesus would be as good for him as it would be for them. And as he had never been to Africa, this seemed like the perfect opportunity for several important factors to coalesce in an exciting soul-winning project. But Greg had his doubts. Could God really use him to reach people with the gospel?

The church was at the far north of a major urban center, on the edge of a newly developed area with limited infrastructure, poor roads, and high unemployment. Those with jobs typically traveled long distances into the city to work.

The meetings were conducted in a field and began well. Electricity for the projector was supplied through a series of long extension cords, and battery-powered lights were used. But one night early in the series of meetings, the unthinkable happened. Greg's projector stopped working part-way through a sermon. He relied on it to prompt him through his presentations, and the pictures and Bible texts aided the people in better understanding the message Greg was presenting. Repeated attempts to coax it back to life failed.

There was only one thing to do. Greg and church members assisting with the meetings gathered together to pray. In faith, they tried the projector again, and this time—it worked! Greg rejoiced, the church members were happy, and the visitors to the meeting were glad they could continue to hear the Word of God.

After the meeting, as they told their story, people were incredulous. "How did your projector work?" they asked. Greg told them, "God answered our prayer." "But *how* did your projector work?" they demanded. "There was a power outage. There was no power in the entire area!"

Immediately Greg understood. It had been a miracle, a miracle to demonstrate that yes, God could use Greg to do a great work for Him.

The Unconventional Evangelist

Preach the word! Be ready in season and out of season.
Convince, rebuke, exhort, with all longsuffering and teaching.
—2 Timothy 4:2

They had requested the best preacher available. Church leaders in Kingston, Jamaica, wanted an evangelist who could expertly train a number of promising ministers in the finer points of public evangelism. Luther Warren was an experienced evangelist, and he earnestly prayed that God would grant him wisdom and strength commensurate with the task he had accepted.

According to the account in the book *Luther Warren,** a large crowd filled the meeting hall to capacity. His opening night presentation was to be on the subject of Daniel 2. The young ministers were eager to see how the American evangelist covered the subject. But after only three or four minutes, Elder Warren had finished his study of Daniel 2 and moved on to another subject. He spoke on the prophecies of the Bible, the second coming of Jesus, the law of God, the Sabbath, and the judgment. Local church leaders were beside themselves! Why was this speaker undoing all the instruction the young pastors had been given?

At the end of his presentation, Elder Warren made an altar call. With tears streaming down his face, he appealed to the congregation to surrender their lives to God. The response was overwhelming as people surged forward to accept Jesus Christ as their Lord and Savior.

Not even Luther Warren understood at the time why he preached the sermon he preached. But the next day, everything became clear. Kingston was struck by a devastating earthquake. Every building in the city was damaged, and around a thousand people were killed. Warren headed to a local hospital to see what he could do to minister to the sick and suffering. He recognized many he had met with at his meeting the night before.

There are times God will lead you in unexpected directions in order to accomplish His will. Luther Warren was close enough to God to be able to discern His unconventional leading. A vital connection with God will prepare His people to be ready to serve Him in surprising ways.

---

* Sharon Boucher, *Luther Warren* (Washington, DC: Review and Herald®, 1959).

Demonstration

"Let your light so shine before men, that they may see
your good works and glorify your Father in heaven."
—Matthew 5:16

The final days of this earth's history are to be characterized by the proclamation of the everlasting gospel, according to the three angels' messages found in Revelation 14. The messages are specific, detailed, and pointed, speaking to the spiritual needs of a planet that for six thousand years has been weighed down by the after-effects of the fall of Adam and Eve in the Garden of Eden. God is striving to restore His image in fallen humanity, preparing sinners for everlasting life. Satan is working tirelessly to keep people from coming to faith in Christ and to occupy the minds of men and women with anything other than the saving principles of the gospel.

But if the mission of the church was simply to proclaim a message, to share words, to alert people to the information contained in a collection of Bible verses, the gospel commission could have been completed many years ago. God, however, is looking to His church to do more than educate. He commissions the church to *demonstrate*.

Like Israel of old, the church has been called into existence to reveal the character of God to the world. Revelation's fourth angel, the messenger who issues the final call to come out of Babylon, reveals the character of God to such an extent it is said that the earth is illuminated with a manifestation of His glory. The angel in Revelation 18 represents the church, suggesting the church has a much broader mandate than simply preaching a litany of doctrines. In *Christ's Object Lessons*, Ellen White states, "It was God's purpose that by the revelation of His character through Israel men should be drawn unto Him."* In Matthew 5:14, Jesus informed His closest friends that *they* were to be "the light of the world. A city that is set on a hill cannot be hidden."

The one who has yielded his or her life to Jesus and is filled with the Holy Spirit will reveal God's character to others. This is the work God has called His people to do. Proclamation of God's end-time message is vital. Living that message is no less important.

---

* Ellen G. White, *Christ's Object Lessons* (Washington, DC: Review and Herald®, 1941), 290.

The Message

*For the time has come for judgment to begin at the house
of God; and if it begins with us first, what will be the end
of those who do not obey the gospel of God?*

—1 Peter 4:17

A number of years ago, I was invited to broadcast my breakfast radio program from a site where military exercises were being carried out cooperatively by several nations. These were highly important simulations of real wartime scenarios.

During our program, my cohost and I recounted our guided tour of the area the night before. "It was fantastic," she said to our audience. "It's the real thing. We were even taken through checkpoints. The guard said, 'Blue,' and our guide said, 'Vilvo,' and we were escorted through." Which is *precisely* what the army did not want her to say. She had just broadcast our hosts' top-secret password. If the "enemy" had heard what she said, it might have jeopardized the entire military exercise.

There are some things that are better left unsaid. But in the last days of this world's history, there are some things that *must* be said. The church has been given a divine mandate to preach the everlasting gospel "to every nation, tribe, tongue, and people" (Revelation 14:6). The messages of holy living, the judgment hour, true worship, the fall of Babylon, and the mark of the beast must be proclaimed to the world. In addition to the proclamation, the character of Jesus will be demonstrated to the world by a people who are fully surrendered to God, a people who have accepted the invitation to share the three angels' messages with the world.

Messages of hope and warning are not ordinarily accepted by everyone. Jeremiah discovered that his popularity plummeted when he shared God's message with Judah. Yet, he could not be quiet. He said,

"His word was in my heart like a burning fire
Shut up in my bones;
I was weary of holding it back,
And I could not" (Jeremiah 20:9).

Driven by love for God and a love for lost souls, God's people will carry forward the gospel before Jesus returns. "This gospel of the kingdom will be preached in all the world as a witness to all the nations, and then the end will come" (Matthew 24:14).

Speaking the Truth

[That we], speaking the truth in love, may grow up
in all things into Him who is the head—Christ.
—Ephesians 4:15

As Pastor Joe and I were driving to make evangelistic-meeting visits, we spotted what looked like smoke coming from a home set back from the road. Something looked a little out of place, so we stopped to investigate. Everything was not OK. Children playing with fireworks had unintentionally set fire to a pile of old belongings that had been piled against the family home. The pile had ignited, and the fire had spread to the house. The house was on fire. We called the fire department, who assured us a fire truck was on its way.

The children's parents were not home, and we were told no one else was nearby. However, the building was a duplex! Was anyone in the other home? The children did not know.

Realizing there was no time to waste, I knocked, opened the door, and entered. The lady who occupied the home was sitting in an easy chair talking on the phone. She was surprised to see me! "Ma'am, I'm sorry, but your home is on fire," I told her calmly. I pointed to the ceiling, through which smoke was entering her living room.

There's no question that I startled the lady and inconvenienced her day. But not knowing her home was on fire would have made her day considerably worse. She was able to save her most valued possessions and make it to safety without any problems.

Before Jesus returns, the church will share an uncomfortable message with the world. A saving message, to be sure, but for those who are comfortable in their sin, or rebellion, or tradition, or ignorance, the message might not initially be welcomed.

How is the church to share a Bible message that might surprise or even startle? In love. Paul told the Ephesians—a small group of believers in the midst of an idolatrous society—that they were to be "speaking the truth in love." The everlasting gospel is God's message—originated by God and inspired by God. Our work is to share it in love. As we do, God will lead many people to safety.

Specific

But Saul and the people spared Agag and the best
of the sheep, the oxen, the fatlings, the lambs, and all
that was good, and were unwilling to utterly destroy them.
But everything despised and worthless, that they utterly destroyed.
—1 Samuel 15:9

It was a daunting commission. The new king of Israel had been instructed by the prophet: "Go and attack Amalek, and utterly destroy all that they have, and do not spare them" (1 Samuel 15:3). Israel had a history with Amalek. It was during a battle with Amalek that Aaron and Hur held up the hands of Moses. At that time, God had said, "I will utterly blot out the remembrance of Amalek from under heaven" (Exodus 17:14) and that "the Lord will have war with Amalek from generation to generation" (verse 16).

In the same prophecy in which he stated, "a Star shall come out of Jacob," Balaam predicted the destruction of Amalek (Numbers 24:17, 20). And Moses wrote of Amalek in Deuteronomy 25:17–19: "Remember what Amalek did to you on the way as you were coming out of Egypt, how he met you on the way and attacked your rear ranks, all the stragglers at your rear, when you were tired and weary; and he did not fear God. Therefore it shall be, when the Lord your God has given you rest from your enemies all around, in the land which the Lord your God is giving you to possess as an inheritance, that you will blot out the remembrance of Amalek from under heaven. You shall not forget."

The day of reckoning had come. After Amalek's repeated refusals to repent, the nation was to be destroyed. "But Saul and the people spared Agag . . . and all that was good. . . . But everything despised and worthless, that they utterly destroyed" (1 Samuel 15:9). Saul thought that to get *close* to what God had requested would be sufficient. But God was very specific, and Saul's disobedience was the beginning of his end.

God's grace, mercy, and kindness should not lead us to believe that obedience is unimportant. It is important to recognize that when God asks for "this," He is not asking for "that." Love for God carries with it a desire to please Him—to live according to His will. The Spirit of God working in your life leads you to obey His specific commands.

The Everlasting Gospel

Then I saw another angel flying in the midst of heaven,
having the everlasting gospel to preach to those who dwell
on the earth—to every nation, tribe, tongue, and people.
—Revelation 14:6

The book of Revelation contains the final gospel message to be shared with the world, a message the Bible assures us will go forward with power. Jesus said that "this gospel of the kingdom will be preached in all the world as a witness to all the nations, and then the end will come" (Matthew 24:14). God's gospel message will go to all the world before Jesus returns.

So what is the everlasting gospel? Some might be tempted to say "the judgment hour message," "the message of true worship," "Babylon is fallen," or "the warning about the mark of the beast." Undoubtedly these are vital components of the messages of the three angels, but it must not be forgotten that the everlasting gospel is the everlasting *gospel*. God's people in earth's final days are called to share the *gospel*.

The apostle Paul gave what may be the most succinct yet comprehensive outline of the gospel in 1 Corinthians 15:1–5. He wrote,

Moreover, brethren, I declare to you the gospel which I preached to you, which also you received and in which you stand. . . .

For I delivered to you first of all that which I also received: that Christ died for our sins according to the Scriptures, and that He was buried, and that He rose again the third day according to the Scriptures, and that He was seen by Cephas, then by the twelve.

In classical Greek, the word *euangelion* means "good news." An "evangelist" is literally a "bringer of good news." God's people in earth's last days have a vital message to share, and the heart of that message is the gospel itself. The spotless, divine Son of God came into the world to offer mercy to sinners and grant the gift of everlasting life. The grave could not contain Him, and He ascended to heaven, where He now ministers as our great High Priest.

The gospel—the saving good news—is a message that must be shared. The various elements that comprise the three angels' messages are of vital importance, especially as they illuminate the gospel message and lead people to faith in Jesus.

The Hour of His Judgment

*"Fear God and give glory to Him, for the hour of His judgment has come;
and worship Him who made heaven and earth, the sea and springs of water."*
—Revelation 14:7

The book of Revelation carefully traces the millennia-long battle between good and evil—the great controversy that has been raging since before the creation of the world. In the heart of the book of Revelation is an appeal from the sovereign God of the universe to His children. God directs us to what the Bible calls the everlasting gospel—a message of grace designed to draw people deep into God's heart of love. The message ultimately achieves its objective, as is revealed by a statement at its conclusion. "Here is the patience of the saints; here are those who keep the commandments of God and the faith of Jesus" (Revelation 14:12). People respond to the everlasting gospel and are saved.

The first angel proclaims with a loud voice, "Fear God and give glory to Him, for the hour of His judgment has come" (verse 7). To fear God and give glory to Him is to live a surrendered life, fully yielded to the will of the Almighty. Understanding that the human family is now living in the time of the antitypical day of atonement should help us to understand the seriousness of the times. The Hebrew Day of Atonement has been described by scholars as a crisis of confession and repentance. God would have His people today be cognizant of the devastating effects of sin, seeking for cleansing, forgiveness, and the indwelling power of the Holy Spirit to keep them yielded to the will of God.

There is no time to waste. The return of Jesus is imminent. The parable of the ten virgins reminds us that not only do we want to have our lamps filled with the oil of the Holy Spirit but also that we must not be asleep when we should be watching and waiting. We are living in the time of the judgment. Jesus is soon to return. Our sins are to be forgiven. Life is to be lived in reference to God. These are important days.

Guilty

For Christ has not entered the holy places made with hands, which are copies of the true, but into heaven itself, now to appear in the presence of God for us.
—Hebrews 9:24

Archie Williams was twenty-two years old when he was arrested. Months later, he was found guilty of having committed a terrible crime and was sentenced by the State of Louisiana to life in prison without the possibility of parole. Thirty-six years later, he was freed. New evidence revealed that what Mr. Williams had claimed since his arrest was true. He did not commit the crime of which he had been accused. Mr. Williams had been wrongfully convicted.*

The Bible speaks of a last-day judgment when it says in Revelation 14:7, "Fear God and give glory to Him, for the hour of His judgment has come." The whole world will be arraigned before the judgment bar of God. In the case of *God v. The People*, there is no question about the guilt or innocence of humanity. The Bible says that "all have sinned and fall short of the glory of God" (Romans 3:23).

What hope is there for the guilty sinner? Every person alive has sinned against God, and "the wages of sin is death" (Romans 6:23). We are guilty of crimes we did, in fact, commit.

But in heaven's judgment, every inhabitant of the earth is entitled to legal representation. When Jesus ascended to heaven, He assumed the role of heavenly High Priest, and in heaven's final judgment, He is our Mediator before God. "Seeing then that we have a great High Priest who has passed through the heavens, Jesus the Son of God, let us hold fast our confession. . . . Let us therefore come boldly to the throne of grace, that we may obtain mercy and find grace to help in time of need" (Hebrews 4:14–16).

In the judgment of earth's last days, we are invited to come with confidence to Jesus, our heavenly Intercessor. Jesus willingly took our punishment when He died on the cross. He now offers us His pardon for sin. You may come to Jesus confident you will obtain mercy and grace.

The judgment is good news. We may be forgiven and cleansed. Jesus appears "in the presence of God *for us*." Jesus invites you to come to Him and be saved.

---

* "Match in National Fingerprint Database Establishes Innocence of Baton Rouge Man After 36 Years in Prison," Innocence Project, March 21, 2019, https://innocenceproject.org/fingerprint-database-match -establishes-archie-williams-innocence/.

The Creator

"Everyone who is called by My name, whom I have created
for My glory; I have formed him, yes, I have made him."
—Isaiah 43:7

The final crisis that comes to the world before the return of Jesus hinges on a certain issue. We are alerted to the nature of this issue in the three angels' messages in Revelation 14. An angel says with a loud voice—indicating this is a message everyone must hear—"Fear God and give glory to Him, for the hour of His judgment has come; and worship Him who made heaven and earth, the sea and springs of water" (verse 7).

Jesus' Creatorship is under relentless attack. Since a twenty-two-year-old scientist sailed on the HMS *Beagle* in the early 1830s, the question of creation has been hotly debated, and God's role in the genesis of the world has been increasingly disputed. However, Bible writers maintain a remarkable harmony on the subject.

Jeremiah was convinced God created the world. "Ah, Lord God! Behold, You have made the heavens and the earth by Your great power and outstretched arm" (Jeremiah 32:17). David agrees with Jeremiah:

By the word of the Lord the heavens were made,
And all the host of them by the breath of His mouth.

For He spoke, and it was done;
He commanded, and it stood fast (Psalm 33:6, 9).

Isaiah repeatedly endorsed the Creation account of the Bible. "The everlasting God, the Lord, the Creator of the ends of the earth, neither faints nor is weary" (Isaiah 40:28). Moses appealed to Israel on the basis of God's Creatorship. "Of the Rock who begot you, you are unmindful, and have forgotten the God who fathered you" (Deuteronomy 32:18).

New Testament writers were no less emphatic. John—who wrote Revelation—begins his New Testament gospel by attributing the creation of the world to Jesus (John 1:1–3).

When Jesus calls us in Revelation 14 to worship Him as Creator, He is echoing the consistency that exists throughout all sixty-six books of Scripture. As our Creator, Jesus is truly worthy of our worship. If Creation did not occur as the Bible says, the messages of the three angels are meaningless.

The Sign

*And He said to them, "The Sabbath was made
for man, and not man for the Sabbath."*
—Mark 2:27

As He draws our attention to a certain, controverted issue in earth's last days, God gives the human family a sign to remind us of who He is and who we are in relationship to Him.

In the everlasting gospel found in Revelation 14, an angel flies in the midst of heaven, attracting the attention of all, and proclaims with a loud voice, "Worship Him who made heaven and earth, the sea and springs of water" (Revelation 14:7). In quoting the fourth commandment, John (the writer of Revelation) calls us to worship Jesus as Creator by observing the seventh-day Sabbath.

Just thirty-three verses into the Bible, we are introduced to the Sabbath. "And on the seventh day God ended His work which He had done, and He rested on the seventh day from all His work which He had done. Then God blessed the seventh day and sanctified it, because in it He rested from all His work which God had created and made" (Genesis 2:2, 3). Jesus—who gave the Sabbath at Creation—stated that "the Sabbath was made for man" (Mark 2:27).

The Sabbath is an eternal sign of God's creative power. In keeping the seventh-day Sabbath, God's people recognize His authority in their lives and their complete dependence upon Him. The Sabbath isn't a work done by Christians to curry favor with God. It is an acceptance of God's goodness, a time to rest from our work just as God rested from His at the conclusion of the Creation week. The Sabbath is a sign of righteousness by faith, as disciples of Jesus allow God's will to be carried out in their lives.

The busyness of life could easily be permitted to squeeze the Sabbath out of a believer's life. But we are called in earth's last days to *remember* the Sabbath day and keep it holy. The Sabbath is time spent with God, our Creator.

Remade

"I also gave them My Sabbaths, to be a sign between them and Me,
that they might know that I am the LORD who sanctifies them."
—Ezekiel 20:12

When John called the attention of the world to the Sabbath of the fourth commandment in Revelation 14, he did more than simply alert humanity to the correct day of worship. And he did more than point out that Jesus is the Creator of the world and that a gracious God has given earth's inhabitants a day away from the demands of the secular world. The Sabbath stands as a memorial of God's creative power. It also serves as a reminder of God's power to *re*-create.

Sin stands as a barrier between human beings and God. Jeremiah wrote that "the heart is deceitful above all things, and desperately wicked; who can know it?" (Jeremiah 17:9). The verse can be translated that the sinful human heart is deceitful above all things and *incurable*. Sin is a terminal illness for which there is no earthly cure.

Following his disgraceful sin, David prayed a sincere and heartfelt prayer, in which he appealed to God for mercy in the wake of his immoral behavior. "Have mercy upon me, O God," he wrote in Psalm 51. "Wash me thoroughly from my iniquity, and cleanse me from my sin." He went on to say, "Create in me a clean heart, O God, and renew a steadfast spirit within me" (Psalm 51:1, 2, 10). David knew that without God intervening to forgive, cleanse, and remake him, he would be a lost man. The god of evolution could offer David no help. He needed to be remade, re-created. Only the Creator God could do the work necessary in David's experience.

Paul expressed a similar sentiment when he wrote, "If anyone is in Christ, he is a new creation; old things have passed away; behold, all things have become new" (2 Corinthians 5:17). "The Lord of the Sabbath" (Mark 2:28) is alone able to restore in fallen humanity the image of God. The Sabbath-keeping Christian is doing more than observing a day. He or she is entering into a saving relationship with a God who gave us not just a day—but His Son, that we, through Him, might be remade.

Re-created

*"I will give you a new heart and put a new spirit within you; I will
take the heart of stone out of your flesh and give you a heart of flesh."*
—Ezekiel 36:26

I tried not to make it obvious I was unimpressed with the home my brother and his wife were considering buying. My sister-in-law saw potential in the home that I couldn't see. "We'll just knock out this wall here, put a doorway there, open up this area over here . . ." They bought the home and, sure enough, transformed it into something I would never have thought possible.

As impressive as it is, this is not what God does in the life of a sinner. A renovation improves an existing home. Start with an old home, add new windows, new floors, a new roof, and fresh paint, and you have . . . an old home with new windows, new floors, a new roof, and fresh paint. It may be a beautiful home. It may be an expensive home. But it's the same old home—remodeled.

God does not renovate fallen human beings. He re-creates them. A home renovation project under God's direction would see the old home totally demolished, the lot completely cleared, and an entirely new home built where the old home used to be. In the plan of salvation, "our old man was crucified with Him, that the body of sin might be done away with, that we should no longer be slaves of sin" (Romans 6:6). In his letter to the Ephesians, Paul stated that God unites a sinner with Jesus and makes, out of the two, "one new" person (Ephesians 2:15).

It isn't God's plan to modify, renovate, or improve a fallen sinner. Instead, God intends to take a fallen sinner and remake him or her as a saint, as described in Revelation 14:12. Sinners come to God with their unrighteousness and receive in its place the righteousness of Jesus. Christ's perfect righteousness is credited to the fallen sinner, and by faith, the sinner receives that righteousness and is made new through Jesus Christ, growing ever more into His likeness. God gives the repentant sinner a *new* heart and puts a *new* spirit within that person. The stony heart is taken away and replaced with a heart of flesh.

God does not renovate. He re-creates.

Babylon Is Fallen

And another angel followed, saying, "Babylon is fallen,
is fallen, that great city, because she has made all nations
drink of the wine of the wrath of her fornication."

—Revelation 14:8

The proclamation of the second angel in Revelation 14 is an urgent message issued by a God of love.

Ancient Babylon was a center of false worship. It was a mighty kingdom. But in spite of King Nebuchadnezzar's remarkable experience with God, his grandson, Belshazzar, was not inclined to follow his example. One night, writing appeared on the wall. That night Babylon's king had taken the holy worship vessels that had been stolen from the temple in Jerusalem and drank intoxicating wine from them in praise of pagan gods. It was then that Babylon fell.

John borrowed imagery from this account in the book of Daniel (and other books of the Old Testament) when writing Revelation. The fall of ancient Babylon provided a striking parallel to events that will take place in the earth's final days. When the message of the first angel has been sounded, and the world has heard of the importance of God's seventh-day Sabbath, then it will be announced that Babylon—representing systems of false worship infused with paganism—is fallen.

Such an uncompromising message may appear to be at odds with the character of a loving God. But for six thousand years, a God of immense love has been appealing to the world to embrace His Word and His will. Prophets came to the world to call God's people to faithfulness. His own Son was sent from heaven, embodying the principles of heaven and revealing to all the true character of His Father. Since that time, the church has been sharing and living God's message, and the Holy Spirit has been persistently convicting hearts.

The time is fast approaching when God will issue His final call. Those in fallen Babylon are to be invited into the full light of God's Word. Many today are responding. We are on the verge of a great ingathering when people the world over take a bold stand for Jesus.

Let the church be determined to live and graciously share the important message for our time.

The Third Angel's Message

Then a third angel followed them, saying with a loud voice, "If anyone worships the beast and his image, and receives his mark on his forehead or on his hand, he himself shall also drink of the wine of the wrath of God."
—Revelation 14:9, 10

It is not easy to fully understand the events that will take place shortly before Jesus returns to this earth. Students of prophecy know that fulfilled prophecy is easier to interpret than unfulfilled prophecy. As we look into the future, God, in His mercy, provides us with an outline of coming events but does not always supply every detail about times that are yet to be.

The messages of the three angels culminate in what is likely the Bible's most solemn warning in history. After being told we are living in the time of heaven's final judgment; after being called to true worship; after being informed of the fall of spiritual Babylon, God alerts the world that those who have chosen to remain unrepentant will receive the mark of the beast and will not be saved.

We cannot yet know exactly what will transpire to bring about the events that lead to the mark of the beast being forced upon the inhabitants of the earth. But we do know that the Sabbath of the fourth commandment will have been made known as the seal of the living God. The claims of God's law will have been presented to the world. The Holy Spirit will have pleaded with individuals all over the planet in an attempt to draw people to surrender to Jesus.

It will be an intense time for all. Lines will have been drawn. The minority who remain faithful to God will have been identified as being in opposition to the majority, who by this time have repeatedly rejected God's appeals. The wrath poured out on those who have the mark of the beast is not from a short-tempered God venting His wrath on the unsuspecting. In a time of immense crisis, God will have done all He could to reach the willfully unrepentant. As David said in Psalm 119:126, "It is time for You to act, O Lord, for they have regarded Your law as void."

Warning after warning has been ignored. Appeal after appeal has been rejected. Those who have determined not to yield their hearts to God will be lost. Only those who have clung to Jesus and His Word will be saved.

The Gift

"If you then, being evil, know how to give good gifts
to your children, how much more will your heavenly
Father give the Holy Spirit to those who ask Him!"

—Luke 11:13

To celebrate his wife's forty-fourth birthday, an Indian businessman bought her a luxury jet worth more than fifty million dollars. The man's brother then bought a luxury yacht for *his* wife, spending more than eighty million dollars. As undoubtedly extravagant as they are, both gifts pale into insignificance when compared to the gift God offers, a gift far too few people choose to receive.

The Holy Spirit brings the personal presence of Jesus into a life, granting access to the limitless power of God. Never has a greater gift been offered to the human family. It is the conviction brought by the Holy Spirit that softens hardened hearts and leads men and women to repentance. The Holy Spirit at work in earth's final days will effect an ingathering of souls such as has never before been seen. And anyone can have this gift. Jesus said that our heavenly Father wants to give us the gift of the Holy Spirit much more than any earthly father desires his children to have good gifts.

The miraculous scenes witnessed at Pentecost spoke of a God who is willing to move heaven and earth to save the lost. "The sword of the Spirit, newly edged with power and bathed in the lightnings of heaven, cut its way through unbelief. Thousands were converted in a day."* As Pentecost was the former rain, the latter rain will achieve larger, more comprehensive results. None should be without the Holy Spirit in their daily life; neither should the church exist independent of the Spirit of the living God. We have the assurance that as we make our request known to God, He will undoubtedly grant the Holy Spirit in rich measure. "The Spirit awaits our demand and reception."†

Heaven possesses sufficient power to enable every church member to live out his or her divine calling and to urge the church forward to complete its work. Only as we receive the Holy Spirit can the gospel commission be fulfilled. Only as God's Spirit takes possession of His children can they reflect the character of Jesus to the world.

---

* Ellen G. White, *The Acts of the Apostles* (Mountain View, CA: Pacific Press®, 1911), 38.
† Ellen G. White, *Christ's Object Lessons* (Washington, DC: Review and Herald®, 1941), 121.

God's Leading

In all your ways acknowledge Him,
and He shall direct your paths.

—Proverbs 3:6

M y wife, Melissa, was giving me directions as we drove. "Turn here." "Straight ahead at the light." "Left here." As we neared our destination, she said, "Right here." I turned right. Her next words were, "No, left!" What she meant to say was, "Turn left, right here." But "right here" means "right here," so I dutifully drove in what turned out to be the wrong direction.

God promises to guide our lives at every step. The Bible makes an emphatic statement in Proverbs 3:5, 6. There is nothing unequivocal in what God has said. "Trust in the LORD . . . and He shall direct." God has promised, and God's promises are sure.

God's willingness to direct the lives of His children is never in question. The believer's unwillingness to follow may sometimes impede the working out of God's plans. Impatience is another hindrance. A young man or woman who grows tired of waiting for the "right" one may simply settle for second-best. An unwillingness to give God adequate time to work out His plans may be the difference between a happy future and a troubled life. A Christian who prays to know God's will but afterward cannot discern His leading typically has not taken the time to become familiar with the sound of God's voice.

Daily connecting with God and continually receiving the gift of the Holy Spirit produces an intimacy with heaven that ensures His voice will be heard. God wishes to lead His church even more than the church wishes to be led. He desires to see the gospel go to the ends of the earth and His children experience growth to full spiritual maturity. The Holy Spirit accomplishes these great works. As the disciple of Jesus receives the Holy Spirit day by day, he or she will better understand the will of God and more completely surrender to His will.

Where Is Your Faith?

Now it happened, on a certain day, that He got into a
boat with His disciples. And He said to them, "Let us cross
over to the other side of the lake." And they launched out.

—Luke 8:22

B ruce found himself stranded on the side of a busy highway in a major city. A truck
driver, Bruce needed to be towed to where his truck could be repaired. He prayed
and asked God for help. Then he got out of his truck, hooked a chain to the front
of his rig, and stretched it out as if a vehicle were already there to tow him. Minutes
later, a vehicle pulled up, connected the chain, and provided Bruce with the help he
desperately needed. The perfect vehicle, with the right driver, in the right place, at
precisely the right time.

Bruce demonstrated real faith, believing not only that God could answer his prayer
but also that God *would* answer his prayer. Faith believes that God is able to do what
God says He can do, simply because God said that it is so.

On one occasion, Jesus got into a boat with His disciples and said, "Let us cross over
to the other side of the lake." However, bad weather developed as they sailed. The Bible
says, "They were filling with water, and were in jeopardy." In a panic, they woke Jesus,
who calmed the stormy seas before inquiring, "Where is your faith?" (Luke 8:22–25).

Moments away from losing their lives, they turned to their Lord for help, and He
rebuked them for their lack of faith! But Jesus had given them every assurance that
they would not lose their lives. He had said to them, "Let us cross over to the other
side of the lake," which meant that irrespective of what occurred, they were, in fact,
going to the other side of the lake. When Jesus said, "Let us go to the other side of the
lake," the disciples simply needed to believe they were going to the other side of the
lake, and it would be so.

Relying on the Word of God to do what it says it will do is faith in action. In their
moment of crisis, the disciples had forgotten Jesus' promise. They were going to the
other side of the lake. Faith believes God will do what He says He will do.

The Rain Continued

*"And whatever things you ask in prayer,
believing, you will receive."*

—Matthew 21:22

H is daughter was desperately ill. Modern drugs were unknown, and those that were commonly prescribed were sometimes poisonous, claiming lives instead of saving lives. Physicians could offer little hope or help. Frances Howland had rheumatic fever. There were fears she might die. But the family knew what to do. They would turn to God and pray, and He would hear their prayer.

Her father, Stockbridge Howland, believed God could heal his daughter. The believers who had gathered in his home fervently prayed that God would restore the young woman to full health. After they had prayed, someone asked if there was a female present who would be willing to go upstairs to encourage Francis to get out of bed. Had she not been healed? The woman who volunteered took Frances by the hand and said, "Sister Frances, in the name of the Lord arise, and be whole." Frances dressed and went downstairs to join the group. She was well!*

It is one thing to pray but another to act on faith. Imagine how many more prayers would be answered in the affirmative if those who prayed truly believed God was able to do what was being asked! As I stood on the platform about to preach at a camp meeting, the sound of the rain falling on the roof of the tent was deafening. In my opening prayer, I prayed that God would stop the rain so the sermon could begin. I could barely be heard, but I prayed in faith, knowing God could cause the rain to stop falling. During the prayer, the deluge went on. But at the exact moment that I said, "Amen," the rain stopped. Immediately!

Not long afterward, I was speaking at another camp meeting, where reports showed there were bad storms in the area. The rain thundered down on the tin roof of the auditorium. As before, I prayed God would stop the rain. But this time, in the back of my mind, I felt it was unlikely the rain would actually stop. I prayed a half-hearted prayer.

The rain continued.

---

* Ellen G. White, *Life Sketches of Ellen G. White* (Mountain View, CA: Pacific Press®, 1943), 74.

The Unlikely Giver

"Give, and it will be given to you: good measure, pressed down, shaken together, and running over will be put into your bosom. For with the same measure that you use, it will be measured back to you."

—Luke 6:38

B ill's one goal was to become a millionaire. He lived a very simple life, forswearing the usual creature comforts in order to protect his rising net worth. He owned a humble home and lived on an everyday street. He drove an old car and never visited a doctor, preferring to save the money he would have spent on doctor's visits. Bill didn't have a cell phone. In fact, he didn't have a phone of any kind.

When a visit to the doctor seemed unavoidable, Bill could not have expected the news he received. He had cancer. His doctor advised Bill to go home and put his affairs in order. He did not have long to live.

But what would become of Bill's money? He wasn't married, had no children, and his extended family hadn't played any part in his life. It was then that he remembered: some years ago, members of a local church had come to his home asking for donations to support the church's humanitarian work. Bill was not a member of any church, but he was impressed by the sincerity of the people who knocked on his door and by the work their church was doing to help others.

He went to a drawer and found papers left for him by the people from the church. The papers explained the humanitarian work and listed several projects. *That's what I should do with my money,* Bill thought to himself. He did a little detective work, found a phone number (and a phone), and called the church's state headquarters. When a representative from the church came to his home, Bill got straight to the point. He was dying, he wanted his money to be used for good, and he wanted to leave 100 percent of it to the church.

The auction to dispose of Bill's possessions raised just short of a million dollars. The church members who visited Bill's home during several Ingathering campaigns could never have known that their visits would lead to such generosity to the church and the advancement of God's kingdom.

Divine Appointments

And Nathanael said to him, "Can anything good come out of Nazareth?"
Philip said to him, "Come and see."

—John 1:46

Warren prayed before he got on the bus that would take him to his new job. "Lord, there must be someone on this bus that I can witness to. Please show me who it is, and give me words to speak that will lead them to You." Finding an open seat, he sat down, smiled at the woman sitting next to him, and said, "Good morning." She didn't respond and turned to face the window. The next day, a similar thing happened. Warren greeted the person he sat next to but was met with stony silence. "Lord," he prayed, "that's two people who probably are not the ones You want me to meet on this bus. Show me whom You want me to share Jesus with."

The next morning he sat next to a young man, said "Good morning," and was met with a cheerful response. The young man smiled. "Good morning!" he replied. They chatted along the bus route until Warren got off at his stop. "I'll see you tomorrow morning," the young man, Tony, said. As they sat together over the following days and weeks, Warren prayed to know the right time to introduce Jesus into the conversation. One morning, the opportunity presented itself.

"I watched a program on television last night about the universe, about the planets and stars," Tony said. "It was incredible!"

Warren asked a simple question. "Did you ever wonder who made it all?"

Tony thought a moment. "Yes!" he said. "I have often wondered about that."

At that moment, a Bible study was born. Warren and Tony frequently met to discuss the teachings of the Bible. Tony even joined Warren and his family at their home for Christmas dinner. Tony studied his way into the truth of the Bible.

Warren was careful not to run ahead of God but prayerfully followed where God was leading. God is looking to His people to share Jesus with others. Petitioning God for opportunities to share your faith will result in many divine appointments.

The Achilles' Heel

Who can understand his errors?
Cleanse me from secret faults.

—Psalm 19:12

A t first, I thought it was a swan. Moments later, I wished it had been.

As I arrived at work late one afternoon, I noticed the picture on the front page of the evening newspaper being read by the receptionist. At first glance, I thought it might have been a photograph of a swan at a nearby lake. Having worked overnight, I was unaware of that day's major international news story. I was soon to discover that the photo in the newspaper was a picture of the space shuttle *Challenger* disintegrating just seventy-three seconds after takeoff from the Kennedy Space Center.

On January 28, 1986, seven astronauts were heading into space on what was to be the *Challenger*'s tenth mission. Among them was Christa McAuliffe, a thirty-seven-year-old social studies teacher at Concord High School in New Hampshire. Her participation in the mission meant schoolchildren from all over the country were watching coverage of the launch. McAuliffe's parents were at the Kennedy Space Center to witness the historic launch.

It was later discovered that the *Challenger* broke up shortly after liftoff because of faulty O-ring seals on the solid-rocket boosters. Due to unusually cold temperatures at Cape Canaveral, the O-rings weren't able to function correctly. They had been designed to work in warmer weather. A vehicle weighing four and a half million pounds was undone by O-rings weighing a few ounces.*

The *Challenger* had a fatal flaw, not unlike many people who possess a spiritual Achilles' heel. Judas was a thief. Solomon, David, and Samson succumbed to lust. Achan, Ananias and Sapphira, and the rich young ruler were covetous, while it was pride that caused the fall of Lucifer and led the world to be trapped in sin. In each case, one sin grew until it consumed an entire life.

Solomon wrote that "the little foxes . . . spoil the vines" (Song of Solomon 2:15). A cherished secret sin will ultimately do great damage if it is not surrendered to God. Far better to yield "little" sins to God than to see a human weakness become a fatal flaw.

---

* Elizabeth Howell, "Challenger: The Shuttle Disaster That Changed NASA," *Space*, May 1, 2019, https://www.space.com/18084-space-shuttle-challenger.html.

"Is This the Man?"

"Those who see you will gaze at you,
And consider you, saying:
" 'Is this the man who made the earth tremble,
Who shook kingdoms . . . ?' "

—Isaiah 14:16

Many of the passengers were nervous. In spite of assurances from the pilot that the sound they were hearing was entirely normal for this particular aircraft, many pressed the call light on the panel above their heads. Flight attendants were kept busy answering the same question from numerous passengers. "What is that noise?"

It was only months after the 9/11 tragedy, and many on the plane were convinced there was a serious problem. To assuage the fears of the concerned, the pilot informed us a mechanic was on the way to inspect the aircraft. Even after the mechanic had performed his investigation and we were informed there was nothing to worry about, twenty-three passengers insisted they be returned to the gate and offloaded with their luggage. The noise was caused by the plane's hydraulic systems and was familiar to frequent fliers, but irrational fear caused a flight to be delayed and many plans to be interrupted.

Although the devil is certainly a powerful enemy, it is important to remember he is a defeated foe. The serpent was told in the Garden of Eden that the Seed of the woman would bruise his head. He would one day be destroyed. John wrote, "He who is in you is greater than he who is in the world" (1 John 4:4).

Isaiah painted a striking picture in Isaiah 14:15–17. Satan is told he will "be brought down . . . to the lowest depths of the pit," and people will stare in disbelief. One day the redeemed will see the originator of sin and ask, "Is this the man? We struggled with sin and self because of *this*?" A condemned devil bereft of his strength will appear as he really is, as he really always has been: defeated, powerless, and infinitely inferior to the great Savior of the world. God's people today may live in confidence that, through Jesus, eternity is theirs.

Through Jesus, victory in the great controversy is yours.

A Timely Message

"Cry aloud, spare not;
Lift up your voice like a trumpet;
Tell My people their transgression,
And the house of Jacob their sins."

—Isaiah 58:1

The king would be heartbroken. His son was dead. But who would inform David of Absalom's demise? Ahimaaz, the son of Zadok, volunteered to convey the tidings to Israel's monarch. "Please let me run and bring the king news that the LORD has freed him from the hand of his enemies!" (2 Samuel 18:19, NASB).

Joab, however, preferred to send a foreigner with the delicate message that the king had lost a child. "Joab said to the Cushite, 'Go, tell the king what you have seen.' So the Cushite bowed to Joab and ran" (verse 21, NASB). But Ahimaaz was insistent, prompting Joab to exclaim, "Why would you run, my son, since you will have no messenger's reward for going?" (verse 22, NASB).

When finally permitted by Joab to take the news to the king, Ahimaaz ran quickly, overtaking the Cushite along the way. When King David asked about the welfare of Absalom, Ahimaaz returned an evasive answer. "I saw a great commotion, but I did not know what it was" (verse 29). In the heat of the moment, Ahimaaz wilted. He elected not to share the timely message.

Late in this world's history, God's people must share a message. As given to John on Patmos two thousand years ago, the three angels' messages were calculated by God to meet the needs of troubled minds immediately prior to the return of Jesus. The everlasting gospel presents Jesus as the hope of the world and proclaims His righteousness as the only remedy for the lost.

Ellen White affirmed, "Several have written to me, inquiring if the message of justification by faith is the third angel's message, and I have answered, 'It is the third angel's message in verity.' "* Every facet of the everlasting gospel points to Jesus as the hope of the world. Only the forgiveness and justification offered to the world in Jesus can prepare a sinner for eternity. Faith lays hold on the righteousness of Jesus and makes salvation a present reality.

God's people have a saving message to share with the world.

---

* Ellen G. White, "Repentance the Gift of God," *Advent Review and Sabbath Herald*, April 1, 1890, 1.

Christ in You

"I am the vine, you are the branches. He who abides in Me,
and I in him, bears much fruit; for without Me you can do nothing."
—John 15:5

U p until that time, I had never faced such a major challenge in the classroom. Any problems I had encountered had been easily resolved. But this was different. Staring at the book in front of me, I tried in vain to figure out the complex math I was wrestling with. But as this was unlike anything I had ever seen, I simply didn't know what to do. I had only just been promoted to the fourth grade and had come up against what appeared to be an impenetrable roadblock.

It was then that Mrs. Mounsey came to my rescue. She was a wonderful, caring teacher who took time to ensure that I understood my work and was making good progress. I had skipped a grade and entered her fourth-grade class just in time to discover I was in over my head when it came to math. But in moments, Mrs. Mounsey's patient, expert instruction solved the arithmetical mystery, and I was running again at full speed.

Christianity operates on a similar principle. Until a follower of Jesus is shown how to unravel the mysteries of living a life of faith, he or she will struggle to make any forward progress. The apostle Paul described the mystery of the gospel as being "Christ in you, the hope of glory" (Colossians 1:27). Without the actual presence of Jesus Himself in a life, the best that can be hoped for is a frustrating up-and-down existence of struggle and failure. A life without "Christ in you" is a life lived by one's own wits. Willpower is the enemy of faith. Until it is understood that the key to successful Christian living is Christ in the heart, a sinner can only fall far short of a consistent Christian experience.

"Christ in you" is the power of Christianity. Jesus brings His righteousness into the life of a believer. He brings His obedience. He brings His peace. When Jesus said, "Without Me you can do nothing" (John 15:5), He meant what He said. The only successful path forward for any follower of Jesus is "Christ in you"—Jesus in the heart.

The Gang

*"I was hungry and you gave Me food; I was thirsty
and you gave Me drink; I was a stranger and you took Me in."*
—Matthew 25:35

They were local boys, most of them, and they lived on the margins of the law. Most of them had a criminal record, and as gang members, they were viewed with suspicion by many people and with fear by some. But when they discovered local children were going to school hungry, the gang members swung into action.

Using their own money, they began making sandwiches and delivering them to a nearby elementary school. Teachers and hungry students were thrilled. Children from homes where there was often not enough food were now being fed regularly. Other schools requested that they also might participate in the sandwich program, and before long, the gang members—who described themselves as "not exactly pillars of society"—were rising early in the morning to prepare hundreds of sandwiches and delivering them to dozens of schools. A former school superintendent commented, saying, "Rich, poor, good or perceived as evil, everyone gets a lift from giving that makes them feel good. Give enough and it's almost selfish because you feel so good about what you're doing for others."*

In Matthew 25, Jesus described genuine Christianity. He said that when He returns, He will acknowledge that some clothed Him, welcomed Him, visited Him, and fed Him. In the story, those He commended were puzzled to learn they had done such things for Jesus. He explained, "Inasmuch as you did it to one of the least of these My brethren, you did it to Me" (verse 40).

The parable contains no affirmation of theology or orthodoxy. Neither church attendance nor faithfulness in giving is mentioned, as important as they undoubtedly are. Jesus speaks here to the importance of demonstrating the love of God, of serving Him as we serve others.

Followers of Jesus can learn from a group of men with criminal records and tattoos. Seeing a need and motivated by compassion for those who were going without, they stepped forward and made a life-altering difference in numerous young lives. Motivated by the love of God and a desire to see people come to know Jesus as Lord and Savior, the church can make an eternal difference when it rises up to bless Jesus in others.

---

* Lisa Suhay, "Why Gangs Are Making Sandwiches in New Zealand," *The Christian Science Monitor*, October 21, 2014, https://www.csmonitor.com/World/Making-a-difference/Change-Agent/2014/1021/Why-gangs-are-making-sandwiches-in-New-Zealand.

The Ultimate Answer

"Behold, I stand at the door and knock. If anyone hears My voice and opens the door, I will come in to him and dine with him, and he with Me."
—Revelation 3:20

Revelation chapter three contains a blunt assessment of the spiritual state of God's people. The letter to the church of Laodicea is a message to the church in earth's last days. In this brief communication, Jesus speaks to people who say, "I am rich, have become wealthy, and have need of nothing." They do not understand that, in actuality, they "are wretched, miserable, poor, blind, and naked" (Revelation 3:17).

Mercifully, Jesus presents the solution for the spiritual inadequacy of His church. "I counsel you to buy from Me gold refined in the fire, that you may be rich; and white garments, that you may be clothed, that the shame of your nakedness may not be revealed; and anoint your eyes with eye salve, that you may see" (verse 18). So how might we receive the faith that works by love, the righteousness of Christ, and the gift of the Holy Spirit that are represented by the gold, white raiment, and eye salve? The answer is shockingly simple.

Jesus says, "I stand at the door and knock" (verse 20). Jesus doesn't force His way into a human heart. He knocks, making us aware of His desire to enter. Jesus knocks in the hope that He will be permitted to come into the life of a sinner.

Although Jesus is appealing to a self-deceived sinner, someone unaware of their tremendous spiritual need, He does not state that upon entering a needy human heart, He will lecture its possessor on how to be a true Christian. Neither does He say that His first priority is to clean the mess He finds. Jesus says to sinners, "If you open your heart to Me, I will come inside, and we will dine together." No judgment. No censure. To those who have not yet found their way to a truly genuine Christian experience, Jesus simply says, "If you let Me into your life, we will spend time together in fellowship."

The ultimate answer for the broken human heart is time spent with Jesus.

November 27

Miracles of Grace

Put on the whole armor of God,
that you may be able to stand against the wiles of the devil.
—Ephesians 6:11

As a child, Timo loved to look at the pictures in The Bible Story series, by Arthur Maxwell. He dreamed of being "up with the angels." As he got older, he attended church and was active in Bible studies with a group of young adults.

As Andrew McChesney, the editor of *Youth and Adult Mission* quarterly, reported, Timo asked his parents about a book he saw on their dining room table. He was told it had been sent by a distant relative, and he was intrigued by what he saw on the cover of the book. The title was *The Great Controversy*, and it was subtitled, "Ancient prophecies are coming true." Remembering the pictures from The Bible Story, Timo took the book and read it in just three days. He read the book twice more before attending a Daniel seminar at a local church. He was baptized months later and went on to become a church pastor.

It was God's providence that led Timo to find the book that would change his life. *The Great Controversy* has led many to faith in Jesus and to a deeper understanding of the Bible. Tracing the history of the great battle between good and evil that began at the origin of sin, *The Great Controversy* chronicles the advance of the gospel, culminating in the proclamation of the three angels' messages and the return of Jesus to this world.

Paul wrote to the Ephesian church that "we do not wrestle against flesh and blood, but against principalities, against powers, against the rulers of the darkness of this age, against spiritual hosts of wickedness in the heavenly places" (Ephesian 6:12). A jealous devil works with supernatural might to draw God's people away from faith in Christ. But our heavenly Father works with unparalleled power to free those who are held captive in sin and reveal His love to the world.

God introduced thoughts of heaven to Timo when he was a young boy. As an adult, he happened upon *The Great Controversy* at exactly the right time. God was at work at every step. He still works to bring people to faith in Jesus. Miracles of grace continue to happen.*

---

* From the story by Andrew McChesney, " 'Great Controversy' Miracle in Finland," Seventh-day Adventist Church News, accessed March 15, 2021, https://www.adventistmission.org/great-controversy-miracle-in-finland.

False Alarm

A time to be born, and a time to die.

—Ecclesiastes 3:2

In January 2018, an emergency alert was issued in Hawaii, warning of an impending missile attack. The message read, "BALLISTIC MISSILE THREAT INBOUND TO HAWAII. SEEK IMMEDIATE SHELTER. THIS IS NOT A DRILL," and was broadcast on radio, television, and via cell phone. People were warned to stay inside or immediately seek shelter if they were outdoors. In the midst of escalating tensions between the United States and North Korea, it was believed North Korea had targeted Hawaii. Surely devastation and loss of life would follow.

But an employee at the Hawaii Emergency Management Agency (HEMA) had sent the report in error. The man was apparently confused by an unscheduled drill that had been conducted within the agency and believed the training exercise to be an actual threat to the United States. News agencies later reported that in the ensuing panic, drivers ran red lights and drove at high speeds to reunite with family members, while many made phone calls convinced it was their final opportunity to hear the voices of loved ones. Messages refuting the emergency alert were not sent out until thirteen minutes after the alarm was first raised, with HEMA officials finally announcing their mistake a full thirty-eight minutes after the original error occurred.*

But what if the reports had been true, and missiles had rained down on Hawaii? Residents would have been facing the end of their life on earth. Were that true, how would they have responded? Would people have been able to say, "I will die in the hope of the first resurrection"? How many people would have been without hope? "If only I had taken my faith seriously." "If only I had truly valued relationships." "If only I had given my heart to Jesus."

One day the alert will be real. If not missiles, then a heart attack, an auto accident, or simply the ravages of time will ensure that, like David, every person alive will "go the way of all the earth" (1 Kings 2:2). One day it will not be a false alarm. Our time on earth will be over.

What then?

---

* Adam Nagourney, David E. Sanger, Johanna Barr, "Hawaii Panics After Alert About Incoming Missile Is Sent in Error," *New York Times*, January 13, 2018, https://www.nytimes.com/2018/01/13/us/hawaii-missile .html?action=click&contentCollection=Asia%20Pacific&module=RelatedCoverage&region=Marginalia& pgtype=article.

The Book

*Bring the cloak that I left with Carpus at Troas when
you come—and the books, especially the parchments.*
—2 Timothy 4:13

D esperate to find meaning in my faith in God, I found myself attending St. Saviour's
Church during a visit to Limerick, Ireland. After many years of trying to make
sense of what I had been taught as a child, I had high hopes that I would finally find
the keys to a life of faith in God.

I walked away from the church service completely disheartened, concluding I would
likely never encounter God in a meaningful way. As I walked along a deserted street that
Sunday morning, I looked into the overcast sky, pointed my finger in what I assumed
was the direction of heaven, and said out loud, "I am not going back to church until
You show me the truth!" I felt a burden lift. I had genuinely tried to find a faith that
worked, and I had genuinely failed. It was God's problem now. If He wanted me to
know the truth about faith and eternity and Jesus and the Bible, He would have to
show me.

Arriving back at my flat in North London, I found a package waiting for me. Eight
years before, my brother, Wayne, had given me a copy of *The Great Controversy*. I started
on the introduction but did not continue reading. Four years later, he gave me a second
copy. I began at the first page but didn't get far before I put the book down. In recent
months, I had asked my brother if he knew where I might find the book in London.
I even visited Charing Cross Road, which at the time was a used-books mecca. Now
here it was, copy number three of *The Great Controversy*. And being temporarily out of
work, I had time to read. Along with history and prophecy, I found a Savior whom I
could receive into my heart by faith. *The Great Controversy* directed me to the Bible, a
lesser light pointing me to the greater light, and my life was changed.

Even in today's high-tech world, the printed page still has the power to change a life.
Sharing literature with others is still an effective way of introducing people to Jesus.

"So Much Wasted Time"

I have not departed from the commandment of His lips; I have treasured the words of His mouth more than my necessary food.
—Job 23:12

One of the biggest stars of the entertainment industry in the 1970s was David Cassidy. The son of an actor, Cassidy was featured in *The Partridge Family*, a hugely successful television musical sitcom that aired between 1970 and 1974. Cassidy became a teen idol and performed sold-out shows before enormous audiences. The hysteria accompanying his 1974 visit to Australia led to official calls to have him deported, and a fourteen-year-old girl lost her life in a stampede at a David Cassidy concert in London the same year.

Cassidy's fan club boasted more members than that of Elvis Presley or the Beatles. Yet, in spite of his popularity, personal challenges took a heavy toll, and he died at the age of sixty-seven. According to his daughter, his last words were, "So much wasted time."*

"So much wasted time." You don't want to say that about your relationship with God. "I could have been closer to God, but so much wasted time." "I could have known the Bible much better and experienced more hope and positivity in my life, but so much wasted time." Time spent in communion with God or in serving others is the best possible use of time. Every person is given twenty-four hours every day, hours that will be invested one way or another. They can be invested for good, or they can be aimlessly frittered away.

"Of no talent He has given will He require a more strict account than of our time."† Yesterday's missed prayers cannot be prayed today. Neglected opportunities to read the Bible cannot be undone. Failure to invest in family time often has very negative long-term consequences. Paul wrote, "Be careful how you walk, not as unwise people but as wise, making the most of your time, because the days are evil" (Ephesians 5:15, 16, NASB). Not one soul will look back over his or her life and regret that too much time was spent in the company of the God of heaven. Prioritizing one's time and putting God first is something no child of God will ever regret.

---

* "Katie Cassidy Shares Father David's Last Words: 'So Much Wasted Time'," *Billboard*, November 26, 2017, https://www.billboard.com/articles/news/8046943/katie-cassidy-shares-father-david-cassidy-last-words-so-much-wasted-time.
† Ellen G. White, *Christ's Object Lessons* (Washington, DC: Review and Herald®, 1941), 342.

The Derecho

"At that time Michael shall stand up,
The great prince who stands watch over the sons of your people;
And there shall be a time of trouble,
Such as never was since there was a nation."

—Daniel 12:1

In August 2020, a powerful storm system known as a derecho made its way from Nebraska to Indiana, leaving behind a seven-hundred-mile-long trail of destruction. The term *derecho* was coined in the 1800s by a professor at Iowa State University and is the Spanish word meaning "straight." According to the *Des Moines Register*, winds reaching speeds of up to 140 miles per hour caused massive damage. In Iowa, the hardest-hit state, houses, farms, businesses, and livestock were destroyed, along with 40 percent of the state's corn and soybean crops. Half a million Iowans were left without power. Several lives were lost, and billions of dollars in damage was inflicted on the Hawkeye State. It was the costliest thunderstorm in the history of the United States.

The Midwest derecho of 2020 struck with unanticipated ferocity, spawning numerous tornadoes and damaging countless trees. Within weeks of the bruising weather event, thousands of Iowans had filed for unemployment benefits. Eight hundred fifty thousand crop acres were lost.*

Writing in *Testimonies for the Church*, volume 8, Ellen White said, "A storm is coming, relentless in its fury." Then she asked the question, "Are we prepared to meet it?"† That which is soon to come upon the earth will be of a far greater magnitude than anything we have ever witnessed. Speaking of the coming "time of trouble," the same author writes, "It is often the case that trouble is greater in anticipation than in reality; but this is not true of the crisis before us. The most vivid presentation cannot reach the magnitude of the ordeal."‡

Those who get news of an approaching hurricane quickly get to work preparing their homes. It is too late to board up windows when the storm is already upon you. Preparation must be done before the storm. Preparing in advance of the return of Jesus—surrendering the will to God, repenting of sin, and pleading for a new heart—will ensure God's people will stand successfully in earth's last days.

---

* Andrea May Sahouri, "$7.5 Billion and Counting: August Derecho That Slammed Iowa Was Most Costly Thunderstorm in US History, Data Shows," *Des Moines Register*, October 17, 2020, https://www.desmoines register.com/story/news/2020/10/17/iowas-august-derecho-most-costly-thunderstorm-us-history-7-5-billion -damages/3695053001/.

† Ellen G. White, *Testimonies for the Church*, vol. 8 (Mountain View, CA: Pacific Press®, 1948), 315.

‡ Ellen G. White, *The Great Controversy Between Christ and Satan* (Mountain View, CA: Pacific Press®, 1950), 622.

One Decision

*"I am the door. If anyone enters by Me, he will be saved,
and will go in and out and find pasture."*

—John 10:9

I n 1914, near the Latin Bridge in Sarajevo in present-day Bosnia and Herzegovina, a desperate act committed by a nineteen-year-old Bosnian changed the course of the world. As a member of an underground military group committed to freeing Bosnia from Austro-Hungarian rule, Gavrilo Princip shot and killed Archduke Franz Ferdinand, the heir to the Austro-Hungarian throne, and his wife, Sophie, the Duchess of Hohenberg. Princip's murderous moment is credited with starting World War I.* If Franz Ferdinand had not been killed, it is reasonable to assume World War I would not have taken place. Consequently, Adolf Hitler would likely have not been elected to power in Germany, and the horrors of the Holocaust would never have happened. The world today would be vastly different but for that one murderous deed.

One act can have significant ramifications. In October 1912, former president Theodore Roosevelt survived and assassination attempt at a campaign event in Milwaukee, Wisconsin. He was shot in the chest at point blank range; he not only survived the attempt on his life, but also delivered a ninety-minute speech before accepting medical attention. The bullet passed through his overcoat, his eyeglass case, and a fifty-page speech he had folded and put in his pocket. He remarked to his hearers, "It takes more than that to kill a bull Moose!"† If Roosevelt had put the speech in another pocket, he would almost certainly have died.

Every person alive has the opportunity to make a decision that will alter the course of eternity. With each new day, every life may be yielded to Jesus as Lord and Savior. A simple prayer of surrender turns the life over to Christ, who makes the heart His home and fills the life with His presence. A simple decision remakes a sinful life, as the grace of Jesus makes a sinner into a "new creation" (2 Corinthians 5:17).

When Jesus returns, the world will be divided into two groups: the saved and the lost. Had they chosen, every lost soul could have been saved. A decision for Jesus changes the trajectory of a life. One decision unites a sinner with Jesus for eternity.

---

* "Gavrilo Princip," Britannica, accessed April 6, 2021, https://www.britannica.com/biography/Gavrilo-Princip.

† Theodore Roosevelt, "It Take More Than That to Kill a Bull Moose," Theodore Roosevelt Association, accessed June 3, 2021, https://www.theodoreroosevelt.org/content.aspx?page_id=22&club_id=991271&module_id=338394.

"In Verity"

Therefore, having been justified by faith, we have peace
with God through our Lord Jesus Christ.

—Romans 5:1

The message to the world found in Revelation 14 is replete with both hope and warning. The three angels' messages speak of judgment and worship, of commitment to God, and of the danger of choosing falsehood over truth. At the eleventh hour of this world's history, the inhabitants of the earth are given a solemn warning. Those who steadfastly refuse to yield their lives to the God of heaven have no hope of eternal salvation and will instead be forever lost.

So where should the focus of the believer be when it comes to the messages of the three angels? Do we emphasize giving glory to God or worshiping Him "who made heaven and earth, the sea and springs of water" (Revelation 14:7)? Is alerting people that Babylon is fallen to be the church's primary burden, or does the church pour its energies into educating people regarding the mark of the beast?

Notice this important insight given by Ellen White: "Several have written to me, inquiring if the message of justification by faith is the third angel's message, and I have answered, 'It is the third angel's message in verity,' "* "What is justification by faith? It is the work of God in laying the glory of man in the dust, and doing for man that which it is not in his power to do for himself."† The message of the three angels is designed by God to bring the righteousness of Christ into the life of the believer. The sinner is to be transformed by the indwelling presence of Jesus. Rightly understood, this is the burden of the three angels' messages.

The three angels' messages are not messages of denunciation. They are messages of hope, showing the world that in a time of crisis, an eternal future is granted in the One who died for the sins of the world. The "everlasting gospel" is the *gospel*. As specific as the three angels' messages are, we must not lose sight of the theme of God's last-day message: justification by faith, in verity.

---

* Ellen G. White, "Repentance the Gift of God," *Advent Review and Sabbath Herald*, April 1, 1890, 1.

† Ellen G. White, *Testimonies to Ministers and Gospel Workers* (Mountain View, CA: Pacific Press®, 1944), 456.

"A Battle and a March"

"Have I not commanded you? Be strong and of good courage; do not be afraid, nor be dismayed, for the Lord your God is with you wherever you go."
—Joshua 1:9

Many are frustrated with their seeming inability to remedy defects of character. Even the most conscientious Christians can find themselves falling short of God's will for their lives. They find that accepting Jesus did not remove temptation and sin. And there are those who believe that to strive against sin would be salvation by works, as though trusting in Jesus spares them the heat of the battle against sin.

Yet, a plain reading of the Bible reveals that Jesus tells His followers to "strive to enter through the narrow gate" (Luke 13:24). And Paul speaks of believers resisting "to the point of shedding blood in your striving against sin" (Hebrews 12:4, NASB). Ellen White puts it this way:

By a momentary act of will, one may place himself in the power of evil; but it requires more than a momentary act of will to break these fetters and attain to a higher, holier life. The purpose may be formed, the work begun; but its accomplishment will require toil, time, and perseverance, patience and sacrifice.

Beset with temptations without number, we must resist firmly or be conquered. Should we come to the close of life with our work undone, it would be an eternal loss.

Paul's sanctification was the result of a constant conflict with self. He said: "I die daily." 1 Corinthians 15:31. His will and his desires every day conflicted with duty and the will of God. Instead of following inclination, he did God's will, however crucifying to his own nature.

God leads His people on step by step. The Christian life is a battle and a march. In this warfare there is no release; the effort must be continuous and persevering. It is by unceasing endeavor that we maintain the victory over the temptations of Satan. Christian integrity must be sought with resistless energy and maintained with a resolute fixedness of purpose.*

James wrote that those who submit themselves to God "resist the devil," knowing that he will flee (James 4:7). Faith in God grants the believer victory over the weaknesses of the fallen nature.

---

* Ellen G. White, *Testimonies for the Church*, vol. 8 (Mountain View, CA: Pacific Press®, 1948), 313.

Never Too Late

*"And they overcame him by the blood of the Lamb
and by the word of their testimony."*

—Revelation 12:11

As the COVID-19 pandemic gripped the United Kingdom, an unlikely hero inspired a nation reeling from its deadly effects. Captain Tom Moore was a ninety-nine-year-old veteran of World War II, having served his country in both India and Burma. Motivated by what he described as the wonderful service he had received from Britain's National Health Service after breaking his hip, Captain Moore launched a fund-raising effort to raise money for the NHS. With his birthday approaching, he planned to walk the length of his backyard one hundred times, a total of one and a half miles before he turned one hundred, ten lengths of his yard a day for ten days. Captain Moore hoped to raise £1,000 (almost $1,400).

Within a month, Captain Moore had raised in excess of £30 million and went on to raise the remarkable total of around £40 million ($55.5 million)! Captain Sir Thomas Moore died at the age of one hundred, six months after being knighted by Queen Elizabeth II.* He also became the oldest Briton to top the UK's pop music charts when a song featuring his spoken words reached number one on his hundredth birthday.†

Captain Tom demonstrated that age need not be a barrier to achievement. The same is true in terms of sharing one's faith. Personal ministry is not only the domain of the young. When I saw Larry for the first time in a couple of years, I remarked at the beautiful walking stick he was using. He told me he had been praying God would give him a soul-winning ministry and was impressed that the walking stick was the entering wedge he needed.

Printing a picture of the walking stick on the front of a flyer he designed, Larry wrote a Bible story, his personal testimony, and a list of ministries to contact for further information. Whenever someone commented on his unique walking stick, Larry gave that person a copy of the flyer and encouraged them to read it and to contact him if they had further questions. Larry was ninety-four years old at the time.

It is never too late to share your faith in Jesus.

---

* "Capt Sir Tom Moore Knighted in 'Unique' Ceremony," *BBC News*, July 17, 2020, https://www.bbc.com/news/uk-england-beds-bucks-herts-53442746.

† Laura Snapes, "Captain Tom Moore Becomes Oldest Artist to Claim UK No. 1 Single," *The Guardian*, April 24, 2020, https://www.theguardian.com/music/2020/apr/24/captain-tom-moore-becomes-oldest-artist-to-claim-uk-no-1-single.

He Hears

*"The Helper, the Holy Spirit, whom the Father will send in My name,
He will teach you all things, and bring to your remembrance
all things that I said to you."*

—John 14:26

Laura was desperate to make it to the shelter. The young mother had lived what she described as "a rough life" and was in an extremely unhealthy relationship. Having fled her home, she was walking in the direction of the local shelter when a car pulled up beside her. A kind lady named Yara asked Laura if she needed a ride, and as they drove, she felt impressed to offer Laura a place to stay. She assured her she would be safe and could stay as long as she needed.

Yara lived next door to the church she attended, which, at the time, was conducting an evangelistic series presented by the evangelist Eric Flickinger. Laura attended the meetings with Yara and experienced the love of God, and for the first time she could remember, a sense of peace in her heart. Before then, Laura had never studied the Bible, and the more she learned, the more she wanted to know. She accepted Jesus as her personal Savior, and before long, made the decision to be baptized. Her baptism took place several weeks after the series concluded. Laura was emphatic. "God has changed my life."

When Laura left her home that day, she did so in the hope of surviving. In addition to saving Laura's life, the God of heaven extended to her the gift of eternal life.

God is constantly working to draw men and women, boys and girls, to His heart of love. Cheryl had been praying for her sister for twenty-five years. Wondering whether her prayers would ever be answered, she invited her sister to watch Hope Awakens, an online evangelistic series I presented in 2020. Cheryl was ecstatic when her sister began watching the nightly presentations. She was overjoyed when her sister was baptized two months after the series concluded.

God is at work in the experience of your loved ones. The Holy Spirit impresses the hearts of those for whom you pray, appealing to them to open their hearts to Jesus and arranging circumstances to give them the best possible chance of accepting salvation. Never stop praying for others. God hears your prayers.

Your Superpower

As you therefore have received Christ Jesus the Lord, so walk in Him.
—Colossians 2:6

He was said to be "Faster than a speeding bullet! More powerful than a locomotive! Able to leap tall buildings in a single bound!" With his ability to fly, to melt steel with his gaze, and to repel bullets with his body, the fictional superhero Superman captured the imagination of the American public when he first appeared in comic books in 1938.*

While he doesn't believe people can bend steel bars with their bare hands, Irish neurologist Dr. Shane O'Mara does claim that every human being possesses what he calls a "superpower." His book, *In Praise of Walking*, describes the remarkable benefits of ambulation. Dr. O'Mara says that walking sharpens the senses, unlocks the cognitive powers of the brain, and provides neurological nourishment.[†] Other experts say walking alleviates depression and fatigue, improves mood, reduces the risk of cancer and other chronic diseases, improves circulation, and is, for many people, a better workout than running. A church leader once told me the two best doctors he had ever met were Left Foot and Right Foot.

Walking is a simple matter of putting one foot in front of another. Faith in Jesus is the same. The English Standard Version renders Revelation 14:12 as follows: "Here is a call for the endurance of the saints, those who keep the commandments of God and their faith in Jesus." In Colossians 2:6, Paul suggests walking in Christ—continued movement in the Christian experience. The Greek word he used for "walk" forms the basis of the English word "peripatetic," which means "traveling from place to place" or "nomadic." Paul expresses the idea that the person who accepts Jesus as Lord and Savior does not stand still. Christianity is about constant advancement.

The disciple of Jesus is ever advancing. He or she will put one foot in front of the other and continue to grow, deepening the Christian experience. Discouragement and failure do not prevent the believer from pressing on the upward way. The Christian's "superpower" is Jesus. Walking in Him is to experience increasingly more of His presence and power.

---

* "Superman," Library of American Comics, accessed April 1, 2021, http://libraryofamericancomics.com /product-category/loac/dccomics/superman/.

† Shane O'Mara, *In Priase of Walking: A New Scientific Exploration* (New York: W. W. Norton, 2019).

Never So Great

*"Now, O Lord my God, You have made Your
servant king instead of my father David, but I am a
little child; I do not know how to go out or come in."*

—1 Kings 3:7

S hortly after he ascended the throne of Israel, Solomon received what may well be the most remarkable offer in all of history. Appearing to him in a dream, the Sovereign of the universe told him, "Ask! What shall I give you?" (1 Kings 3:5).

At that moment, Solomon recognized his great lack. Instead of requesting wealth or military success, he answered the God of heaven with true humility. Ellen White wrote, "Solomon was never so rich or so wise or so truly great as when he confessed, 'I am but a little child: I know not how to go out or come in.' "* Solomon's distrust of self led him to ask of God "an understanding heart to judge Your people, that I may discern between good and evil" (1 Kings 3:9). As long as Solomon remained cognizant of his smallness in light of the vastness of the Almighty, he and Israel were secure.

Ellen White described justification by faith as "the work of God in laying the glory of man in the dust, and doing for man that which it is not in his power to do for himself. When men see their own nothingness, they are prepared to be clothed with the righteousness of Christ."†

Looking in faith to God and away from self enables the sinner to truly experience the presence of God in his or her life. Those who are enamored with self and whose lives are governed by self-interest cannot receive the righteousness of Christ because, like Adam and Eve in the Garden of Eden, they are determined to save themselves by their own works.

When God's people recognize the depth of their spiritual need, heaven's power will be brought to bear in their lives. Solomon simply admitted the truth. He was inadequate to fulfill the position to which God had called him. As long as his sufficiency was of Christ, God could use him for His glory. The same is still true. Those—and only those—who distrust self and look in faith to the Savior can live for the glory of God.

---

* Ellen G. White, *Prophets and Kings* (Mountain View, CA: Pacific Press®, 1943), 30.
† Ellen G. White, *The Faith I Live By* (Washington, DC: Review and Herald®, 1958), 111.

The Great Conspirator

For the word of the LORD is right,
and all His work is done in truth.

—Psalm 33:4

Even in the church, conspiracy theories fascinate large numbers of people. Whether side issues such as date setting and reinterpreting prophecy or out-and-out conspiracy theories regarding chemtrails or the "faked" moon landing, Christian believers can allow their time and energy to be absorbed by subjects that have no redemptive value and that have nothing to do with proclaiming the everlasting gospel.

For a series of television programs on the subject of the great controversy, I interviewed individuals who believe in modern-day conspiracies. One man was convinced of the existence of Sasquatch, which he claimed to have seen on more than one occasion. Another was an outspoken advocate of the flat earth theory. What was fascinating about both men was that they appeared to believe in *all* conspiracy theories. Nothing seemed to be too outlandish. In their understanding, flying pterodactyls, tears in the space-time continuum, the existence of aliens, and innumerable government cover-ups were all very much in play. They were convinced the government is lying about virtually everything and that no one is to be trusted. They didn't believe in just one conspiracy theory. They seemed to believe them all.

God's end-time people should shun all unverifiable conspiracy theories. While it is true there are myriad mysteries and unanswered questions in the world, these are not the burden for those who have been called by God to live and proclaim the three angels' messages. There is, however, undoubtedly, a vast conspiracy unfolding before our eyes. The world is being conditioned daily to receive the mark of the beast and reject the seal of the living God. The great conspirator is Satan, pulling strings behind the scenes like a master marionettist and pressing the world toward earth's last, great crisis.

Let God's people be fixated on the Cross, committed to reflecting the character of Jesus, and dedicated to proclaiming and living the everlasting gospel. Speculation, a manufactured excitement, and an infatuation with shadowy theories do not prepare people for translation. They have the opposite effect. We want the truth, and we want Jesus. Anything less hinders spiritual growth.

Balloon Boy

For He made Him who knew no sin to be sin for us,
that we might become the righteousness of God in Him.

—2 Corinthians 5:21

They called 911 to report the emergency. Their homemade, helium-filled balloon had lifted off from the backyard of their Fort Collins, Colorado, home with their six-year-old son on board. Emergency services reacted swiftly to reports that something was seen falling from the balloon, which reached heights of up to seven thousand feet. Military helicopters were deployed, commercial aircraft were rerouted, and a massive search operation was launched.

But before long, the entire episode was declared to be a hoax. The young boy—who was found hiding in the attic of the family home—appeared to say on live television that the entire saga was "for the show," interpreted to mean it was cooked up to generate publicity for the family. The boy's father had been trying to secure his own reality television program but, along with his wife, was sentenced to jail time and community service.*

Eleven years later, the couple was pardoned by the state of Colorado. In the executive order pardoning the couple, Governor Jared Polis wrote, "Not everyone earns the privilege of a second chance. But you have demonstrated that you deserve one."†

Fortunately for sinners, the grace of God operates differently. The Bible is clear that "all have sinned and fall short of the glory of God" (Romans 3:23) and that "the wages of sin is death" (Romans 6:23). Sinners do not deserve a second chance. Yet, "God so loved the world that He gave His only begotten Son, that whoever believes in Him should not perish but have everlasting life" (John 3:16). Paul wrote that "Christ died for our sins" (1 Corinthians 15:3) and that God "made Him who knew no sin to be sin for us, that we might become the righteousness of God in Him" (2 Corinthians 5:21).

The thief on the cross died the tragic death of a common criminal. King Manasseh sacrificed his children to the devil and led Israel into apostasy. Yet both men will be raised from the dead when Jesus returns at the Second Coming. God still forgives the undeserving. All who trust in Him by faith receive the gift of salvation.

---

* Reese Oxner, " 'Balloon Boy' Parents Pardoned By Colorado Governor for 2009 Hoax," NPR News, December 24, 2020, https://www.npr.org/2020/12/24/950074173/balloon-boy-parents-pardoned-by-colorado -governor-for-2009-hoax.

† 2020 Clemency–Executive Orders–Letters of Jared Polis, Governor of Colorado, accessed April 6, 2021, https://drive.google.com/drive/folders/1QGXeiThyHWQtY4S_nA5JkEFEUueM71bv.

Running to Win

Do you not know that those who run in a race all run,
but only one receives the prize? Run in such a way that you may win.
—1 Corinthians 9:24, NASB

One winter morning in 1977, Luis Rios jogged almost three and a half miles in Prospect Park, Brooklyn. He ran again the next day and the next, eventually logging well over 200,000 miles. He participated in more than fifty marathons and over two hundred ultra-races and multiday events and, in his sixties, was still running 150 miles a week.* Mr. Rios was committed to running.

Faith in Jesus requires consistency. There is no power in a Bible that is not read, and unprayed prayers are not answered. Psalm 42:1 states, "As the deer pants for the water brooks, so pants my soul for You, O God." The psalmist expressed a longing for God. A life of faith affects a believer's entire existence. Jesus becomes a constant companion, the Bible a daily guide, and prayer a regular connection between heaven and earth.

Even though he was facing the death penalty, Daniel made a decided stand for God. Informed that he must worship no other god save the king himself, Daniel "went home. And in his upper room, with his windows open toward Jerusalem, he knelt down on his knees three times that day, and prayed and gave thanks before his God" (Daniel 6:10).

What could give Daniel such firmness of conviction? The secret to Daniel's faithfulness is found at the end of Daniel 6:10. The verse concludes, "As was his custom since early days." Even when his life was on the line, Daniel prayed to God because that is what he always did. For Daniel, not praying would be like Luis Rios not running. Faithfulness to God defined Daniel's life.

Those running the Christian race have been called to "run in such a way that you may win" (1 Corinthians 9:24, NASB). Competitive runners give everything to achieve their goals. Followers of Jesus surrender everything so that God's will can be done in their lives.

* Peter Gambaccini, "35 Years of Running Around Brooklyn," *Runners World*, August 10, 2012, https://www.runnersworld.com/races-places/a20806740/35-years-of-running-around-brooklyn/.

The Invitation

Likewise you also, reckon yourselves to be dead indeed to sin,
but alive to God in Christ Jesus our Lord.

—Romans 6:11

One of the great paradoxes of successful Christian living is that life follows death. Life in Jesus begins once a person dies to sin. In Romans 6, Paul explains that the person "who has died has been freed from sin" (Romans 6:7). A dead person cannot possibly sin. Anyone who has had the sobering experience of being in close proximity to a lifeless body knows there is no noise loud enough to wake the dead. Tempting a dead person elicits no response. It cannot. The individual is dead.

This truth is what makes Paul's counsel so important in the day-to-day Christian life. He says, "Reckon yourselves to be dead indeed to sin, but alive to God in Christ Jesus our Lord" (verse 11). In the physical realm, no person can declare himself or herself to be dead. But in the spiritual life, we are instructed to do so. We are to "reckon" that we are dead to sin. And the reckoning makes it so.

The man who is tempted to slander his neighbor can find nothing within himself to keep him from falling into that sin. The woman tempted to lie may feel compelled to do so, recognizing her complete inability to do otherwise. But should that person be dead to sin, the sin will not be committed. In fact, it cannot without the individual, at that moment, choosing to let go of faith in Jesus. The question that needs to be answered is, "How does a person experience 'deadness' in that crucial moment?" The answer is, one "reckons" one is dead. When you believe it is so, then it is so. Those who reckon they are dead to sin are indeed dead to sin through the working of the Holy Spirit.

When tempted to sin, reckon—believe—that you are dead to sin, and sin shall not "reign in your mortal body, that you should obey it in its lusts" (verse 12). An essential key to a successful Christian life is considering yourself to be dead to sin and allowing Jesus to be alive in you.

Still There

And such were some of you. But you were washed, but you were sanctified, but you were justified in the name of the Lord Jesus and by the Spirit of our God.
—1 Corinthians 6:11

M any years after becoming a Christian, I found myself back in Limerick, Ireland, the city in which I once handed God an ultimatum that would ultimately change my life. "I am never going back to church," I told Him, "until You show me the truth." Twenty-five years later, I visited the church in which I had broken with my past and decided to stop in at the pub where I stayed during that time.

It appeared little had changed since my last visit a quarter of a century earlier, apart from the addition of video games and television screens. Greeting a man seated at the bar, I asked him if he visited often. "I've been sitting in this same spot for thirty years," the man told me. "I could count on one hand the weekends I haven't stopped in." I was stunned. "I visited here early in 1991. You would have been here at the time," I said. "No question about it," he replied. "I would have been sitting right here."

Unaware of the circumstances of his life, I certainly didn't want to pass judgment. But for three decades, the man had been frequenting the same watering hole, drinking the same beer with more or less the same people. I realized in that encounter what God had saved me from. There was little reason to believe my life would have been substantively different had God not intervened to put me on an altogether different path.

In 1 Corinthians 6, Paul catalogs various sins he states will keep people out of the kingdom of heaven, including the sin of drunkenness. Then he reminds the believers in Corinth, "And such were some of you. But you were washed, but you were sanctified, but you were justified in the name of the Lord Jesus and by the Spirit of our God" (verse 11).

Faith in the death of Jesus transforms the life of the believer. Whatever a person's struggles, God looks forward to saying, "Such were some of you." One's past does not have to define one's future. Jesus offers a new start and a bright tomorrow.

The Two Crowns

Now behold, one came and said to Him,
"Good Teacher, what good thing shall I do that I may have eternal life?"
—Matthew 19:16

In *Testimonies for the Church*, volume 1, Ellen White relates a vision in which she saw two crowns. One was offered by God and bore the inscription, "All who win me are happy, and shall have everlasting life." Upon the other crown were the words, "Earthly treasure. Riches is power. All who win me have honor and fame." She wrote that a "vast multitude" rushed forward to obtain this crown, even trampling over others in order to do so. She wrote that many "would look wishfully upon the heavenly crown, and would often seem charmed with its beauty, yet they had no true sense of its value and glory. While with one hand they were reaching forth languidly for the heavenly, with the other they reached eagerly for the earthly, determined to possess that; and in their earnest pursuit for the earthly, they lost sight of the heavenly."*

The same attitude is exhibited in the experience of the rich young ruler. When this young man asked what he needed to do in order to "have eternal life," Jesus replied, "If you want to enter into life, keep the commandments" (Matthew 19:17). Quoting those commandments that deal with a believer's relationship with his or her fellow humans, Jesus chose not to mention the tenth commandment. Undoubtedly the young man spotted the deliberate omission. Although convicted by Jesus' injunction to sell his possessions and donate the proceeds to the poor, he went away both sorrowful and lost.

Jesus certainly is not opposed to wealth, and it isn't only the wealthy who may be trapped by their possessions. Wealth that has been consecrated to God brings blessings to both its possessor and to the work of the gospel, while even a little that is kept from God becomes a curse to its possessor.

God asks, "Have your possessions been placed on the altar before heaven?" Those who seek earthly riches at the expense of surrender to God will find that while they have something in this world, they will have no place in the world to come.

---

* Ellen G. White, *Testimonies for the Church*, vol. 1 (Mountain View, CA: Pacific Press®, 1948), 347–349.

Inclination and Preference

If then you were raised with Christ, seek those things which are above,
where Christ is, sitting at the right hand of God.
—Colossians 3:1

A person might naturally like ice cream, french fries, bananas, or burgers, some of which are more healthful than others. Similarly, a reader might favor novels, biographies, thrillers, or science fiction. A movie watcher might enjoy westerns, action movies, romantic comedies, or documentaries.

Everyone has preferences. But what are we to do with them? The Christian who enjoys horror movies knows they fall outside the will of God. The same is true for violent movies, occult books, and sexually suggestive television programs. These are real-world issues for masses of people. What is a person to do if they naturally enjoy the things that the Bible does not approve?

The apostle Paul answered this when he wrote, "Seek those things which are above, where Christ is" (Colossians 3:1). Followers of Jesus are encouraged to focus their attention on "things above" rather than "things on the earth" (verse 2). Paul suggests we exercise our God-given freedom of choice to govern what occupies the mind and wins the affections. When a lifestyle preference is not in harmony with God's principles, His people are to choose alternatives that are not counter to the will of heaven. As Paul stated in Romans 8:5, "Those who live according to the flesh set their minds on the things of the flesh, but those who live according to the Spirit, the things of the Spirit."

Natural inclinations are too frequently allowed to determine what constitutes appropriate Christian living. There is much in the world today that is spiritually dangerous but almost universally accepted even among Christians. Worldly standards are readily adopted by the church, with new generations of believers freely led into practices that hinder Christian growth.

There are times difficult choices must be made that run counter to one's natural inclination. Those who continue to grow in the grace of God will find Jesus' strength will increasingly become their own. Their affections are set on things above, not on things on the earth.

Life

"He who eats My flesh and drinks My blood abides in Me, and I in him."
—John 6:56

Met with kindness rather than the hostility he expected, a morbidly obese man browsing a bodybuilding website experienced a change he neither anticipated nor thought possible. Weighing almost seven hundred pounds, he hadn't left his house in years and was not able to fit into his shower. In time, he lost an incredible four hundred pounds and credits the support he was given by website users for his remarkable transformation. Speaking to those who supported him on his journey, he said, "I'm standing here as an example of someone whose life you gave back."

The follower of Jesus recognizes Jesus did more than give life. Jesus *is* life. Writing to the church at Colossae, Paul said, "When Christ who is our life appears, then you also will appear with Him in glory" (Colossians 3:4). A more literal reading of the passage would say, "When Christ our life appears . . ." Paul echoed the words of Moses in Deuteronomy 30:20, when Moses said of God, "He is your life and the length of your days." Addressing philosophers gathered on Mars' Hill in Athens, Paul co-opted the words of a Greek poet when he said of Jesus, "In Him we live and move and have our being" (Acts 17:28).

Jesus is more than the Giver of good gifts and the Provider of daily needs. Jesus is the very life of the believer. As the Originator of life, "by Him all things were created that are in heaven and that are on earth, visible and invisible" (Colossians 1:16). As the Savior of the world, "He who eats My flesh and drinks My blood abides in Me, and I in him" (John 6:56). As the sustainer of life, He issues the gracious invitation, "Come to Me, all you who labor and are heavy laden, and I will give you rest" (Matthew 11:28). And to a world longingly waiting for sin to be no more, Jesus says, "I will come again and receive you to Myself; that where I am, there you may be also" (John 14:3).

The heart that is open to receive Him will recognize Jesus as life itself. Maker, Redeemer, and soon-coming King, Jesus is life to all who accept Him by faith.

Magic?

Can the Ethiopian change his skin or the leopard its spots?
Then may you also do good who are accustomed to do evil.
—Jeremiah 13:23

I was fascinated as I watched the magician ply his trade. He had our small group enthralled at his ability to do the seemingly impossible. At one point, he set fire to some paper he had placed on a small stand. He placed a cover over the paper to extinguish the flames, then lifted the cover to reveal four white mice!

Have you ever seen a magician produce a coin from behind someone's ear, pull a rabbit out of a hat, or cut a woman in half? The answer, of course, is no. The magician may have made it look as though he or she did so, but that is all. Magicians are illusionists, highly skilled in the art of misdirection. While your attention is "here," the illusionist does something "there," leading you to the erroneous conclusion that something miraculous occurred.

Illusionists seem to do what is apparently impossible. But in spite of their tremendous skill and showmanship, they do not. God, however, does what is truly impossible. The prophet Jeremiah says it is as impossible for evil people to do good as for an Ethiopian to change his skin or a leopard its spots. The same prophet said, "O Lord, I know the way of man is not in himself; it is not in man who walks to direct his own steps" (Jeremiah 10:23). A few chapters later we find this thought. "The heart is deceitful above all things, and desperately wicked; who can know it?" (Jeremiah 17:9). In this verse, Jeremiah uses a word that means "incurable." "The heart is deceitful above all things, and *incurable*." Who can restore an impossibly lost sinner to union with the God of heaven?

Paul wrote, "There is therefore now no condemnation to those who are in Christ Jesus, who do not walk according to the flesh, but according to the Spirit" (Romans 8:1). In Christ is found the remedy for the sin-sick heart. In Christ, the one who is accustomed to doing evil can find a new direction. The soul surrendered to the indwelling of Jesus Christ finds new hope and new life. Jesus can do the impossible in your life.

Good Advice

Where is the flock that was given
to you, your beautiful sheep?

—Jeremiah 13:20

I t was too good an opportunity. I might never see him again, and as he was one of the most prominent evangelists in the denomination, I felt I had to act while I could.

"Pastor," I began, "would you mind giving me some advice?"

A look of concern crossed his face. "Why, of course," he replied, his brow furrowing. "Advice about what? Is there a problem?"

"No, not at all," I responded. "I'd just appreciate it if you could give me some advice—about anything at all."

He looked away momentarily before looking back to me and saying, "Put your family first." He then repeated himself. "Put your family first."

As he elaborated briefly, those four words etched themselves into my mind. My wife and I had no children at the time, but knowing something of the elderly evangelist's personal experience, I felt this was advice worth heeding, advice he wished his own father might have taken. "Put your family first."

God has been very clear in communicating with members of the church their great responsibility to reach the world with the gospel. " 'You are My witnesses,' says the Lord, 'And My servant whom I have chosen' " (Isaiah 43:10). "You are the light of the world," Jesus said in Matthew 5:14, during the Sermon on the Mount. And in the Great Commission, Jesus charged His disciples throughout all ages, saying, "Go therefore and make disciples of all the nations" (Matthew 28:19).

In light of all this, however, God will one day ask of parents, "Where is the flock that was given to you, your beautiful sheep?" (Jeremiah 13:20). Children are "a heritage from the Lord" (Psalm 127:3). No greater gift could be committed to the care of a husband and wife. And while perfect parents can never be found, God desires parents to make the home their primary field of evangelistic labor. Efforts made to reach children with the gospel and to model the love of God will be richly repaid. Of all the questions God could ask, few could be more important. "Where is the beautiful flock that was given you?"

The Advent

For the Lord Himself will descend from heaven with a shout,
with the voice of an archangel, and with the trumpet of God.
And the dead in Christ will rise first.

—1 Thessalonians 4:16

That first Christmas two thousand or so years ago is referred to as the first advent of Jesus. Jesus came to the world as a baby in a manger. The Creator Himself was born a helpless, dependent infant. Two millennia have passed since the day Jesus was born in Bethlehem. While we can only imagine what it was like when Jesus was born, it seems almost certain that many people alive today will witness the *second* advent of Jesus.

The first time Jesus came to the earth, the vast majority of people had no idea the Messiah had been born. A nation was awaiting the advent of the Messiah, but when He was born in their midst, the populace was oblivious to the fact that the greatest event since the creation of the world had taken place. There was no need for anyone to have been unprepared. The coming of the Messiah was Israel's great hope. And the people of Israel possessed the knowledge that should have alerted them to the wondrous event.

When the wise men arrived in Jerusalem inquiring about the One who had been born King of the Jews, it set the city astir. Herod was agitated and asked the chief priests where the Messiah was to be born. They replied, "In Bethlehem of Judea," and cited Micah 5:2.

It seems incomprehensible that a people anticipating the arrival of its Messiah would be unaware the Son of God was in their midst. But will it be any different at the time of the Second Coming? God invites all to welcome Jesus when He returns to our world, not as a dependent child but as a conquering King. Preparation must be made for the long-awaited return of Jesus. Faith in God and dependence on His Word will ensure that this time, children of God are ready to meet the Messiah.

Jesus will return to the earth as a conquering King, as King of kings and Lord of lords. Paul says, "The Lord Himself will descend from heaven with a shout" (1 Thessalonians 4:16).

Christmas Gifts

My son, give me your heart,
and let your eyes observe my ways.

—Proverbs 23:26

I once asked my father what he considered to be the most special gift he had ever received. He paused, reflected for a few moments, and spoke with some certainty. He said, "While I consider every gift I've ever received to be special, there is one that stands out."

He told me about a Christmas some years before I was born when one of my older brothers bought him a very simple gift. "He was only young. Maybe four years old. He wanted to buy something for his daddy and managed to scrape together enough coins to buy me a little bar of shaving soap." I listened as my father continued. "It couldn't have cost much at all. It was a small bar of soap, but what made it special is that it was given with love. A young boy wanted to do something special for his father. I have never forgotten that." Over the years, Dad received gifts of much greater monetary value. In fact, the shaving soap was almost certainly the least expensive gift he had ever been given, but no gift ever touched his heart like the inexperience gift given him by a boy barely out of infancy.

While waiting to go onto the platform to preach one Sabbath during the Christmas season, I asked the same question of several women who were waiting to participate in the church service. The answers I received were essentially the same. One said, "I remember my daughter made something for me that I treasured for years." Another told me about a gift her three children had worked together to make. The third woman said essentially the same thing. Her children had given her something they had made. It was simple and inexpensive, but it came from the heart.

As Christmas approaches and people check off their shopping lists, it is possible to miss out on recognizing the greatest gift that can be given. In Proverbs, God says, "My son, give me your heart" (Proverbs 23:26). Don't forget God this Christmas. You already know what He wants most. He wants the simple gift of your heart.

Ditto

Godliness with contentment is great gain.
—1 Timothy 6:6

Every Christmas season, houses across the land are brightly arrayed with lights and ornaments, blow-up characters, and a seemingly endless array of creative and not-so-creative decorations. The front yard of a certain man would be spectacularly lit every Christmas and was inevitably the biggest and brightest display in his neighborhood. Knowing she could never match the light show over her fence, the lady next door placed a small sign on her house that simply said "Ditto," along with a lighted arrow pointing to her neighbor's property.

"Ditto" is all she said, with obvious good humor. What she realized is that she couldn't match the Christmas display next door and that maybe she shouldn't attempt to. There was no point in her trying to keep up with the neighbors.

How many people spend unnecessarily just to keep pace with what others are doing? Just to be seen as relevant or important or impressive as someone else? There are good reasons to buy a nice vehicle, but the fact that someone else has one is not one of them. Many factors go into the decision to buy a home, but buying a certain home merely to keep up appearances is neither wise nor necessary and is out of harmony with the character of Jesus.

Keeping up with the Joneses has ruined a lot of people, financially and emotionally. Paul told Timothy, "Godliness with contentment is great gain" (1 Timothy 6:6). There is certainly nothing wrong with bettering your lot, but a person needs to know where to draw the line. Many people would be far happier if they chose to be content with what they have.

The Holy Spirit will grant wisdom so that you may discern whether you are buying to gratify yourself or whether there is a nobler reason to spend God-given resources. No Christian will walk on the streets of gold and regret having given too much to the cause of God, but it could be that many will rue that they did not invest more in the salvation of souls. How much more could be done for the gospel if we weren't trying to keep up with others?

Stuff

*"Take heed and beware of covetousness, for one's life does
not consist in the abundance of the things he possesses."*

—Luke 12:15

The Christmas season is often marked by conspicuous consumption. It is a good time of year to ask ourselves whether we really need so much stuff.

Storage units have sprung up like mushrooms in recent years because people need somewhere to put all of their stuff. Houses and garages don't seem to be big enough anymore, and people find they must rent space in order to have somewhere to keep their possessions. Meanwhile, Marie Kondo has become famous worldwide for being an "organizing consultant." Her book *The Life-Changing Magic of Tidying Up* has been published in three dozen countries. Ms. Kondo—whose methods are inspired in part by her Shinto religion—has become a media sensation for the simple reason that so many people have so much stuff they can't figure out what to do with it all.

Many people have all the possessions they really need. The majority of people have enough money to get by but are challenged by the concept of living within their means. "Getting by" means different things to different people. There is certainly nothing wrong with having possessions, but it is wise to reflect on how deeply we are immersed in the culture of "have."

Christmas offers us an opportunity to remember to bring our gifts to Jesus, to consider how we might spend less on ourselves and invest more in God's cause. Consider whether you are giving God enough of your money, time, and attention. While we indulge ourselves with things we really don't need, the cause of Christ suffers for lack of means.

As church leaders struggle to fund gospel workers and ministry initiatives, we should keep in mind that Christian stewardship is not only the domain of the wealthy. Everyone is called upon by God to return tithes and offerings. God says, "Bring all the tithes into the storehouse" (Malachi 3:10). When Jesus returns, we won't reflect on how much we had in this world. But we likely will reflect on how much more we could have done to advance His work.

Christmas Every Day

For God so loved the world that He gave His only begotten Son,
that whoever believes in Him should not perish but have everlasting life.
—John 3:16

It is hard to resist. 'Tis the season to receive catalogs from companies you never knew existed. 'Tis the season for glossy advertisements peddling gifts your loved ones absolutely don't have to have. 'Tis the season for people to spend money they don't have on things they don't need because society tells us that's what they're supposed to do. There isn't a commandment that says you have to celebrate Christmas, which means there certainly isn't a commandment that says you have to get sucked into the vortex of get, get, get, have, have, have.

What really is the most important thing? When the truck has come to take away the trash, and the tree has been taken down, and the relatives are gone, and the kids have gone back to college or have returned home with their own families; when all the food has been eaten, and the lights have been taken down, and the stores have stopped playing Christmas music—what will you be left with?

If Christmas is all about getting, you will be happy just until your gifts lose their luster. If Christmas is all about giving, you'll soon forget what you gave to whom and how much you spent on which present—until the credit card statement arrives. But if Christmas is about accepting the gift God gave the world, then you have something that will stay with you.

If your focus is in the right place, it can be Christmas every day. God so loved the world that, two thousand years ago, He gave His only begotten Son. And long before that, He pledged to give Jesus to the world should humanity fall into sin. That's a gift you can truly appreciate. And it's a gift everybody needs. If you remember the great gift of God and commit to sharing that gift with others, every day can be Christmas day.

Silent Night

And suddenly there was with the angel a multitude
of the heavenly host praising God and saying: "Glory to God
in the highest, and on earth peace, goodwill toward men!"

—Luke 2:13, 14

One thing I have always loved about Christmas is Christmas music. Not the incessant, grating Christmas music you hear at shopping malls, but the many Christmas songs that are powerful and meaningful. Handel's *Messiah* is often sung at Christmas, and there are few works that could claim the majesty and power captured by Handel and librettist Charles Jennens.

> O come all ye faithful, joyful and triumphant,
> O come ye, O come ye to Bethlehem!
> Come and behold Him, born the King of angels!
>
> O come, let us adore Him, . . . Christ, the Lord!

It's a hopeful, inspiring message wrapped in a beautiful melody, proclaiming Jesus has been born! Christ the Lord has come to the world!

"Silent Night" was originally written as "Stille Nacht" in Austria in the 1800s.

> Silent night, holy night!
> Shepherds quake at the sight:
> Glories stream from heaven afar,
> Heavenly hosts sing "Alleluia!
> Christ the Savior is born!"

The words of the classic Christmas hymn take you to a hillside in Israel where humble shepherds witnessed heavenly visitors in all their splendor—when angel choirs sang the good news that the Messiah had come into the world.

The advent of the Savior was such a momentous, historic, joyful occasion that angel choirs not only sang but were heard by mortals. In a world where there is no shortage of sadness and bad news, there is still something to sing about. Two thousand years ago, Jesus came to this world. Born as a baby in humble circumstances, He came with the mission to save humanity from sin and give to the world the gift of everlasting life.

It was history's greatest moment. Jesus had come into the world! When He comes into your heart, you, too, will have something to sing about.

Merry Christmas!

"The glory of the LORD shall be revealed, and all flesh shall see
it together; for the mouth of the LORD has spoken."

—Isaiah 40:5

C hristmas Day is a reminder to the world that God is a God who keeps His promises. In the third chapter of the Bible, God promised a Deliverer would bruise the head of the serpent (Genesis 3:15). Satan would be defeated by One who would come into the world to save fallen human beings. Jeremiah 31:31 assured the world that a new covenant would one day come into effect, a covenant that would be ratified by Jesus the Messiah. The prophet Daniel specified the Messiah would come to the earth in harmony with a divine timetable (Daniel 9:24–27). Isaiah wrote that the Messiah would be "despised and rejected by men, a Man of sorrows and acquainted with grief" (Isaiah 53:3). And the same prophet predicted that the Messiah would be born of a virgin (Isaiah 7:14).

So many biblical predictions were made about the advent of the Messiah, and not one of them proved to be inaccurate. The psalmist said the hands and feet of the Messiah would be pierced and that not one of His bones would be broken (Psalms 22:16; 34:20). Zechariah speaks of the wounds in Jesus' hands. He also declared that the Messiah would come riding on a donkey (Zechariah 9:9). Dozens of predictions were made about the Messiah.

In other words, dozens of predictions made by God about the Messiah were fulfilled, and every promise was kept. Still, other promises made in relation to the ministry of Jesus have not yet been fulfilled. Jesus promised He would return to the earth. While He has yet to do so, the proliferation of fulfilled predictions and promises must suggest those that are not yet fulfilled will be fulfilled one soon day. The Bible predicts the end of sin, the Holy City coming to earth, and an eternity without sickness, sadness, or sin.

The God who has never broken a promise pledges to us today that just as He has always kept His promises in the past, He will do so in the future. Jesus is coming back soon!

Unwanted Gifts

From that time many of His disciples went back
and walked with Him no more.

—John 6:66

Following Christmas Day in 2014, $284 billion worth of Christmas gifts were returned to stores in the United States.* Unwanted gifts. No doubt, many of the returned gifts were carefully selected and given with love, but for some reason, they weren't desired.

In John 6, Jesus offered a priceless gift when He told a crowd He was the "bread of life." Jesus came to the world when Israel was in a difficult place. Occupied by the armies of Rome, Israel did not appear to be a nation that had been chosen by God. The oppressed Jewish people were not in charge of their own destiny and were subject to the dictates and caprice of an occupying force. When Jesus announced He was the bread of life, Israel could have taken hold of a certain future. But, incredibly, Jesus' announcement that Israel's long-hoped-for Messiah was in their midst was neither comprehended nor appreciated.

Jesus offered the Jewish people the greatest gift ever imagined, and they chose to reject it. They exchanged everlasting life for everlasting death. Jesus had come to Israel with hope for their hopelessness, light for their darkness, and courage to endure difficulties. He came to the world "to give them beauty for ashes, the oil of joy for mourning, the garment of praise for the spirit of heaviness" (Isaiah 61:3). He raised the dead, gave sight to the blind, fed the multitudes, healed lepers, turned water into juice, and showed compassion to all. And still, the people of His day returned the gift Jesus came to the world to give them. They said to Jesus, "Thanks, but no thanks. We don't want this."

They wanted a Messiah, but not *that* kind of Messiah. A Messiah who would conquer the Romans would have been welcomed, but a Messiah who offered a new heart was not what they were looking for.

God offers you the gift of eternity. Hold on to it tightly. It is the one gift you never want to return.

---

* Tom DiChristopher, "Your Holiday Gift Returns Cost Retailers Billions," CNBC, December 28, 2015, https://www.cnbc.com/2015/12/28/your-holiday-gift-returns-cost-retailers-billions.html.

No Condemnation

There is therefore now no condemnation to those who are in Christ Jesus,
who do not walk according to the flesh, but according to the Spirit.
—Romans 8:1

L iterature is replete with famous quotes. William Shakespeare wrote in *Romeo and Juliet*, "But soft! what light through yonder window breaks? It is the east, and Juliet is the sun."* Charles Dickens's *A Tale of Two Cities* opens with the famous line, "It was the best of times, it was the worst of times."† But the opening words of Romans chapter eight far exceed the power and beauty of anything found in secular literature.

In Romans chapter 7, Paul had discussed the condition of the person whose life is not surrendered to the indwelling Christ. "For what I am doing," Paul had written, "I do not understand. For what I will to do, that I do not practice; but what I hate, that I do" (Romans 7:15). Recognizing the futility of a life that is not yielded to Jesus, Paul asked the desperate question, "O wretched man that I am! Who will deliver me from this body of death?" (verse 24). If the book of Romans had ended there, it would be one of the most discouraging books ever written. But Paul went on to present the solution to human selfishness. "I thank God—through Jesus Christ our Lord!" (verse 25).

Then follows the majestic statement that offers hope to the entire human family. "There is therefore now no condemnation." For whom? "To those who are in Christ Jesus." And who are they? Those "who do not walk according to the flesh, but according to the Spirit" (Romans 8:1). The surrendered life is lived "according to the Spirit," and for that life, there is "no condemnation."

More profound words have scarcely been written. Better news has never been heard by a struggling child of God. Those who make room for the Holy Spirit in their lives live a completely new life without condemnation. Sin cannot govern the life that has been yielded to Jesus. Jesus lives in the heart. The believer lives a life of hope and assurance.

---

* William Shakespeare, *Romeo and Juliet* 2.2. References are to act and scene, http://shakespeare.mit.edu /romeo_juliet/romeo_juliet.2.2.html.

† Charles Dickens, *A Tale of Two Cities: A Story of the French Revolution*, Project Gutenberg eBook, last up-dated December 20, 2020, https://www.gutenberg.org/files/98/98-h/98-h.htm.

"Do You Believe in Miracles?"

Now when He had said these things,
He cried with a loud voice, "Lazarus, come forth!"

—John 11:43

At the Winter Olympics in Lake Placid, New York, in February 1980, the United States ice hockey team—made up of mostly amateurs—wasn't expected to win a medal. The Soviet Union was the best team in the world and was expected to win gold easily. The United States met the Goliaths of international hockey in their second to last game. The day before, the *New York Times* reported, "Unless the ice melts, or unless the United States team or another team performs a miracle . . . the Russians are expected to easily win the Olympic gold medal for the sixth time in the last seven tournaments."*

Eight and a half thousand people crowded into the Olympic Center ice rink to see the United States play the Soviet Union, and as America won the game four goals to three, television announcer Al Michaels famously exclaimed, "Do you believe in miracles?!" It was such a shocking win that *Sports Illustrated* called it the "top sports moment of the 20th century." The game became known as "The Miracle on Ice."

What a question. Do you believe in miracles? The win over the Soviets wasn't a miracle. It was a game, and as in all hockey games, the team that scores the most points wins. Usually, it's the better team. Sometimes there are upsets, a surprise winner, but a game is a game. The Bible talks about *real* miracles. John 11:43 says that when Jesus stood before the tomb of Lazarus, He called out, "Lazarus, come forth," and Lazarus came forth from the dead. A true miracle! Jesus healed the lame, cast out demons, and fed the multitudes. Jesus turned water to wine, caused the deaf to hear, and restored sight to the blind. These were real miracles. God is the God of the supernatural. He is able to work miracles. They don't always happen when and where we wish, but God is still in the miracle-working business. Is it time you expected more from God? Have faith in God today. He is able.

Do you believe in miracles?

---

* Jane Rogers, "Do You Believe in Miracles (on Ice)?" National Museum of American History, February 21, 2014, https://americanhistory.si.edu/blog/2014/02/do-you-believe-in-miracles-on-ice.html.

Deep-Seated

And Samson said to his father,
"Get her for me, for she pleases me well."

—Judges 14:3

Those who have become trapped in sin understand it exerts powerful, merciless control. In Judges 14, Samson informs his parents that he is attracted to a certain Philistine woman. "Then his father and mother said to him, 'Is there no woman among the daughters of your brethren, or among all my people, that you must go and get a wife from the uncircumcised Philistines?' " But Samson insisted, "Get her for me, for she pleases me well" (Judges 14:3).

Instead of obeying God, Samson obeyed his desires. Samson was a slave to those desires for much of his life. Sins of a moral nature can take a very strong hold as they are deep-seated and associated with strong emotional and chemical impulses. Impurity ruins lives, marriages, and families. Although Samson had an impressive record of defeating his foes, lust was an enemy he could not conquer. Failing to resolve his issues with impurity led ultimately to losing his life.

The devil is well acquainted with how individuals are wired and what their peculiar weaknesses are. He knows some people genuinely struggle with what they eat or drink, and he works to defeat them in that area. Another person might not be tempted whatsoever by appetite but instead has a short fuse and struggles to keep their temper under control. Another may be prone to pride, while another person struggles with covetousness or dishonesty.

Everyone battles temptation in some form. According to the apostle Paul, "All have sinned and fall short of the glory of God" (Romans 3:23). All of humanity finds itself weakened by sin. But while Satan endeavors to insinuate himself into every life, God reminds us that deliverance from sin is offered in Jesus. Paul wrote to the Corinthians that God will not allow us to be tempted beyond our ability to resist and that for every temptation, He makes a way of escape (1 Corinthians 10:13).

Jesus is that way of escape. The indwelling power of the God of heaven could have made Samson as mighty spiritually as he was physically. Learning from Samson's errors will keep us from repeating his mistakes.

No Time at All

You do not know what will happen tomorrow. For what is your life?
It is even a vapor that appears for a little time and then vanishes away.
—James 4:14

People beyond a certain age remember looking forward to the year 2000 and calculating how old they would be at the turn of the millennium. Now we look back and realize the turn of the millennium came and went years ago. I once asked a 100-year-old woman how long it felt for her to reach that milestone. She smiled thoughtfully and said, "Not long at all."

James wrote that life is like "a vapor that appears for a little time and then vanishes away" (James 4:14). Life is extremely short, and years fly by. The average life span in the United States is roughly 78½ years. In Great Britain, it is a little over 81, while in Japan—which boasts the longest average life span of any country—a person can expect to live a little beyond 84. The person who has lived longest in modern times is a French woman, Jeanne Calment, who is said to have lived to be 122 before dying in 1997. But compared to the life span of the patriarchs of the Bible, Ms. Calment was just getting started! Noah lived to 950. Jared, the grandfather of Methuselah, lived to be 962, while Methuselah became the oldest man to have ever died when he passed away at 969. The oldest man to have ever lived is Enoch, Methuselah's father, who, at the age of 365, was taken to heaven without seeing death.

God's plan is that His children live forever. Eternity will give us all the time we need to learn, develop, meet new people, and explore new worlds. And all the while, we will reflect the character of God more and more and experience true happiness as God sees it. But eternity is rapidly approaching. God grants us this life so we may develop characters that will be ready for the return of Jesus. A soul is a terrible thing to waste.

If this life was all you had, life would be little more than futile. God gives meaning to your life. Through Jesus, you can live forever.

New Beginnings

*Put on the new man which was created according
to God, in true righteousness and holiness.*

—Ephesians 4:24

A new year promises new beginnings. With less than twenty-four hours until a new year rolls around, a lot of people are looking ahead and hoping for better things than they experienced this year. Others are hopeful that the blessings of this year continue into the next. Maybe an investment portfolio will increase in value. Perhaps there will be professional advancement. A new relationship might flourish, there could be opportunities for travel, or it may be that the new year will be the year in which weight is lost or that time is found to spend with family.

But it doesn't take a new year for the greatest "new start" to take place. Every day presents the opportunity to come to Jesus and experience transformation. Paul expressed it like this in Ephesians 4:22–24: "Put off, concerning your former conduct, the old man which grows corrupt according to the deceitful lusts, and be renewed in the spirit of your mind, and that you put on the new man which was created according to God, in true righteousness and holiness."

In Jesus, every day is a new day. God grants us the opportunity to be "renewed in the spirit of" our minds, putting off what we were and putting on a new self which has been created by God "in righteousness and true holiness." It is important to notice that God does not say that we are to renew our own minds but that God Himself creates us after His own image. Surrender to God results in God drawing us deep into His heart and making us new.

Many years have gone down in history as being notable. In 1492, Christopher Columbus discovered the New World. In 1620, the pilgrims landed at Plymouth Rock. The US Declaration of Independence was signed in 1776. World War II began in 1939 and ended in 1945. The year 1969 is remembered as the time that a person first walked on the moon. What will make this next year memorable is that it will be the year in which you are "renewed in the spirit of your mind" again and again. Every year is a good year when your life is yielded to God.